WOMEN'S WRI
OF THE
EARLY MODERN PERIOD
1588–1688:
AN ANTHOLOGY

For my maternal grandmother,
Mary Harding (1907–1977)

WOMEN'S WRITING
OF THE
EARLY MODERN PERIOD
1588–1688:
AN ANTHOLOGY

Edited by

Stephanie Hodgson-Wright

EDINBURGH UNIVERSITY PRESS

Edinburgh University Press
22 George Square, Edinburgh

Typeset in Bulmer
by Pioneer Associates, Perthshire, and
printed and bound in Great Britain by
MPG Books Ltd, Bodmin

A CIP record for this book is available from the
British Library

ISBN 0 7486 1096 0 (hardback)
ISBN 0 7486 1097 9 (paperback)

CONTENTS

INTRODUCTION

We need a reading which acknowledges that we start now, from here; but which re-awakens the dormant signification of past literature to its first readers. Such reading seeks intense meaning embedded in semantics, plot, formal and generic properties, conditions of production. These have been overlaid by the sequent pasts and by our present concerns which cannot be obliterated, but we need to explore both likeness and difference. Such reading gives room to both scepticism and immersion. (Spender 1986, 69)

Dale Spender's call, although over fifteen years old, is still pertinent to both the processes of compiling and reading an anthology such as this, as the compiler and reader alike must negotiate a position between respecting the 'pastness' of sixteenth- and seventeenth-century women's writing, and allowing it to signify in the present; recognising its historical specificity without closing off new ways of reading. Perhaps this type of anthology should bear the warning 'handle with care' – not as an injunction to think kindly of the contents or the editor, but rather to the reader to be careful how they interpret what is within, lest they do damage to themselves.

The selections contained herein primarily comprise 'literature' as discussed and defined by Widdowson:

'the literary' is distinguished by its own sense of being '*of* the literary'. This apparently circular definition means that writing which presents itself as being 'creative', 'imaginative' and 'artificial' (i.e. composed of and by artifice) simultaneously conceives of itself as being different to other kinds of writing which do not so conceive of themselves. (Widdowson 1999, 96)

Those texts which do not so 'signal' themselves as literature have been selected partly because of the ways in which they employ a particular 'literary' quality also identified by Widdowson:

'Revisionary' writing, then, is a crucial component of 'the literary' as a contemporary 'counter-culture of the imagination', which in 'writing back' to historical texts, and to the historical conjunctures which shaped them, re-writes authorised history by way of revising its 'master narratives'. (Widdowson 1999, 166)

For example, whilst not self-consciously presented as a work of the imagination, Rachel Speght's pamphlet *A Muzzle for Melastomus* is as radically 're-visionary' as Margaret Cavendish's play *The Convent of Pleasure*, and I hope that the reader will make similar comparisons and connections between the other texts in this anthology. Elaine Hobby, in her pioneering work *Virtue of Necessity: English Women's Writing 1649–88*, wrote:

We need to ask a different sort of question about writing from the past. I am much more interested in what women's writings show us about female struggles within and against the demands made of them, than I am in their use of rhyme or complexity of characterisation (to take some extreme examples of the narrowness of conventional literary-critical concerns). (Hobby 1988, 25)

Many years of subsequent scholarship mean that the student is now able to consider both/and rather than either/or and my selections have been made precisely to facilitate this kind of investigation.

This anthology has therefore been compiled with the aim of providing a coherent selection of texts that can form the basis for a course in women's writing 1588–1688. The period saw massive political and social change within England and in its relationship with the rest of the world. In 1588, England was ruled by Elizabeth I, a monarch appointed by Divine Right, was largely isolated from the rest of Europe and was facing invasion by the Spanish. In 1688, England deposed its King, James II, and offered its crown to a foreign prince, William of Orange, on terms negotiated with Parliament; party politics had replaced Divine Right. In the intervening time, Civil Wars had split the country from 1641–1649, until the incumbent King, Charles I, was executed. For a brief time, the country had been governed by Parliament, before Charles II was restored to the throne in 1660. Furthermore, by 1688, England had established itself as a major colonial power in the New World and, as J. R. Jones has argued, this year marked the beginning of its political and intellectual influence upon Europe (Jones 1980, 59). The texts included in this anthology represent the ways in which women engaged with the political, social and cultural developments of the period and are, to a large extent, *about* the period as well as *from it*.[1] The texts have been chosen partly for their relevance to issues current in academic debates (specifically, but not exclusively) about women in the Early Modern period and partly because they act as effective intertexts for each other. I would hope that the reader will consider the texts alongside each other, rather than as discrete documents.

Elizabeth I produced a great body of writings in her lifetime, although, as the editors of her complete works argue, they have not hitherto been considered as a whole oeuvre, something which they seek to rectify (Marcus, Mueller and Rose 2000, xi). Of her numerous works, three speeches have been selected for inclusion, in keeping with the anthology's theme of published writing, and also because, as Frances Teague argues, 'in Elizabeth's speeches we see her writing at its best' (Teague 1987, 531). Furthermore, as with many of the other writers in this anthology, Elizabeth's published speeches constitute carefully constructed performances of a particular, and not necessarily consistent, persona. The three speeches see her variously invoking her physical limitations (Speech to the Troops at Tilbury), dynastic legitimacy (Speech at the Dissolving of Parliament) and great love for her people (The Golden Speech). As Marcus, Mueller and Rose succinctly point out:

> Elizabeth's identity as princess and monarch cannot be separated from her identity as author. . . . Her writings present an interesting and valuable example of the ways in which individual agency intersects with various cultural domains in the creation of literary texts. (2000, xiii–xiv)

Jane Anger's *Her Protection for Women* was written in the same year as Elizabeth delivered her Tilbury speech, although it was not published until 1589. Anger joins a literary debate about women, which had developed from the medieval European *Querelle des Femmes*, and writes in response to a misogynistic tract entitled *Boke, His Surfeit in Love* (now lost). Hitherto this genre had been a masculine preserve in England and so, arguably, Anger's work is the earliest piece of English feminist polemic (see, for example, Henderson and MacManus 1985, 27–31 and Magnusson 1991, 269–82; Benson 1992, 223–30 offers a different view). The terms upon which she bases her case are rather removed from the feminism of later centuries, and are bound up with contemporary notions of essential differences between men and women. Unfortunately, limitations of space would not allow reproduction of the whole text. The four sections, respectively, give Anger's reasons for publishing, an attack on the genre of misogynistic pamphlets, a counter-attack on the vices of men, a Biblically-based defence of women's virtues and, finally, a warning to all women about the vices of men.

The œuvre of Mary Sidney Herbert, Countess of Pembroke, (published and manuscript) mainly comprises translation, the most culturally acceptable form of literary production for women in the sixteenth century. The first selection is taken from her translation of Philippe Du Plessis Mornay's *The Discourse of Life and Death*, an example of *ars moriendi* (art of dying) literature which was popular during the Renaissance. Mary Ellen Lamb suggests that the Countess may have been attracted to Mornay's work because of its emphasis on Senecan Stoicism, a philosophy which idealises 'passive endurance rather than heroic action, which honors withdrawal and inner composure as positive virtues, ennobles the behaviour that was expected of women anyway' (Lamb 1986, 213). Of course, there is a certain irony in the Countess of Pembroke's publication of this work, when the work itself enjoins the reader to eschew public life. The second selection departs considerably from the first, being both original to the author and a poem of celebration. 'A Dialogue between two shepherds, Thenot and Piers, in praise of Astrea' literally inserted the Countess of Pembroke into the male-dominated publishing mainstream, being printed alongside poems by a number of leading male poets in a volume edited by Francis Davison. Written as a pastoral entertainment for Elizabeth (although we do not have details of its performance), it is highly conventional in its praise of the monarch and is one of a number of works in this anthology which takes Elizabeth I as its subject matter.

Aemilia Lanyer's volume entitled *Salve Deus Rex Judaeorum* is an early example of a woman writer seeking to attract the material benefits of patronage. The main poem is prefaced by dedicatory poems to eight powerful women, including Queen Anna, wife of James VI and I. For reasons of space, I have had to omit these poems, although I have included the highly feminist 'To the virtuous reader' which, Lewalski argues, 'extends the community constructed in the dedications . . . and makes a vigorous contribution to the centuries-old *querelles des femmes*' (Lewalski 1991, 102). Lanyer thereby combined a specific agenda, based upon personal need for patronage, with a wider ideological agenda. The main poem offers a notably feminist reworking of key passages from Genesis, the Gospels and Revelations, highlighting the importance of women in the ministry, death and resurrection of Jesus. It also questions the culpability of Eve, frequently cited as a means to denigrate all women, thereby sharing the strategies of the pamphlets by Jane Anger and Rachel Speght. Moreover, as Achsah Guibbory argues, the poem shows Lanyer's 'recognition of the fundamental contradiction or discontinuity between Christ's teachings, which subverted the social order of Roman and Jewish society and emphasized the equality of the sexes, and those interpretations of Christ's message by his disciples that perpetuated the subjection of women' (Guibbory 1996, 121). The sense of an exclusively female Eden is created in 'To Cookeham', included partly for reasons of reassessing literary history. Internal evidence suggests that it was commissioned by Lanyer's main dedicatee, Margaret Clifford, Countess of Cumberland, rendering it the earliest example of the English country-house poem genre, long assumed to have been initiated by Ben Jonson's 'To Penshurst'.

Elizabeth Cary's *The Tragedy of Mariam* is the earliest surviving original female-authored drama in English. Probably composed in the early years of James VI and I's reign, it deals with the consequences of masculine tyranny within the home and within the state. The play begins with an unfounded rumour of Herod's death, which leads to various members of the royal household taking advantage of their new-found freedom. When Herod returns, several suffer immediately, but his final atrocity is to have Mariam executed because he mistakenly believes that she has committed adultery with a servant. Issues of marriage, divorce, male privilege and the place of the female voice are put under close scrutiny in this play, which has generated a wealth of criticism focusing upon these issues. More recently, critics have begun to consider the importance of social class, dynasty and ethnicity in the play (see, for example, Callaghan 1994; Purkiss 1998; Raber 1995; Shannon 1994). Furthermore, whilst the play was dismissed by early critics as a closet drama not intended for acting, it has since been proved to be a highly vigorous piece of writing, entirely suited for the stage (Findlay, Hodgson-Wright and Williams 1999a, 1999b and 2000) and less like the earlier 'closet' dramas upon which it had been considered to be modelled (Gutierrez 1991).

Rachel Speght's *A Muzzle for Melastomus*, like Jane Anger's pamphlet, is an early piece of feminist polemic. It is the first of three replies to a misogynist attack on women, Joseph Swetnam's *The Arraignment of Lewd, Idle, Froward and Unconstant Women* (1615), the other two being Esther Sowernam's *Esther Hath Hanged Haman* and Constantia Munda's *A Sop for Cerberus*. Its tone is slightly more restrained, being less rooted in the observed behaviour of men and women and more concerned with re-interpreting Biblical and Classical authority to prove her point. As with Anger's piece, the terms of her argument may seem limited in comparison with current feminisms, but her interpretative skills work impressively within those limits. The extract reproduced here is the central section of the pamphlet, in which Speght constructs her Scriptural exegesis around the Aristotelian theory of causes, marshalling two sources of masculine authority to evolve a feminist argument. Indeed, as Lewalski notes, it:

> breaks the mold of the *Querelle's rhetorical game*. If Speght's language and argument are in some ways less daring than those of Sowernam or Munda, her undertaking is more serious: to make the authoritative Protestant discourse of biblical exegesis yield a more expansive and equitable concept of gender. (Lewalski 1997, 140)

Lady Mary Wroth appropriated a genre which had previously been the preserve of the masculine poetic voice and used, for the most part, to objectify a female beloved. Her sonnet sequence *Pamphilia to Amphilanthus* has both familial and stylistic links with *Astrophel and Stella* (by her uncle, Sir Philip Sidney), which itself constituted a break from tradition by expressing the frustrations of unfulfilled physical desire in a genre originally devoted to the contemplation of an unattainable woman. Written over twenty years later, *Pamphilia to Amphilanthus* departs from tradition even further; not only does the sequence deal with physical passion, but the poetic voice is female. Moreover, the sequence contemplates the feelings of the female narrator rather than the beauty of her beloved. In Mary Wroth's sonnet sequence, the woman is still the primary focus, but as lover, rather than the beloved, constituting both subject and object of her own poetic voice. Finally, as Miller notes, Wroth 'uses imagery standard to the genre, only to re-present that same imagery with a new twist later in the sequence, manipulating the conventional discourse of the sonnet tradition towards her own ends' (Miller 1990, 299).

The three selections from Diana Primrose's *A Chain of Pearl* (there were ten in all, the others being Justice, Chastity, Prudence, Clemency, Science, Patience and Bounty) show a woman writer appropriating the past to comment upon the present, and, as Lisa Gim argues, portraying Elizabeth 'as the most appropriate intellectual and ethical model for her sex, and to affirm conceptual connections between this powerful female authority and women who might follow her example' (Gim 1999, 188). In addition to its function as a panegyric to Elizabeth I, this poem criticises Charles I by comparison. Primrose praises both Elizabeth's opposition to Roman Catholicism and her refusal to be swayed by court favourites. At the time, Queen Henrietta Maria and her entourage openly practised their Catholic faith and Charles I had only recently been relieved of the excessive influence of the Duke of Buckingham, who was assassinated in 1628. Written at the beginning of what was to be an eleven-year rule without

Parliament, Primrose delineates by implication some of the sources of discontent which were to lead to the outbreak of the English Civil War. By the time *A True Copy of the Petition of Gentlewomen* was published, the subtle criticism of the court offered by the previous selection had been overtaken by the increasingly vocal opposition between the King and the Parliament he was obliged to call in 1640. Charles I's failure to contain the threat posed by the Queen's overt Catholicism and to execute the disgraced Archbishop of Canterbury William Laud (a follower of Arminianism, which was a version of Protestantism very close to Catholicism) and are criticised heavily by the otherwise unknown Anne Stagg and a company of gentlewomen. They petitioned Parliament in fear that the terrors of Bishops' Wars in Scotland and the Irish Rebellion may be visited upon England. The text emphasises the physical vulnerability of women in armed conflict, particularly to the threat of rape. Unfortunately for the petitioners, their attempt to prevent war was unsuccessful although how they fared in the ensuing conflict remains unknown.

The authors of the next two selections delivered their material orally before it was committed to print. Elizabeth Poole's *A Vision: Wherein is Manifested the Disease and Cure of the Kingdom* was addressed to Cromwell and the General Council and contributed to the debate over whether or not it would be lawful to execute the now defeated Charles I, a King appointed by God. The theory of the Divine Right of Kings, promoted particularly in the Stuart period, still held considerable weight and despite her radical sectarian views, Elizabeth Poole cannot support Charles I's execution, although she does advocate his trial. She uses the politically charged analogy of husband/wife and King/State to argue that the King cannot be separated from his State by violent means. Instead, as Gillespie notes (1999, n.p.), she proposes the radical solution of the State 'divorcing' the King, tying her argument against tyrannicide 'explicitly to a wife's right to withdraw sexual and marital consent in the event of abuse'. Conversely, Anna Trapnel was a member of the Fifth Monarchist movement, which supported the execution of Charles I as a step towards the imminent arrival of Christ to resume power over the Earth: the 'Fifth Monarchy'. Drawing upon the books of Daniel and Revelations, *Strange and Wonderful News from Whitehall* severely criticises Oliver Cromwell and his self-appointed position as Lord Protector. Like Elizabeth Poole, Trapnel's words are recorded by a third party 'the Relator' after the event of her prophecy. Unlike Poole, Trapnel does not make a speech but is seized by the prophesying spirit 'in a little room near the Council door' and then returns to her lodgings. Drawing upon Habermasian notions of the public and private spheres, Gillespie identifies Trapnel's strategy as part of a mid-seventeenth-century dynamic whereby 'sectarian women converted the private spaces of the home and their attendant domestic subject positions and discourses into sites for the production of a female public voice' (1997, 59).

The Restoration of Charles II in 1660 did not manage to reverse the unsettling social effects of the previous years and Mary Carleton chose to take advantage of these effects by reinventing herself. In 1663 she was brought to trial for bigamy as a result, although she was acquitted. *The Case of Madam Mary Carleton* was one of a number of publications surrounding her trial, although it is only one of two attributed to her. The selections have been taken from the beginning and end of the text, omitting the trial which, as a transcript of events, owes the least to Mary Carleton's imagination. The dedications are both audacious and express an understandable sense of injustice. The first sections from the main text show her creating herself as the heroine of romance travel narrative; the final sections are an indictment of English manners and the legal system. Although presented as a true story, Carleton's German origins were fictitious; Mary Jo Kietzman identifies her particular strategy as:

> 'serial subjectivity' . . . a viable mode of self-fashioning in which the conventional opposition between the private and public, the unconscious and the conscious, the personal/unknowable and the universal/comprehensible, is displaced and re-anchored in a new conception of situation or context as both psychic and historical. (Kietzman 1999, 678)

In a less overt fashion, Katherine Philips proved to be adept at creating an alternative identity for herself. Claudia A. Limbert has noted that she was, in effect, two women: the first a daughter and wife within the merchant class, Puritan in religion and Parliamentarian in politics, and the second the unconventional poet Orinda, essentially Royalist in her inclinations, with a wide circle of Royalist friends (Limbert 1991, 27). Katherine's interest in and sympathy for the Royal family can been seen in the selection of poems included here, which amounts to about a fifth of her total printed oeuvre. She also wrote poems about her familial relationships and her elegies for her son and mother-in-law are also included. However, the majority of the poems selected concern the passionate celebration of emotional bonds between women, the subject which has attracted most attention in recent scholarship (see, for example, Andreadis 1989 and 1999; Easton 1990; Hobby 1991; Mintz 1998 and Revard 1997). Whilst subtly undermining marriage as the primary relationship in a woman's life, the poems also draw on and manipulate the hitherto heterosexual courtly love conventions. But whilst Orinda describes her *relationships* with Lucasia and Rosania, we are never offered a physical description of them; the blazon is omitted and so the women are not judged against a predetermined aesthetic.

Bonds between women are also celebrated in Margaret Cavendish, Duchess of Newcastle's *The Convent of Pleasure*. The rich heiress Lady Happy chooses to avoid marriage and set up a convent, devoted to intellectual, artistic and sensual indulgence. The convent receives a new devotee, 'the Princess', and who turns out to be a Prince in disguise; this revelation is kept from Lady Happy until she has fallen in love with him/her and their first kiss occurs whilst the disguise is still in place. The possibilities of same-sex love give way to something equally radical – a feminine man who is able to accept, and is acceptable to, the feminine sensibilities of the heroine. He is contrasted with the bullish and crude male characters who are appalled, excluded and therefore threatened by the convent. Like *The Tragedy of Mariam*, the performability of Margaret Cavendish's plays was doubted by many critics. However, Gweno Williams's work on Cavendish's plays, which has given rise to a number of video productions, has successfully challenged this view (see Findlay, Hodgson-Wright and Williams 1999a, 1999b and 2000). As Misty G. Anderson summarises, 'Cavendish's montage dramatic style resists narrative unity, causality and closure by changing scene and topic without regard to a realist standard of objectivity . . . amenable to the contemporary technologically rich media of film' (Anderson 1999, 336).

Although neither cloistered nor opulent, Bathsua Makin's school advertised in *An Essay to Revive the Ancient Education of Gentlewomen* gave young women an opportunity to develop their talents. The selections included here offer the main points of Makin's argument, that educated women are essentially more useful creatures and that God would never have given them the capacity for learning if they were not meant to use it. Makin offers a counter-argument to John Milton's *Of Education* (1644, reissued 1673). Although, as Teague cautions, the closeness in publication dates may be coincidence, both treat the same topics in diametrically opposed ways and Makin's pamphlet 'echoes and mocks' the phrase 'one tongue is enough for a woman', reputedly a favourite of Milton's (Teague 1998, 100). Unfortunately, limited space means that one of Makin's methods of supporting her argument, the chronology of learned women from Classical, Biblical and recent European history, has been omitted; significantly, the chronology includes Elizabeth I and the author of the next selection, Anne Bradstreet (Makin 1673, C2r).

Bathsua Makin would have been aware of Bradstreet's work through the 1650 pirated edition, *The Tenth Muse Lately Sprung up in America*. The selection here is taken from the second edition of 1678, entitled *Several Poems*, which claims to have been revised and expanded by the author. The Prologue is both apologetic and assertive. Whilst acknowledging the 'precedency' of male poets, against which the poetic efforts of women should not be judged, it also claims the right for women to write poetry on their own terms. 'The Author to her Book' indicates her feelings about the pirated edition, expressed by the delicate metaphor of a mother having her sickly and unprepossessing child put out into the world prematurely; her editorial improvements are described in terms of maternal reparations to her 'rambling brat'. The selections from her 'Quarternions' are largely backward looking, drawing upon the history, geography and climate of England. However, the sense of a new start and an emergent separate identity for the New England are present in the 'Dialogue Between Old and New England', which expresses the division between the political history and current political strife of Old England, on the one hand, and New England's colonial future, on the other, as a subversive mother–daughter relationship, with the latter advising the former. Gillespie suggests that with such a representation of the 'transfer of power from motherland to daughter colony in naturalising, familial terms, Bradstreet shifts the locus of the maternal production of the body politic . . . to New England, suggesting that the daughter is imminently poised to take her mother's place as the locus of wisdom and the generation of a new English body politic' (Gillespie 1999a, 111).

The final two selections are by Aphra Behn. From the later part of her career, they both address the issues surrounding the 1688 Revolution in England via New World settings; scholars have recently begun to explore the links between them (see, for example, Frohock 1996). They are also based (or claim to be based) upon actual historical events; both are examples of Behn's later work and both are mixed-genre. As Gallagher succinctly states, in *Oroonoko* Behn aimed 'to blend three popular forms of Restoration literature; the New World travel story, the courtly romance, and the heroic tragedy' (Gallagher 2000, 13). Although dubbed a 'tragicomedy' *The Widow Ranter* is actually a combination of a tragic plot and a comic plot. The hero of the former, Nathaniel Bacon, has been identified by Zook as the cavalier who has had his day (Zook 1999, 90) and furthermore, Todd notes his likeness to the rash Duke of Monmouth, natural son of Charles II, who tried to lead a rebellion against James II and was executed for his trouble (Todd 1999, 75). In contrast to Bacon's outdated and out of place sentiments, the *modus operandi* of the good-natured and pragmatic Widow proves successful. Arguably a 'serial subject' (see page xiv), she easily reinvents and asserts herself amongst the self-deluding, lazy and incompetent men of Virginian society. Behn's detrimental characterisation of the colonial male is a particularly striking feature of both texts: vicious in *Oroonoko*, ridiculous in *The Widow Ranter*, dishonest and cowardly in both.

Any reader who expects (sceptically or otherwise) this anthology to be a definitive collection of women's writing from the period is liable to be disappointed, for such a collection is a chimera.[2] Furthermore, the role of anthology has changed. When published in an environment where students have access to a vast array of sixteenth- and seventeeth-century materials via CD-ROM and the World Wide Web, plus numerous scholarly editions now residing in University libraries, the anthology is clearly no longer the monolithic structure it was once (however mistakenly) perceived to be. A student can find the rest of Behn's oeuvre or the remainder of *A Muzzle for Melastomus* far more easily than they could ten years ago, and so the particular selection is not necessarily the only source at the student's disposal. Most of the texts herein exist in fine scholarly editions too expensive for classroom use; some exist in other anthologies; others in classroom editions that, if bought separately, would still prove expensive.[3] This anthology is not an attempt to present an authoritative selection of the 'best' or 'most important' texts by women of the period. The editorial decision to select from only printed works immediately debars it from such status (if such status were indeed attainable by any collection).[4] Quite apart from the pragmatic decision to cover one mode of transmission reasonably well, rather than two modes badly, the difference between manuscript and print ought to be highlighted rather than occluded. Whilst some scholars have argued, quite rightly, that manuscript circulation was an important means of 'publishing', such 'publishing' is limited to *a* public, it does not make the texts available to *the* public, which, as envisaged by Habermas (1962, trans. 1989),[5] had begun to emerge in the period covered by the anthology. Paula McDowell summarises the key features thus:

> Mass-distributed texts addressed invisible publics from afar, generating new collective identities and silent adherents to a cause. And even with sharp restrictions on women's potential participation in public affairs through print, it may be said that print allowed for a more polyphonic engagement of individuals in controversy. (McDowell 1998, 291)

Indeed, the anxieties expressed by and about women of the period being writers are less concerned with the creative act itself and more about making the fruits of that act available for public scrutiny via the printing press. Ezell notes that:

> In prefaces of books by women, certain patterns emerge. Those women who printed under their own names took great pains to assure their readers that it was not a desire for personal fame and fortune that prompted them to print. (Ezell 1987, 87)

Whilst 'fortunes' were unlikely to be made by the woman writer, 'fame' is a different matter. Print was recognised as a valuable means of preservation as well as distribution. John Davies prefaced his *The Muse's Sacrifice* (1612) with a dedicatory poem that mildly admonished three women writers – Lucy Russell, Countess of Bedford; Mary Sidney Herbert, Countess of Pembroke; and Elizabeth Cary – for leaving their works in manuscript rather than having them published. His specific advice to the latter is telling:

> Such nervy Limbes of Art, and Straines of Wit
> 　　Times past ne'er knew the weaker sex to have;
> And Times to come, will hardly credit it,
> 　　if thus thou give thy Workes both Birth and Grave.
> 　　　　　　　　　　　　　　(Davies 1612, ***3ᵛ)[6]

Arguably, appearance in subsequent editions, or in an anthology of this nature, is the logical progression of an initial venture into print. Indeed, as Ingram notes, Margaret Cavendish's refusal to make modest excuses for publishing her *Poems, and Fancies* (1653) points to that very future:

> [I]f male poets imagined fame according to classical commonplace, as perpetuated through a monumental book that endures far beyond the author's lifetime, Cavendish proposed in "To All Noble, and Worthy Ladies" a definition of fame that depends less upon the lasting of a printed object: "For all I desire is Fame, and Fame is nothing but a great noise, and noise lives most in a multitude; wherefore I wish my Book may set a worke every Tongue" (A3ʳ). Fame so described is less *preserved* in Cavendish's folio than *initiated* by it; by setting tongues working, her book *begins* rather than completes a process. (Ingram 2000, 115–16, my emphasis)

Cavendish, the great self-publicist, is less concerned with the sanctity of the work than the survival of the text through intellectual engagement. In keeping with the overt motives of Cavendish and, by logical extension, the implicit ones of the other writers included here, this anthology is offered to keep further generations of tongues 'a worke', in the classroom and beyond.

Editorial Matters

The aim of this anthology is to make the texts user-friendly to the first-time reader. Therefore, I have not always retained the orthography and punctuation of the originals, choosing to prioritise accessibility of the text as read, over the idiosyncrasies of the physical work (Barthes 1977, 156–7). The textual notes indicate the location of copy-texts and also give microfilm references; the reader is, therefore, invited to compare my emendations with the originals.

The following conventions apply:

- **Spelling**

Spelling has been modernised throughout the anthology where it does not make a substantive difference to the pronunciation of original, especially where the letter represents the neutral vowel. For example, spelling of than/then and prefixes en/in and em/im have been standardised according to modern conventions, but prefixes un/in have not been, so 'imploy' becomes 'employ', but 'unconstant' has not been changed to 'inconstant'.

i/j and u/v substitutions have been standardised.

Where spellings of particular words are inconsistent within a text they have been standardised to the most modern usage within that text.

- **Punctuation**

Punctuation has been changed where necessary to clarify the meaning.

Where a colon is followed by a capital letter, it had been emended to a full stop.

- **Layout**

The use of capitals and italics has been standardised according to modern conventions.

Layout of the texts has been altered to match the housestyle of the series.

Where Biblical references are provided in the original, these are included in the main body of the text in round parentheses.

Where I have added Biblical references, these are included in the main body of the text in square parentheses [ ]. All references are taken from the King James Authorised Version, 1611.

Except in the case of stage directions in the three play texts, any other editorial additions have also been indicated in square parentheses [ ].

• Emendations

Where major emendations have been made, these have been listed in the textual notes.

• Explanatory notes

Brief explanatory notes are included on the first occurrence of the word/phrase/reference in each individual text.

Long explanatory notes are included on the first occurrence of the word/phase/reference in the whole anthology; for subsequent occurrences the reader is directed to the first note.

• Textual selection

All the selections are based upon the first editions, with the exception of the poems by Katherine Philips and Anne Bradstreet, which are based upon the authorised second editions.

Prefatory material not by the writers of the main texts has been omitted in all cases; prefatory material by the writers of the main texts has been omitted in cases where it has minimal relationship to the main text.

In each case the copy-text has been collated with another exemplar, and with the most recent modern editions, where available.

Notes

1. Hence the inclusion of Behn's *The Widow Ranter*, which technically falls just outside the terminal dates, being performed in 1689 and published in 1690; nevertheless Behn was writing it in 1688 and in the light of the events of that year rather than any subsequent years. And the reader may wish to compare this text, in which two of the leading female characters go into battle dressed as men, with the first selection, in which Queen Elizabeth addresses her army, whilst acknowledging her gendered exclusion from the battlefield.

2. Despite the obvious value of the anthology format, the anguished reaction 'what about [x]?' inevitably occurs in most readers as they realise that their favourite piece by Margaret Cavendish or Aphra Behn has been left out. I write from the experience of having such reactions myself and have adopted the most credible means of rejoinder, by compiling an anthology of my own. That said, the extent to which this collection is my own is questionable. The final version results partly from suggestions by colleagues and publishers' readers, and demands from the publishers themselves. Together these have transformed what was originally a personal selection (out went *The Countess of Lincoln's Nursery* and the full text of *A Muzzle for Melastomus*, in came *Oroonoko*) into a collection designed to take account of wider academic, pedagogic and commercial interests.

3. I write as an editor of one of those editions and therefore with a full appreciation that they have a flexibility that larger collections do not.

4. This should not be read as an implicit hierarchising of print over manuscript; the reader who takes it to be so is at best mistaken and at worst wilful in their interpretation.

5. Although Habermas takes little account of gender issues, the potential usefulness of his theories has been recognised by feminist scholars; see, for example Meehan (ed.) (1995).
   Gillespie makes particularly effective use of Habermasian theories in her work on Anna Trapnel (Gillespie 1997).

6. The fact that the publication of *The Tragedy of Mariam* occurred a year later suggests that Elizabeth Cary took Davies's advice.

ACKNOWLEDGEMENTS

Financial support for this project was gratefully received from the University of Sunderland, the Newberry Library and the British Academy. Moral support from colleagues at The University of Gloucestershire and the University of Sunderland, especially Valerie Sanders and Alison Younger, was equally appreciated. For helpful suggestions and comments I would like to thank Michael G. Brennan, Gordon Campbell, Alison Findlay, Neil Keeble, Susan J. Owen and Gweno Williams. For their patience and encouragement I would like to thank Jackie Jones and Carol MacDonald at Edinburgh University Press.

When the first scholarly anthology of women's writing of this period was published, I was ten years old; therefore, this anthology is much indebted to the work of a whole generation of scholars before me, many of whom are cited in the bibliography. I should like to thank them and especially my first tutors, Ann Thompson, Helen Wilcox and Marion Wynne-Davies. Finally, for her love, support and inspiration, I thank my mother, Barbara Wright.

CHRONOLOGY

1588   Repulsion of the Spanish Armada; war with Spain continues; Elizabeth I addresses the troops at Tilbury

1589   Premiere of Christopher Marlowe's *Dr Faustus*; Jane Anger's *Her Protection for Women*

1590   Virginia colony found abandoned by relief expedition; Edmund Spenser, *The Faerie Queene* (Books 1 to 3)

1591   Sir Philip Sidney, *Astrophil and Stella*

1592   Plague in London; Mary Sidney Herbert's translation of Mornay's *A Discourse of Life and Death*

1593   Rebellion in Ireland; death of Christopher Marlowe; dissolving of Parliament and speech by Elizabeth I

1594   Alleged plot to murder the Queen by her physician Dr Lopez

1596   Blackfriars Theatre opened in London

1597   Francis Bacon, *Essays*

1599   Globe Theatre opened in London; premiere of William Shakespeare's *Julius Caesar*; James VI *Basilikon Doron*

1600   East India Company founded; Fortune Theatre opened

1601   Earl of Essex's revolt against Elizabeth I fails and he is executed; Elizabeth I's Golden Speech

1602   Premiere of William Shakespeare's *Hamlet*; Mary Sidney Herbert 'A Dialogue between two shepherds, Thenot and Piers, in Praise of Astraea'

1603   Death of Queen Elizabeth I; accession of James VI of Scotland to the English throne; James and his wife, Queen Anna, journey south; end of Irish rebellion

1604   James proclaimed King of 'Great Britain'; peace made with Spain; first publication of William Shakespeare's *Hamlet*

1605   The Gunpowder Plot to blow up the Houses of Parliament and James I foiled

1606   Expedition departs to recolonise Virginia (originally established in 1585); premiere of Ben Jonson's *Volpone*

1607   Establishment of English colony at Jamestown in Virginia

harsh measures against those with Puritan sympathies; John Donne and George Herbert both publish books of poetry; William Prynne's attack on the theatre, *Histriomastix*

1634 Star Chamber and the Court of High Commission begin to treat political and religious opposition with increasing severity

1635 War declared between France and Spain

1637 Death of Ben Jonson

1638 Sir William Davenant made Poet Laureate

1639 First Bishops' War against the Scots, concluded without fighting

1640 Thomas Wentworth, chief adviser to the King, created Earl of Strafford; Second Bishops' War, in which English forces are defeated by the Scots; Long Parliament meets and the Commons impeach Laud and Strafford

1641 Execution of Strafford; Parliamentary supporters gain control of the government of London; Anne Stagg et al petition parliament

1642 Beginning of hostilities between supporters of the King (Royalists/ Cavaliers) and supporters of Parliament (Parliamentarians/ Roundheads); the indecisive Battle of Edge Hill fought; Long Parliament orders the closure of the London theatres; publication of Anne Stagg et al's *A True Copy of the Petition of Gentlewomen, and Tradesmen's Wives*

1643 Royalist forces succeeding in North and West of England; Parliamentary victory at Gloucester; indecisive battle at Newbury; Parliament secures the support of the Scots; Parliament revives censorship

1644 Royalist Parliament summoned at Oxford; parliamentary victory at Marston Moor; royalist victory at Lostwithiel; another indecisive battle at Newbury; John Milton, *Areopagitica*

1645 Execution of Laud; creation of New Model Army; parliamentary victories at Naseby and Langport

1646 Charles I surrenders to the Scots; Oxford surrenders to Parliament; end of the First Civil War.

1647 Scots hand Charles I over to Parliament; Parliament disbands the army without pay; the army seizes Charles I; Charles I escapes from the army to the Isle of Wight; makes a treaty with the Scots; beginning of Leveller movement

1648 Scots invade England on behalf of Charles I and are defeated at the battle of Preston; Second Civil War ends with the Treaty of Newport; Thirty Years War on the Continent ends with the Peace of Westphalia; Elizabeth Poole, *A Vision: Wherein is Manifested the Disease and Cure of the Kingdom*

1649 Trial and execution of Charles I; Charles II proclaimed King in Edinburgh; Cromwell leads successful seiges on Drogheda and Wexford in Ireland

1650 Cromwell returns from Ireland to become Lord General; Charles II lands in Scotland; Digger movement and Ranter movements at their height

1651 Charles II crowned King of Scots at Scone; Charles II escapes to France

1652 War with the United Provinces (the Dutch); American colonies recognise Parliamentary authoritiy

1653 Height of Fifth Monarchist movement

1654 Trial of Vavasor Powell; treaty of Westminster secures peace with the United Provinces; publication of Elizabeth I's Speech to the Troops at Tilbury in *Cabala, Mysteries of State*; Anna Trapnel, *Strange and Wonderful News from Whitehall*

1655 War with Spain in the colonies; Cromwell's treaty with France forces out exiled Royal family; readmission of the Jews to England

1657 Cromwell refuses the Crown but undergoes an Inauguration Ceremony with all regalia except the Crown

1658 Death of Cromwell; his son Richard succeeds him as Lord Protector

1659 Richard Cromwell resigns

1660 Charles II restored to the throne and arrives in London on 29 May, with Edward Hyde, Earl of Clarendon as chief minister; re-opening of the London theatres, with actresses appearing for the first time; Sir William Davenant and Thomas Killigrew, are given royal patents to establish theatre companies; establishment of the Royal Society; Samuel Pepys begins his *Diary*

1662 Charles II married Catherine of Braganza; playing of women's parts by male actors forbidden by Act of Parliament

1663 Premiere of Katherine Philip's translation of *Pompey* in Dublin; Mary Carleton, *The Case of Madam Mary Carleton*

1665 The Great Plague in London

1666 The Great Fire of London

1667 Fall of Clarendon; Charles rules with the aid of five ministers known as the 'Cabal'; John Milton, *Paradise Lost*; Katherine Philips, *Poems*

1668 Death of William Davenant; John Dryden succeeds him as Poet Laureate; Margaret Cavendish, *The Convent of Pleasure*

1669 James, Duke of York, converts to Catholicism; premiere of Frances Boothby's *Marcelia*, first original play by a woman playwright to be performed on the London stage

1670   Charles II secretly allies with the French via the Treaty of Dover; premiere of Aphra Behn's first play, *The Forced Marriage*
1672   Charles II's Declaration of Indulgence allows toleration to dissenters, Catholic and Puritan alike; Bathsua Makin, *An Essay to Revive the Ancient Education of Gentlewomen*
1673   First Test Act prevents non-Anglicans from holding public office
1674   Death of John Milton
1675   John Bunyan, imprisoned in Bedford Gaol, begins *The Pilgrim's Progress*
1676   Premiere of George Etherege's *The Man of Mode*
1677   Marriage of William of Orange and Mary, daughter of James, Duke of York
1678   Titus Oates alleges a 'Popish Plot' to murder Charles II; this precipitates attempts, led by the Earl of Shaftesbury, to exclude the Catholic James, Duke of York, from the succession in favour of Charles's illegitimate son, the Duke of Monmouth; Anne Bradstreet, *Several Poems*
1679   The Second Test Act excludes non-Anglicans from sitting in either House of Parliament
1680   Sir Robert Filmer, *Patriarcha*
1681   John Dryden, *Absalom and Achitophel*
1685   Death of Charles II; accession of James II; Monmouth's rebellion fails and he is executed; arrival of exiled Huguenots from the increasingly absolutist regime of Louise XIV in France increases alarm at the consequences for England of a Catholic King
1687   James II's Declaration of Indulgence, suspending the law in all matters ecclesiastical
1688   Arrival of William of Orange's army and entourage; deposition of James II; accession William and Mary, to reign jointly as William III and Mary II, although only William has regal power; Aphra Behn, *Oroonoko, or The Royal Slave*
1689   Premiere of Aphra Behn's *The Widow Ranter*
1690   Publication of *The Widow Ranter*

1588

1. Elizabeth I
Speech to the Troops at Tilbury
(published 1654)

My loving people, we have been persuaded by some, that are careful of our safety, to take heed how we commit our self to armed multitudes for fear of treachery; but I assure you, I do not desire to live to distrust my faithful, and loving people. Let tyrants fear, I have always so behaved myself, that under God I have placed my chiefest strength, and safeguard in the loyal hearts and good will of my subjects. And therefore I am come amongst you as you see, at this time, not for my recreation, and disport, but being resolved in the midst, and heat of the battle to live, or die amongst you all, to lay down for my God, and for my kingdom, and for my people, my honour, and my blood even in the dust. I know I have the body but of a weak and feeble woman, but I have the heart and stomach of a king, and of a king of England too, and think foul scorn that Parma or Spain, or any Prince of Europe should dare to invade the borders of my realm, to which rather than any dishonour shall grow by me, I myself will take up arms, I myself will be your General, Judge, and rewarder of every one of your virtues in the field. I know already for your forwardness, you have deserved rewards and crowns, and we do assure you in the word of a Prince, they shall be duly paid you. In the meantime my Lieutenant General shall be in my stead, than whom never Prince commanded a more noble or worthy subject, not doubting but by your obedience to my General, by your concord in the camp, and your valour in the field, we shall shortly have a famous victory over those enemies of my God, of my Kingdoms, and of my people.

1589

2. Jane Anger

from *Jane Anger, her Protection for Women. To defend
them against the scandalous reports of a late surfeiting lover,
and all other like venerians that complain so to be
overcloyed with women's kindness.*

To the gentlewomen of England, health.

Gentlewomen, though it is to be feared that your settled wits will advisedly
condemn that, which my choleric vein hath rashly set down, and so perchance, Anger shall reap anger for not agreeing with diseased persons. Yet
(if with indifferency of censure, you consider of the head of the quarrel) I
hope you will rather show yourselves defendants of the defender's title,
than complainants of the plaintiff's wrong. I doubt judgement before trial,
which were injurious to the law, and I confess that my rashness deserveth
no less, which was a fit of my extremity. I will not urge reasons because
your wits are sharp and will soon conceive my meaning, nor will I be
tedious lest I prove too, too troublesome, nor over dark in my writing, for
fear of the name of a riddler. But (in a word) for my presumption I crave
pardon, because it was Anger that did write it: committing your protection, and myself, to the protection of yourselves, and the judgement of the
cause to the censures of your just minds.
Yours ever at commandment,
Ja: A.

To all women in general, and gentle reader whatsoever.

Fie on the falsehood of men, whose minds go oft a madding, and whose
tongues cannot so soon be wagging, but straight they fall a railing. Was
there ever any so abused, so slandered, so railed upon, or so wickedly
handled undeservedly, as are we women? Will the Gods permit it, the
Goddesses stay their punishing judgements, and we ourselves not pursue
their undoings for such devilish practises? O Paul's steeple and Charing
Cross! A halter hold all such persons. Let the streams of the channels in
London streets run so swiftly, as they may be able alone to carry them from
that sanctuary. Let the stones be as ice, the soles of their shoes as glass, the
ways steep like Ætna, and every blast a whirl-wind puffed out of Boreas his
long throat, that these may hasten their passage to the Devil's haven. Shall
surfeiters rail on our kindness, you stand still and say nought, and shall not
Anger stretch the veins of her brains, the strings of her fingers, and the lists

of her modesty, to answer their surfeitings? Yes truly. And herein I conjure all you to aid and assist me in defence of my willingness, which shall make me rest at your commands. Fare you well.
Your friend,
Ja. A.

A Protection for Women

The desire that every man hath to show his true vein in writing is unspeakable, and their minds are so carried away with the manner, as no care at all is had of the matter: they run so into rhetoric, as often times they overrun the bounds of their own wits, and go they know not whither. If they have stretched their invention so hard on a last, as it is at a stand, there remains but one help, which is, to write of us women. If they may once encroach so far into our presence, as they may but see the lining of our outermost garment, they straight think that Apollo honours them, in yielding so good a supply to refresh their sore overburdened heads, through studying for matters to indict of. And therefore that the God may see how thankfully they receive his liberality, (their wits whetted, and their brains almost broken with botching his bounty) they fall straight to dispraising and slandering our silly sex. But judge what the cause should be, of this their so great malice towards simple women. Doubtless the weakness of our wits, and our honest bashfulness, by reason whereof they suppose that there is not one amongst us who can, or dare reprove their slanders and false reproaches: their slanderous tongues are so short, and the time wherein they have lavished out their words freely, hath been so long, that they know we cannot catch hold of them to pull them out, and they think we will not write to reprove their lying lips: which conceits have already made them cocks and would (should they not be cravened) make themselves among themselves be thought to be of the game. They have been so daintily fed with our good natures, that like jades (their stomachs are grown so queasy) they surfeit of our kindness. If we will not suffer them to smell on our smocks, they will snatch at our petticoats: but if our honest natures cannot away with that uncivil kind of jesting then we are coy: yet if we bear with their rudeness, and be somewhat modestly familiar with them, they will straight make matter of nothing, blazing abroad that thy have surfeited with love, and then their wits must be shown in telling the manner how.

❀ ❀ ❀ ❀

Their eyes are so curious, as be not all women equal with Venus for beauty, they cannot abide the sight of them: their stomachs so queasy, as do they taste but twice of one dish they straight surfeit, and needs must a new diet be provided for them. We are contrary to men, because they are contrary to that which is good: because they are purblind, they cannot see into our natures, and we too well (though we had but half an eye) into their conditions, because they are so bad: our behaviours alter daily, because men's virtues decay hourly. If Hesiodus had with equity as well looked into the life of man, as he did precisely search out the qualities of us women, he would have said, that if a woman trust unto a man, it shall fare as well with her, as if she had a weight of a thousand pounds tied about her neck, and then cast into the bottomless seas: for by men are we confounded though they by us are sometimes crossed. Our tongues are light, because earnest in reproving men's filthy vices, and our good counsel is termed nipping injury, in that it accords not with their foolish fancies. Our boldness rash, for giving noddies nipping answers, our dispositions naughty, for not agreeing with their vile minds, and our fury dangerous, because it will not bear with their knavish behaviours. If our frowns be so terrible, and our anger so deadly, men are too foolish in offering occasions of hatred, which shunned, a terrible death is prevented. There is a continual deadly hatred between the wild boar and tame hounds, I would there were the like betwixt women and men unless they amend their manners, for so strength should predominate, where now flattery and dissimulation hath the upper hand. The lion rageth when he is hungry, but man raileth when he is glutted. The tiger is robbed of her young ones, when she is ranging abroad, but men rob women of their honour undeservedly under their noses. The viper stormeth when his tail is trodden on, and may not we fret when all our body is a footstool to their vile lust? Their unreasonable minds which know not what reason is, make them nothing better than brute beasts. But let us grant that Clytemnestra, Ariadna, Delilah, and Jezebel were spotted with crimes: shall not Nero with others innumerable, and therefore unnameable join hands with them and lead the dance?

✵ ✵ ✵ ✵

The creation of man and woman at the first, he being formed *In principio* of dross and filthy clay, did so remain until God saw that in him his work-manship was good, and therefore by the transformation of the dust which was loathsome unto flesh, it became purified. Then lacking a help for him, God making woman of man's flesh, that she might be purer than he, doth evidently show, how far we women are more excellent than men. Our bodies are fruitful, whereby the world increaseth, and our care wonderful, by which man is preserved. From woman sprang man's salvation. A woman was the first that believed, and a woman likewise the first that repented of sin. In women is only true fidelity: (except in her) there is [no] constancy, and without her no huswifery. In the time of their sickness we cannot be wanted, and when they are in health we for them are most necessary. They are comforted by our means: they are nourished by the meats we dress: their bodies freed from diseases by our cleanliness, which otherwise would surfeit unreasonably through their own noisomeness. Without our care they lie in their beds as dogs in litter, and go like lousy mackerel swimming in the heat of summer. They love to go handsomely in their apparel, and rejoice in the pride thereof, yet who is the cause of it, but our carefulness, to see that everything about them be curious. Our virginity makes us virtuous, our conditions courteous, and our chastity maketh our trueness of love manifest. They confess we are necessary, but they would have us likewise evil. That they cannot want us I grant: yet evil I deny: except only in the respect of man, who, hating all good things, is only desirous of that which is ill, through whose desire, in estimation of conceit we are made ill. But lest some should snarl on me, barking out this reason: that none is good but God, and therefore women are ill. I must yield that in that respect we are ill, and affirm that men are no better, seeing we are so necessary unto them. It is most certain, that if we be ill, they are worse: for *Malum malo additum efficit malum peius*: and they that use ill worse than it should be, are worse than the ill. And therefore if they will correct *Magnificat*, they must first learn the signification thereof. That we are liberal, they will not deny sithence that many of them have (*ex confessio*) received more kindness in one day at our hands, than they can repay in a whole year: and some have so glutted themselves with our liberality as they cry 'No more'. But if they shall avow that women are fools, we may safely give them the lie: for myself have heard some of them confess that we have more wisdom than need is, and therefore no fools: and they less than they should have, and therefore fools. It hath been affirmed by some of their sex, that to shun a shower of rain, and to know the way to our husband's bed is wisdom sufficient for us women: but in this year of '88, men are grown so fantastical, that unless we can make them fools, we are accounted unwise. And now (seeing I speak to none but to you which are of mine own sex,) give me leave like a scholar to prove our wisdom more excellent than theirs, though I never knew what sophistry meant. There is no wisdom but it comes by grace, this is a principle, and *Contra principium non est disputandum*: but grace was first given to a woman, because to Our Lady: which premises conclude that women are wise. Now *Primum est optimum*, and therefore women are wiser than men. That we are more witty which comes by nature, it cannot better be proved, than that by our answers, men are often driven to *Non plus*, and if their talk be of worldly affairs, with our resolutions they must either rest satisfied, or prove themselves fools in the end.

❀ ❀ ❀

At the end of men's fair promises there is a labyrinth, and therefore ever hereafter stop your ears when they protest friendship, lest they come to an end before you are aware, whereby you fall without redemption. The path which leadeth thereunto, is man's wit, and the miles' ends are marked with these trees: Folly, Vice, Mischief, Lust, Deceit, and Pride. These to deceive you shall be clothed in the raiments of Fancy, Virtue, Modesty, Love, Truemeaning, and Handsomeness. Folly will bid you welcome on your way, and tell you his fancy, concerning the profit which may come to you by this journey, and direct you to Vice who is more crafty. He with a company of protestations will praise the virtues of women, showing how many ways men are beholden unto us: but our backs once turned, he falls a railing. Then Mischief he pries into every corner of us, seeing if he can espy a cranny, that getting in his finger into it, he may make it wide enough for his tongue to wag in. Now being come to Lust: he will fall a railing on lascivious looks, and will ban Lechery, and with the collier will say, the devil take him though he never means it. Deceit will give you fair words, and pick your pockets: nay he will pluck out your hearts, if you be not wary. But when you hear one cry out against lawns, drawn-works, peri-wigs, against the attire of courtesans, and generally of the pride of all women: then know him for a wolf clothed in sheep's raiment, and be sure you are fast by the lake of destruction. Therefore take heed of it, which you shall do, if you shun men's flattery, the forerunner of our undoing. If a jade be galled, will he not winch? And can you find fault with a horse that springeth when he is spurred? The one will stand quietly when his back is healed, and the other go well when his smart ceaseth. You must bear with the old Lover his Surfeit, because he was diseased when he did write it, and peradventure hereafter, when he shall be well amended, he will repent himself of his slanderous speeches against our sex, and curse the dead man which was the cause of it, and make a public recantation: For the faltering in his speech at the latter end of his book affirmeth, that already he half repenteth of his bargain, and why? Because his melody is past: but believe him not, though he should out swear you, for although a jade may be still in a stable when his gall back is healed, yet he will show himself in his kind when he is travelling: and man's flattery bites secretly, from which I pray God keep you and me too. Amen.

1592

3. Mary Sidney Herbert, Countess of Pembroke
from *A Discourse of Life and Death*

It seems to me strange, and a thing much to be marvelled, that the labourer to repose himself hasteneth as it were the course of the sun, that the mariner rows with all force to attain the port, and with a joyful cry salutes the descried land, that the traveller is never quiet nor content till he be at the end of his voyage, and that we in the meanwhile tied in this world to a perpetual task, tossed with continual tempest, tired with a rough and cumbersome way, cannot yet see the end of our labour but with grief, nor behold our port but with tears, nor approach our home and quiet abode but with horror and trembling. This life is but a Penelope's web, wherein we are always doing and undoing; a sea open to all winds, which sometime within, sometime without never cease to torment us: a weary journey through extreme heats, and colds, over high mountains, steep rocks, and thievish deserts. And so we term it in weaving at this web, in rowing at this oar, in passing this miserable way. Yet lo when death comes to end our work, when she stretcheth out her arms to pull us into the port, when after so many dangerous passages, and loathsome lodgings she would conduct us to our true home and resting place, instead of rejoicing at the end of our labour, of taking comfort at the sight of our land, of singing at the approach of our happy mansion, we would fain, (who would believe it?) retake our work in hand, we would again hoist sail to the wind, and willingly undertake our journey anew. No more then remember we our pains, our shipwrecks and dangers are forgotten; we fear no more the travails nor the thieves. Contrariwise, we apprehend death as an extreme pain, we doubt it as a rock, we fly it as a thief. We do as little children, who all the day complain, and when the medicine is brought them, are no longer sick, as they who all the week long run up and down the streets with pain of the teeth, and seeing the barber coming to pull them out, feel no more pain, as those tender and delicate bodies, who in pricking pleurisy complain, cry out, and cannot stay for a surgeon, and when they see him whetting his lancet to cut the throat of the disease, pull in their arms, and hide them in the bed, as if he were come to kill them. We fear more the cure than the disease, the surgeon than the pain, the stroke than the impostume. We have more sense of the medicine's bitterness soon gone, than of a bitter languishing long continued, more feeling of death the end of our miseries, than the endless misery of our life. And whence proceedeth this folly and simplicity? We neither know life, nor death. We fear that we ought to hope for, and wish for that we ought to fear. We call life a continual death, and death the issue of a living death, and the entrance of a never dying life. Now what good, I pray you, is there in life, that we should so much pursue it? Or what evil is there in death, that we should so much eschew it? Nay what evil is there not in life, and what good is there not in death? Consider all the periods of this life. We enter it in tears, we pass it in sweat, we end it in sorrow. Great and little, rich and poor, not one in the whole world, that can plead immunity from this condition.

❈ ❈ ❈

At a word, whatsoever happiness can be in that ambition promiseth, is but suffering much ill, to get ill. Men think by daily climbing higher to pluck themselves out of this ill, and the height whereunto they so painfully aspire, is the height of misery itself. I speak not here of the wretchedness of them who all their life have held out their cap to receive the alms of court fortune, and can get nothing (often with incredible heart grief, seeing some by less pains taken have riches fall into their hands), of them, who jostling one another to have it, lose it, and cast it into the hands of a third, of those, who holding it in their hands to hold it faster, have lost it through their fingers. Such by all men are esteemed unhappy, and are indeed so, because they judge themselves so. It sufficeth that all these liberalities which the Devil casteth us as out at a window, are but baits, all these pleasures but ambushes, and that he doth but make his sport of us, who strive one with another for such things, as most unhappy is he, that hath best hap to find them. Well now, you will say, the Covetous in all his goods, hath no good, the Ambitious at the best he can be, is but ill. But may there not be some, who supplying the place of Justice, or being near about a prince, may without following such unbridled passions, pleasantly enjoy their goods, joining honour with rest and contentment of mind? Surely in former ages (there yet remaining among men some sparks of sincerity) in some sort it might be so, but being of that composition they now are, I see not how it may be in any sort. For deal you in affairs of estate in these times, either you shall do well, or you shall do ill. If ill, you have God for your enemy, and your own conscience for a perpetually tormenting executioner. If well, you have men for your enemies, and of men, the greatest whose envy and malice will spy you out, and whose cruelty and tyranny will evermore threaten you. Please the people you please a beast, and pleasing such, ought to be displeasing to yourself. Please yourself, you displease God; please him, you incur a thousand dangers in the world, with purchase of a thousand displeasures. Whereof it grows, that if you could hear the talk of the wisest and least discontent of this kind of men, whether they speak advisedly, or their words pass them by force of truth, one would gladly change garment with his tenant; another preacheth how goodly an estate it is to have nothing; a third, complaining that his brains are broken with the noise of court or palace, hath no other thought, but as soon as he may to retire himself thence. So that you shall not see any but is displeased with his own calling, and envieth that of another, ready nevertheless to repent him, if a man should take him at his word. None but is weary of the businesses whereunto his age is subject, and wisheth not to be elder, to free himself of them, albeit otherwise he keepeth of old age as much as in him lieth.

What must we then do in so great a contrariety and confusion of minds? Must we to find true humanity, fly the society of men, and hide us in forests among wild beasts? To avoid these unruly passions, eschew the assembly of creatures supposed reasonable? To pluck us out of the evils of the world, sequester ourselves from the world? Could we in so doing live at rest, it were something.

But alas, men cannot take herein what part they would: and even they which do, find not there all the rest they sought for.

❋ ❋ ❋ ❋

They fly the court, and a court follows them on all sides; they endeavour to escape the world, and the world pursues them to death. Hardly in this world can they find a place where the world finds them not, so greedily it seeks to murther them.

And if by some special grace of God they seem for a while free from these dangers, they have some poverty that troubles them, some domestical debate that torments them, or some familiar spirit that tempts them. Briefly the world daily in some sort or other makes itself felt of them. But the worst is, when we are out of these external wars and troubles, we find greater civil war within ourselves: the flesh against the spirit, passion against reason, earth against heaven, the world within us fighting for the world, evermore so lodged in the bottom of our own hearts, that on no side we can fly from it. I will say more: he makes profession to fly the world who seeks thereby the praise of the world; he feigneth to run away who according to the proverb 'By drawing back sets himself forward', he refuseth honours, that would thereby be prayed to take them and hides him from men to the end they should come to seek him. So the world often harbours in disguised attire among them that fly the world. This is an abuse. But follow we the company of men, the world hath his court among them. Seek we the deserts, it hath there his dens and places of resort, and in the desert itself tempteth Christ Jesus. Retire we ourselves into ourselves, we find it there as unclean as anywhere. We cannot make the world die in us, but by dying ourselves. We are in the world, and the world in us, and to separate us from the world, we must separate us from ourselves. Now this separation is called death. We are, we think, come out of the contagious city, but we are not advised that we have sucked the bad air, that we carry the plague with us, that we so participate with it, that through rocks, through deserts, through mountains, it ever accompanieth us. Having avoided the contagion of others, yet we have it in ourselves. We have withdrawn us out of men, but not withdrawn man out of us. The tempestuous sea torments us; we are grieved at the heart, and desirous to vomit and to be discharged thereof; we remove out of one ship into another, from a greater to less; we promise ourselves rest in vain, they being always the same winds that blow, the same waves that swell, the same humours that are stirred. To all no other port, no other mean of tranquillity but only death. We were sick in a chamber near the street, or near the market; we caused ourselves to be carried into some backer closet, where the noise was not so great. But though there the noise was less, yet was the fever there nevertheless and thereby lost nothing of his heat. Change bed, chamber, house, country, again and again we shall everywhere find the same unrest, because everywhere we find ourselves and seek not so much to be others, as to be otherwheres. We follow solitariness, to fly carefulness. We retire us (so say we) from the wicked but carry with us our avarice, our ambition, our riotousness, all our corrupt affections[.]

❀ ❀ ❀ ❀

Behold, now comes Death unto us. Behold her, whose approach we so much fear. We are now to consider whether she be such as we are made believe and whether we ought so greatly to fly her, as commonly we do. We are afraid of her, but like little children of a vizard, or of the images of Hecate. We have her in horror, but because we conceive her not such as she is, but ugly, terrible, and hideous, such as it pleaseth the painters to represent unto us on a wall. We fly before her, but it is because, foretaken with such vain imaginations, we give not ourselves leisure to mark her. But stay we, stand we steadfast, look we her in the face, we shall find her quite other than she is painted us and altogether of other countenance than our miserable life. Death makes an end of this life. This life is a perpetual misery and tempest. Death then is the issue of our miseries and entrance of the port where we shall ride in safety from all winds. And should we fear that which withdraweth us from misery, or which draws us into our haven? Yea, but you will say, it is a pain to die. Admit it be: so is there in curing of a wound. Such is the world, that one evil cannot be cured but by another; to heal a contusion, must be made an incision. You will say, there is difficulty in the passage: so is there no haven, no port, whereinto the entrance is not strait and cumbersome. No good thing is to be bought in this world with other than the coin of labour and pain. The entrance indeed is hard, if ourselves make it hard, coming thither with a tormented spirit, a troubled mind, a wavering and irresolute thought. But bring we quietness of mind, constancy, and full resolution, we shall not find any danger or difficulty at all. Yet what is the pain that death brings us? Nay, what can she do with those pains we feel? We accuse her of all the evils we abide in ending our life, and consider not how many more grievous wounds or sicknesses we have endured without death, or how many more vehement pains we have suffered in this life, in the which we called even her to our succour. All the pains our life yields us at the last hour we impute to death, not marking that life begun and continued in all sorts of pain, must also necessarily end in pain. Not marking (I say) that it is the remainder of our life, not death, that tormenteth us, the end of our navigation that pains us, not the haven we are to enter, which is nothing else but a safeguard against all winds. We complain of death, where we should complain of life, as if one having been long sick, and beginning to be well, should accuse his health of his last pains, and not the relics of his disease. Tell me, what is it else to be dead, but to be no more living in the world? Absolutely and simply not to be in the world, is it any pain? Did we then feel any pain, when as yet we were not? Have we ever more resemblance of death, than when we sleep? Or ever more rest than at that time? Now if this be no pain, why accuse we death of the pains our life gives us at our departure, unless also we will fondly accuse the time when as yet we were not, of the pains we felt at our birth? If the coming in be with tears, is it wonder that such be the going out? If the beginning of our being, be the beginning of our pain, is it marvel that such be the ending? But if our not being in times past hath been without pain, and all this being contrariwise full of pain, whom should we by reason accuse of the last pains, the not being to come, or the remnant of this present being? We think we die not, but when we yield up our last gasp. But if we mark well, we die every day, every hour, every moment. We apprehend death as a thing unusual to us and yet have nothing so common in us. Our living is but continual dying. Look how much we live, we die; how much we increase, our life decreases. We enter not a step into life, but we enter a step into death. Who hath lived a third part of his years, hath a third part of himself dead. Who half his years, is already half dead. Of our life, all the time past is dead, the present lives and dies a once, and the future likewise shall die. The past is no more, the future is not yet, the present is, and no more is. Briefly, this whole life is but a death. It is as a candle lighted in our bodies: in one the wind makes it melt away, and in another blows it clean out many times ere it be half burned, in others it endureth to the end. Howsoever it be, look how much it shineth, so much it burneth: her shining is her burning, her light a vanishing smoke, her last fire, her last wick, and her last drop of moisture. So is it in the life of man, life and death in man is all one. If we call the last breath death, so must we all the rest, all proceeding from one place, and all in one manner. One only difference there is between this life, and that we call death: that during the one, we have always whereof to die and after the other, there remaineth only whereof to live. In sum, even he that thinketh death simply to be the end of man, ought not to fear it: inasmuch as who desireth to live longer, desireth to die longer and who feareth soon to die, feareth (to speak properly) lest he may not longer die.

❀ ❀ ❀

Now to end well this life, is only to end it willingly, following with full consent the will and direction of God, and not suffering us to be drawn by the necessity of destiny. To end it willingly, we must hope, and not fear death. To hope for it, we must certainly look after this life, for a better life. To look for that, we must fear God, whom whoso well feareth, feareth indeed nothing in this world, and hopes for all things in the other. To one well resolved in these points death can be but sweet and agreeable, knowing that through it he is to enter into a place of all joys. The grief that may be therein shall be allayed with sweetness, the sufferance of ill, swallowed in the confidence of good, the sting of death itself shall be dead, which is nothing else but fear. Nay, I will say more. Not only all the evils conceived in death shall be to him nothing, but he shall even scorn all the mishaps men redoubt in this life, and laugh at all these terrors. For I pray what can he fear, whose death is his hope? Think we to banish him his country? He knows he hath a country other-where, whence we cannot banish him, and that all these countries are but inns, out of which he must part at the will of his host. To put him in prison? A more strait prison he cannot have, than his own body, more filthy, more dark, more full of racks and torments. To kill him and take him out of the world? That is it he hopes for, that is it with all his heart he aspires unto. By fire, by sword, by famine, by sickness: within three years, within three days, within three hours, all is one to him, all is one at what gate, or at what time he pass out of this miserable life. For his businesses are ever ended, his affairs all dispatched, and by what way he shall go out, by the same he shall enter into a most happy and everlasting life. Men can threaten him but death, and death is all he promiseth himself.

The worst they can do is to make him die, and that is the best he hopes for. The threatenings of tyrants are to him promises, the swords of his greatest enemies drawn in his favour: forasmuch as he knows that threatening him death, they threaten him life and the most mortal wounds can make him but immortal. Who fears God, fears not death and who fears it not, fears not the worst of this life.

By this reckoning, you will tell me death is a thing to be wished for and to pass from so much evil, to so much good, a man should as it seemeth cast away his life. Surely, I fear not, that for any good we expect, we will hasten one step the faster: though the spirit aspire, the body it draws with it, withdraws it ever sufficiently towards the earth. Yet is it not that I conclude. We must seek to mortify our flesh in us, and to cast the world out of us, but to cast ourselves out of the world is in no sort permitted us. The Christian ought willingly to depart out of this life but not cowardly to run away. The Christian is ordained by God to fight therein and cannot leave his place without incurring reproach and infamy. But if it please the grand Captain to recall him, let him take the retrait in good part, and with good will obey it. For he is not born for himself, but for God: of whom he holds his life at farm, as his tenant at will, to yield him the profits. It is in the landlord to take it from him, not in him to surrender it, when a conceit takes him. Diest thou young? Praise God as the mariner that hath had a good wind, soon to bring him to port. Diest thou old? Praise him likewise, for if thou hast had less wind, it may be thou hast also had less waves. But think not at thy pleasure to go faster or softer: for the wind is not in thy power, and instead of taking the shortest way to the haven, thou mayest happily suffer shipwreck. God calleth home from his work, one in the morning, another at noon, and another at night. One he exerciseth till the first sweat, another he sunburneth, another he roasteth and drieth throughly. But of all His He leaves not one without, but brings them all to rest, and gives them all their hire, every one in his time. Who leaves his work before God call him, loses it, and who importunes him before the time, loses his reward. We must rest us in his will, who in the midst of our troubles sets us at rest.

To end, we ought neither to hate this life for the toils therein, for it is sloth and cowardice; nor love it for the delights, which is folly and vanity; but serve us of it, to serve God in it, who after it shall place us in true quietness, and replenish us with pleasures which shall never more perish. Neither ought we to fly death, for it is childish to fear it and in flying from it, we meet it. Much less to seek it, for that is temerity; nor everyone that would die, can die. As much despair in the one, as cowardice in the other; in neither any kind of magnanimity. It is enough that we constantly and continually wait for her coming, that she may never find us unprovided. For as there is nothing more certain than death, so is there nothing more uncertain than the hour of death, known only to God, the only Author of life and death, to whom we all ought endeavour both to live and die. Die to live, live to die.

———

1593

4. Elizabeth I

Speech at the Dissolving of Parliament
(printed 1615)

My Lords, and you, my Commons of the Lower House, were it not that I know no speeches presented by any other, nor words delivered by any substitute, can be so deeply imprinted into your minds, as spoken by herself, whose order and direction was but followed and delivered by the Lord Keeper, I could be content to spare speech, whom silence better pleaseth than to speak. And because much hath been spoken, much less shall I now need to speak of mine own indisposition in nature, and small desire in private respect to be enriched by you present, which words shall not witness, but deeds, by your former experience, having expended what I have received, to the preservation and defence of yourselves. And thus much I dare assure you, that the care you have taken for myself, yourselves, and the commonweal, that you do it for a prince that neither careth for any particular – no, not for life – but so to live that you may flourish. For before God and in my conscience, I protest, whereunto many that know me can witness, that the great expense of my time, the labour of my studies, and the travail of my thoughts chiefly tendeth to God's service and the government of you, to live in a flourishing and happy estate; God forbid you should ever know any change thereof. Many wiser princes than myself you have had, but one only excepted, none more careful over you (whom in the duty of a child I must regard and to whom I must acknowledge myself far shallow). I may truly say none whose love and care can be greater, or whose desire can be more to fathom deeper for prevention of danger to come or resisting of dangers, if attempted towards you, shall ever be found to exceed myself in love, I say, towards you and care over you. You have heard in the beginning of this Parliament some doubt of danger, more than I would have you to fear. Doubt only should be if not prevented; and fear, if not provided for.

For mine own part, I protest I never feared; and what fear was, my heart never knew. For I knew that my cause was ever just, and it standeth upon a sure foundation that I should not fail, God assisting the quarrel of the rightwise, and such as are but to defend. Glad might that king, my greatest enemy, be to have the like advantage against me, if in truth for his own actions he might truly so say. For in ambition of glory I have never sought to enlarge the territories of my land, nor thereby to advance you. If I have used my forces to keep the enemy far from you, I have thereby thought your safety the greater and your danger the less. If you suppose I have done it for fear of the enemy, or in doubt of his revenge, I know his power is not to prevail, nor his force to fear me, having so mighty a Protector on my side. I would not have you returning into the country to strike fear into the minds of any of my people, as some, upon the arrival of the late navy, dwelling in a maritane shire fled for fear farther into the middle of the land. But if I had been by him, I would sure have taught him to have showed so base and cowardly a courage, for even our enemies hold our nature resolute and valiant, which though they will not outwardly show, they inwardly know. And whensoever the malice of our enemies shall cause them to make any attempt against us, I doubt not but we shall have the greater glory, God fighting for those that truly serve Him with the justness of their quarrel. Only let them know to be wary, and not to be found sleeping; so shall they show their own valour and frustrate the hopes of the enemies. And thus far let me charge you that be lieutenants and you that in shires have the leading of the most choice and serviceable men under your bands: that you see them sufficiently exercised and trained so oft as need shall require, that the wants of any of them be supplied by others to be placed in their rooms, and that all decays of armour be presently repaired and made sufficient. The enemy, finding yor care such and so great to provide for him, will with the less courage think of your disturbance. To conclude, that I may show my thankful mind, in my conscience never having been willing to draw from you but what you should contentedly give, and that for yourselves, and having my head by years and experience better stayed – whatsoever any shall suppose to the contrary – than that you may easily believe that I will enter into any idle expenses: now must I give you all as great thanks as ever prince gave to loving subjects, assuring you that my care for you hath, and shall, exceed all my other cares of worldly causes whatsoever.

1601

5. Elizabeth I
The Golden Speech

Mr Speaker, we perceive by you, whom we did constitute the mouth of our Lower House, how with even consent they are fallen into the due consideration of the precious gift of thankfulness, most usually least esteemed, where it is best deserved. And therefore we charge you tell them how acceptable such sacrifice is worthily received of a loving king who doubteth much whether the given thanks can be of more poise than the owed is to them; and suppose that they have done more for us than they themselves believe. And this is our reason: who keeps their sovereign from the lapse of error, in which, by ignorance and not by intents they might have fallen, what thanks they deserve, we know, though you may guess. And as nothing is more dear to us than the loving conservation of our subjects' hearts, what an undeserved doubt might we have incurred if the abusers of our liberality, the thrallers of our people, the wringers of the poor, had not been told us! Which, ere our heart or hand should agree unto, we wish we had neither, and do thank you the more, supposing that such griefs touch not some amongst you in particular. We trust there resides in their conceits of us no such simple cares of their good, whom we so dearly prize, that our hand should pass aught that might injure any, though they doubt not it is lawful for our kingly state to grant gifts of sundry sorts of whom we make election, either for service done or merit to be deserved, as being for a king to make choice on whom to bestow benefits, more to one than another.

You must not beguile yourselves, nor wrong us, to think that the glozing lustre of a glistering glory of a king's title may so extol us that we think all is lawful what we list, not caring what we do. Lord, how far should you be off from our conceits! For our part we vow unto you that we suppose physicians' aromatical savours, which in the top of their potion they deceive the patient with, or gilded drugs that they cover their bitter sweet with, are not more beguilers of senses than the vaunting boast of a kingly name may deceive the ignorant of such an office. I grant that such a prince as cares but for the dignity, nor passes not how the reins be guided, so he rule, to such a one it may seem an easy business. But you are cumbered (I dare assure) with no such prince, but such a one as looks how to give account afore another tribunal seat than this world affords, and that hopes that if we discharge with conscience what He bids, will not lay to our charge the fault that our substitutes (not being our crime) fall in. We think ourselves most fortunately born under such a star, as we have been enabled by God's power to have saved you under our reign from foreign foes, from tyrants' rule, and from your own ruin; and do confess that we pass not so much to be a queen as to be a queen of such subjects, for whom (God is witness, without boast or vaunt) we would willingly lose our life ere see such to perish. I bless God, He hath given me never this fault of fear; for He knows best whether ever fear possessed me, for all my dangers. I know it is His gift, and not to hide His glory, I say it. For were it not for conscience and for your sake, I would willingly yield another my place; so great is my pride in reigning as she that wisheth no longer to be than best and most would have me so. You know our presence cannot assist each action, but must distribute in sundry sorts to diverse kinds our commands. If they (as the greatest number be commonly the worst) should (as I doubt not but some do) abuse their charge, annoy whom they should help, and dishonour their king, whom they should serve, yet we verily believe that all you will (in your best judgement) discharge us from such guilts. Thus we commend us to your constant faith, and yourselves to your best fortunes.

⊏══⊐

1602

6. Mary Sidney Herbert, Countess of Pembroke
A Dialogue between two shepherds, Thenot and Piers,
in praise of Astrea

Thenot
I sing divine Astrea's praise,
O Muses! help my wits to raise,
   And heave my verses higher.
Piers
Thou needst the truth but plainly tell,
Which much I doubt thou canst not well,
   Thou art so oft a liar.

Thenot
If in my song no more I show,
Than Heav'n, and Earth, and sea do know,
   Then truly I have spoken.

Piers
Sufficeth not no more to name,
But being no less, the like, the same,
    Else laws of truth be broken.

Thenot
Then say, she is so good, so fair,
With all the Earth she may compare,
    Not Momus' self denying.
Piers
Compare may think where likeness holds,
Nought like to her the earth enfolds,
    I looked to find you lying.

Thenot
Astrea sees with wisdom's sight,
Astrea works by virtue's might,
    And jointly both do stay in her.
Piers
Nay take from them, her hand, her mind,
The one is lame, the other blind,
    Shall still your lying stain her?

Thenot
Soon as Astrea shows her face,
Straight every ill avoids the place,
    And every good aboundeth.
Piers
Nay long before her face doth show,
The last doth come, the first doth go,
    How loud this lie resoundeth!

Thenot
Astrea is our chiefest joy,
Our chiefest guard against annoy,
    Our chiefest wealth, our treasure.
Pier
Where chiefest are, three others be,
To us none else but only she;
    When wilt thou speak in measure?

Thenot
Astrea may be justly said,
A field in flow'ry robe arrayed,
    In season freshly springing.
Piers
That spring endures but shortest time,
This never leaves Astrea's clime,
    Thou liest, instead of singing.

Thenot
As heavenly light that guides the day,
Right so doth thine each lovely ray,
    That from Astrea flieth.
Piers
Nay, darkness oft that light enclouds,
Astrea's beams no darkness shrouds;
    How loudly Thenot lieth!

Thenot
Astrea rightly term I may,
A manly palm, a maiden bay,
    Her verdure never dying.
Piers
Palm oft is crooked, bay is low,
She still upright, still high doth grow,
    Good Thenot leave thy lying.

Thenot
Then Piers, of friendship tell me why,
My meaning true, my words should lie,
    And strive in vain to raise her.
Piers
Words from conceit do only rise,
Above conceit her honour flies;
    But silence, nought can praise her.

1611

7. Aemilia Lanyer

from *Salve Deus Rex Judæorum*. Containing,
*1 The Passion of Christ. 2 Eve's Apology in defence of Women.
3 The Tears of the Daughters of Jerusalem.
4. The Salutation and Sorrow of the Virgin Mary.*
With diverse other things not unfit to be read

To the virtuous reader

Often have I heard, that it is the property of some women, not only to emulate the virtues and perfections of the rest, but also by all their powers of ill speaking, to eclipse the brightness of their deserved fame. Now contrary to this custom, which men I hope unjustly lay to their charge, I have written this small volume, or little book, for the general use of all virtuous ladies and gentlewomen of this kingdom; and in commendation of some particular persons of our own sex, such as for the most part, are so well known to myself, and others, that I dare undertake Fame dares not to call any better. And this have I done, to make known to the world, that all women deserve not to be blamed though some forgetting they are women themselves, and in danger to be condemned by the words of their own mouths, fall into so great an error, as to speak unadvisedly against the rest of their sex; which if it be true, I am persuaded they can show their own imperfection in nothing more: and therefore could wish (for their own ease, modesties, and credit) they would refer such points of folly, to be practised by evil disposed men, who forgetting they were born of women, nourished of women, and that if it were not by the means of women, they would be quite extinguished out of the world, and a final end of them all, do like vipers deface the wombs wherein they were bred, only to give way and utterance to their want of discretion and goodness. Such as these, were they that dishonoured Christ his Apostles and Prophets, putting them to shameful deaths. Therefore we are not to regard any imputations, that they undeservedly lay upon us, no otherwise than to make use of them to our own benefits, as spurs to virtue, making us fly all occasions that may colour their unjust speeches to pass current. Especially considering that they have tempted even the patience of God himself, who gave power to wise and virtuous women, to bring down their pride and arrogance. As was cruel Sisera by the discreet counsel of noble Deborah, Judge and Prophetess of Israel, and resolution of Jael wife of Heber the Kenite; wicked Haman, by the divine prayers and prudent proceedings of beautiful

Esther; blasphemous Holofernes, by the invincible courage, rare wisdom, and confident carriage of Judith; and the unjust Judges, by the innocency of chaste Susanna; with infinite others, which for brevity's sake I will omit. As also in respect it pleased our Lord and Saviour Jesus Christ, without the assistance of man, being free from original and all other sins, from the time of his conception, till the hour of his death, to be begotten of a woman, born of a woman, nourished of a woman, obedient to a woman; and that he healed women, pardoned women, comforted women: yea, even when he was in his greatest agony and bloody sweat, going to be crucified, and also in the last hour of his death, took care to dispose of a woman. After his resurrection, appeared first to a woman, sent a woman to declare his most glorious resurrection to the rest of his disciples. Many other examples I could allege of diverse faithful and virtuous women, who have in all ages, not only been confessors, but also endured most cruel martyrdom for their faith in Jesus Christ. All which is sufficient to enforce all good Christians and honourable minded men to speak reverently of our sex, and especially of all virtuous and good women. To the modest censures of both which, I refer these my imperfect endeavours, knowing that according to their own excellent dispositions, they will rather, cherish, nourish, and increase the least spark of virtue where they find it, by their favourable and best interpretations, than quench it by wrong constructions. To whom I wish all increase of virtue, and desire their best opinions.

Salve Deus Rex Judæorum

Sith Cynthia is ascended to that rest
Of endless joy and true eternity,
That glorious place that cannot be expressed
By any wight clad in mortality,
In her almighty love so highly blessed,
And crowned with everlasting sov'reignty;
Where saints and angels do attend her throne,
And she gives glory unto God alone.

To thee great Countess now I will apply
My pen, to write thy never dying fame;
That when to Heav'n thy blessèd soul shall fly,
These lines on earth record thy reverend name:
And to this task I mean my muse to tie,
Though wanting skill I shall but purchase blame:

Pardon (dear lady) want of woman's wit
To pen thy praise, when few can equal it.

And pardon (madam) though I do not write
Those praiseful lines of that delightful place,
As you commanded me in that fair night,
When shining Phoebe gave so great a grace,
Presenting Paradise to your sweet sight,
Unfolding all the beauty of her face
With pleasant groves, hills, walks and stately trees,
Which pleasures with retirèd minds agrees.

Whose eagle's eyes behold the glorious sun
Of th'all-creating providence, reflecting
His blessèd beams on all by Him begun;
Increasing, strength'ning, guiding and directing
All worldly creatures their due course to run,
Unto His powerful pleasure all subjecting:
And thou (dear lady) by His special grace,
In these His creatures dost behold His face.

Whose all-reviving beauty yields such joys
To thy sad soul, plunged in waves of woe,
That worldly pleasures seems to thee as toys,
Only thou seek'st eternity to know,
Respecting not the infinite annoys
That Satan to thy well-staid mind can show;
Ne can he quench in thee, the Spirit of Grace,
Nor draw thee from beholding Heaven's bright face.

Thy mind so perfect by thy Maker framed,
No vain delights can harbour in thy heart,
With his sweet love, thou art so much inflamed,
As of the world thou seem'st to have no part;
So, love Him still, thou need'st not be ashamed,
'Tis He that made thee, what thou wert, and art:
'Tis He that dries all tears from orphans' eyes,
And hears from Heav'n the woeful widows' cries.

'Tis He that doth behold thy inward cares,
And will regard the sorrows of thy soul;
'Tis He that guides thy feet from Satan's snares,

And in his wisdom, doth thy ways control:
He through afflictions, still thy mind prepares,
And all thy glorious trials will enrol:
That when dark days of terror shall appear,
Thou as the sun shalt shine; or much more clear.

The Heav'ns shall perish as a garment old,
Or as a vesture by the maker changed,
And shall depart, as when a scroll is rolled;
Yet thou from Him shalt never be estranged,
When He shall come in glory, that was sold
For all our sins; we happily are changed,
Who for our faults put on His righteousness,
Although full oft His laws we do transgress.

Long may'st thou joy in this almighty love,
Long may thy soul be pleasing in His sight,
Long may'st thou have true comforts from above,
Long may'st thou set on him thy whole delight,
And patiently endure when he doth prove,
Knowing that He will surely do thee right:
Thy patience, faith, long suff'ring, and thy love,
He will reward with comforts from above.

With majesty and honour is He clad,
And decked with light, as with a garment fair;
He joys the meek, and makes the mighty sad,
Pulls down the proud, and doth the humble rear:
Who sees this Bridegroom, never can be sad;
None lives that can his wondrous works declare:
Yea, look how far the east is from the west,
So far he sets our sins that have transgressed.

He rides upon the wings of all the winds,
And spreads the Heav'ns with his all pow'rful hand;
Oh who can loose when the Almighty binds?
Or in his angry presence dares to stand?
He searcheth out the secrets of all minds;
All those that fear Him, shall possess the land:
He is exceeding glorious to behold,
Ancient of Times; so fair, and yet so old.

He of the wat'ry clouds his chariot frames,
And makes His blessèd angels powerful spirits,
His ministers are fearful fiery flames,
Rewarding all according to their merits;
The righteous for an heritage He claims,
And registers the wrongs of humble spirits:
Hills melt like wax, in presence of the Lord,
So do all sinners, in his sight abhorred.

He in the waters lays His chamber beams,
And clouds of darkness compass Him about,
Consuming fire shall go before in streams,
And burn up all his en'mies round about:
Yet on these judgements worldlings never dreams,
Nor of these dangers never stand in doubt:
While He shall rest within His holy hill,
That lives and dies according to His will.

But woe to them that double-hearted be,
Who with their tongues the righteous souls do slay;
Bending their bows to shoot at all they see,
With upright hearts their Maker to obey;
And secretly do let their arrows flee,
To wound true hearted people any way:
The Lord will root them out that speak proud things,
Deceitful tongues are but false slander's wings.

Froward are th'ungodly from their birth,
No sooner born, but they do go astray;
The Lord will root them out from off the earth,
And give them to their en'mies for a prey,
As venomous as serpents is their breath,
With poisoned lies to hurt in what they may
The innocent: who as a dove shall fly
Unto the Lord, that He his cause may try.

The righteous Lord doth righteousness allow,
His countenance will behold the thing that's just;
Unto the mean He makes the mighty bow,
And raiseth up the poor out of the dust:

Yet makes no count to us, nor when, nor how,
But pours His grace on all, that puts their trust
In Him: that never will their hopes betray,
Nor lets them perish that for mercy pray.

He shall within His tabernacle dwell,
Whose life is uncorrupt before the Lord,
Who no untruths of innocents doth tell,
Nor wrongs his neighbour, nor in deed, nor word,
Nor in his pride with malice seems to swell,
Nor whets his tongue more sharper than a sword,
To wound the reputation of the just;
Nor seeks to lay their glory in the dust.

That great Jehova, King of Heav'n and earth,
Will rain down fire and brimstone from above,
Upon the wicked monsters in their berth
That storm and rage at those whom He doth love:
Snares, storms, and tempests He will rain, and dearth,
Because He will himself almighty prove:
And this shall be their portion they shall drink,
That thinks the Lord is blind when He doth wink.

Pardon (good madam) though I have digressed
From what I do intend to write of thee,
To set his glory forth whom thou lov'st best,
Whose wondrous works no mortal eye can see;
His special care on those whom He hath blessed
From wicked worldlings, how He sets them free:
And how such people He doth overthrow
In all their ways, that they His power may know.

The meditation of this Monarch's love,
Draws thee from caring what this world can yield;
Of joys and griefs both equal thou dost prove,
They have no force, to force thee from the field:
Thy constant faith like to the turtle dove
Continues combat, and will never yield
To base affliction; or proud pomps desire,
That sets the weakest minds so much on fire.

Thou from the court to the country art retired,
Leaving the world, before the world leaves thee:
That great enchantress of weak minds admired,
Whose all-bewitching charms so pleasing be
To worldly wantons; and too much desired
Of those that care not for eternity:
But yield themselves as preys to lust and sin,
Losing their hopes of Heav'n, Hell pains to win.

But thou, the wonder of our wanton age
Leav'st all delights to serve a Heav'nly King:
Who is more wise? Or who can be more sage,
Than she that doth affection subject bring;
Not forcing for the world, or Satan's rage,
But shrouding under the Almighty's wing;
Spending her years, months, days, minutes, hours,
In doing service to the Heav'nly powers.

Thou fair example, live without compare,
With honour's triumphs seated in thy breast;
Pale envy never can thy name impair,
When in thy heart thou harbour'st such a guest:
Malice must live for ever in despair;
There's no revenge where virtue still doth rest:
All hearts must needs do homage unto thee,
In whom all eyes such rare perfection see.

That outward beauty which the world commends,
Is not the subject I will write upon,
Whose date expired, that tyrant Time soon ends,
Those gaudy colours soon are spent and gone:
But those fair virtues which on thee attends
Are always fresh, they never are but one:
They make thy beauty fairer to behold,
Than was that Queen's for whom proud Troy was sold.

As for those matchless colours red and white,
Or perfect features in a fading face,
Or due proportion pleasing to the sight;
All these do draw but dangers and disgrace:

A mind enriched with virtue, shines more bright,
Adds everlasting beauty, gives true grace,
Frames an immortal goddess on the earth,
Who though she dies, yet Fame gives her new birth.

That pride of Nature which adorns the fair,
Like blazing comets to allure all eyes,
Is but the thread, that weaves their web of care,
Who glories most, where most their danger lies;
For greatest perils do attend the fair,
When men do seek, attempt, plot and devise,
How they may overthrow the chastest dame,
Whose beauty is the white whereat they aim.

'Twas beauty bred in Troy the ten years' strife,
And carried Helen from her lawful lord;
'Twas beauty made chaste Lucrece lose her life,
For which proud Tarquin's fact was so abhorred:
Beauty the cause Antonius wronged his wife,
Which could not be decided but by sword:
Great Cleopatra's beauty and defects
Did work Octavia's wrongs, and his neglects.

What fruit did yield that fair forbidden tree,
But blood, dishonour, infamy, and shame?
Poor blinded Queen, couldst thou no better see,
But entertain disgrace, instead of fame?
Do these designs with Majesty agree.
To stain thy blood, and blot thy royal name?
That heart that gave consent unto this ill,
Did give consent that thou thyself shouldst kill.

Fair Rosamund, the wonder of her time,
Had been much fair, had she not been fair;
Beauty betrayed her thoughts, aloft to climb,
To build strong castles in uncertain air,
Where th'infection of a wanton crime
Did work her fall; first poison, then despair,
With double death did kill her perjured soul,
When Heavenly justice did her sin control.

Holy Matilda in a hapless hour
Was born to sorrow and to discontent,
Beauty the cause that turned her sweet to sour,
While chastity sought folly to prevent.
Lustful King John refused, did use his power,
By fire and sword, to compass his content:
But friends' disgrace, nor father's banishment,
Nor death itself, could purchase her consent.

Here beauty in the height of all perfection,
Crowned this fair creature's everlasting fame,
Whose noble mind did scorn the base subjection
Of fears, or favours, to impair her name:
By Heavenly grace, she had such true direction,
To die with honour, not to live in shame;
And drink that poison with a cheerful heart,
That could all Heavenly grace to her impart.

This grace, great lady, doth possess thy soul,
And makes thee pleasing in thy Maker's sight;
This grace doth all imperfect thoughts control,
Directing thee to serve thy God aright;
Still reckoning Him, the Husband of thy soul,
Which is most precious in his glorious sight:
Because the world's delights she doth deny
For him, who for her sake vouchsafed to die.

And dying made her dowager of all;
Nay more, co-heir of that eternal bliss
That angels lost, and we by Adam's fall
Mere castaways, raised by a Judas kiss.
Christ's bloody sweat, the vinegar, and gall,
The spear, sponge, nails, his buffeting with fists,
His bitter passion, agony, and death,
Did gain us Heaven when He did lose his breath.

These high deserts invites my lowly muse
To write of Him, and pardon crave of thee,
For time so spent, I need make no excuse,
Knowing it doth with thy fair mind agree

So well, as thou no labour wilt refuse,
That to thy holy love may pleasing be:
His death and passion I desire to write,
And thee to read, the blessèd soul's delight.

But my dear muse, now whither wouldst thou fly,
Above the pitch of thy appointed strain?
With Icarus thou seekest now to try,
Not waxen wings, but thy poor barren brain,
Which far too weak, these silly lines descry;
Yet cannot this thy forward mind restrain,
But thy poor infant verse must soar aloft,
Not fearing threat'ning dangers, happening oft.

Think when the eye of wisdom shall discover
Thy weakling muse to fly, that scarce could creep,
And in the air above the clouds to hover,
When better 'twere mewed up, and fast asleep;
They'll think with Phaeton, thou canst near recover,
But helpless with that poor young lad to weep:
The little world of thy weak wit on fire,
Where thou wilt perish in thine own desire.

But yet the weaker thou dost seem to be
In sex, or sense, the more His glory shines,
That doth infuse such powerful grace in thee,
To show thy love in these few humble lines;
The widow's mite, with this may well agree,
Her little all more worth than golden mines,
Being more dearer to our loving Lord,
Than all the wealth that kingdoms could afford.

Therefore I humbly for his grace will pray,
That He will give me power and strength to write,
That what I have begun, so end I may,
As His great glory may appear more bright;
Yea in these lines I may no further stray,
Than His most Holy Spirit shall give me light:
That blindest weakness be not over-bold,
The manner of His passion to unfold.

In other phrases than may well agree
With His pure doctrine, and most holy writ,
That Heaven's clear eye, and all the world may see,
I seek his glory, rather than to get
The vulgar's breath, the seed of vanity,
Nor Fame's loud trumpet care I to admit;
But rather strive in plainest words to show,
The matter which I seek to undergo.

A matter far beyond my barren skill,
To show with any life this map of death,
This story; that whole worlds with books would fill,
In these few lines, will put me out of breath,
To run so swiftly up this mighty hill,
I may behold it with the eye of faith;
But to present this pure unspotted Lamb,
I must confess, I far unworthy am.

Yet if He please t'illuminate my spirit,
And give me wisdom from his holy hill,
That I may write part of his glorious merit,
If He vouchsafe to guide my hand and quill,
To show His death, by which we do inherit
Those endless joys that all our hearts do fill;
Then will I tell of that sad black faced night,
Whose mourning mantle covered Heavenly light.

That very night our Saviour was betrayed,
Oh night! Exceeding all the nights of sorrow,
When our most blessèd Lord, although dismayed,
Yet would not he one minute's respite borrow,
But to Mount Olives went, though sore afraid,
To welcome night, and entertain the morrow;
And as He oft unto that place did go,
So did He now, to meet his long nursed woe.

He told his dear disciples that they all
Should be offended by Him, that self night,
His grief was great, and theirs could not be small,
To part from Him who was their sole delight;

Saint Peter thought his faith could never fall,
No mote could happen in so clear a sight:
Which made him say, though all men were offended,
Yet would he never, though his life were ended.

But his dear Lord made answer, that before
The cock did crow, he should deny Him thrice;
This could not choose but grieve him very sore,
That his hot love should prove more cold than ice,
Denying Him he did so much adore;
No imperfection in himself he spies,
But faith again, with Him he'll surely die,
Rather than his dear Master once deny.

And all the rest (did likewise say the same)
Of His disciples, at that instant time;
But yet poor Peter, he was most to blame,
That thought above them all, by faith to climb;
His forward speech inflicted sin and shame,
When wisdom's eyes did look and check his crime:
Who did foresee, and told it him before,
Yet would he needs aver it more and more.

Now went our Lord unto that holy place,
Sweet Gethsemane hallowed by his presence,
That blessèd garden, which did now embrace
His Holy Corpse, yet could make no defence
Against those vipers, objects of disgrace,
Which sought that pure eternal love to quench:
Here His disciples willèd He to stay,
Whilst He went further, where He meant to pray.

None were admitted with their Lord to go,
But Peter, and the sons of Zebed'us,
To them good Jesus opened all His woe,
He gave them leave His sorrows to discuss,
His deepest griefs, He did not scorn to show
These three dear friends, so much He did entrust:
Being sorrowful, and overcharged with grief,
He told it them, yet looked for no relief.

Sweet Lord, how couldst thou thus to flesh and blood
Communicate thy grief? Tell of thy woes?
Thou knew'st they had no power to do Thee good,
But were the cause Thou must endure these blows,
Being the scorpions bred in Adam's mud,
Whose poisoned sins did work among thy foes,
To re-o'ercharge Thy over-burdened soul,
Although the sorrows now they do condole.

Yet didst Thou tell them of Thy troubled state,
Of Thy soul's heaviness unto the death,
So full of love, so free wert Thou from hate,
To bid them stay, whose sins did stop Thy breath,
When Thou wert ent'ring at so strait a gate,
Yea en'tring even into the door of Death,
Thou bidst them tarry there, and watch with Thee,
Who from Thy precious bloodshed were not free.

Bidding them tarry, Thou didst further go,
To meet affliction in such graceful sort,
As might move pity both in friend and foe,
Thy sorrows such, as none could them comport,
Such great endurements who did ever know,
When to th'Almighty Thou didst make resort?
And falling on Thy face didst humbly pray,
If 'twere His will that cup might pass away.

Saying, not my will, but Thy will Lord be done.
When as thou prayedst an Angel did appear
From Heaven, to comfort Thee God's only Son,
That Thou Thy suff'rings might'st the better bear,
Being in an agony, Thy glass near run,
Thou prayedst more earnestly, in so great fear,
That precious sweat came trickling to the ground,
Like drops of blood Thy senses to confound.

Lo here His will, not Thy will, Lord was done,
And Thou content to undergo all pains,
Sweet Lamb of God, His dear belovèd Son,
By this great purchase, what to thee remains?

Of Heaven and Earth thou hast a Kingdom won,
Thy Glory being equal with thy gains,
In ratifying God's promise on the Earth,
Made many hundred years before Thy birth.

But now returning to Thy sleeping friends,
That could not watch one hour for love of Thee,
Even those three friends, which on Thy Grace depends,
Yet shut those eyes that should their Maker see;
What colour, what excuse, or what amends,
From thy displeasure now can set them free?
Yet Thy pure piety bids them watch and pray,
Lest in temptation they be led away.

Although the spirit was willing to obey,
Yet what great weakeness in the flesh was found!
They slept in ease, whilst Thou in pain didst pray;
Lo, they in sleep, and Thou in sorrow drowned:
Yet God's right hand was unto Thee a stay,
When horror, grief, and sorrow did abound:
His angel did appear from Heaven to Thee,
To yield Thee comfort in extremity.

But what could comfort then Thy troubled mind,
When Heaven and Earth were both against Thee bent?
And Thou no hope, no ease, no rest couldst find,
But must restore that life, which was but lent;
Was ever creature in the world so kind,
But He that from eternity was sent?
To satisfy for many worlds of sin,
Whose matchless torments did but then begin.

If one man's sin doth challenge death and Hell,
With all the torments that belong thereto:
If for one sin such plagues on David fell,
As grieved him, and did his seed undo:
If Solomon, for that he did not well,
Falling from grace, did lose his Kingdom too:
Ten tribes being taken from his wilful son
And sin the cause that they were all undone.

What could Thy innocency now expect,
When all the sins that ever were committed,
Were laid to Thee, whom no man could detect?
Yet far Thou wert of man from being pitied,
The judge so just could yield Thee no respect,
Nor would one jot of penance be remitted;
But greater horror to Thy soul must rise,
Than heart can think, or any wit devise.

Now draws the hour of Thy affliction near,
And ugly death presents himself before Thee;
Thou now must leave those friends thou held'st so dear,
Yea those disciples, who did most adore Thee;
Yet in Thy countenance doth no wrath appear,
Although betrayed to those that did abhor Thee:
Thou didst vouchsafe to visit them again,
Who had no apprehension of Thy pain.

Their eyes were heavy, and their hearts asleep,
Nor knew they well what answer then to make thee;
Yet thou as watchman, hadst a care to keep
Those few from sin, that shortly would forsake thee;
But now Thou bidst them henceforth rest and sleep,
Thy hour is come, and they at hand to take Thee:
The Son of God to sinners made a prey,
Oh hateful hour! Oh blessed! Oh cursèd day!

Lo here Thy great humility was found,
Being King of Heaven, and Monarch of the Earth,
Yet well content to have Thy glory drowned,
By being counted of so mean a birth;
Grace, love, and mercy did so much abound,
Thou entertaindst the cross, even to the death:
And namedst Thyself, the Son of Man to be,
To purge our pride by Thy humility.

But now thy friends whom Thou didst call to go,
Heavy spectators of Thy hapless case,
See Thy betrayer, whom too well they know,
One of the twelve, now object of disgrace,

A trothless traitor, and a mortal foe,
With feignèd kindness seeks Thee to embrace;
And gives a kiss, whereby he may deceive Thee,
That in the hands of sinners he might leave Thee.

Now muster forth with swords, with staves, with bills,
High Priests and Scribes, and Elders of the land,
Seeking by force to have their wicked wills,
Which Thou didst never purpose to withstand;
Now Thou mak'st haste unto the worst of ills,
And who they seek, Thou gently dost demand;
This didst Thou Lord, t'amaze these fools the more,
T''inquire of that, Thou knew'st so well before.

When lo these monsters did not shame to tell,
His name they sought, and found, yet could not know
Jesus of Nazareth, at whose feet they fell,
When Heavenly wisdom did descend so low
To speak to them: they knew they did not well,
Their great amazement made them backward go:
Nay, though He said unto them 'I am He',
They could not know Him, whom their eyes did see.

How blind were they could not discern the light!
How dull! If not to understand the truth,
How weak! If meekness overcame their might;
How stony hearted, if not moved to ruth:
How void of pity, and how full of spite,
'Gainst Him that was the Lord of Light and Truth:
Here insolent boldness checked by love and grace,
Retires, and falls before our Maker's face.

For when He spake to this accursèd crew,
And mildly made them know that it was He:
Presents Himself, that they might take a view;
And what they doubted they might clearly see;
Nay more, to reassure that it was true,
He said: 'I say unto you, I am He.'
If Him they sought, He's willing to obey,
Only desires the rest might go their way.

Thus with a heart preparèd to endure
The greatest wrongs impiety could devise,
He was content to stoop unto their lure,
Although his greatness might do otherwise:
Here grace was seizèd on with hands impure,
And virtue now must be suppressed by vice,
Pure innocency made a prey to sin,
Thus did his torments and our joys begin.

Here fair obedience shined in His breast,
And did suppress all fear of future pain;
Love was His leader unto this unrest,
Whilst righteousness doth carry up His train;
Mercy made way to make us highly blessed,
When patience beat down sorrow, fear and pain:
Justice sat looking with an angry brow,
On blessèd misery appearing now.

More glorious than all the conquerors
Than ever lived within this Earthly round,
More powerful than all Kings, or Governors
That ever yet within this world were found;
More valiant than the greatest soldiers
That ever fought, to have their glory crowned:
For which of them, that ever yet took breath,
Sought t'endure the doom of Heaven and Earth?

But our sweet Saviour whom these Jews did name;
Yet could their learnèd ignorance apprehend
No light of grace, to free themselves from blame:
Zeal, laws, religion, now they do pretend
Against the truth, untruths they seek to frame:
Now all their powers, their wits, their strengths, they bend
Against one silly, weak, unarmèd man,
Who no resistance makes, though much He can,

To free Himself from these unlearnèd men,
Who called Him Saviour in his blessèd name;
Yet far from knowing Him their Saviour then,
That came to save both them and theirs from blame;

Though they retire and fall, they come again
To make a surer purchase of their shame:
With lights and torches now they find the way,
To take the Shepherd whilst the sheep do stray.

Why should unlawful actions use the light?
Iniquity in darkness seeks to dwell;
Sin rides his circuit in the dead of night,
Teaching all souls the ready ways to Hell;
Satan comes armed with all the powers of spite,
Heartens his champions, makes them rude and fell;
Like rav'ning wolves, to shed His guiltless blood,
Who thought no harm, but died to do them good.

Here falsehood bears the show of formal right,
Base treachery hath got a guard of men;
Tyranny attends, with all his strength and might,
To lead this silly Lamb to lion's den;
Yet He unmoved in this most wretched plight,
Goes on to meet them, knows the hour, and when
The power of darkness must express God's ire,
Therefore to save these few was his desire.

These few that wait on poverty and shame,
And offer to be sharers in his ills;
These few that will be spreaders of his fame,
He will not leave to tyrant's wicked wills;
But still desires to free them from all blame,
Yet fear goes forward, anger patience kills:
A saint is movèd to revenge a wrong,
And mildness doth what doth to wrath belong.

For Peter grieved at what might then befall,
Yet knew not what to do, nor what to think,
Thought something must be done, now, if at all,
To free his Master, that He might not drink
This poisoned draught, far bitterer than gall,
For now he sees Him at the very brink
Of grisly death, who 'gins to show his face,
Clad in all colours of a deep disgrace.

And now those hands, that never used to fight,
Or draw a weapon in his own defence,
Too forward is, to do his Master right,
Since of his wrongs, he feels so true a sense:
But ah poor Peter now thou wantest might,
And He's resolved, with them He will go hence:
To draw thy sword in such a helpless cause,
Offends thy Lord, and is against the laws.

So much He hates revenge, so far from hate,
That He vouchsafes to heal, whom thou dost wound;
His paths are peace, with none He holds debate,
His patience stands upon so sure a ground,
To counsel thee, although it comes too late:
Nay, to His foes, His mercies so abound,
That He in pity doth thy will restrain,
And heals the hurt, and takes away the pain.

For willingly He will endure this wrong,
Although His prayers might have obtained such grace,
As to dissolve their plots though ne'er so strong,
And bring these wicked actors in worse case
Than Egypt's King on whom God's plagues did throng,
But that foregoing Scriptures must take place:
If God by prayers had an army sent
Of powerful angels, who could them prevent?

Yet mighty Jesus meekly asked, 'Why they
With swords and staves do come as to a thief?'
He teaching in the Temple day by day
None did offend, or give Him cause of grief.
Now all are forward, glad is he that may
Give most offence, and yield him least relief:
His hateful foes are ready now to take Him,
And all his dear disciples do forsake Him.

Those dear disciples that He most did love,
And were attendant at his beck and call,
When trial of affliction came to prove,
They first left Him, who now must leave them all:

For they were earth, and He came from above,
Which made them apt to fly, and fit to fall:
Though they protest they never will forsake Him,
They do like men, when dangers overtake them.

And He alone is bound to loose us all,
Whom with unhallowed hands they led along,
To wicked Caiaphas in the judgement hall,
Who studies only how to do Him wrong;
High Priests and Elders, people great and small,
With all reproachful words about Him throng:
False witnesses are now called in apace,
Whose trothless tongues must make pale death embrace

The Beauty of the World, Heaven's chiefest glory;
The Mirror of Martyrs, Crown of Holy Saints;
Love of th'Almighty, Blessèd Angel's story;
Water of Life, which none that drinks it, faints;
Guide of the Just, where all our light we borrow;
Mercy of Mercies; Hearer of Complaints;
Triumpher over Death; Ransomer of Sin;
Falsely accused: now His pains begin.

Their tongues do serve Him as a passing bell,
For what they say is certainly believed;
So sound a tale unto the judge they tell,
That He of life must shortly be bereaved;
Their share of Heaven, they do not care to sell,
So His afflicted heart be throughly grieved:
They tell His words, though far from his intent,
And what His speeches were, not what He meant.

That He God's Holy Temple could destroy,
And in three days could build it up again;
This seemed to them a vain and idle toy,
It would not sink into their sinful brain:
Christ's blessèd body, all true Christians joy,
Should die, and in three days revive again:
This did the Lord of Heaven and Earth endure,
Unjustly to be charged by tongues impure.

And now they all do give attentive ear,
To hear the answer, which He will not make;
The people wonder how He can forbear,
And these great wrongs so patiently can take;
But yet He answers not, nor doth He care,
Much more He will endure for our sake:
Nor can their wisdoms any way discover,
Who He should be that proved so true a Lover.

To entertain the sharpest pangs of death,
And fight a combat in the depth of Hell,
For wretched worldlings made of dust and earth,
Whose hardened hearts, with pride and malice swell;
In midst of bloody sweat, and dying breath,
He had compassion on these tyrants fell:
And purchased them a place in Heav'n forever,
When they His soul and body sought to sever.

Sin's ugly mists, so blinded had their eyes,
That at noonday's they could discern no light;
These were those fools, that thought themselves so wise,
The Jewish wolves, that did our Saviour bite;
For now they use all means they can devise,
To beat down truth, and go against all right:
Yea now they take God's holy name in vain,
To know the truth, which truth they do profane.

The chiefest Hell-hounds of this hateful crew,
Rose up to ask what answer He could make,
Against those false accusers in His view;
That by His speech, they might advantage take:
He held His peace, yet knew they said not true,
No answer would His Holy Wisdom make,
Till He was charged in His glorious name,
Whose pleasure 'twas He should endure this shame.

Then with so mild a Majesty He spake,
As they might eas'ly know from whence He came,
His harmless tongue doth no exceptions take,
Nor Priests, nor people, means He now to blame;

But answers folly, for true wisdom's sake,
Being charged deeply by His powerful name,
To tell if Christ the Son of God He be,
Who for our sins must die, to set us free.

To thee, O Caiaphas doth He answer give,
That thou hast said, what thou desir'st to know,
And yet thy malice will not let Him live,
So much thou art unto thyself a foe;
He speaketh truth, but thou wilt not believe,
Nor canst thou apprehend it to be so:
Though He express His Glory unto thee,
Thy owly eyes are blind, and cannot see.

Thou rend'st thy clothes, instead of thy false heart,
And on the guiltless lay'st thy guilty crime;
For thou blasphem'st, and he must feel the smart:
To sentence death, thou think'st it now high time;
No witness now thou need'st, for this foul part,
Thou to the height of wickedness canst climb:
And give occasion to the ruder sort,
To make afflictions sorrows, follies sport.

Now when the dawn of day 'gins to appear,
And all your wicked counsels have an end,
To end His life, that holds you all so dear,
For to that purpose did your studies bend;
Proud Pontius Pilate must the matter hear,
To your untroths his ears he now must lend:
Sweet Jesus bound, to him you led away,
Of His most precious blood to make your prey.

Which, when that wicked caitiff did perceive,
By whose lewd means He came to this distress;
He brought the price of blood he did receive,
Thinking thereby to make his fault seem less,
And with these Priests and Elders did it leave,
Confessed his fault, wherein he did transgress:
But when he saw repentance unrespected,
He hanged himself; of God and man rejected.

By this example, what can be expected
From wicked man, which on the Earth doth live?
But faithless dealing, fear of God neglected;
Who for their private gain cares not to sell
The innocent blood of God's most dear elected,
As did that caitiff wretch, now damned in Hell:
If in Christ's school, he took so great a fall,
What will they do, that come not there at all?

Now Pontius Pilate is to judge the cause
Of faultless Jesus, who before him stands;
Who neither hath offended Prince, nor laws,
Although He now be brought in woeful bands:
O noble Governor, make thou yet a pause,
Do not in innocent blood imbrue thy hands;
But hear the words of thy most worthy wife,
Who sends to thee, to beg her Saviour's life.

Let barb'rous cruelty far depart from thee,
And in true justice take affliction's part;
Open thine eyes, that thou the truth may'st see,
Do not the thing that goes against thy heart,
Condemn not Him that must thy Saviour be;
But view His holy life, His good desert.
Let not us women glory in men's fall,
Who had power given to over-rule us all.

Till now your indiscretion sets us free,
And makes our former fault much less appear;
Our mother Eve, who tasted of the tree,
Giving to Adam what she held most dear,
Was simply good, and had no power to see,
The after-coming harm did not appear:
The subtle Serpent that our sex betrayed,
Before our fall so sure a plot had laid.

That undiscerning ignorance perceived
No guile, or craft that was by him intended;
For had she known, of what we were bereaved,
To his request she had not condescended.

But she (poor soul) by cunning was deceived,
No hurt therein her harmless heart intended:
For she alleged God's word, which he denies,
That they should die, but even as Gods, be wise.

But surely Adam cannot be excused,
Her fault though great, yet he was most to blame;
What weakness offered, strength might have refused,
Being Lord of all, the greater was his shame:
Although the Serpent's craft had her abused,
God's holy word ought all his actions frame,
For he was Lord and King of all the Earth,
Before poor Eve had either life or breath.

Who being framed by God's eternal hand,
The perfect'st man that ever breathed on earth;
And from God's mouth received that strait command,
The breach whereof he knew was present death:
Yea having power to rule both sea and land,
Yet with one apple won to lose that breath
Which God had breathèd in his beauteous face,
Bringing us all in danger and disgrace.

And then to lay the fault on patience' back,
That we (poor women) must endure it all;
We know right well he did discretion lack,
Being not persuaded thereunto at all;
If Eve did err, it was for knowledge sake,
The fruit being fair persuaded him to fall:
No subtle Serpent's falsehood did betray him,
If he would eat it, who had power to stay him?

Not Eve, whose fault was only too much love,
Which made her give this present to her dear,
That what she tasted, he likewise might prove,
Whereby his knowledge might become more clear;
He never sought her weakness to reprove,
With those sharp words, which he of God did hear:
Yet men will boast of knowledge, which he took
From Eve's fair hand, as from a learnèd book.

If any evil did in her remain,
Being made of him, he was the ground of all;
If one of many worlds could lay a stain
Upon our sex, and work so great a fall
To wretched man, by Satan's subtle train;
What will so foul a fault amongst you all?
Her weakness did the Serpent's words obey;
But you in malice God's dear Son betray.

Whom, if unjustly you condemn to die,
Her sin was small, to what you do commit;
All mortal sins that do for vengeance cry,
Are not to be comparèd unto it:
If many worlds would altogether try,
By all their sins the wrath of God to get;
This sin of yours, surmounts them all as far
As doth the sun, another little star.

Then let us have our liberty again,
And challenge to yourselves no sov'reignty;
You came not in the world without our pain,
Make that a bar against your cruelty;
Your fault being greater, why should you disdain
Our being your equals, free from tyranny?
If one weak woman simply did offend,
This sin of yours, hath no excuse, nor end.

To which (poor souls) we never gave consent,
Witness thy wife (O Pilate) speaks for all;
Who did but dream, and yet a message sent,
That thou shouldst have nothing to do at all
With that just man; which, if thy heart relent,
Why wilt thou be a reprobate with Saul,
To seek the death of Him that is so good,
For thy soul's health to shed His dearest blood?

Yea, so thou may'st these sinful people please,
Thou art content against all truth and right,
To seal this act, that may procure thine ease
With blood, and wrong, with tyranny, and might;

The multitude thou seekest to appease,
By base dejection of this Heavenly light:
Demanding which of these that thou shouldst lose,
Whether the thief, or Christ King of the Jews.

Base Barrabas, the thief, they all desire,
And thou more base than he, perform'st their will;
Yet when thy thoughts back to themselves retire,
Thou art unwilling to commit this ill:
Oh that thou couldst unto such grace aspire,
That thy polluted lips might never kill
That honour, which right judgement ever graceth,
To purchase shame, which all true worth defaceth.

Art thou a judge, and asketh what to do
With one, in whom no fault there can be found?
The death of Christ wilt thou consent unto,
Finding no cause, no reason, nor no ground?
Shall He be scourged, and crucifièd too?
And must His miseries by thy means abound?
Yet not ashamed to ask what he hath done,
When thine own conscience seeks this sin to shun.

Three times thou ask'st, 'What evil hath He done?'
And sayst, thou find'st in Him no cause of death.
Yet wilt thou chasten God's belovèd Son,
Although to thee no word of ill He saith?
For wrath must end, what malice hath begun,
And thou must yield to stop His guiltless breath.
This rude tumultuous rout doth press so sore,
That thou condemnest Him thou shouldst adore.

Yet Pilate, this can yield thee no content,
To exercise thine own authority,
But unto Herod He must needs be sent,
To reconcile thyself by tyranny:
Was this the greatest good in Justice meant,
When thou perceiv'st no fault in Him to be?
If thou must make thy peace by virtue's fall,
Much better 'twere not to be friends at all.

Yet neither thy stern brow, nor His great place,
Can draw an answer from the Holy One:
His false accusers, nor His great disgrace,
Nor Herod's scoffs; to Him they are all one:
He neither cares, nor fears His own ill case,
Though being despised and mocked of everyone:
King Herod's gladness gives Him little ease,
Neither his anger seeks He to appease.

Yet this is strange, that base impiety
Should yield those robes of honour, which were due;
Pure white, to show His great integrity,
His innocency, that all the world might view;
Perfection's height in lowest penury,
Such glorious poverty as they never knew:
Purple and scarlet well might Him beseem,
Whose precious blood must all the world redeem.

And that imperial crown of thorns He wore,
Was much more precious than the diadem
Of any king that ever lived before,
Or since His time, their honour's but a dream
To His eternal glory, being so poor,
To make a purchase of that Heavenly realm;
Where God with all his angels lives in peace,
No griefs, nor sorrows, but all joys increase.

Those royal robes, which they in scorn did give,
To make Him odious to the common sort,
Yield light of Grace to those whose souls shall live
Within the harbour of this Heavenly port;
Much do they joy, and much more do they grieve,
His death, their life, should make His foes such sport:
With sharpest thorns to prick his blessèd face,
Our joyful sorrow, and His greater grace.

Three fears at once possessèd Pilate's heart;
The first, Christ's innocence, which so plain appears;
The next, that He which now must feel this smart,
Is God's dear Son, for anything he hears:

But that which proved the deepest wounding dart,
Is people's threat'nings, which he so much fears,
That he to Cæsar could not be a friend,
Unless he sent sweet Jesus to His end.

Now Pilate thou art proved a painted wall,
A golden sepulchre with rotten bones;
From right to wrong, from equity to fall:
If none upbraid thee, yet the very stones
Will rise against thee, and in question call
His blood, His tears, His sighs, His bitter groans:
All these will witness at the latter day,
When water cannot wash thy sin away.

Canst thou be innocent, that 'gainst all right,
Wilt yield to what thy conscience doth withstand?
Being a man of knowledge, power, and might,
To let the wicked carry such a hand,
Before thy face to blindfold Heav'n's bright light,
And thou to yield to what they did demand?
Washing thy hands, thy conscience cannot clear,
But to all worlds this stain must needs appear.

For lo, the guilty doth accuse the just,
And faulty judge condemns the innocent;
And wilful Jews to exercise their lust,
With whips and taunts against their Lord are bent;
He basely used, blasphemed, scorned, and cursed,
Our Heavenly King to death for us they sent:
Reproaches, slanders, spittings in His face,
Spite doing all her worst in His disgrace.

And now this long expected hour draws near,
When blessèd saints with angels do condole;
His holy march, soft pace, and heavy cheer,
In humble sort to yield His glorious soul,
By His deserts the foulest sins to clear;
And in th'eternal book of Heaven to enrol
A satisfaction till the general doom,
Of all sins past, and all that are to come.

They that had seen this pitiful procession,
From Pilate's palace to Mount Calvary,
Might think He answered for some great transgression,
Being in such odious sort condemned to die;
He plainly showed that His own profession
Was virtue, patience, grace, love, piety;
And how by suffering He could conquer more
Than all the kings that ever lived before.

First went the crier with open mouth proclaiming
The heavy sentence of iniquity,
The hangman next, by his base office claiming
His right in Hell, where sinners never die,
Carrying the nails, the people still blaspheming
Their maker, using all impiety;
The thieves attending Him on either side,
The sergeants watching, while the women cried.

Thrice happy women that obtained such grace
From Him whose worth the world could not contain;
Immediately to turn about His face,
As not rememb'ring His great grief and pain,
To comfort you, whose tears poured forth apace
On Flora's banks, like showers of April's rain:
Your cries enforcèd mercy, grace, and love
From Him, whom greatest princes could not move:

To speak one word, nor once to lift his eyes
Unto proud Pilate, no nor Herod, King;
By all the questions that they could devise,
Could make Him answer to no manner of thing;
Yet these poor women, by their piteous cries
Did move their Lord, their Lover, and their King,
To take compassion, turn about, and speak
To them whose hearts were ready now to break.

Most blessèd daughters of Jerusalem,
Who found such favour in your Saviour's sight,
To turn His face when you did pity Him;
Your tearful eyes, beheld His eyes more bright;

Your faith and love unto such grace did climb,
To have reflection from this Heav'nly light:
Your eagle's eyes did gaze against this Sun,
Your hearts did think, He dead, the world were done.

When spiteful men with torments did oppress
Th'afflicted body of this innocent Dove,
Poor women seeing how much they did transgress,
By tears, by sighs, by cries entreat, nay prove,
What may be done among the thickest press,
They labour still these tyrants' hearts to move;
In pity and compassion to forbear
Their whipping, spurning, tearing of His hair.

But all in vain, their malice hath no end,
Their hearts more hard than flint, or marble stone;
Now to His grief, His greatness they attend,
When He (God knows) had rather be alone;
They are His guard, yet seek all means t'offend:
Well may He grieve, well may He sigh and groan,
Under the burthen of a heavy cross
He faintly goes to make their gain His loss.

His woeful Mother waiting on her Son,
All comfortless in depth of sorrow drowned;
Her griefs extreme, although but new begun,
To see His bleeding body oft she swooned;
How could she choose but think herself undone,
He dying, with whose glory she was crowned?
None ever lost so great a loss as she,
Being Son, and Father of Eternity.

Her tears did wash away His precious blood,
That sinners might not tread it under feet
To worship Him, and that it did her good
Upon her knees, although in open street,
Knowing He was the Jesse flower and bud,
That must be gath'red when it smelled most sweet:
Her Son, her Husband, Father, Saviour, King,
Whose death killed Death, and took away his sting.

Most blessèd Virgin, in whose faultless fruit,
All nations of the Earth must needs rejoice,
No creature having sense though ne'er so brute,
But joys and trembles when they hear His voice;
His wisdom strikes the wisest persons mute,
Fair chosen vessel, happy in His choice:
Dear Mother of our Lord, whose reverend name,
All people Blessèd call, and spread thy fame.

For the Almighty magnifièd thee,
And lookèd down upon thy mean estate;
Thy lowly mind, and unstained chastity,
Did plead for love at great Jehova's gate,
Who sending swift-winged Gabriel unto thee,
His holy will and pleasure to relate;
To thee most beauteous Queen of woman-kind,
The angel did unfold his Maker's mind.

He thus began, 'Hail Mary full of grace,
Thou freely art belovèd of the Lord,
He is with thee, behold thy happy case;'
What endless comfort did these words afford
To thee that saw'st an angel in the place
Proclaim thy virtue's worth, and to record
Thee blessèd among women: that thy praise
Should last so many worlds beyond thy days.

Lo, this high message to thy troubled spirit,
He doth deliver in the plainest sense;
Says, 'Thou shouldst bear a Son that shall inherit
His Father David's throne, free from offence,'
Calls Him that Holy thing, by whose pure merit
We must be saved, tells what He is, of whence;
His worth, His greatness, what His name must be,
Who should be called the Son of the most High.

He cheers thy troubled soul, bids thee not fear;
When thy pure thoughts could hardly apprehend
This salutation, when he did appear;
Nor couldst thou judge, whereto those words did tend;

His pure aspect did move thy modest cheer
To muse, yet joy that God vouchsafed to send
His glorious angel; who did thee assure
To bear a child, although a Virgin pure.

Nay more, thy Son should rule and reign forever;
Yea, of his Kingdom there should be no end;
Over the house of Jacob, Heaven's great giver
Would give Him power, and to that end did send
His faithful servant Gabriel to deliver
To thy chaste ears no word that might offend:
But that this blessèd Infant born of thee,
Thy Son, the only Son of God should be.

When on the knees of thy submissive heart
Thou humbly didst demand, 'How that should be?'
Thy virgin thoughts did think, none could impart
This great good hap, and blessing unto thee;
Far from desire of any man thou art,
Knowing not one, thou art from all men free:
When he, to answer this thy chaste desire,
Gives thee more cause to wonder and admire.

That thou a Blessèd Virgin shouldst remain,
Yea that the Holy Ghost should come on thee
A maiden mother, subject to no pain,
For highest power should overshadow thee:
Could thy fair eyes from tears of joy refrain,
When God looked down upon thy poor degree?
Making thee servant, mother, wife, and nurse
To Heaven's bright King, that freed us from the curse.

Thus being crowned with glory from above,
Grace and perfection resting in thy breast,
Thy humble answer doth approve thy love,
And all these sayings in thy heart do rest:
Thy Child a Lamb, and thou a turtle dove,
Above all other women highly blessed;
To find such favour in his glorious sight,
In whom thy heart and soul do most delight.

What wonder in the world more strange could seem,
Than that a virgin could conceive and bear
Within her womb a Son, that should redeem
All nations on the earth, and should repair
Our old decays: who in such high esteem,
Should prize all mortals, living in his fear;
As not to shun death, poverty, and shame,
To save their souls, and spread His glorious name.

And partly to fulfil His Father's pleasure,
Whose powerful hand allows it not for strange,
If he vouchsafe the riches of his treasure,
Pure righteousness to take such ill exchange;
On all iniquity to make a seizure,
Giving His snow-white weed for ours in change;
Our mortal garment in a scarlet dye,
Too base a robe for immortality.

Most happy news, that ever yet was brought,
When poverty and riches met together,
The wealth of Heaven, in our frail clothing wrought
Salvation by His happy coming hither:
Mighty Messiah, who so dearly bought
Us slaves to sin, far lighter than a feather:
Tossed to and fro with every wicked wind,
The world, the flesh, or Devil gives to blind.

Who on His shoulders our black sins doth bear
To that most blessèd, yet accursèd cross;
Where fast'ning them, He rids us of our fear,
Yea for our gain He is content with loss,
Our ragged clothing scorns He not to wear,
Though foul, rent, torn, disgraceful, rough and gross,
Spun by that monster Sin, and weaved by Shame,
Which grace itself, disgraced with impure blame.

How canst thou choose (fair Virgin) then but mourn,
When this sweet offspring of thy body dies,
When thy fair eyes behold His body torn,
The people's fury, hears the women's cries;

His holy name profaned, He made a scorn,
Abused with all their hateful slanderous lies:
Bleeding and fainting in such wondrous sort,
As scarce His feeble limbs can Him support.

Now Simon of Cyrene passeth them by,
Whom they compel sweet Jesus' cross to bear
To Golgotha, there do they mean to try
All cruel means to work in Him despair:
That odious place, where dead men's skulls did lie,
There must our Lord for present death prepare:
His sacred blood must grace that loathsome field,
To purge more filth, than that foul place could yield.

For now arrived unto this hateful place,
In which His cross erected needs must be,
False hearts, and willing hands come on apace,
All pressed to ill, and all desire to see:
Graceless themselves, still seeking to disgrace;
Bidding Him, if the Son of God He be,
To save Himself, if He could others save,
With all th'opprobrious words that might deprave.

His harmless hands unto the cross they nailed,
And feet that never trod in sinner's trace,
Between two thieves, unpitied, unbewailed,
Save of some few possessors of His grace,
With sharpest pangs and terrors thus appalled,
Stern death makes way, that life might give Him place:
His eyes with tears, His body full of wounds,
Death last of pains His sorrows all confounds.

His joints disjointed, and His legs hang down,
His alabaster breast, His bloody side,
His members torn, and on His head a crown
Of sharpest thorns, to satisfy for pride:
Anguish and pain do all His senses drown,
While they His holy garments do divide:
His bowels dry, His heart full fraught with grief,
Crying to Him that yields Him no relief.

This with the eye of faith thou mayst behold,
Dear spouse of Christ, and more than I can write;
And here both grief and joy thou mayst unfold,
To view thy Love in this most heavy plight,
Bowing His head, His bloodless body cold;
Those eyes wax dim that gave us all our light,
His count'nance pale, yet still continues sweet,
His blessed blood wat'ring his piercèd feet.

O glorious miracle without compare!
Last, but not least which was by Him effected;
Uniting death, life, misery, joy and care,
By His sharp passion in His dear elected:
Who doth the badges of like liveries wear,
Shall find how dear they are of Him respected.
No joy, grief, pain, life, death, was like to His,
Whose infinite dolours wrought eternal bliss.

What creature on the Earth did then remain,
On whom the horror of this shameful deed
Did not inflict some violent touch, or strain,
To see the Lord of all the world to bleed?
His dying breath did rend huge rocks in twain,
The Heavens betook them to their mourning weed:
The sun grew dark, and scorned to give them light,
Who durst eclipse a glory far more bright.

The moon and stars did hide themselves for shame,
The Earth did tremble in her loyal fear,
The temple veil did rent to spread His fame,
The monuments did open everywhere;
Dead saints did rise forth of their graves, and came
To diverse people that remained there
Within that holy city; whose offence,
Did put their Maker to this large expense.

Things reasonable, and reasonless possessed
The terrible impression of this fact;
For His oppression made them all oppresssed,
When with His blood He sealed so fair an act,

In restless misery to procure our rest;
His glorious deeds that dreadful prison sacked:
When Death, Hell, Devils, using all their power,
Were overcome in that most blessèd hour.

Being dead, He killed Death, and did survive
That proud insulting tyrant: in whose place
He sends bright immortality to revive
Those whom his iron arms did long embrace;
Who from their loathsome graves brings them alive
In glory to behold their Saviour's face:
Who took the keys of all Death's power away,
Opening to those that would His name obey.

O wonder, more than man can comprehend,
Our joy and grief both at one instant framed,
Compounded: Contrarieties contend
Each to exceed, yet neither to be blamed.
Our grief to see our Saviour's wretched end,
Our joy to know both Death and Hell He tamed:
That we may say, 'O Death, where is thy sting?
Hell, yield thy victory to thy conqu'ring King.'

Can stony hearts refrain from shedding tears,
To view the life and death of this sweet Saint?
His austere course in young and tender years,
When great endurements could not make Him faint:
His wants, His pains, His torments, and His fears,
All which He undertook without constraint,
To show that infinite goodness must restore,
What infinite justice looked for, and more.

Yet, had He been but of a mean degree,
His suff'rings had been small to what they were;
Mean minds will show of what mean moulds they be;
Small griefs seem great, yet use doth make them bear:
But ah! 'tis hard to stir a sturdy tree;
Great dangers hardly puts great minds in fear:
They will conceal their griefs which mighty grow
In their stout hearts until they overflow.

If then an Earthly prince may ill endure
The least of those afflictions which he bear,
How could this all-commanding King procure
Such grievous torments with His mind to square,
Legions of angels being at His lure?
He might have lived in pleasure without care:
None can conceive the bitter pains He felt,
When God and man must suffer without guilt.

Take all the suff'rings thoughts can think upon,
In ev'ry man that this huge world hath bred;
Let all those pains and suff'rings meet in one,
Yet are they not a mite to that He did
Endure for us: Oh let us think thereon,
That God should have His precious blood so shed:
His greatness clothèd in our frail attire,
And pay so dear a ransom for the hire.

Lo, here was glory, misery, life and death,
An union of contraries did accord;
Gladness and sadness here had one berth,
This wonder wrought the Passion of our Lord,
He suff'ring for all the sins of all th'Earth,
No satisfaction could the world afford:
But this rich jewel, which from God was sent,
To call all those that would in time repent.

Which I present (dear lady) to your view,
Upon the cross deprived of life or breath,
To judge if ever Lover were so true,
To yield Himself unto such shameful death:
Now blessèd Joseph doth both beg and sue,
To have His body who possessed his faith,
And thinks, if he this small request obtains,
He wins more wealth than in the world remains.

Thus honourable Joseph is possessed,
Of what his heart and soul so much desired,
And now he goes to give that body rest,
That all His life, with griefs and pains was tired;

He finds a tomb, a tomb most rarely blessed,
In which was never creature yet interred;
There this most precious body he encloses,
Embalmed and decked with lilies and with roses.

Lo here the Beauty of Heav'n and Earth is laid,
The purest colours underneath the sun,
But in this place He cannot long be stayed,
Glory must end what horror hath begun;
For He the fury of the Heavens obeyed,
And now He must possess what He hath won:
The Marys do with precious balms attend,
But being come, they find it to no end.

For He is ris'n from death t'eternal life,
And now those precious ointments He desires
Are brought unto Him, by His faithful wife
The Holy Church; who in those rich attires,
Of patience, love, long suff'ring, void of strife,
Humbly presents those ointments He requires:
The oils of mercy, charity, and faith,
She only gives that which no other hath.

These precious balms do heal his grievous wounds,
And water of compunction washeth clean
The sores of sins, which in our souls abounds;
So fair it heals, no scar is ever seen;
Yet all the glory unto Christ redounds,
His precious blood is that which must redeem;
Those well may make us lovely in His sight,
But cannot save without His powerful might.

This is that Bridegroom that appears so fair,
So sweet, so lovely in His spouse's sight,
That unto snow we may His face compare,
His cheeks like scarlet, and His eyes so bright
As purest doves that in the rivers are,
Washed with milk, to give the more delight;
His head is likened to the finest gold,
His curled locks so beauteous to behold;

Black as a raven in her blackest hue;
His lips like scarlet threads, yet much more sweet
Than is the sweetest honey dropping dew,
Or honeycombs, where all the bees do meet;
Yea, He is constant, and His words are true,
His cheeks are beds of spices, flowers sweet;
His lips like lilies, dropping down pure myrrh,
Whose love, before all worlds we do prefer.

Ah! give me leave (good lady) now to leave
This task of beauty which I took in hand,
I cannot wade so deep, I may deceive
Myself, before I can attain the land;
Therefore (good madam) in your heart I leave
His perfect picture, where it still shall stand,
Deeply engraved in that holy shrine,
Environed with love and thoughts divine.

There may you see Him as a God in glory,
And as a Man in miserable case;
There may you read His true and perfect story,
His bleeding body there you may embrace,
And kiss His dying cheeks with tears of sorrow,
With joyful grief, you may entreat for grace;
And all your prayers, and your alms-deeds
May bring to stop His cruel wounds that bleeds.

Oft times hath He made trial of your love,
And in your faith hath took no small delight,
By crosses and afflictions He doth prove,
Yet still your heart remaineth firm and right;
Your love so strong, as nothing can remove,
Your thoughts being placed on Him both day and night,
Your constant soul doth lodge between her breasts,
This sweet of sweets, in which all glory rests.

Sometime H'appears to thee in shepherd's weed,
And so presents Himself before thine eyes,
A good old man; that goes his flock to feed;
Thy colour changes, and thy heart doth rise;

Thou call'st, He comes, thou find'st 'tis He indeed,
Thy soul conceives that He is truly wise:
Nay more, desires that He may be the book,
Whereon thine eyes continually may look.

Sometime imprisoned, naked, poor, and bare,
Full of diseases, impotent, and lame,
Blind, deaf, and dumb, He comes unto His fair,
To see if yet she will remain the same;
Nay sick and wounded, now thou dost prepare
To cherish Him in thy dear Lover's name:
Yea thou bestow'st all pains, all cost, all care,
That may relieve Him, and His health repair.

These works of mercy are so sweet, so dear
To Him that is the Lord of life and love,
That all thy prayers He vouchsafes to hear,
And sends His Holy Spirit from above;
Thy eyes are opened, and thou seest so clear,
No worldly thing can thy fair mind remove;
Thy faith, thy prayers, and His special grace
Doth open Heav'n, where thou behold'st His face.

These are those keys Saint Peter did possess,
Which with a spiritual power are giv'n to thee,
To heal the souls of those that do transgress,
By thy fair virtues; which, if once they see,
Unto the like they do their minds address,
Such as thou art, such they desire to be:
If they be blind, thou giv'st to them their sight;
If deaf or lame, they hear, and go upright.

Yea, if possessed with any evil spirits,
Such power thy fair examples have obtained
To cast them out, applying Christ's pure merits,
By which they are bound, and of all hurt restrained:
If strangely taken, wanting sense or wits,
Thy faith applied unto their souls so pained,
Healeth all griefs, and makes them grow so strong,
As no defects can hang upon them long.

Thou being thus rich, no riches dost respect,
Nor dost thou care for any outward show;
The proud that do fair virtue's rules neglect,
Desiring place, thou sittest them below:
All wealth and honour thou dost quite reject,
If thou perceiv'st that once it proves a foe
To virtue, learning, and the powers divine,
Thou may'st convert, but never wilt incline

To foul disorder, or licentiousness
But in thy modest veil dost sweetly cover
The stains of other sins, to make themselves,
That by this means thou may'st in time recover
Those weak lost sheep that did so long transgress,
Presenting them unto thy dearest Lover;
That when He brings them back unto His fold,
In their conversion then He may behold

Thy beauty shining brighter than the sun,
Thine honour more than ever monarch gained,
Thy wealth exceeding his that kingdoms won,
Thy love unto His spouse, thy faith unfeigned,
Thy constancy in what thou hast begun,
Till thou His Heavenly Kingdom have obtained;
Respecting worldly wealth to be but dross,
Which, if abused, doth prove the owner's loss.

Great Cleopatra's love to Anthony,
Can no way be comparèd unto thine;
She left her love in his extremity,
When greatest need should cause her to combine
Her force with his, to get the victory:
Her love was earthly, and thy love divine;
Her love was only to support her pride,
Humility thy love and thee doth guide.

That glorious part of death, which last she played,
T'appease the ghost of her deceasèd love,
Had never needed, if she could have stayed
When his extremes made trial, and did prove

Her leaden love unconstant, and afraid:
Their wicked wars the wrath of God might move
To take revenge for chaste Octavia's wrongs,
Because she enjoys what unto her belongs.

No Cleopatra, though thou wert as fair
As any creature in Antonius' eyes;
Yea though thou wert as rich, as wise, as rare,
As any pen could write, or wit devise;
Yet with this lady canst thou not compare,
Whose inward virtues all thy worth denies:
Yet thou a black Egyptian dost appear;
Thou false, she true; and to her love more dear.

She sacrificeth to her dearest love,
With flowers of faith, and garlands of good deeds;
She flies not from Him when afflictions prove,
She bears His cross, and stops His wounds that bleeds;
She loves and lives chaste as the turtle dove,
She attends upon Him, and His flock she feeds;
Yea for one touch of death which thou didst try,
A thousand deaths she every day doth die.

Her virtuous life exceeds thy worthy death,
Yea, she hath richer ornaments of state,
Shining more glorious than in dying breath
Thou didst; when either pride, or cruel fate,
Did work thee to prevent a double death;
To stay the malice, scorn, and cruel hate
Of Rome; that joyed to see thy pride pulled down,
Whose beauty wrought the hazard of her crown.

Good madam, though your modesty be such,
Not to acknowledge what we know and find;
And that you think these praises overmuch,
Which do express the beauty of your mind;
Yet pardon me although I give a touch
Unto their eyes, that else would be so blind,
As not to see thy store, and their own wants,
From whose fair seeds of virtue spring these plants.

And know, when first into this world I came,
This charge was giv'n me by th'Eternal powers,
The everlasting trophy of thy fame,
To build and deck it with the sweetest flowers
That virtue yields; then madam, do not blame
Me, when I show the world but what is yours,
And deck you with that crown which is your due,
That of Heav'n's beauty Earth may take a view.

Though famous women elder times have known,
Whose glorious actions did appear so bright,
That powerful men by them were overthrown,
And all their armies overcome in fight;
The Scythian women by their power alone,
Put King Darius unto shameful flight:
All Asia yielded to their conqu'ring hand,
Great Alexander could not their power withstand.

Whose worth, though writ in lines of blood and fire,
Is not to be comparèd unto thine;
Their power was small to overcome desire,
Or to direct their ways by virtue's line:
Were they alive, they would thy life admire,
And unto thee their honours would resign:
For thou a greater conquest dost obtain,
Than they who have so many thousands slain.

Wise Deborah that judgèd Israel,
Nor valiant Judith cannot equal thee,
Unto the first, God did his will reveal,
And gave her power to set his people free;
Yea Judith had the power likewise to quell
Proud Holofernes, that the just might see
What small defence vain pride, and greatness hath
Against the weapons of God's word and faith.

But thou far greater war dost still maintain,
Against that many headed monster sin,
Whose mortal sting hath many thousand slain,
And every day fresh combats do begin;

Yet cannot all his venom lay one stain
Upon thy soul, thou dost the conquest win,
Though all the world he daily doth devour,
Yet over thee he never could get power.

For that one worthy deed by Deb'rah done,
Thou hast performèd many in thy time;
For that one conquest that fair Judith won,
By which she did the steps of honour climb;
Thou hast the conquest of all conquests won,
When to thy conscience Hell can lay no crime:
For that one head that Judith bore away,
Thou tak'st from sin a hundred heads a day.

Though virtuous Hester fasted three days' space,
And spent her time in prayers all that while,
That by God's power she might obtain such grace,
That she and hers might not become a spoil
To wicked Haman, in whose crabbèd face
Was seen the map of malice, envy, guile;
Her glorious garments though she put apart,
So to present a pure and single heart

To God, in sack-cloth, ashes, and with tears;
Yet must fair Hester needs give place to thee,
Who hath continued days, weeks, months, and years,
In God's true service, yet thy heart being free
From doubt of death, or any other fears:
Fasting from sin, thou pray'st thine eyes may see
Him that hath full possession of thine heart,
From whose sweet love thy soul can never part.

His love, not fear, makes thee to fast and pray,
No kinsman's counsel needs thee to advise;
The sack-cloth thou dost wear both night and day,
Is worldly troubles, which thy rest denies;
The ashes are the vanities that play
Over thy head, and steal before thine eyes;
Which thou shak'st off when mourning time is past,
That royal robes thou may'st put on at last.

Joachim's wife; that fair and constant dame,
Who rather chose a cruel death to die,
Than yield to those two Elders void of shame,
When both at once her chastity did try,
Whose innocency bore away the blame,
Until th'Almighty Lord had heard her cry;
And raised the spirit of a child to speak,
Making the powerful judgèd of the weak.

Although her virtue do deserve to be
Writ by that hand that never purchased blame;
In holy writ, where all the world may see
Her perfect life, and ever honoured name:
Yet was she not to be compared to thee,
Whose many virtues do increase thy fame:
For she opposed against old doting lust,
Who with life's danger she did fear to trust.

But your chaste breast, guarded with strength of mind,
Hates the embracements of unchaste desires;
You loving God, live in yourself confined
From unpure love, your purest thoughts retires,
Your perfect sight could never be so blind,
To entertain the old or young desires
Of idle lovers; which the world presents,
Whose base abuses worthy minds prevents.

Even as the constant laurel, always green,
No parching heat of Summer can deface,
Nor pinching Winter ever yet was seen,
Whose nipping frosts could wither, or disgrace:
So you (dear lady) still remain as Queen,
Subduing all affections that are base,
Unalterable by the change of times,
Not following, but lamenting others' crimes.

No fear of death, or dread of open shame,
Hinders your perfect heart to give consent;
Nor loathsome age, whom time could never tame
From ill designs, whereto their youth was bent;

But love of God, care to preserve your fame,
And spend that precious time that God hath sent,
In all good exercises of the mind,
Whereto your noble nature is inclined.

That Ethiopian Queen did gain great fame,
Who from the Southern world, did come to see
Great Solomon; the glory of whose name
Had spread itself o'er all the Earth, to be
So great, that all the princes thither came,
To be spectators of his royalty:
And this fair Queen of Sheba came from far,
To reverence this new appearing star.

From th'utmost part of all the Earth she came,
To hear the wisdom of this worthy King;
To try if wonder did agree with fame,
And many fair rich presents did she bring:
Yea many strange hard questions did she frame,
All which were answered by this famous King:
Nothing was hid that in her heart did rest,
And all to prove this King so highly blessed.

Here majesty with majesty did meet,
Wisdom to wisdom yielded true content,
One beauty did another beauty greet,
Bounty to bounty never could repent;
Here all distaste is trodden under feet,
No loss of time, where time was so well spent
In virtuous exercises of the mind,
In which this Queen did much contentment find.

Spirits affect where they do sympathise,
Wisdom desires wisdom to embrace,
Virtue covets her like, and doth devise
How she her friends may entertain with grace;
Beauty sometime is pleased to feed her eyes,
With viewing beauty in another's face:
Both good and bad in this point do agree,
That each desireth with his like to be.

And this desire did work a strange effect,
To draw a Queen forth of her native land,
Not yielding to the niceness and respect
Of woman-kind; she passed both sea and land,
All fear of dangers she did quite neglect,
Only to see, to hear, and understand
That beauty, wisdom, majesty, and glory,
That in her heart impressed his perfect story.

Yet this fair map of majesty and might,
Was but a figure of thy dearest love,
Born t'express that true and Heavenly light,
That doth all other joys imperfect prove;
If this fair Earthly star did shine so bright,
What doth that glorious Son that is above?
Who wears th'imperial crown of Heaven and Earth,
And made all Christians blessèd in His birth.

If that small spark could yield so great a fire,
As to inflame the hearts of many Kings
To come to see, to hear, and to admire
His wisdom, tending but to worldly things;
Then much more reason have we to desire
That Heav'nly wisdom, which salvation brings;
The Son of righteousness, that gives true joys,
When all they fought for, were but Earthly toys.

No travels ought th'affected soul to shun,
That this fair Heavenly Light desires to see:
This King of kings to whom we all should run,
To view His glory and His majesty;
He without whom we all had been undone,
He that from sin and death hath set us free,
And overcome Satan, the world, and sin,
That by His merits we those joys might win.

Prepared by Him, whose everlasting throne
Is placed in Heaven, above the starry skies,
Where He that sat, was like the Jasper stone,
Who rightly knows Him shall be truly wise,

A rainbow round about His glorious throne;
Nay more, those wingèd beasts so full of eyes,
That never cease to glorify His Name,
Who was, and will be, and is now the same.

This is that great almighty Lord that made
Both Heaven and Earth, and lives for evermore;
By Him the world's foundation first was laid:
He framed the things that never were before:
The sea within His bounds by Him is stayed,
He judgeth all alike, both rich and poor:
All might, all majesty, all love, all law
Remains in Him that keeps all worlds in awe.

From His eternal throne the lightning came,
Thund'rings and voices did from thence proceed;
And all the creatures glorified his name,
In Heaven, in Earth, and seas, they all agreed,
When lo that spotless Lamb so void of blame,
That for us died, whose sins did make Him bleed:
That true physician that so many heals,
Opened the book, and did undo the seals.

He only worthy to undo the book
Of our charged souls, full of iniquity,
Where with the eyes of mercy He doth look
Upon our weakness and infirmity;
This is that cornerstone that was forsook,
Who leaves it, trusts but to uncertainty:
This is God's Son, in whom He is well pleased,
His dear belovèd, that His wrath appeased.

He that had power to open all the seals,
And summon up our sins of blood and wrong,
He unto whom the righteous souls appeals,
That have been martyred, and do think it long,
To whom in mercy He His will reveals,
That they should rest a little in their wrong,
Until their fellow servants should be killed,
Even as they were, and that they were fulfilled.

Pure thoughted lady, blessèd be thy choice
Of this Almighty, everlasting King;
In thee His saints and angels do rejoice,
And to their Heav'nly Lord do daily sing
Thy perfect praises in their loudest voice;
And all their harps and golden vials bring
Full of sweet odours, even thy holy prayers
Unto that spotless Lamb, that all repairs.

Of whom that heathen Queen obtained such grace,
By honouring but the shadow of His love,
That great judicial day to have a place,
Condemning those that do unfaithful prove;
Among the hapless, happy is her case,
That her dear Saviour spake for her behove;
And that her memorable act should be
Writ by the hand of true eternity.

Yet this rare Phoenix of that worn-out age,
This great majestic Queen comes short of thee
Who to an Earthly Prince did then engage
Her hearts desires, her love, her liberty,
Acting her glorious part upon a stage
Of weakness, frailty, and infirmity:
Giving all honour to a creature, due
To her Creator, whom she never knew.

But lo, a greater thou hast sought and found
Than Solomon in all his royalty;
And unto Him thy faith most firmly bound
To serve and honour Him continually;
That glorious God, whose terror doth confound
All sinful workers of iniquity:
Him hast thou truly servèd all thy life,
And for His love, lived with the world at strife.

To this great Lord, thou only art affected,
Yet came He not in pomp or royalty,
But in an humble habit, base, dejected;
A King, a God, clad in mortality,

He hath thy love, thou art by Him directed,
His perfect path was fair humility:
Who being Monarch of Heav'n, Earth, and seas,
Endured all wrongs, yet no man did displease.

Then how much more art thou to be commended,
That seek'st thy love in lowly shepherd's weed?
A seeming tradesman's son, of none attended,
Save of a few in poverty and need;
Poor fishermen that on His love attended,
His love that makes so many thousands bleed:
Thus did He come, to try our faiths the more,
Possessing worlds, yet seeming extreme poor.

The pilgrim's travels, and the shepherd's cares,
He took upon Him to enlarge our souls,
What pride hath lost, humility repairs,
For by His glorious death He us enrols
In deep characters, writ with blood and tears,
Upon those blessèd everlasting scrolls;
His hands, His feet, His body, and His face,
Whence freely flowed the rivers of His grace.

Sweet holy rivers, pure celestial springs,
Proceeding from the fountain of our life;
Swift sugared currents that salvation brings,
Clear crystal streams, purging all sin and strife,
Fair floods, where souls do bathe their snow-white wings,
Before they fly to true eternal life:
Sweet nectar and ambrosia, food of saints,
Which, whoso tasteth, never after faints.

This honey dropping dew of holy love,
Sweet milk, wherewith we weaklings are restored,
Who drinks thereof, a world can never move,
All Earthly pleasures are of them abhorred;
This love made martyrs many deaths to prove,
To taste His sweetness, whom they so adored:
Sweetness that makes our flesh a burthen to us,
Knowing it serves but only to undo us.

His sweetness sweet'ned all the sour of death,
To faithful Stephen His appointed saint;
Who by the river stones did lose his breath,
When pains nor terrors could not make him faint:
So was this blessèd martyr turned to earth,
To glorify his soul by death's attaint:
This holy Saint was humbled and cast down,
To win in Heaven an everlasting crown.

Whose face replete with majesty and sweetness,
Did as an angel unto them appear,
That sat in Counsel hearing his discreetness,
Seeing no change, or any sign of a fear;
But with a constant brow did there confess
Christ's high deserts, which were to him so dear:
Yea when these tyrants' storms did most oppress,
Christ did appear to make his grief the less.

For being fillèd with the Holy Ghost,
Up unto Heav'n he looked with steadfast eyes,
Where God appeared with his Heavenly host
In glory to this Saint before he dies;
Although he could no Earthly pleasures boast,
At God's right hand sweet Jesus he espies;
Bids them behold Heavens open, he doth see
The Son of Man at God's right hand to be.

Whose sweetness sweet'ned that short sour of life,
Making all bitterness delight his taste,
Yielding sweet quietness in bitter strife,
And most contentment when he died disgraced;
Heaping up joys where sorrows were most rife;
Such sweetness could not choose but be embraced:
The food of souls, the spirit's only treasure,
The Paradise of our celestial pleasure.

This Lamb of God, who died, and was alive,
Presenting us the bread of life eternal,
His bruised body powerful to revive
Our sinking souls, out of the pit infernal;

For by this blessèd food He did contrive
A work of grace, by this His gift external,
With Heav'nly manna, food of His elected,
To feed their souls, of whom He is respected.

This wheat of Heav'n the blessèd angel's bread,
Wherewith He feeds His dear adopted heirs;
Sweet food of life that doth revive the dead,
And from the living takes away all cares;
To taste this sweet Saint Laurence did not dread,
The broiling gridiron cooled with holy tears:
Yielding his naked body to the fire,
To taste this sweetness, such was his desire.

Nay, what great sweetness did th'Apostles taste,
Condemned by counsel, when they did return;
Rejoicing that for Him they died disgraced,
Whose sweetness made their hearts and souls so burn
With holy zeal and love most pure and chaste;
For Him they sought from whom they might not turn:
Whose love made Andrew go most joyfully,
Unto the cross, on which he meant to die.

The Princes of th'Apostles were so filled
With the delicious sweetness of His grace,
That willingly they yielded to be killed,
Receiving deaths that were most vile and base,
For His name sake, that all might be fulfilled.
They with great joy all torments did embrace:
The ugliest face that death could ever yield,
Could never fear these champions from the field.

They still continued in their glorious fight,
Against the enemies of flesh and blood;
And in God's law did set their whole delight,
Suppressing evil, and erecting good:
Not sparing kings in what they did not right;
Their noble acts they sealed with dearest blood:
One chose the gallows, that unseemly death,
The other by the sword did lose his breath.

His head did pay the dearest rate of sin,
Yielding it joyfully unto the sword,
To be cut off as he had never been,
For speaking truth according to God's word,
Telling King Herod of incestuous sin,
That hateful crime of God and man abhorred:
His brother's wife, that proud licentious dame,
Cut off his head to take away his shame.

Lo madam, here you take a view of those,
Whose worthy steps you do desire to tread,
Decked in those colours which our Saviour chose;
The purest colours both of white and red,
Their freshest beauties would I fain disclose,
By which our Saviour most was honourèd:
But my weak Muse desireth now to rest,
Folding up all their beauties in your breast.

Whose excellence hath raised my sprites to write,
Of what my thoughts could hardly apprehend;
Your rarest virtues did my soul delight,
Great lady of my heart: I must commend
You that appear so fair in all men's sight:
On your deserts my Muses do attend:
You are the Arctic Star that guides my hand,
All what I am, I rest at your command.

The Description of Cookeham

Farewell (sweet Cookeham) where I first obtained
Grace from that grace where perfect grace remained:
And where the Muses gave their full consent,
I should have power the virtuous to content:
Where princely Pallas willed me to indict,
The sacred story of the soul's delight.
Farewell (sweet place) where virtue then did rest,
And all delights did harbour in her breast:
Never shall my sad eyes again behold
Those pleasures which my thoughts did then unfold:
Yet you (great lady) mistress of that place,

From whose desires did spring this work of grace;
Vouchsafe to think upon those pleasures past,
As fleeting worldly joys that could not last:
Or, as dim shadows of celestial pleasures,
Which are desired above all Earthly treasures.
Oh how (methought) against you thither came,
Each part did seem some new delight to frame!
The house received all ornaments to grace it,
And would endure no foulness to deface it.
The walks put on their summer liveries,
And all things else did hold like similes:
The trees with leaves, with fruits, with flowers clad,
Embraced each other, seeming to be glad,
Turning themselves to beauteous canopies,
To shade the bright sun from your brighter eyes:
The crystal streams with silver spangles graced,
While by the glorious sun they were embraced:
The little birds in chirping notes did sing,
To entertain both you and that sweet Spring.
And Philomela with her sundry lays,
Both you and that delightful place did praise.
Oh how methought each plant, each flower, each tree
Set forth their beauties then to welcome thee:
The very hills right humbly did descend,
When you to tread upon them did intend.
And as you set your feet, they still did rise,
Glad that they could receive so rich a prize.
The gentle winds did take delight to be
Among those woods that were so graced by thee.
And in sad murmur uttered pleasing sound,
That pleasure in that place might more abound:
The swelling banks delivered all their pride,
When such a Phoenix once they had espied.
Each arbor, bank, each seat, each stately tree,
Thought themselves honoured in supporting thee.
The pretty birds would oft come to attend thee,
Yet fly away for fear they should offend thee:
The little creatures in the burrow by
Would come abroad to sport them in your eye;
Yet fearful of the bow in your fair hand,
Would run away when you did make a stand.

Now let me come unto that stately tree,
Wherein such goodly prospects you did see;
That oak that did in height his fellows pass,
As much as lofty trees, low growing grass:
Much like a comely cedar straight and tall,
Whose beauteous stature far exceeded all:
How often did you visit this fair tree,
Which seeming joyful in receiving thee,
Would like a palm tree spread his arms abroad,
Desirous that you there should make abode:
Whose fair green leaves much like a comely veil,
Defended Phoebus when he would assail:
Whose pleasing boughs did yield a cool fresh air,
Joying his happiness when you were there.
Where being seated, you might plainly see,
Hills, vales, and woods, as if on bended knee
They had appeared, your honour to salute,
Or to prefer some strange unlooked for suit:
All interlaced with brooks and crystal springs,
A prospect fit to please the eyes of kings:
And thirteen shires appeared all in your sight,
Europe could not afford much more delight.
What was there then but gave you all content,
While you the time in meditation spent,
Of their Creator's power, which there you saw,
In all His creatures held a perfect law;
And in their beauties did you plain descry,
His beauty, wisdom, grace, love, majesty.
In these sweet woods how often did you walk,
With Christ and His Apostles there to talk;
Placing His holy writ in some fair tree,
To meditate what you therein did see:
With Moses you did mount his holy hill,
To know his pleasure, and perform his will.
With lovely David you did often sng,
His holy hymns to Heaven's eternal King.
And in sweet music did your soul delight,
To sound his praises, morning, noon, and night.
With blessèd Joseph you did often feed
Your pinèd brethren, when they stood in need.
And that sweet lady sprung from Clifford's race,

Of noble Bedford's blood, fair stem of grace;
To honourable Dorset now espoused,
In whose fair breast true virtue then was housed:
Oh what delight did my weak spirits find
In those pure parts of her well-framèd mind:
And yet it grieves me that I cannot be
Near unto her, whose virtues did agree
With those fair ornaments of outward beauty,
Which did enforce from all both love and duty.
Unconstant Fortune, thou art most to blame,
Who casts us down into so low a frame:
Where our great friends we cannot daily see,
So great a difference is there in degree.
Many are placèd in those orbs of state,
Partners in honour, so ordained by Fate;
Nearer in show, yet farther off in love,
In which, the lowest always are above.
But whither am I carried in conceit?
My wit too weak to conster of the great.
Why not? Although we are but born of earth,
We may behold the Heavens, despising death;
And loving Heaven that is so far above,
May in the end vouchsafe us entire love.
Therefore sweet memory do thou retain
Those pleasures past, which will not turn again:
Remember beauteous Dorset's former sports,
So far from being touched by ill reports;
Wherein myself did always bear a part,
While reverend love presented my true heart:
Those recreations let me bear in mind,
Which her sweet youth and noble thoughts did find:
Whereof deprived, I evermore must grieve,
Hating blind Fortune, careless to relieve.
And you sweet Cookeham, whom these ladies leave,
I now must tell the grief you did conceive
At their departure; when they went away,
How everything retained a sad dismay:
Nay long before, when once an inkling came,
Methought each thing did unto sorrow frame:
The trees that were so glorious in our view,
Forsook both flowers and fruit, when once they knew

Of your depart, their very leaves did wither,
Changing their colours as they grew together.
But when they saw this had no power to stay you,
They often wept, though speechless, could not pray you;
Letting their tears in your fair bosoms fall,
As if they said, 'Why will ye leave us all?'
This being vain, they cast their leaves away,
Hoping that pity would have made you stay:
Their frozen tops, like age's hoary hairs,
Shows their disasters, languishing in fears:
A swarthy rivelled ryne all over spread,
Their dying bodies half alive, half dead.
But your occasions called you so away,
That nothing there had power to make you stay:
Yet did I see a noble grateful mind,
Requiting each according to their kind,
Forgetting not to turn and take your leave
Of these sad creatures, powerless to receive
Your favour when with grief you did depart,
Placing their former pleasures in your heart;
Giving great charge to noble memory,
There to preserve their love continually:
But specially the love of that fair tree,
That first and last you did vouchsafe to see:
In which it pleased you oft to take the air,
With noble Dorset, then a virgin fair:
Where many a learned book was read and scanned
To this fair tree, taking me by the hand,
You did repeat the pleasures which had passed,
Seeming to grieve they could no longer last.
And with a chaste, yet loving kiss took leave,
Of which sweet kiss I did it soon bereave:
Scorning a senseless creature should possess
So rare a favour, so great happiness.
No other kiss it could receive from me,
For fear to give back what it took of thee:
So I ingrateful creature did deceive it,
Of that which you vouchsafed in love to leave it.
And though it oft had giv'n me much content,
Yet this great wrong I never could repent:
But of the happiest made it most forlorn,

To show that nothing's free from Fortune's scorn,
While all the rest with this most beauteous tree,
Made their sad consort sorrow's harmony.
The flowers that on the banks and walks did grow,
Crept in the ground, the grass did weep for woe.
The winds and waters seemed to chide together,
Because you went away they know not whither:
And those sweet brooks that ran so fair and clear,
With grief and trouble wrinkled did appear.
Those pretty birds that wonted were to sing,
Now neither sing, nor chirp, nor use their wing;
But with their tender feet on some bare spray,
Warble forth sorrow, and their own dismay.
Fair Philomela leaves her mournful ditty,
Drowned in dead sleep, yet can procure no pity:
Each arbor, bank, each seat, each stately tree,
Looks bare and desolate now for want of thee;
Turning green tresses into frosty grey,
While in cold grief they wither all away.
The sun grew weak, his beams no comfort gave,
While all green things did make the earth their grave:
Each brier, each bramble, when you went away,
Caught fast your clothes, thinking to make you stay:
Delightful Echo wonted to reply
To our last words, did now for sorrow die:
The house cast off each garment that might grace it,
Putting on dust and cobwebs to deface it.
All desolation then there did appear,
When you were going whom they held so dear.
This last farewell to Cookeham here I give,
When I am dead thy name in this may live,
Wherein I have performed her noble hest,
Whose virtues lodge in my unworthy breast,
And ever shall, so long as life remains,
Tying my heart to her by those rich chains.

1613

8. Elizabeth Cary

The Tragedy of Mariam, the Fair Queen of Jewry

The names of the speakers

Herod, King of Judea
Doris, his first wife
Mariam, his second wife
Salome, Herod's sister
Antipater, his son by Doris
Alexandra, Mariam's mother
Silleus, Prince of Arabia
Constabarus, husband to Salome
Pheroras, Herod's brother
Graphina, his love
Baba's first son
Baba's second son
Ananell, the High Priest
Sohemus, a counsellor to Herod
Nuntio, a messenger
Bu[tler], another messenger
Chorus, a company of Jews
[Silleus' man
Soldiers and Attendants]

The Argument

Herod, the son of Antipater (an Idumean) having crept, by the favour of the Romans, into the Jewish monarchy, married Mariam the [grand]daughter of Hircanus, the rightful King and priest, and for her (besides her high blood, being of singular beauty) he repudiated Doris, his former wife, by whom he had children.

This Mariam had a brother called Aristobolus, and next him and Hircanus his grandfather, Herod in his wife's right had the best title. Therefore to remove them, he charged the first with treason and put him to death; and drowned the second under colour of sport. Alexandra, daughter to the one, and mother to the other, accused him for their deaths before Antony.

So when he was forced to go answer this accusation at Rome, he left the custody of his wife to Josephus, his uncle, that had married his sister Salome, and out of a violent affection (unwilling any should enjoy her after him) he gave strict and private commandment that if he were slain, she should be put to death. But he returned with much honour, yet found his wife extremely discontented, to whom Josephus had (meaning it for the best, to prove Herod loved her) revealed his charge.

So by Salome's accusation he put Josephus to death, but was reconciled to Mariam, who still bore the death of her friends exceeding hardly.

In this mean time Herod was again necessarily to revisit Rome, for Caesar having overthrown Antony, his great friend was likely to make an alteration of his fortune.

In his absence, news came to Jerusalem that Caesar had put him to death. Their willingness it should be so, together with the likelihood, gave this rumour so good credit as Sohemus that had suceeded in Josephus' charge, succeeded him likewise in revealing it. So at Herod's return which was speedy and unexpected, he found Mariam so far from joy, that she showed apparent signs of sorrow. He still desiring to win her to a better humour; she being very unable to conceal her passion, fell to upbraiding him with her brother's death. As they were thus debating, came in a fellow with a cup of wine, who, hired by Salome, said first it was a love potion, which Mariam desired to deliver to the King; but afterwards he affirmed that it was a poison, and that Sohemus had told her somewhat which procured the vehement hate in her.

The King hearing this, more moved with jealousy of Sohemus, than with this intent of poison, sent her away and presently after by the instigation of Salome, she was beheaded. Which rashness was afterward punished in him, with an intolerable and almost frantic passion for her death.

I.i

Enter Mariam

Mariam How oft have I, with public voice run on
To censure Rome's last hero for deceit?
Because he wept when Pompey's life was gone,
Yet when he lived, he thought his name too great.
But now I do recant and, Roman lord,
Excuse too rash a judgement in a woman:
My sex pleads pardon, pardon then afford,
Mistaking is with us but too, too common.
Now do I find by self experience taught,

One object yields both grief and joy.
You wept indeed when on his worth you thought,
But joyed that slaughter did your foe destroy.
So at his death your eyes true drops did rain,
Whom dead, you did not wish alive again.
When Herod lived, that now is done to death,
Oft have I wished that I from him were free,
Oft have I wished that he might lose his breath,
Oft have I wished his carcass dead to see.
Then rage and scorn had put my love to flight,
That love which once on him was firmly set;
Hate hid his true affection from my sight,
And kept my heart from paying him his debt.
And blame me not, for Herod's jealousy
Had power ev'n constancy itself to change:
For he by barring me from liberty,
To shun my ranging, taught me first to range.
But yet too chaste a scholar was my heart
To learn to love another than my lord;
To leave his love, my lesson's former part,
I quickly learned, the other I abhorred.
But now his death to memory doth call
The tender love that he to Mariam bore,
And mine to him. This makes those rivers fall,
Which by another thought unmoist'nèd are.
For Aristobolus, the loveliest youth
That ever did in angel's shape appear,
The cruel Herod was not moved to ruth,
Then why grieves Mariam Herod's death to hear?
Why joy I not the tongue no more shall speak
That yielded forth my brother's latest doom?
Both youth and beauty might thy fury break,
And both in him did ill befit a tomb.
And, worthy grandsire, ill did he requite
His high ascent, alone by thee procured,
Except he murdered thee to free the sprite
Which still he thought on Earth too long immured.
How happy was it that Sohemus' mind
Was moved to pity my distressed estate?
Might Herod's life a trusty servant find,
My death to his had been unseparate.
These thoughts have power his death to make me bear;

Nay more, to wish the news may firmly hold.
Yet cannot this repulse some falling tear
That will against my will some grief unfold.
And more I owe him for his love to me,
The deepest love that ever yet was seen;
Yet had I rather much a milkmaid be,
Than be the monarch of Judea's Queen.
It was for nought but love he wished his end
Might to my death but the vaunt-courier prove.
But I had rather still be foe than friend
To him that saves for hate and kills for love.
Hard-hearted Mariam! At thy discontent,
What floods of tears have drenched his manly face?
How canst thou then so faintly now lament
Thy truest lover's death, a death's disgrace?
Aye, now mine eyes you do begin to right
The wrongs of your admirer and my lord.
Long since you should have put your smiles to flight!
Ill doth a widowed eye with joy accord.
Why now methinks the love I bore him then,
When virgin freedom left me unrestrained,
Doth to my heart begin to creep again:
My passion now is far from being feigned.
But tears fly back and hide you in your banks,
You must not be to Alexandra seen,
For if my moan be spied, but little thanks
Shall Mariam have from that incensèd Queen.

I.ii

Enter Alexandra

Alexandra What means these tears? My Mariam doth mistake.
The news we heard did tell the tyrant's end!
What, weepst thou for thy brother's murd'rer's sake?
Will ever wight a tear for Herod spend?
My curse pursue his breathless trunk and spirit,
Base Edomite, the damnèd Esau's heir.
Must he ere Jacob's child the crown inherit?
Must he, vile wretch, be set in David's chair?
No, David's soul, within the bosom placed
Of our forefather Abram, was ashamed
To see his seat with such a toad disgraced,

That seat that hath by Judah's race been famed.
Thou fatal enemy to royal blood,
Did not the murder of my boy suffice
To stop thy cruel mouth that gaping stood,
But must thou dim the mild Hircanus' eyes?
My gracious father, whose too ready hand
Did lift this Idumean from the dust.
And he, ungrateful caitiff, did withstand
The man that did in him most friendly trust.
What kingdom's right could cruel Herod claim?
Was he not Esau's issue, heir of hell?
Then what succession can he have but shame?
Did not his ancestor his birth-right sell?
O yes, he doth from Edom's name derive
His cruel nature, which with blood is fed.
That made him me of sire and son deprive;
He ever thirsts for blood, and blood is red.
Weepst thou because his love to thee was bent?
And readst thou love in crimson characters?
Slew he thy friends to work thy heart's content?
No, hate may justly call that action hers.
He gave the sacred priesthood for thy sake
To Aristobolus, yet doomed him dead
Before his back the ephod warm could make,
And ere the mitre settled on his head.
Oh, had he given my boy no less than right,
The double oil should to his forehead bring
A double honour, shining doubly bright:
His birth anointed him both priest and King.
And say my father and my son he slew,
To royalize, by right your prince-born breath;
Was love the cause, can Mariam deem it true,
That Herod gave commandment for her death?
I know by fits, he showed some signs of love,
And yet not love, but raging lunacy,
And this his hate to thee may justly prove
That sure he hates Hircanus' family.
Who knows if he, unconstant wavering lord,
His love to Doris had renewed again
And that he might his bed to her afford?
Perchance he wished that Mariam might be slain?

Mariam Doris? Alas her time of love was past,
Those coals were raked in embers long ago,
If Mariam's love, and she, was now disgraced.
Nor did I glory in her overthrow.
He not a whit his first born son esteemed,
Because as well as his he was not mine:
My children only for his own he deemed.
These boys that did descend from royal line,
These did he style his heirs to David's throne.
My Alexander, if he live, shall sit
In the majestic seat of Solomon.
To will it so, did Herod think it fit.
Alexandra Why? Who can claim from Alexander's brood
That gold-adornèd lion-guarded chair?
Was Alexander not of David's blood?
And was not Mariam Alexander's heir?
What more than right could Herod then bestow?
And who will think, except for more than right?
He did not raise them, for they were not low,
But born to wear the crown in his despite.
Then send those tears away that are not sent
To thee by reason, but by passion's power.
Thine eyes to cheer, thy cheeks to smiles be bent,
And entertain with joy this happy hour.
Felicity, if when she comes, she finds
A mourning habit and a cheerless look,
Will think she is not welcome to thy mind,
And so perchance her lodging will not brook.
Oh keep her whilst thou hast her; if she go
She will not easily return again.
Full many a year have I endured in woe,
Yet still have sued her presence to obtain.
And did not I to her as presents send
A table, that best art did beautify
Of two, to whom Heaven did best feature lend,
To woo her love by winning Antony?
For when a prince's favour we do crave,
We first their minions' loves do seek to win.
So I, that sought felicity to have,
Did with her minion Antony begin.
With double sleight I sought to captivate

The warlike lover, but I did not right.
For if my gift had borne but half the rate,
The Roman had been overtaken quite.
But now he fared like a hungry guest,
That to some plenteous festival is gone;
Now this, now that, he deems to eat were best,
Such choice doth make him let them all alone.
The boy's large forehead first did fairest seem,
Then glanced his eye upon my Mariam's cheek,
And that without comparison did deem.
What was in either, but he most did seek,
And thus distracted, either's beauties' might
Within the other's excellence was drowned:
Too much delight did bar him from delight,
For either's love, the other's did confound.
Where if thy portraiture had only gone,
His life from Herod, Antony had taken.
He would have loved thee, and thee alone,
And left the brown Egyptian clean forsaken.
And Cleopatra then to seek had been
So firm a lover of her wanèd face;
Then great Antonius' fall we had not seen,
By her that fled to have him hold the chase.
Then Mariam in a Roman's chariot set,
In place of Cleopatra might have shown
A mart of beauties in her visage met,
And part in this, that they were all her own.
Mariam Not to be empress of aspiring Rome,
Would Mariam like to Cleopatra live:
With purest body will I press my tomb,
And wish no favours Antony could give.
Alexandra Let us retire us, that we may resolve
How now to deal in this reversèd state.
Great are th'affairs that we must now revolve,
And great affairs must not be taken late.

I.iii

Enter Salome

Salome More plotting yet? Why? Now you have the thing
For which so oft you spent your suppliant breath.

And Mariam hopes to have another king,
Her eyes do sparkle joy for Herod's death.
Alexandra If she desired another king to have,
She might, before she came in Herod's bed,
Have had her wish. More kings than one did crave
For leave to set a crown upon her head.
I think with more than reason she laments
That she is freed from such a sad annoy.
Who is't will weep to part from discontent?
And if she joy, she did not causeless joy.
Salome You durst not thus have given your tongue the rein,
If noble Herod still remained in life.
Your daughter's betters far, I dare maintain,
Might have rejoiced to be my brother's wife.
Mariam My betters far? Base woman, 'tis untrue.
You scarce have ever my superiors seen,
For Mariam's servants were as good as you,
Before she came to be Judea's Queen.
Salome Now stirs the tongue that is so quickly moved,
But more than once your choler have I born.
Your fumish words are sooner said than proved,
And Salome's reply is only scorn.
Mariam Scorn those that are for thy companions held!
Though I thy brother's face had never seen,
My birth thy baser birth so far excelled,
I had to both of you the Princess been.
Thou parti-Jew, and parti-Edomite,
Thou mongrel, issued from rejected race!
Thy ancestors against the heavens did fight,
And thou like them wilt heavenly birth disgrace.
Salome Still twit you me with nothing but my birth?
What odds betwixt your ancestors and mine?
Both born of Adam, both were made of earth,
And both did come from holy Abr'ham's line.
Mariam I favour thee when nothing else I say.
With thy black acts I'll not pollute my breath,
Else to thy charge I might full justly lay
A shameful life, besides a husband's death.
Salome 'Tis true indeed, I did the plots reveal,
That passed betwixt your favourites and you.
I meant not I, a traitor to conceal,

Thus Salome your minion Joseph slew.
Mariam Heaven, dost thou mean this infamy to smother?
Let slandered Mariam ope thy closèd ear.
Self-guilt hath ever been suspicion's mother,
And therefore I this speech with patience bear.
No, had not Salome's unsteadfast heart
In Joseph's stead her Constabarus placed,
To free herself she had not used the art
To slander hapless Mariam for unchaste.
Alexandra Come Mariam, let us go: it is no boot
To let the head contend against the foot.

                                    Exeunt Mariam, Alexandra

I.iv

Salome Lives Salome to get so base a style
As foot to the proud Mariam? Herod's spirit
In happy time for her endured exile,
For did he live she should not miss her merit.
But he is dead, and though he were my brother,
His death such store of cinders cannot cast
My coals of love to quench, for though they smother
The flames a while, yet will they out at last.
Oh blessed Arabia, in best climate placed!
I by the fruit will censure of the tree:
'Tis not in vain, thy happy name thou hast,
If all Arabians like Silleus be.
Had not my fate been too, too contrary,
When I on Constabarus first did gaze,
Silleus had been object to mine eye,
Whose looks and personage must all eyes amaze.
But now ill-fated Salome, thy tongue
To Constabarus by itself is tied,
And now, except I do the Hebrew wrong
I cannot be the fair Arabian's bride.
What childish lets are these? Why stand I now
On honourable points? 'Tis long ago
Since shame was written on my tainted brow,
And certain 'tis that shame is honour's foe.
Had I upon my reputation stood,
Had I affected an unspotted life,

Josephus' veins had still been stuffed with blood,
And I to him had lived a sober wife.
Then had I never cast an eye of love
On Constabarus' now detested face,
Then had I kept my thoughts without remove,
And blushed at motion of the least disgrace.
But shame is gone and honour wiped away,
And impudency on my forehead sits.
She bids me work my will without delay,
And for my will I will employ my wits.
He loves, I love. What then can be the cause
Keeps me from being the Arabian's wife?
It is the principles of Moses' laws,
For Constabarus still remains in life.
If he to me did bear as earnest hate
As I to him, for him there were an ease:
A separating bill might free his fate
From such a yoke that did so much displease.
Why should such privilege to men be given?
Or given to them, why barred from women then?
Are men than we in greater grace with heaven?
Or cannot women hate as well as men?
I'll be the custom-breaker, and begin
To show my sex the way to freedom's door.
And with an off'ring will I purge my sin –
The law was made for none but who are poor.
If Herod had lived, I might to him accuse
My present lord. But for the future's sake,
Then would I tell the King he did refuse
The sons of Baba in his power to take.
But now I must divorce him from my bed,
That my Silleus may possess his room.
Had I not begged his life he had been dead,
I curse my tongue the hind'rer of his doom.
But then my wand'ring heart to him was fast,
Nor did I dream of change. Silleus said
He would be here, and see he comes at last:
Had I not named him longer had he stayed.

I.v

Enter Silleus

Silleus Well found fair Salome, Judea's pride!
Hath thy innated wisdom found the way
To make Silleus deem him deified,
By gaining thee, O more than precious, pray?
Salome I have devised the best I can devise,
A more imperfect means was never found,
But what cares Salome? It doth suffice
If our endeavours with their end be crowned.
In this our land we have an ancient use,
Permitted first by our law-giver's head:
Who hates his wife, though for no just abuse,
May with a bill divorce her from his bed.
But in this custom women are not free,
Yet I for once will wrest it. Blame not thou
The ill I do, since what I do's for thee.
Though others blame, Silleus should allow.
Silleus Thinks Salome Silleus hath a tongue
To censure her fair actions? Let my blood
Bedash my proper brow, for such a wrong,
The being yours, can make even vices good.
Arabia joy! Prepare thy earth with green!
Thou never happy wert indeed till now!
Now shall thy ground be trod by beauty's Queen,
Her foot is destined to depress thy brow.
Thou shalt, fair Salome, command as much
As if the royal ornament were thine:
The weakness of Arabia's King is such,
The kingdom is not his so much as mine.
My mouth is our Obodas' oracle,
Who thinks not aught but what Silleus will.
And thou rare creature, Asia's miracle,
Shalt be to me as it: Obodas still.
Salome 'Tis not for glory I thy love accept;
Judea yields me honour's worthy store.
Had not affection in my bosom crept,
My native country should my life deplore.
Were not Silleus he with whom I go,
I would not change my Palestine for Rome.

Much less would I, a glorious state to show,
Go far to purchase an Arabian tomb.
Silleus Far be it from Silleus so to think.
I know it is thy gratitude requites
The love that is in me, and shall not shrink
Till death do sever me from Earth's delights.
Salome But whist! Methinks the wolf is in our talk.
Be gone Silleus. Who doth here arrive?
'Tis Constabarus that doth hither walk.
I'll find a quarrel, him from me to drive.
Silleus Farewell. But were it not for thy command,
In his despite Silleus here would stand.

Exit

I.vi

Enter Constabarus

Constabarus Oh Salome, how much you wrong your name,
Your race, your country, and your husband most.
A stranger's private conference is shame;
I blush for you, that have your blushing lost.
Oft have I found, and found you to my grief,
Consorted with this base Arabian here.
Heaven knows that you have been my comfort chief;
Then do not now my greater plague appear.
Now by the stately carvèd edifice,
That on Mount Sion makes so fair a show,
And by the altar fit for sacrifice,
I love thee more than thou thyself dost know.
Oft with a silent sorrow have I heard
How ill Judea's mouth doth censure thee,
And did I not thine honour much regard,
Thou shouldst not be exhorted thus for me.
Didst thou but know the worth of honest fame,
How much a virtuous woman is esteemed,
Thou wouldst like hell eschew deservèd shame,
And seek to be both chaste and chastely deemed.
Our wisest Prince did say, and true he said,
A virtuous woman crowns her husband's head.
Salome Did I for this uprear thy low estate?
Did I for this requital beg thy life,

That thou hadst forfeited to hapless fate,
To be to such a thankless wretch the wife?
This hand of mine hath lifted up thy head,
Which many a day ago had fallen full low,
Because the sons of Baba are not dead;
To me thou dost both life and fortune owe.
Constabarus You have my patience often exercised,
Use makes my choler keep within the banks,
Yet boast no more, but be by me advised:
A benefit upbraided, forfeits thanks.
I prithee Salome dismiss this mood,
Thou dost not know how ill it fits thy place.
My words were all intended for thy good,
To raise thine honour and to stop disgrace.
Salome To stop disgrace? Take thou no care for me.
Nay do thy worst, thy worst I set not by.
No shame of mine is like to light on thee,
Thy love and admonitions I defy.
Thou shalt no hour longer call me wife.
Thy jealousy procures my hate so deep
That I from thee do mean to free my life,
By a divorcing bill before I sleep.
Constabarus Are Hebrew women now transformed to men?
Why do you not as well our battles fight
And wear our armour? Suffer this, and then
Let all the world be topsy-turvèd quite.
Let fishes graze, beasts swim, and birds descend,
Let fire burn downwards whilst the Earth aspires,
Let winter's heat and summer's cold offend,
Let thistles grow on vines, and grapes on briers.
Set us to spin or sow, or at the best,
Make us wood-hewers, water-bearing wights,
For sacred service let us take no rest,
Use us as Joshua did the Gibonites.
Salome Hold on your talk till it be time to end!
For me, I am resolved it shall be so.
Though I be first that to this course do bend,
I shall not be the last, full well I know.
Constabarus Why then be witness heav'n, the judge of sins,
Be witness spirits that eschew the dark,
Be witness angels, witness cherubins,

Whose semblance sits upon the holy Ark,
Be witness Earth, be witness Palestine,
Be witness David's city, if my heart
Did ever merit such an act of thine.
Or if the fault be mine that makes us part,
Since mildest Moses, friend unto the Lord,
Did work his wonders in the land of Ham,
And slew the first-born babes without a sword,
In sign whereof we eat the holy lamb;
Till now that fourteen hundred years are past,
Since first the law with us hath been in force,
You are the first, and will, I hope, be last,
That ever sought her husband to divorce!
Salome I mean not to be led by precedent,
My will shall be to me instead of law.
Constabarus I fear me much you will too late repent
That you have ever lived so void of awe.
This is Silleus' love that makes you thus
Reverse all order. You must next be his.
But if my thoughts aright the cause discuss,
In winning you, he gains no lasting bliss.
I was Silleus, and not long ago
Josephus then was Constabarus now:
When you became my friend you proved his foe,
As now for him you break to me your vow.
Salome If once I loved you, greater is your debt,
For certain 'tis that you deserved it not.
And undeservèd love we soon forget,
And therefore that to me can be no blot.
But now fare ill my once belovèd lord,
Yet never more beloved than now abhorred.

                                                        Exit

Constabarus Yet Constabarus biddeth thee farewell.
Farewell light creature, Heaven forgive thy sin!
My prophesying spirit doth foretell
Thy wavering thoughts do yet but new begin.
Yet I have better 'scaped than Joseph did.
But if our Herod's death had been delayed,
The valiant youths that I so long have hid,
Had been by her, and I for them betrayed.
Therefore in happy hour did Caesar give

The fatal blow to wanton Antony,
For had he lived, our Herod then should live,
But great Antonius' death made Herod die.
Had he enjoyed his breath, not I alone
Had been in danger of a deadly fall,
But Mariam had the way of peril gone,
Though by the tyrant most beloved of all.
The sweet faced Mariam as free from guilt
As Heaven from spots! Yet had her lord come back
Her purest blood had been unjustly spilt,
And Salome it was would work her wrack.
Though all Judea yield her innocent,
She often hath been near to punishment.

Exit

Chorus

Those minds that wholly dote upon delight,
Except they only joy in inward good,
Still hope at last to hop upon the right,
And so from sand they leap in loathsome mud.
    Fond wretches, seeking what they cannot find,
    For no content attends a wavering mind.

If wealth they do desire, and wealth attain,
Then wondrous fain would they to honour leap.
If mean degree they do in honour gain,
They would but wish a little higher step.
    Thus step to step, and wealth to wealth they add,
    Yet cannot all their plenty make them glad.

Yet oft we see that some in humble state,
Are cheerful, pleasant, happy and content,
When those indeed that are of higher state,
With vain additions do their thoughts torment.
    Th'one would to his mind his fortune bind,
    Th'other to his fortune frames his mind.

To wish variety is sign of grief,
For if you like your state as now it is,
Why should an alteration bring relief?
Nay, change would then be feared as loss of bliss.

That man is only happy in his fate,
That is delighted in a settled state.

Still Mariam wished she from her lord were free,
For expectation of variety.
Yet now she sees her wishes prosperous be,
She grieves, because her lord so soon did die.
    Who can those vast imaginations feed,
    Where in a property, contempt doth breed?

Were Herod now perchance to live again,
She would again as much be grieved at that.
All that she may, she ever doth disdain,
Her wishes guide her to she knows not what.
    And sad must be their looks, their honour sour,
    That care for nothing being in their power.

II.i

Enter Pheroras and Graphina

Pheroras 'Tis true Graphina, now the time draws nigh
Wherein the holy priest with hallowed rite,
The happy long-desirèd knot shall tie,
Pheroras and Graphina to unite.
How oft have I with lifted hands implored
This blessèd hour, till now implored in vain,
Which hath my wishèd liberty restored,
And made my subject self my own again?
Thy love, fair maid, upon mine eye doth sit,
Whose nature hot doth dry the moisture all,
Which were, in nature and in reason, fit
For my monarchal brother's death to fall.
Had Herod lived, he would have plucked my hand
From fair Graphina's palm perforce, and tied
The same in hateful and despisèd band,
For I had had a baby to my bride.
Scarce can her infant tongue with easy voice
Her name distinguish to another's ear;
Yet had he lived, his power, and not my choice
Had made me solemnly the contract swear.
Have I not cause in such a change to joy?

What though she be my niece, a princess born?
Near blood's without respect, high birth a toy,
Since love can teach [us] blood and kindred's scorn.
What booted it that he did raise my head
To be his realm's co-partner, kingdom's mate?
Withal, he kept Graphina from my bed,
More wished by me than thrice Judea's state.
Oh, could not he be skilful judge in love,
That doted so upon his Mariam's face?
He, for his passion, Doris did remove;
I needed not a lawful wife displace.
It could not be but he had power to judge!
But he that never grudged a kingdom's share,
This well-known happiness to me did grudge,
And meant to be therein without compare,
Else had I been his equal in love's host.
For though the diadem on Mariam's head
Corrupt the vulgar judgements, I will boast
Graphina's brow's as white, her cheeks as red.
Why speakst thou not fair creature? Move thy tongue,
For silence is a sign of discontent.
It were to both our loves too great a wrong
If now this hour do find thee sadly bent.
Graphina Mistake me not my lord. Too oft have I
Desired this time to come with wingèd feet,
To be enwrapped with grief when 'tis too nigh.
You know my wishes ever yours did meet.
If I be silent, 'tis no more but fear
That I should say too little when I speak,
But since you will my imperfections bear,
In spite of doubt I will my silence break.
Yet might amazement tie my moving tongue,
But that I know before Pheroras' mind,
I have admirèd your affection long,
And cannot yet therein a reason find.
Your hand hath lifted me from lowest state
To highest eminency, wondrous grace,
And me, your hand-maid, have you made your mate,
Though all but you alone do count me base.
You have preserved me pure at my request,
Though you so weak a vassal might constrain

To yield to your high will. Then, last not best,
In my respect a princess you disdain.
Then need not all these favours study crave,
To be requited by a simple maid?
And study still, you know, must silence have:
Then be my cause for silence justly weighed.
But study cannot boot, nor I requite,
Except your lowly hand-maid's steadfast love
And fast obedience may your mind delight:
I will not promise more than I can prove.
Pheroras That study needs not. Let Graphina smile,
And I desire no greater recompense.
I cannot vaunt me in a glorious style,
Nor show my love in far-fetched eloquence.
But this believe me: never Herod's heart
Hath held his prince-born beauty famèd wife
In nearer place than thou, fair virgin, art
To him that holds the glory of his life.
Should Herod's body leave the sepulchre
And entertain the severed ghost again,
He should not be my nuptial hinderer,
Except he hindered it with dying pain.
Come fair Graphina, let us go in state,
This wish-endearèd time to celebrate.

Exeunt

II.ii

Enter Constabarus and Baba's sons

Baba's 1 son Now, valiant friend, you have our lives redeemed,
Which lives as saved by you, to you are due.
Command and you shall see yourself esteemed;
Our lives and liberties belong to you.
This twice six years, with hazard of your life,
You have concealed us from the tyrant's sword;
Though cruel Herod's sister were your wife,
You durst in scorn of fear this grace afford.
In recompense we know not what to say;
A poor reward were thanks for such a merit.
Our truest friendship at your feet we lay,
The best requital to a noble spirit.

Constabarus Oh, how you wrong our friendship valiant youth!
With friends there is not such a word as debt,
Where amity is tied with bond of truth,
All benefits are there in common set.
Then is the Golden Age with them renewed:
All names of properties are banished quite,
Division, and distinction are eschewed,
Each hath to what belongs to others, right.
And 'tis not, sure, so full a benefit,
Freely to give, as freely to require.
A bounteous act hath glory following it:
They cause the glory that the act desire.
All friendship should the pattern imitate
Of Jesse's son and valiant Jonathan,
For neither sovereign's nor father's hate,
A friendship fixed on virtue sever can.
Too much of this; 'tis written in the heart,
And needs no amplifying with the tongue.
Now may you from your living tomb depart,
Where Herod's life hath kept you over long;
Too great an injury to a noble mind
To be quick buried. You had purchased fame
Some years ago, but that you were confined,
While thousand meaner did advance their name.
Your best of life, the prime of all your years,
Your time of action, is from you bereft.
Twelve winters have you overpassed in fears,
Yet if you use it well, enough is left.
And who can doubt but you will use it well?
The sons of Baba have it by descent,
In all their thoughts each action to excel,
Boldly to act, and wisely to invent.
Baba's 2 son Had it not like the hateful cuckoo been,
Whose riper age his infant nurse doth kill,
So long we had not kept ourselves unseen,
But Constabarus' safety crossed our will.
For had the tyrant fixed his cruel eye
On our concealèd faces, wrath had swayed
His justice so, that he had forced us die.
And dearer price than life we should have paid,
For you, our truest friend, had fall'n with us,

And we, much like a house on pillars set,
Had clean depressed our prop. And therefore thus
Our ready will with our concealment met.
But now that you, fair lord, are dangerless,
The sons of Baba shall their rigour show,
And prove it was not baseness did oppress
Our hearts so long, but honour kept them low.
Baba's 1 son Yet I do fear this tale of Herod's death
At last will prove a very tale indeed.
It gives me strongly in my mind, his breath
Will be preserved to make a number bleed.
I wish not therefore to be set at large
Yet peril to myself I do not fear.
Let us for some days longer be your charge,
Till we of Herod's state the truth do hear.
Constabarus What, art thou turned a coward noble youth,
That thou beginst to doubt undoubted truth?
Baba's 1 son Were it my brother's tongue that cast this doubt,
I from his heart would have the question out
With this keen fauchion! But 'tis you my lord
Against whose head I must not lift a sword,
I am so tied in gratitude.
Constabarus   Believe
You have no cause to take it ill.
If any word of mine your heart did grieve,
The word dissented from the speaker's will.
I know it was not fear the doubt begun,
But rather valour and your care of me:
A coward could not be your father's son.
Yet know I doubts unnecessary be,
For who can think that in Antonius' fall,
Herod, his bosom friend, should 'scape unbruised?
Then, Caesar, we might thee an idiot call,
If thou by him shouldst be so far abused.
Baba's 2 son Lord Constabarus, let me tell you this:
Upon submission Caesar will forgive.
And therefore though the tyrant did amiss,
It may fall out that he will let him live.
Not many years ago it is since I,
Directed thither by my father's care,
In famous Rome for twice twelve months did live,

My life from Hebrew's cruelty to spare.
There, though I were but yet of boyish age,
I bent mine eye to mark, mine ears to hear,
Where I did see Octavius, then a page,
When first he did to Julius' sight appear.
Methought I saw such mildness in his face,
And such a sweetness in his looks did grow
Withal, commixed with so majestic grace,
His phys'nomy his fortune did foreshow.
For this I am indebted to mine eye,
But then mine ear received more evidence.
By that I knew his love to clemency,
How he with hottest choler could dispense.
Constabarus But we have more than barely heard the news!
It hath been twice confirmed. And though some tongue
Might be so false, with false report t'abuse,
A false report hath never lasted long.
But be it so that Herod have his life,
Concealement would not then a whit avail,
For certain 'tis, that she that was my wife,
Would not to set her accusation fail.
And therefore now as good the venture give,
And free ourselves from blot of cowardice,
As show a pitiful desire to live,
For who can pity but they must despise?
Baba's 1 son I yield, but to necessity I yield.
I dare upon this doubt engage mine arm,
That Herod shall again this kingdom wield,
And prove his death to be a false alarm.
Baba's 2 son I doubt it too. God grant it be an error;
'Tis best without a cause to be in terror.
And rather had I, though my soul be mine,
My soul should lie, than prove a true divine.
Constabarus Come, come, let fear go seek a dastard's nest,
Undaunted courage lies in a noble breast.
                                                    Exeunt

II.iii

Enter Doris and Antipater

Doris You royal buildings bow your lofty sides,
And stoop to her that is by right your Queen;

Let your humility upbraid the pride
Of those in whom no due respect is seen.
Nine times have we with trumpet's haughty sound,
And banishing sour leaven from our taste,
Observed the feast that takes the fruit from ground
Since I, fair city, did behold thee last.
So long it is since Mariam's purer cheek
Did rob from mine the glory. And so long
Since I returned my native town to seek,
And with me nothing but the sense of wrong,
And thee, my boy, whose birth though great it were,
Yet have thy after fortunes proved but poor.
When thou wert born how little did I fear
Thou shouldst be thrust from forth thy father's door.
Art thou not Herod's right begotten son?
Was not the hapless Doris Herod's wife?
Yes, ere he had the Hebrew kingdom won,
I was companion to his private life.
Was I not fair enough to be a queen?
Why, ere thou wert to me, false monarch, tied,
My lake of beauty might as well be seen,
As after I had lived five years thy bride.
Yet then thine oaths came pouring like the rain,
Which all affirmed my face without compare,
And that if thou mightst Doris' love obtain,
For all the world besides thou didst not care.
Then was I young, and rich, and nobly born,
And therefore worthy to be Herod's mate.
Yet thou, ungrateful, cast me off with scorn
When Heaven's purpose raised your meaner fate.
Oft have I begged for vengeance for this fact,
And with dejected knees, aspiring hands,
Have prayed the highest power to enact
The fall of her that on my trophy stands.
Revenge I have according to my will,
Yet where I wished this vengeance did not light.
I wished it should high-hearted Mariam kill,
But it against my whilom lord did fight.
With thee sweet boy I came, and came to try
If thou, before his bastards, might be placed
In Herod's royal seat and dignity.

But Mariam's infants here are only graced,
And now for us there doth no hope remain.
Yet we will not return till Herod's end
Be more confirmed. Perchance he is not slain;
So glorious fortunes may my boy attend.
For if he live, he'll think it doth suffice
That he to Doris shows such cruelty,
For as he did my wretched life despise,
So do I know I shall despisèd die.
Let him but prove as natural to thee,
As cruel to thy miserable mother.
His cruelty shall not upbraided be,
But in thy fortunes I his faults will smother.
Antipater Each mouth within the city loudly cries
That Herod's death is certain. Therefore, we
Had best some subtle hidden plot devise,
That Mariam's children might subverted be
By poison's drink, or else by murderous knife;
So we may be advanced, it skills not how.
They are but bastards, you were Herod's wife,
And foul adultery blotteth Mariam's brow.
Doris They are too strong to be by us removed,
Or else revenge's foulest spotted face
By our detested wrongs might be approved.
But weakness must to greater power give place.
But let us now retire to grieve alone,
For solitariness best fitteth moan.

Exeunt

II.iv

Enter Silleus and Constabarus, meeting

Silleus Well met Judean lord, the only wight
Silleus wished to see. I am to call
Thy tongue to strict account.
Constabarus   For what despite?
I ready am to hear, and answer all.
But if directly at the cause I guess
That breeds this challenge, you must pardon me,
And now some other ground of fight profess,
For I have vowed, vows must unbroken be.

Silleus What may be your exception? Let me know.
Constabarus Why, aught concerning Salome. My sword
Shall not be wielded for a cause so low;
A blow for her my arm will scorn t'afford.
Silleus It is for slandering her unspotted name.
And I will make thee in thy vow's despite,
Suck up the breath that did my mistress blame,
And swallow it again to do her right.
Constabarus I prithee give some other quarrel ground.
To find beginning, rail against my name,
Or strike me first, or let some scarlet wound
Inflame my courage. Give me words of shame;
Do thou our Moses' sacred laws disgrace;
Deprave our nation, do me some despite;
I'm apt enough to fight in any case,
But yet for Salome I will not fight.
Silleus Nor I for aught but Salome. My sword,
That owes his service to her sacred name,
Will not an edge for other cause afford;
In other fight I am not sure of fame.
Constabarus For her, I pity thee enough already.
For her, I therefore will not mangle thee.
A woman with a heart so most unsteady,
Will of herself sufficient torture be.
I cannot envy for so light a gain.
Her mind with such unconstancy doth run,
As with a word thou didst her love obtain,
So with a word she will from thee be won.
So light, as her possession's for most, day
Is her affections lost. To me 'tis known.
As good go hold the wind as make her stay.
She never loves, but till she call her own.
She merely is a painted sepulchre,
That is both fair and vilely foul at once:
Though on her outside graces garnish her,
Her mind is filled with worse than rotten bones,
And ever ready lifted is her hand,
To aim destruction at a husband's throat.
For proofs, Josephus and myself do stand,
Though once on both of us she seemed to dote.
Her mouth, though serpent-like, it never hisses,

Yet like a serpent, poisons where it kisses.
Silleus Well, Hebrew, well! Thou bark'st, but wilt not bite.
Constabarus I tell thee still, for her I will not fight.
Silleus Why then I call thee coward.
Constabarus   From my heart
I give thee thanks. A coward's hateful name
Cannot to valiant minds a blot impart
And therefore I with joy receive the same.
Thou know'st I am no coward. Thou wert by
At the Arabian battle th'other day,
And saw'st my sword with daring valiancy
Amongst the faint Arabians cut my way.
The blood of foes no more could let it shine,
And 'twas enamellèd with some of thine.
But now have at thee! Not for Salome
I fight, but to discharge a coward's style.
Here 'gins the fight that shall not parted be,
Before a soul or two endure exile!

                                              They fight

Silleus Thy sword hath made some windows for my blood,
To show a horrid crimson phys'nomy.
To breathe for both of us methinks 'twere good,
The day will give us time enough to die.
Constabarus With all my heart take breath. Thou shalt have time,
And if thou list a twelvemonth. Let us end.
Into thy cheeks there doth a paleness climb;
Thou canst not from my sword thyself defend.
What needest thou for Salome to fight?
Thou hast her, and may'st keep her, none strives for her.
I willingly to thee resign my right,
For in my very soul I do abhor her.
Thou seest that I am fresh, unwounded yet,
Then not for fear I do this offer make.
Thou art, with loss of blood, to fight unfit,
For here is one, and there another take.
Silleus I will not leave, as long as breath remains
Within my wounded body. Spare your words.
My heart in blood's stead, courage entertains;
Salome's love no place for fear affords.
Constabarus Oh could thy soul but prophesy like mine,
I would not wonder thou shouldst long to die.

For Salome, if I aright divine,
Will be than death a greater misery.
Silleus Then list, I'll breathe no longer.
Constabarus   Do thy will.
I hateless fight, and charitably kill.

                                        They fight

Pity thyself Silleus. Let not death
Intrude before his time into thy heart!
Alas it is too late to fear! His breath
Is from his body now about to part.
How far'st thou brave Arabian?
Silleus   Very well.
My leg is hurt, I can no longer fight.
It only grieves me that so soon I fell,
Before fair Salom's wrongs I came to right.
Constabarus Thy wounds are less than mortal. Never fear,
Thou shalt a safe and quick recovery find.
Come, I will thee unto my lodging bear,
I hate thy body, but I love thy mind.
Silleus Thanks noble Jew, I see a courteous foe.
Stern enmity to friendship can no art.
Had not my heart and tongue engaged me so,
I would from thee no foe, but friend depart.
My heart to Salome is tied too fast
To leave her love for friendship, yet my skill
Shall be employed to make your favour last,
And I will honour Constabarus still.
Constabarus I ope my bosom to thee, and will take
Thee in, as friend, and grieve for thy complaint.
But if we do not expedition make,
Thy loss of blood I fear will make thee faint.
                                        Exeunt

Chorus

To hear a tale with ears prejudicate,
It spoils the judgement, and corrupts the sense,
That human error giv'n to every state,
Is greater enemy to innocence.
    It makes us foolish, heady, rash, unjust;
    It makes us never try before we trust.

It will confound the meaning, change the words,
For it our sense of hearing much deceives.
Besides, no time to judgement it affords,
To weigh the circumstance our ear receives.
  The ground of accidents it never tries,
  But makes us take for truth ten thousand lies.

Our ears and hearts are apt to hold for good,
That we ourselves do most desire to be,
And then we drown objections in the flood
Of partiality. 'Tis that we see
  That makes false rumours long with credit past,
  Though they like rumours must conclude at last.

The greatest part of us prejudicate,
With wishing Herod's death do hold it true.
The being once deluded doth not bate
The credit to a better likelihood due.
  Those few that wish it not, the multitude
  Do carry headlong, so they doubts conclude.

They not object the weak uncertain ground,
Whereon they built this tale of Herod's end,
Whereof the author scarcely can be found,
And all because their wishes that way bend.
  They think not of the peril that ensu'th,
  If this should prove contrary to the truth.

On this same doubt, on this so light a breath,
They pawn their lives and fortunes. For they all
Behave them as the news of Herod's death
They did of most undoubted credit call.
  But if their actions now do rightly hit,
  Let them commend their fortune, not their wit.

III.i

Enter Pheroras and Salome

Pheroras Urge me no more Graphina to forsake,
Not twelve hours since I married her for love.
And do you think a sister's power can make

A resolute decree so soon remove?
Salome Poor minds they are that honour not affects.
Pheroras Who hunts for honour, happiness neglects.
Salome You might have been both of felicity
And honour too, in equal measure seized.
Pheroras It is not you can tell so well as I
What 'tis can make me happy, or displeased.
Salome To match, for neither beauty nor respects,
One mean of birth, but yet of meaner mind,
A woman full of natural defects,
I wonder what your eye in her could find.
Pheroras Mine eye found loveliness, mine ear found wit,
To please the one, and to enchant the other.
Grace on her eye, mirth on her tongue doth sit,
In looks a child, in wisdom's house a mother.
Salome But say you thought her fair, as none thinks else,
Knows not Pheroras beauty is a blast?
Much like this flower which today excels,
But longer than a day it will not last.
Pheroras Her wit exceeds her beauty.
Salome   Wit may show
The way to ill, as well as good you know.
Pheroras But wisdom is the porter of her head,
And bars all wicked words from issuing thence.
Salome But of a porter, better were you sped,
If she against their entrance made defence.
Pheroras But wherefore comes the sacred Ananell,
That hitherward his hasty steps doth bend?
Great sacrificer y'are arrivèd well,
Ill news from holy mouth I not attend.

III. ii

Enter Ananell

Ananell My lips, my son, with peaceful tidings blessed,
Shall utter honey to your list'ning ear.
A word of death comes not from priestly breast,
I speak of life: in life there is no fear.
And for the news I did the Heavens salute,
And filled the temple with my thankful voice,
For though that mourning may not me pollute,

At pleasing accidents I may rejoice.
Pheroras Is Herod then revived from certain death?
Salome What, can your news restore my brother's breath?
Ananell Both so, and so: the King is safe and sound,
And did such grace in royal Caesar meet,
That he with larger style than ever crowned,
Within this hour Jerusalem will greet.
I did but come to tell you, and must back
To make preparitives for sacrifice.
I knew his death, your hearts like mine did rack,
Though to conceal it, proved you wise.

                                                              Exit

Salome How can my joy sufficiently appear?
Pheroras A heavier tale did never pierce mine ear.
Salome Now Salome of happiness may boast.
Pheroras But now Pheroras is in danger most.
Salome I shall enjoy the comfort of my life.
Pheroras And I shall lose it, losing of my wife.
Salome Joy heart, for Constabarus shall be slain!
Pheroras Grieve soul, Graphina shall from me be ta'en!
Salome Smile cheeks, the fair Silleus shall be mine.
Pheroras Weep eyes, for I must with a child combine.
Salome Well brother, cease your moans. On one condition
I'll undertake to win the King's consent,
Graphina still shall be in your tuition,
And her with you be ne'er the less content.
Pheroras What's the condition? Let me quickly know,
That I as quickly your command may act,
Were it to see what herbs in Ophir grow,
Or that the lofty Tyrus might be sacked.
Salome 'Tis not so hard a task. It is no more
But tell the King that Constabarus hid
The sons of Baba, doomed to death before;
And 'tis no more than Constabarus did.
And tell him more, that I for Herod's sake,
Not able to endure our brother's foe,
Did with a bill our separation make,
Though loth from Constabarus else to go.
Pheroras Believe this tale for told. I'll go from hence,
In Herod's ear the Hebrew to deface.

And I that never studied eloquence,
Do mean with eloquence this tale to grace.

Exit

Salome This will be Constabarus' quick dispatch,
Which from my mouth would lesser credit find.
Yet shall he not decease without a match,
For Mariam shall not linger long behind.
First jealousy, if that avail not, fear
Shall be my minister to work her end.
A common error moves not Herod's ear,
Which doth so firmly to his Mariam bend.
She shall be chargèd with so horrid crime,
As Herod's fear shall turn his love to hate.
I'll make some swear that she desires to climb,
And seeks to poison him for his estate.
I scorn that she should live my birth t'upbraid,
To call me base and hungry Edomite.
With patient show her choler I betrayed,
And watched the time to be revenged by slight.
Now tongue of mine with scandal load her name,
Turn hers to fountains, Herod's eyes to flame.
Yet first I will begin Pheroras' suit,
That he my earnest business may effect;
And I of Mariam will keep me mute,
Till first some other doth her name detect.

Enter Silleus' man

Who's there? Silleus' man? How fares your lord,
That your aspects do bear the badge of sorrow?
Silleus' man He hath the marks of Constabarus' sword,
And for a while desires your sight to borrow.
Salome My heavy curse the hateful sword pursue,
My heavier curse on the more hateful arm
That wounded my Silleus. But renew
Your tale again. Hath he no mortal harm?
Silleus' man No sign of danger doth in him appear,
Nor are his wounds in place of peril seen.
He bids you be assured you need not fear;
He hopes to make you yet Arabia's Queen.
Salome Commend my heart to be Silleus' charge.
Tell him, my brother's sudden coming now

Will give my foot no room to walk at large.
But I will see him yet ere night, I vow.

Exeunt

III. iii

Enter Mariam and Sohemus

Mariam Sohemus, tell me what the news may be
That makes your eyes so full, your cheeks so blue?
Sohemus I know not how to call them. Ill for me
'Tis sure they are: not so I hope for you.
Herod –
Mariam Oh, what of Herod?
Sohemus   Herod lives.
Mariam How! Lives? What, in some cave or forest hid?
Sohemus Nay, back returned with honour. Caesar gives
Him greater grace than e'er Antonius did.
Mariam Foretell the ruin of my family,
Tell me that I shall see our city burned,
Tell me I shall a death disgraceful die,
But tell me not that Herod is returned.
Sohemus Be not impatient madam, be but mild,
His love to you again will soon be bred.
Mariam I will not to his love be reconciled,
With solemn vows I have forsworn his bed.
Sohemus But you must break those vows.
Mariam   I'll rather break
The heart of Mariam. Cursèd is my fate –
But speak no more to me, in vain ye speak –
To live with him I so profoundly hate!
Sohemus Great Queen, you must to me your pardon give,
Sohemus cannot now your will obey.
If your command should me to silence drive,
It were not to obey but to betray.
Reject, and slight my speeches, mock my faith,
Scorn my observance, call my counsel nought.
Though you regard not what Sohemus saith,
Yet will I ever freely speak my thought.
I fear ere long I shall fair Mariam see
In woeful state, and by herself undone.

Yet for your issue's sake more temp'rate be,
The heart by affability is won.
Mariam And must I to my prison turn again?
Oh, now I see I was an hypocrite!
I did this morning for his death complain,
And yet do mourn, because he lives ere night.
When I his death believed, compassion wrought,
And was the stickler 'twixt my heart and him.
But now that curtain's drawn from off my thought,
Hate doth appear again with visage grim
And paints the face of Herod in my heart,
In horrid colours with detested look.
Then fear would come, but scorn doth play her part,
And saith that scorn with fear can never brook.
I know I could enchain him with a smile
And lead him captive with a gentle word.
I scorn my look should ever man beguile,
Or other speech, than meaning to afford.
Else Salome in vain might spend her wind,
In vain might Herod's mother whet her tongue,
In vain had they complotted and combined,
For I could overthrow them all ere long.
Oh what a shelter is mine innocence,
To shield me from the pangs of inward grief.
'Gainst all mishaps it is my fair defence,
And to my sorrows yields a large relief.
To be commandress of the triple earth,
And sit in safety from a fall secure,
To have all nations celebrate my birth,
I would not that my spirit were impure.
Let my distressèd state unpitied be,
Mine innocence is hope enough for me.

Exit

Sohemus Poor guiltless Queen! Oh that my wish might place
A little temper now about thy heart!
Unbridled speech is Mariam's worst disgrace,
And will endanger her without desert.
I am in greater hazard. O'er my head
The fatal axe doth hang unsteadily.
My disobedience once discoverèd,

Will shake it down. Sohemus so shall die.
For when the King shall find we thought his death
Had been as certain as we see his life,
And marks withal I slighted so his breath,
As to preserve alive his matchless wife –
Nay more, to give to Alexandra's hand
The regal dignity, the sovereign power,
How I had yielded up at her command,
The strength of all the city, David's tower –
What more than common death may I expect,
Since I too well do know his cruelty?
'Twere death a word of Herod's to neglect,
What then to do directly contrary?
Yet, life, I quit thee with a willing spirit,
And think thou couldst not better be employed.
I forfeit thee for her that more doth merit,
Ten such were better dead than she destroyed.
But fare thee well chaste Queen. Well may I see
The darkness palpable, and rivers part
The sun stand still, nay more, retorted be,
But never woman with so pure a heart.
Thine eyes' grave majesty keeps all in awe,
And cuts the wings of every loose desire.
Thy brow is table to the modest law,
Yet though we dare not love, we may admire.
And if I die, it shall my soul content,
My breath in Mariam's service shall be spent.

Exit

Chorus

'Tis not enough for one that is a wife
To keep her spotless from an act of ill,
But from suspicion she should free her life,
And bare her self of power as well as will.
   'Tis not so glorious for her to be free,
    As by her proper self restrained to be.

When she hath spacious ground to walk upon,
Why on the ridge should she desire to go?
It is no glory to forbear alone
Those things that may her honour overthrow.

But 'tis thank-worthy, if she will not take
All lawful liberties for honour's sake.

That wife her hand against her fame doth rear,
That more than to her lord alone will give
A private word to any second ear.
And though she may with reputation live,
    Yet though most chaste, she doth her glory blot,
    And wounds her honour, though she kills it not.

When to their husbands they themselves do bind,
Do they not wholly give themselves away?
Or give they but their body not their mind,
Reserving that, though best, for others, pray?
    No sure, their thoughts no more can be their own,
    And therefore should to none but one be known.

Then she usurps upon another's right,
That seeks to be by public language graced;
And though her thoughts reflect with purest light,
Her mind if not peculiar is not chaste.
    For in a wife it is no worse to find,
    A common body, than a common mind.

And every mind though free from thought of ill,
That out of glory seeks a worth to show,
When any's ears but one therewith they fill,
Doth in a sort her pureness overthrow.
    Now Mariam had, but that to this she bent,
    Been free from fear, as well as innocent.

IV. i

Enter Herod and his attendants

Herod Hail happy city! Happy in thy store,
And happy that thy buildings such we see;
More happy in the temple where w'adore,
But most of all that Mariam lives in thee.

Enter Nuntio

Art thou returned? How fares my Mariam?

Nuntio She's well my lord, and will anon be here
As you commanded.
Herod   Muffle up thy brow,
Thou day's dark taper! Mariam will appear,
And where she shines, we need not thy dim light.
Oh haste thy steps rare creature, speed thy pace,
And let thy presence make the day more bright,
And cheer the heart of Herod with thy face.
It is an age since I from Mariam went,
Methinks our parting was in David's days,
The hours are so increased by discontent.
Deep sorrow, Joshua-like the season stays
But when I am with Mariam, time runs on:
Her sight can make months minutes, days of weeks.
An hour is then no sooner come than gone,
When in her face mine eye for wonders seeks.
You world-commanding city, Europe's grace,
Twice hath my curious eye your streets surveyed,
And I have seen the statue-fillèd place,
That once if not for grief had been betrayed.
I, all your Roman beauties have beheld,
And seen the shows your Ediles did prepare;
I saw the sum of what in you excelled,
Yet saw no miracle like Mariam rare.
The fair and famous Livia, Caesar's love,
The world's commanding mistress, did I see,
Whose beauties both the world and Rome approve,
Yet, Mariam, Livia is not like to thee.
Be patient but a little while, mine eyes,
Within your compassed limits be contained;
That object straight shall your desires suffice,
From which you were so long a while restrained.
How wisely Mariam doth the time delay,
Lest sudden joy my sense should suffocate.
I am prepared, thou needst no longer stay.

                                              Exit Nuntio

Who's there? My Mariam, more than happy fate?
Oh no, it is Pheroras. Welcome brother!
Now for a while, I must my passion smother.

IV.ii

Enter Pheroras

Pheroras All health and safety wait upon my lord,
And may you long in prosperous fortunes live,
With Rome-commanding Caesar at accord,
And have all honours that the world can give.
Herod Oh brother, now thou speakst not from thy heart!
No, thou hast struck a blow at Herod's love
That cannot quickly from my memory part,
Though Salome did me to pardon move.
Valiant Phasaelus, now to thee farewell,
Thou wert my kind and honourable brother
Oh hapless hour, when you self-stricken fell,
Thou father's image, glory of thy mother
Had I desired a greater suit of thee,
Than to withhold thee from a harlot's bed,
Thou wouldst have granted it. But now I see
All are not like that in a womb are bred.
Thou wouldst not, hadst thou heard of Herod's death,
Have made his burial time thy bridal hour;
Thou wouldst with clamours, not with joyful breath,
Have showed the news to be not sweet but sour.
Pheroras Phasaelus' great worth I know did stain
Pheroras' petty valour, but they lie
(Excepting you yourself) that dare maintain
That he did honour Herod more than I.
For what I showed, love's power constrained me show,
And pardon loving faults for Mariam's sake.
Herod Mariam, where is she?
                                Nay, I do not know,
Pheroras But absent use of her fair name I make.
You have forgiven greater faults than this.
For Constabarus, that against your will
Preserved the sons of Baba, lives in bliss,
Though you commanded him the youths to kill.
Herod Go, take a present order for his death,
And let those traitors feel the worst of fears!
Now Salome will whine to beg his breath,
But I'll be deaf to prayers and blind to tears.
Pheroras He is, my lord, from Salome divorced,

Though her affection did to leave him grieve,
Yet was she by her love to you enforced
To leave the man that would your foes relieve.
Herod Then haste them to their death. I will requite
                                        Exeunt Pheroras, attendants
Thee gentle Mariam – Salome I mean.
The thought of Mariam doth so steal my spirit,
My mouth from speech of her I cannot wean.

V.iii

Enter Mariam

Herod And here she comes indeed! Happily met,
My best and dearest half. What ails my dear?
Thou dost the difference certainly forget
'Twixt dusky habits and a time so clear.
Mariam My lord, I suit my garment to my mind,
And there no cheerful colours can I find.
Herod Is this my welcome? Have I longed so much
To see my dearest Mariam discontent?
What is't that is the cause thy heart to touch?
Oh speak, that I thy sorrow may prevent.
Art thou not Jewry's Queen, and Herod's too?
Be my commandress, be my sovereign guide;
To be by thee directed I will woo,
For in thy pleasure lies my highest pride.
Or if thou think Judea's narrow bound
Too strict a limit for thy great command,
Thou shalt be Empress of Arabia crowned,
For thou shalt rule, and I will win the land.
I'll rob the holy David's sepulchre
To give thee wealth, if thou for wealth do care.
Thou shalt have all they did with him inter,
And I for thee will make the temple bare.
Mariam I neither have of power nor riches want,
I have enough, nor do I wish for more.
Your offers to my heart no ease can grant
Except they could my brother's life restore.
No, had you wished the wretched Mariam glad,
Or had your love to her been truly tied,
Nay, had you not desired to make her sad,

My brother nor my grandsire had not died.
Herod Wilt thou believe no oaths to clear thy lord?
How oft have I with execration sworn?
Thou art by me beloved, by me adored,
Yet are my protestations heard with scorn.
Hircanus plotted to deprive my head
Of this long settlèd honour that I wear,
And therefore I did justly doom him dead,
To rid the realm from peril, me from fear.
Yet I for Mariam's sake do so repent
The death of one whose blood she did inherit,
I wish I had a kingdom's treasure spent,
So I had ne'er expelled Hircanus' spirit.
As I affected that same noble youth,
In lasting infamy my name enrol
If I not mourned his death with hearty truth.
Did I not show to him my earnest love
When I to him the priesthood did restore?
And did for him a living priest remove
Which never had been done but once before.
Mariam I know that moved by importunity
You made him priest, and shortly after die.
Herod I will not speak, unless to be believed!
This froward humour will not do you good.
It hath too much already Herod grieved
To think that you on terms of hate have stood.
Yet smile my dearest Mariam, do but smile,
And I will all unkind conceits exile.
Mariam I cannot frame disguise, nor never taught
My face a look dissenting from my thought.
Herod By Heav'n you vex me, build not on my love!
Mariam I will not build on so unstable ground.
Herod Nought is so fixed, but peevishness may move.
Mariam 'Tis better slightest cause than none were found.
Herod Be judge yourself, if ever Herod sought
Or would be moved a cause of change to find.
Yet let your look declare a milder thought,
My heart again you shall to Mariam bind.
How oft did I for you my mother chide,
Revile my sister, and my brother rate,
And tell them all my Mariam they belied?
Distrust me still, if these be signs of hate.

IV.iv

Enter Butler

Herod What hast thou here?
Butler   A drink procuring love.
The Queen desired me to deliver it.
Mariam Did I? Some hateful practice this will prove!
Yet can it be no worse than Heavens permit.
Herod Confess the truth, thou wicked instrument
To her outrageous will! 'Tis poison sure!
Tell true, and thou shalt 'scape the punishment,
Which if thou do conceal, thou shalt endure.
Butler I know not, but I doubt it be no less,
Long since the hate of you her heart did seize.
Herod Know'st thou the cause thereof?
Butler   My lord, I guess
Sohemus told the tale that did displease.
Herod Oh Heaven! Sohemus false? Go let him die –
Stay not to suffer him to speak a word.

                                         Exit Butler

Oh damnèd villain, did he falsify
The oath he swore ev'n of his own accord?
Now do I know thy falsehood, painted devil,
Thou white enchantress. Oh thou art so foul,
That Hyssop cannot cleanse thee, worst of evil.
A beauteous body hides a loathsome soul.
Your love, Sohemus, moved by his affection,
Though he have ever heretofore been true,
Did blab, forsooth, that I did give direction,
If we were put to death to slaughter you.
And you in black revenge attended now
To add a murder to your breach of vow.
Mariam Is this a dream?
Herod   Oh Heaven, that 'twere no more!
I'll give my realm to who can prove it so!
I would I were like any beggar poor,
So I for false my Mariam did not know;
Foul pith contained in the fairest rind,
That ever graced a cedar. Oh thine eye
Is pure as Heaven, but impure thy mind,
And for impurity shall Mariam die.

Why didst thou love Sohemus?
Mariam   They can tell
That say I loved him, Mariam says not so.
Herod Oh cannot impudence the coals expel,
That for thy love in Herod's bosom glow?
It is as plain as water, and denial
Makes of thy falsehood but a greater trial.
Hast thou beheld thyself, and couldst thou stain
So rare perfection? Even for love of thee
I do profoundly hate thee. Wert thou plain,
Thou shouldst the wonder of Judea be.
But oh, thou art not. Hell itself lies hid
Beneath thy heavenly show. Yet never wert thou chaste.
Thou mightst exalt, pull down, command, forbid,
And be above the wheel of fortune placed.
Hadst thou complotted Herod's massacre,
That so thy son a monarch might be styled,
Not half so grievous such an action were,
As once to think that Mariam is defiled.
Bright workmanship of nature-sullied ore,
With pitchèd darkness now thine end shall be.
Thou shalt not live, fair fiend, to cozen more,
With heav'nly semblance, as thou coz'nedst me.
Yet must I love thee in despite of death,
And thou shalt die in the despite of love,
For neither shall my love prolong thy breath,
Nor shall thy loss of breath my love remove.
I might have seen thy falsehood in thy face –
Where couldst thou get thy stars that served for eyes
Except by theft? And theft is foul disgrace.
This had appeared before, were Herod wise.
But I'm a sot, a very sot, no better;
My wisdom long ago a-wand'ring fell.
Thy face encount'ring it, my wit did fetter,
And made me for delight my freedom sell.
Give me my heart false creature! 'Tis a wrong
My guiltless heart should now with thine be slain.
Thou hadst no right to lock it up so long,
And with usurper's name I Mariam stain.

Enter Butler

Herod Have you designed Sohemus to his end?
Butler I have my lord.
Herod   Then call our royal guard
To do as much for Mariam. They offend
                                              Exit Butler
Leave ill unblamed, or good without reward.

Enter Soldiers

Here take her to her death. Come back! Come back!
What? Meant I to deprive the world of light,
To muffle Jewry in the foulest black,
That ever was an opposite to white?
Why whither would you carry her?
Soldiers   You bade
We should conduct her to her death, my lord.
Herod Why, sure I did not? Herod was not mad.
Why should she feel the fury of the sword?
Oh now the grief returns into my heart,
And pulls me piecemeal! Love and hate do fight:
And now hath love acquired the greater part,
Yet now hath hate affection conquered quite.
And therefore bear her hence! And, Hebrew, why
Seize you with lion's paws the fairest lamb
Of all the flock? She must not, shall not, die!
Without her I most miserable am;
And with her more than most! Away, away!
But bear her but to prison not to death.
                              Exeunt Soldiers with Mariam
And is she gone indeed – stay, villains, stay!
Her looks alone preserved your sovereign's breath.
Well let her go, but yet she shall not die.
I cannot think she meant to poison me,
But certain 'tis she lived too wantonly,
And therefore shall she never more be free.
                                              Exit

IV.v

Enter Butler

Butler Foul villain, can thy pitchy-coloured soul
Permit thine ear to hear her causeless doom,

And not enforce thy tongue that tale control
That must unjustly bring her to her tomb?
Oh Salome thou hast thyself repaid,
For all the benefits that thou hast done.
Thou art the cause I have the Queen betrayed,
Thou hast my heart to darkest falsehood won.
I am condemned. Heav'n gave me not my tongue
To slander innocents, to lie, deceive,
To be the hateful instrument to wrong,
The Earth of greatest glory to bereave.
My sin ascends and doth to Heaven cry:
'It is the blackest deed that ever was!'
And there doth sit an angel notary
That doth record it down in leaves of brass.
Oh how my heart doth quake! Achitophel,
Thou foundst a means thyself from shame to free,
And sure my soul approves thou didst not well;
All follow some, and I will follow thee.

Exit

IV.vi

Enter Constabarus, Baba's sons and their guard

Constabarus Now here we step our last, the way to death,
We must not tread this way a second time.
Yet let us resolutely yield our breath,
Death is the only ladder, Heav'n to climb.
Baba's 1 son With willing mind I could myself resign,
But yet it grieves me, with a grief untold,
Our death should be accompanied with thine,
Our friendship we to thee have dearly sold.
Constabarus Still wilt thou wrong the sacred name of friend?
Then shouldst thou never style it friendship more,
But base mechanic traffic, that doth lend,
Yet will be sure they shall the debt restore.
I could with needless compliment return,
This for thy ceremony I could say:
' 'Tis I that made the fire your house to burn,
For but for me she would not you betray.'
Had not the damnèd woman sought mine end,
You had not been the subject of her hate.

You never did her hateful mind offend,
Nor could your deaths have freed our nuptial fate.
Therefore fair friends, though you were still unborn,
Some other subtlety devised should be,
Whereby my life, though guiltless, should be torn.
Thus have I proved, 'tis you that die for me,
And therefore should I weakly now lament.
You have but done your duties. Friends should die
Alone, their friends' disaster to prevent,
Though not compelled by strong necessity.
But now farewell, fair city. Never more
Shall I behold your beauty shining bright!
Farewell of Jewish men the worthy store,
But no farewell to any female wight.
You wavering crew, my curse to you I leave!
You had but one to give you any grace,
And you yourselves will Mariam's life bereave.
Your commonwealth doth innocency chase.
You creatures made to be the human curse,
You tigers, lionesses, hungry bears,
Tear massacring hyenas! Nay far worse,
For they for prey do shed their feignèd tears.
But you will weep (you creatures cross to good)
For your unquenchèd thirst of human blood.
You were the angels cast from Heav'n for pride,
And still do keep your angels' outward show,
But none of you are inly beautified,
For still your Heav'n-depriving pride doth grow.
Did not the sins of man require a scourge,
Your place on earth had been by this withstood,
But since a flood no more the world must purge,
You stayed in office of a second flood.
You giddy creatures, sowers of debate,
You'll love today, and for no other cause,
But for you yesterday did deeply hate.
You are the wreck of order, breach of laws,
Your best are foolish, froward, wanton, vain;
Your worst adulterous, murderous, cunning, proud;
And Salome attends the latter train,
Or rather, she their leader is allowed.
I do the sottishness of men bewail,

That do with following you enhance your pride.
'Twere better that the human race should fail,
Than be by such a mischief multiplied.
Cham's servile curse to all your sex was given,
Because in Paradise you did offend.
Then do we not resist the will of Heaven,
When on your wills like servants we attend?
You are to nothing constant but to ill,
You are with nought but wickedness endued;
Your loves are set on nothing but your will,
And thus my censure I of you conclude:
You are the least of goods, the worst of evils,
Your best are worse than men, your worst than devils.
Baba's 2 son Come let us to our death. Are we not blessed?
Our death will freedom from these creatures give –
Those trouble-quiet sowers of unrest.
And this I vow: That had I leave to live,
I would forever lead a single life,
And never venture on a devilish wife.

Exeunt

IV.vii

Enter Herod and Salome

Herod Nay, she shall die.
Salome Die quoth you?
Herod That she shall!
But for the means, the means! Methinks 'tis hard
To find a means to murder her withal,
Therefore I am resolved she shall be spared.
Salome Why, let her be beheaded.
Herod That were well,
Think you that swords are miracles, like you?
Her skin will ev'ry curtlax edge refell,
And then your enterprise you well may rue.
What if the fierce Arabian notice take,
Of this your wretched weaponless estate?
They answer, when we bid resistance make,
That Mariam's skin their fauchions did rebate.
Beware of this, you make a goodly hand,
If you of weapons do deprive our land.

Salome Why, drown her then.
Herod   Indeed a sweet device!
Why, would not every river turn her course
Rather than do her beauty prejudice,
And be reverted to the proper source?
So not a drop of water should be found
In all Judea's quondam fertile ground.
Salome Then let the fire devour her.
Herod   'Twill not be.
Flame is from her derived into my heart.
Thou nursest flame, flame will not murder thee,
My fairest Mariam, fullest of desert.
Salome Then let her live for me.
Herod   Nay, she shall die.
But can you live without her?
Salome   Doubt you that?
Herod I'm sure I cannot. I beseech you try.
I have experience but I know not what.
Salome How should I try?
Herod   Why let my love be slain,
But if we cannot live without her sight,
You'll find the means to make her breathe again,
Or else you will bereave my comfort quite.
Salome Oh aye, I warrant you.

                                                            Exit

Herod   What, is she gone,
And gone to bid the world be overthrown?
What, is her heart's composure hardest stone?
To what a pass are cruel women grown?

Enter Salome

She is returned already. Have you done?
Is't possible you can command so soon
A creature's heart to quench the flaming sun,
Or from the sky to wipe away the moon?
Salome If Mariam be the sun and moon, it is,
For I already have commanded this.
Herod But have you seen her cheek?
Salome   A thousand times.
Herod But did you mark it too?
Salome   Aye, very well.

Herod What is't?

Salome   A crimson bush that ever limes
The soul whose foresight doth not much excel.

Herod Send word she shall not die. Her cheek a bush!
Nay then I see indeed you marked it not.

Salome 'Tis very fair, but yet will never blush,
Though foul dishonours do her forehead blot.

Herod Then let her die, 'tis very true indeed,
And for this fault alone shall Mariam bleed.

Salome What fault my lord?

Herod   What fault is't? You that ask?
If you be ignorant I know of none.
To call her back from death shall be your task.
I'm glad that she for innocent is known.
For on the brow of Mariam hangs a fleece,
Whose slenderest twine is strong enough to bind
The hearts of kings. The pride and shame of Greece,
Troy-flaming Helen's, not so fairly shined.

Salome 'Tis true indeed, she lays them out for nets,
To catch the hearts that do not shun a bait.
'Tis time to speak, for Herod sure forgets
That Mariam's very tresses hide deceit.

Herod Oh do they so? Nay, then you do but well!
In sooth I thought it had been hair.
Nets call you them? Lord, how they do excel!
I never saw a net that showed so fair.
But have you heard her speak?

Salome   You know I have.

Herod And were you not amazed?

Salome   No, not a whit.

Herod Then 'twas not her you heard. Her life I'll save,
For Mariam hath a world-amazing wit.

Salome She speaks a beauteous language, but within
Her heart is false as powder and her tongue
Doth but allure the auditors to sin,
And is the instrument to do you wrong.

Herod It may be so. Nay, 'tis so! She's unchaste!
Her mouth will ope to ev'ry stranger's ear.
Then let the executioner make haste,
Lest she enchant him, if her words he hear.
Let him be deaf, lest she do him surprise,

That shall to free her spirit be assigned.
Yet what boots deafness if he have his eyes?
Her murderer must be both deaf and blind,
For if he see, he needs must see the stars
That shine on either side of Mariam's face,
Whose sweet aspect will terminate the wars;
Wherewith he should a soul so precious chase?
Her eyes can speak, and in their speaking move.
Oft did my heart with reverence receive
The world's mandates. Pretty tales of love
They utter, which can human bondage weave.
But shall I let this Heaven's model die,
Which for a small self-portraiture she drew?
Her eyes like stars, her forehead like the sky,
She is like Heaven, and must be heavenly true.
Salome Your thoughts do rave with doting on the Queen.
Her eyes are ebon-hewed, and you'll confess
A sable star hath been but seldom seen.
Then speak of reason more, of Mariam less.
Herod Yourself are held a goodly creature here,
Yet so unlike my Mariam in your shape,
That when to her you have approachèd near,
Myself hath often ta'en you for an ape;
And yet you prate of beauty! Go your ways,
You are to her a sunburnt blackamoor!
Your paintings cannot equal Mariam's praise:
Her nature is so rich, you are so poor.
Let her be stayed from death, for if she die,
We do we know not what to stop her breath.
A world cannot another Mariam buy.
Why stay you ling'ring? Countermand her death.
Salome Then you'll no more remember what hath passed.
Sohemus' love and hers shall be forgot.
'Tis well in truth, that fault may be her last,
And she may mend, though yet she loves you not.
Herod Oh God, 'tis true! Sohemus! Earth and Heav'n,
Why did you both conspire to make me cursed
In coz'ning me with shows, and proofs unev'n?
She showed the best, and yet did prove the worst.
Her show was such, as had our singing king,
The holy David, Mariam's beauty seen,

The Hittite had then felt no deadly sting,
Nor Bethsabe had never been a queen.
Or had his son, the wisest man of men,
Whose fond delight did most consist in change,
Beheld her face, he had been stayed again;
No creature having her, can wish to range.
Had Asuerus seen my Mariam's brow,
The humble Jew, she might have walked alone.
Her beauteous virtue should have stayed below,
Whiles Mariam mounted to the Persian throne.
But what avails it all? For in the weight
She is deceitful, light as vanity!
Oh she was made for nothing but a bait
To train some hapless man to misery.
I am the hapless man that have been trained
To endless bondage. I will see her yet!
Methinks I should discern her if she feigned.
Can human eyes be dazed by woman's wit?
Once more these eyes of mine with hers shall meet
Before the headsman do her life bereave.
Shall I forever part from thee, my sweet,
Without the taking of my latest leave?
Salome You had as good resolve to save her now!
I'll stay her death, 'tis well determinèd.
For sure she never more will break her vow,
Sohemus and Josephus are both dead.
Herod She shall not live, nor will I see her face.
A long-healed wound, a second time doth bleed!
With Joseph I remember her disgrace,
A shameful end ensues a shameful deed.
Oh that I had not called to mind anew
The discontent of Mariam's wavering heart.
'Twas you! You foul mouthed Ate, none but you
That did the thought hereof to me impart.
Hence from my sight, my black tormentor hence!
For hadst thou not made Herod unsecure
I had not doubted Mariam's innocence,
But still had held her in my heart for pure.
Salome I'll leave you to your passion. 'Tis no time
To purge me now, though of a guiltless crime.

Exit

Herod Destruction take thee! Thou hast made my heart
As heavy as revenge. I am so dull,
Methinks I am not sensible of smart,
Though hideous horrors at my bosom pull.
My head weighs downwards, therefore will I go
To try if I can sleep away my woe.

Exit

IV.viii

Enter Mariam

Mariam Am I the Mariam that presumed so much,
And deemed my face must needs preserve my breath?
Aye, I it was that thought my beauty such,
As it alone could countermand my death.
Now death will teach me: he can pale as well
A cheek of roses, as a cheek less bright,
And dim an eye whose shine doth most excel,
As soon as one that casts a meaner light.
Had not myself against myself conspired,
No plot, no adversary from without,
Could Herod's love from Mariam have retired,
Or from his heart have thrust my semblance out.
The wanton Queen that never loved for love,
False Cleopatra, wholly set on gain,
With all her sleights did prove, yet vainly prove,
For her the love of Herod to obtain.
Yet her allurements, all her courtly guile,
Her smiles, her favours, and her smooth deceit,
Could not my face from Herod's mind exile,
But were with him of less than little weight.
That face and person that in Asia late
For beauty's goddess, Paphos' Queen, was ta'en,
That face that did captive great Julius' fate,
That very face that was Antonius' bane,
That face that to be Egypt's pride was born,
That face that all the world esteemed so rare,
Did Herod hate, depsise, neglect, and scorn,
When with the same he Mariam's did compare.
This made that I improvidently wrought,
And on the wager even my life did pawn,

Because I thought, and yet but truly thought,
That Herod's love could not from me be drawn.
But now, though out of time, I plainly see
It could be drawn, though never drawn from me.
Had I but with humility been graced,
As well as fair I might have proved me wise,
But I did think because I knew me chaste,
One virtue for a woman might suffice.
That mind for glory of our sex might stand,
Wherein humility and chastity
Do march with equal paces hand in hand.
But if one single seen, who setteth by?
And I had singly one, but 'tis my joy,
That I was ever innocent, though sour,
And therefore can they but my life destroy;
My soul is free from adversary's power.

Enter Doris unseen by Mariam

You princes great in power and high in birth,
Be great and high, I envy not your hap.
Your birth must be from dust, your power on Earth,
In Heav'n shall Mariam sit in Sara's lap.
Doris In Heav'n! Your beauty cannot bring you thither.
Your soul is black and spotted, full of sin.
You in adult'ry lived nine years together,
And Heav'n will never let adult'ry in.
Mariam What art thou that dost poor Mariam pursue?
Some spirit sent to drive me to despair?
Who sees for truth that Mariam is untrue?
If fair she be, she is as chaste as fair.
Doris I am that Doris that was once beloved,
Beloved by Herod, Herod's lawful wife.
'Twas you that Doris from his side removed,
And robbed from me the glory of my life.
Mariam Was that adult'ry? Did not Moses say
That he that being matched did deadly hate,
Might by permission put his wife away
And take a more beloved to be his mate?
Doris What did he hate me for? For simple truth?
For bringing beauteous babes for love to him?
For riches, noble birth, or tender youth,

Or for no stain did Doris' honour dim?
Oh tell me Mariam, tell me if you know,
Which fault of these made Herod Doris' foe.
These thrice three years have I with hands held up,
And bowèd knees fast nailèd to the ground,
Besought for thee the dregs of that same cup,
That cup of wrath that is for sinners found,
And now thou art to drink it! Doris' curse
Upon thyself did all this while attend,
But now it shall pursue thy children worse.
Mariam Oh Doris, now to thee my knees I bend,
That heart that never bowed, to thee doth bow.
Curse not mine infants, let it thee suffice,
That Heav'n doth punishment to me allow.
Thy curse is cause that guiltless Mariam dies.
Doris Had I ten thousand tongues, and ev'ry tongue
Inflamed with poison's power and steeped in gall,
My curses would not answer for my wrong,
Though I in cursing thee employed them all.
Hear thou that didst Mount Gerarim command
To be a place whereon with cause to curse,
Stretch thy revenging arm, thrust forth thy hand,
And plague the mother much, the children worse.
Throw flaming fire upon the baseborn heads
That were begotten in unlawful beds.
But let them live till they have sense to know
What 'tis to be in miserable state;
Then be their nearest friends their overthrow,
Attended be they by suspicious hate.
And Mariam, I do hope this boy of mine
Shall one day come to be the death of thine.

Exit

Mariam Oh, Heaven forbid! I hope the world shall see
This curse of thine shall be returned on thee!
Now Earth farewell, though I be yet but young,
Yet I, methinks, have known thee too, too long.

Exit

Chorus

The fairest action of our human life,
Is scorning to revenge an injury;

For who forgives without a further strife,
His adversary's heart to him doth tie.
   And 'tis a firmer conquest truly said,
    To win the heart, than overthrow the head.

If we a worthy enemy do find,
To yield to worth, it must be nobly done;
But if of baser metal be his mind,
In base revenge there is no honour won.
   Who would a worthy courage overthrow,
    And who would wrestle with a worthless foe?

We say our hearts are great and cannot yield,
Because they cannot yield it proves them poor;
Great hearts are tasked beyond their power but seld.
The weakest lions will the loudest roar.
   Truth's school for certain doth this same allow,
    High heartedness doth sometimes teach to bow.

A noble heart doth teach a virtuous scorn,
To scorn to owe a duty over-long,
To scorn to be for benefits forborne,
To scorn to lie, to scorn to do a wrong,
   To scorn to bear an injury in mind,
    To scorn a free-born heart slave-like to bind.

But if for wrongs we needs revenge must have,
Then be our vengeance of the noblest kind.
Do we his body from our fury save,
And let our hate prevail against his mind?
   What can 'gainst him a greater vengeance be,
    Than make his foe more worthy far than he?

Had Mariam scorned to leave a due unpaid,
She would to Herod then have paid her love,
And not have been by sullen passion swayed.
To fix her thoughts all injury above
   Is virtuous pride. Had Mariam thus been proud,
    Long famous life to her had been allowed.

V.i

Enter Nuntio

Nuntio When, sweetest friend, did I so far offend
Your heavenly self, that you my fault to quit
Have made me now relator of her end,
The end of beauty, chastity and wit?
Was none so hapless in the fatal place
But I, most wretched, for the Queen to choose?
'Tis certain I have some ill-boding face
That made me culled to tell this luckless news.
And yet no news to Herod. Were it new
To him, unhappy 'thad not been at all.
Yet do I long to come within his view,
That he may know his wife did guiltless fall.
And here he comes. Your Mariam greets you well.

Enter Herod

Herod What, lives my Mariam? Joy, exceeding joy!
She shall not die.
Nuntio   Heav'n doth your will repel.
Herod Oh do not with thy words my life destroy!
I prithee tell no dying-tale. Thine eye
Without thy tongue doth tell but too, too much.
Yet let thy tongue's addition make me die,
Death welcome comes to him whose grief is such.
Nuntio I went amongst the curious gazing troop,
To see the last of her that was the best,
To see if death had heart to make her stoop,
To see the sun admiring Phoenix' nest.
When there I came, upon the way I saw
The stately Mariam not debased by fear;
Her look did seem to keep the world in awe,
Yet mildly did her face this fortune bear.
Herod Thou dost usurp my right! My tongue was framed
To be the instrument of Mariam's praise.
Yet speak. She cannot be too often famed;
All tongues suffice not her sweet name to raise.
Nuntio But as she came she Alexandra met,
Who did her death (sweet Queen) no whit bewail,
But as if nature she did quite forget,

She did upon her daughter loudly rail.
Herod Why stopped you not her mouth? Where had she words
To darken that, that Heaven made so bright?
Our sacred tongue no epithet affords,
To call her other than the world's delight.
Nuntio She told her that her death was too, too good,
And that already she had lived too long;
She said she shamed to have a part in blood
Of her that did the princely Herod wrong.
Herod Base pick-thank devil! Shame? 'Twas all her glory,
That she to noble Mariam was the mother!
But never shall it live in any story
Her name, except to infamy, I'll smother.
What answer did her princely daughter make?
Nuntio She made no answer, but she looked the while,
As if thereof she scarce did notice take,
Yet smiled a dutiful, though scornful, smile.
Herod Sweet creature, I that look to mind do call;
Full oft hath Herod been amazed withal.
Go on.
Nuntio She came unmoved with pleasant grace,
As if to triumph her arrival were,
In stately habit, and with cheerful face,
Yet ev'ry eye was moist, but Mariam's there.
When justly opposite to me she came,
She picked me out from all the crew.
She beckoned to me, called me by my name,
For she my name, my birth, and fortune knew.
Herod What, did she name thee? Happy, happy man!
Wilt thou not ever love that name the better?
But what sweet tune did this fair dying swan
Afford thine ear? Tell all, omit no letter.
Nuntio Tell thou my lord, said she -
Herod   Me, meant she me?
Is't true? The more my shame, I was her lord,
Were I not made her lord, I still should be,
But now her name must be by me adored.
Oh say, what said she more? Each word she said
Shall be the food whereon my heart is fed.
Nuntio Tell thou my lord thou saw'st me lose my breath.
Herod Oh that I could that sentence now control!

Nuntio If guiltily eternal be my death.

Herod I hold her chaste ev'n in my inmost soul!

Nuntio By three days hence, if wishes could revive,

I know himself would make me oft alive.

Herod Three days? Three hours, three minutes, not so much:

A minute in a thousand parts divided!

My penitency for her death is such,

As in the first I wished she had not died.

But forward in thy tale.

Nuntio   Why on she went,

And after she some silent prayer had said,

She died as if to die she were content,

And thus to Heav'n her heav'nly soul is fled.

Herod But art thou sure there doth no life remain?

Is't possible my Mariam should be dead?

Is there no trick to make her breathe again?

Nuntio Her body is divided from her head.

Herod Why yet methinks there might be found, by art,

Strange ways of cure. 'Tis sure rare things are done

By an inventive head, and willing heart.

Nuntio Let not, my lord, your fancies idly run.

It is as possible it should be seen

That we should make the holy Abraham live,

Though he entombed two thousand years had been,

As breath again to slaughtered Mariam give.

But now for more assaults prepare your ears.

Herod There cannot be a further cause of moan;

This accident shall shelter me from fears.

What can I fear? Already Mariam's gone.

Yet tell ev'n what you will.

Nuntio   As I came by

From Mariam's death, I saw, upon a tree,

A man that to his neck a cord did tie,

Which cord he had designed his end to be.

When me he once discerned, he downwards bowed,

And thus with fearful voice he cried aloud,

'Go tell the King he trusted ere he tried,

I am the cause that Mariam causeless died!'

Herod Damnation take him, for it was the slave

That said she meant with poison's deadly force

To end my life, that she the crown might have,

Which tale did Mariam from herself divorce.
Oh pardon me, thou pure unspotted ghost!
My punishment must needs sufficient be,
In missing that content I valued most,
Which was thy admirable face to see.
I had but one inestimable jewel,
Yet one I had, no monarch had the like,
And therefore may I curse myself as cruel,
'Twas broken by a blow myself did strike.
I gazed thereon and never thought me blessed,
But when on it my dazzled eye might rest.
A precious mirror made by wondrous art,
I prized it ten times dearer than my crown,
And laid it up fast folded in my heart,
Yet I in sudden choler cast it down
And pashed it all to pieces. 'Twas no foe
That robbed me of it, no Arabian host,
Nor no Armenian guide hath used me so,
But Herod's wretched self hath Herod crossed.
She was my graceful moi'ty, me accursed,
To slay my better half and save my worst.
But sure she is not dead? You did but jest,
To put me in perplexity a while.
'Twere well indeed if I could so be 'dressed,
I see she is alive, methinks you smile.
Nuntio If sainted Abel yet deceasèd be,
'Tis certain Mariam is as dead as he.
Herod Why then, go call her to me, bid her now
Put on fair habit, stately ornament,
And let no frown o'ershade her smoothest brow,
In her doth Herod place his whole content.
Nuntio She'll come in stately weeds to please your sense,
If now she come attired in robe of Heaven.
Remember you yourself did send her hence,
And now to you she can no more be given.
Herod She's dead! Hell take her murderers! She was fair.
Oh what a hand she had, it was so white,
It did the whiteness of the snow impair.
I never more shall see so sweet a sight.
Nuntio Tis true, her hand was rare.
Herod   Her hand? Her hands!

She had not singly one of beauty rare,
But such a pair as here where Herod stands,
He dares the world to make to both compare.
Accursèd Salome! Hadst thou been still,
My Mariam had been breathing by my side.
Oh never had I, had I had my will,
Sent forth command that Mariam should have died.
But Salome thou didst with envy vex,
To see thyself out-matchèd in thy sex.
Upon your sex's forehead Mariam sat,
To grace you all like an imperial crown,
But you, fond fool, have rudely pushed thereat,
And proudly pulled your proper glory down.
One smile of hers – nay not so much – a look
Was worth a hundred thousand such as you.
Judea how canst thou the wretches brook,
That robbed from thee the fairest of the crew?
You dwellers in the now deprivèd land,
Wherein the matchless Mariam was bred,
Why grasp not each of you a sword in hand,
To aim at me, your cruel sovereign's head?
Oh when you think of Herod as your King,
And owner of the pride of Palestine,
This act to your remembrance likewise bring,
'Tis I have overthrown your royal line.
Within her purer veins the blood did run,
That from her grandam Sara she derived,
Whose beldame age the love of kings hath won.
Oh that her issue had as long been lived!
But can her eye be made by death obscure?
I cannot think but it must sparkle still.
Foul sacrilege to rob those lights so pure,
From out a temple made by heav'nly skill.
I am the villain that have done the deed,
The cruel deed, though by another's hand;
My word though not my sword made Mariam bleed.
Hircanus' grandchild died at my command;
That Mariam that I once did love so dear,
The partner of my now detested bed.
Why shine you sun with an aspect so clear?
I tell you once again my Mariam's dead.

You could but shine, if some Egyptian blowse,
Or Ethiopian dowdy lose her life.
This was (then wherefore bend you not your brows?)
The King of Jewry's fair and spotless wife.
Deny thy beams, and moon refuse thy light,
Let all the stars be dark, let Jewry's eye
No more distinguish which is day and night,
Since her best birth did in her bosom die.
Those fond idolaters, the men of Greece,
Maintain these orbs are safely governèd,
That each within themselves have gods apiece
By whom their steadfast course is justly led.
But were it so, as so it cannot be,
They all would put their mourning garments on.
Not one of them would yield a light to me,
To me that is the cause that Mariam's gone.
For though they fame their Saturn melancholy,
Of sour behaviours, and of angry mood,
They fame him likewise to be just and holy,
And justice needs must seek revenge for blood.
Their Jove, if Jove he were, would sure desire
To punish him that slew so fair a lass,
For Leda's beauty set his heart on fire,
Yet she not half so fair as Mariam was.
And Mars would deem his Venus had been slain,
Sol to recover her would never stick,
For if he want the power her life to gain,
Then physic's god is but an empiric.
The Queen of Love would storm for beauty's sake,
And Hermes too, since he bestowed her wit,
The night's pale light for angry grief would shake,
To see chaste Mariam die in age unfit.
But oh, I am deceived, she passed them all
In every gift, in every property;
Her excellencies wrought her timeless fall,
And they rejoiced, not grieved, to see her die.
The Paphian goddess did repent her waste,
When she to one such beauty did allow;
Mercurius thought her wit his wit surpassed,
And Cynthia envied Mariam's brighter brow.
But these are fictions, they are void of sense,

The Greeks but dream, and dreaming, falsehoods tell;
They neither can offend nor give defence,
And not by them it was my Mariam fell.
If she had been like an Egyptian black,
And not so fair, she had been longer lived.
Her overflow of beauty turnèd back,
And drowned the spring from whence it was derived.
Her heav'nly beauty 'twas that made me think
That it with chastity could never dwell,
But now I see that Heav'n in her did link
A spirit and a person to excel.
I'll muffle up myself in endless night,
And never let mine eyes behold the light.
Retire thyself, vile monster, worse than he
That stained the virgin earth with brother's blood,
Still in some vault or den enclosèd be,
Where with thy tears thou may'st beget a flood,
Which flood in time may drown thee. Happy day,
When thou at once shalt die and find a grave.
A stone upon the vault, someone shall lay,
Which monument shall an inscription have,
And these shall be the words it shall contain:
'Here Herod lies, that hath his Mariam slain.'

Chorus

Who ever hath beheld with steadfast eye,
The strange events of this one only day?
How many were deceived, how many die,
That once today did grounds of safety lay?
   It will from them all certainty bereave,
   Since twice six hours so many can deceive.

This morning Herod held for surely dead,
And all the Jews on Mariam did attend,
And Constabarus rise from Salom's bed,
And neither dreamed of a divorce or end.
   Pheroras joyed that he might have his wife,
   And Baba's sons for safety of their life.

Tonight our Herod doth alive remain,
The guiltless Mariam is deprived of breath,

Stout Constabarus both divorced and slain,
The valiant sons of Baba have their death.
  Pheroras sure his love to be bereft,
  If Salome her suit unmade had left,

Herod this morning did expect with joy,
To see his Mariam's much belovèd face
And yet ere night he did her life destroy,
And surely thought she did her name disgrace.
  Yet now again so short do humours last,
  He both repents her death and knows her chaste.

Had he with wisdom now her death delayed,
He at his pleasure might command her death,
But now he hath his power so much betrayed,
As all his woes cannot restore her breath,
 Now doth he strangely lunaticly rave
 Because his Mariam's life he cannot save.

This day's events were certainly ordained,
To be the warning to posterity,
So many changes are therein contained,
So admirably strange variety.
  This day alone, our sagest Hebrews shall
  In after times the school of wisdom call.

1617

9. Rachel Speght

from *A Muzzle For Melastomus, the cynical baiter of, and
foul mouthed barker against, Evah's Sex* (1617)

*Of woman's excellency, with the causes of her creation, and of the
sympathy which ought to be in man and wife each toward other.*

The work of creation being finished, this approbation thereof was given by
God himself, that 'All was very good' (Gen. 1:31). If all, then woman, who,

excepting man, is the most excellent creature under the canopy of Heaven. But if it be objected by any:

First, that woman, though created good, yet by giving ear to Satan's temptations, brought death and misery upon all her posterity.

Secondly, that 'Adam was not deceived, but that the woman was deceived, and was in the transgression' (1 Tim. 2:14).

Thirdly, that Saint Paul saith, 'It were good for a man not to touch a woman' (1 Cor. 7:1).

Fourthly, and lastly, that of Solomon, who seems to speak against all of our sex; 'I have found one man of a thousand, but a woman among them all have I not found' (Eccles. 7:30), whereof in it due place.

To the first of these objections I answer that Satan first assailed the woman because where the hedge is lowest, most easy it is to get over, and she being the weaker vessel was with more facility to be seduced: like as a crystal glass sooner receives a crack than a strong stone pot. Yet we shall find the offence of Adam and Eve almost to parallel. For as an ambitious desire of being made like unto God, was the motive which caused her to eat, so likewise was it his; as may plainly appear by that Ironica 'Behold, man is become as one of us' (Gen. 3:22). Not that he was so indeed, but hereby his desire to attain a greater perfection than God had given him, was reproved. Woman sinned, it is true, by her infidelity in not believing the Word of God, but giving credit to Satan's fair promises, that 'she should not die' (Gen. 3:4), but so did the man too. And if Adam had not approved of that deed which Eve had done, and been willing to tread the steps which she had gone, he being her head would have reproved her, and have made the commandment a bit to restrain him from breaking his Maker's injunction. For if a man burn his hand in the fire, the bellows that blowed the fire are not to be blamed, but himself rather, for not being careful to avoid the danger, yet if the bellows had not blowed, the fire had not burnt. No more is woman simply to be condemned for man's transgression, for by the free will, which before his fall he enjoyed, he might have avoided and been free from being burnt, or singed with that fire which was kindled by Satan, and blown by Eve. It therefore served not his turn a whit, afterwards to say, 'The woman which thou gavest me, gave me of the tree, and I did eat' (Gen. 3:12), for a penalty was inflicted upon him, as well as on the woman, the punishment of her transgression being particular to her own sex, and to none but the female kind. But for the sin of man the whole Earth was cursed. And he being better able, than the woman, to have resisted temptation (Gen. 3:17), because the stronger vessel, was first called to account, to show that to whom much is given, of them much is required, and that he who was the sovereign of all creatures visible, should have yielded greatest obedience to God.

True it is (as it already confessed) that woman first sinned, yet find we no mention of spiritual nakedness till man had sinned. Then it is said, 'Their eyes were opened' (Gen. 3:7), the eyes of their mind and conscience; and then perceived they themselves naked, that is, not only bereft of that integrity, which they originally had, but felt the rebellion and disobedience of their members in the disordered motions of their now corrupt nature, which made them for shame to cover their nakedness. Then (and not afore) is it said that they saw it, as if sin were imperfect, and unable to bring a deprivation of a blessing received, or death on all mankind, till man (in whom lay the active power of generation) had transgressed. The offence therefore of Adam and Eve is by Saint Au[gu]stin thus distinguished, the man sinned against God and himself, the woman against God, herself, and her husband, yet in her giving of the fruit to eat had she no malicious intent towards him, but did therein show a desire to make her husband partaker of that happiness, which she thought by their eating they should both have enjoyed. This her giving Adam of that sauce, wherewith Satan had served her, whose sourness afore he had eaten, she did not perceive, was that which made her sin to exceed his. Wherefore, that she might not of him, who ought to honour her, be abhorred (1 Pet. 3:7), the first promise that was made in Paradise, God makes to woman, that by her seed should the Serpent's head be broken (Gen. 3:15). Whereupon Adam calls her Hevah, life, that as the woman had been an occasion of his sin, so should woman bring forth the Saviour from sin, which was in the fullness of time accomplished. By which was manifested, that he is a Saviour of believing women, no less than of men (Galat. 4:4), that so the blame of sin may not be imputed to his creature, which is good, but to the will by which Eve sinned. And yet by Christ's assuming the shape of man was it declared, that his mercy was equivalent to both sexes; so that by Hevah's blessed seed (as Saint Paul affirms) it is brought to pass, that 'male and female are all one in Christ Jesus' (Galat. 3:28).

To the second objection I answer, that the Apostle doth not hereby exempt man from sin, but only giveth to understand, that the woman was the primary transgressor, and not the man. But that man was not at all deceived was far from his meaning, for he afterward expressly saith, that as in Adam all die, so in Christ shall all be made alive (1 Cor. 15:22).

For the third objection, 'It is good for a man not to touch a woman'. The Apostle makes it not a positive prohibition, but speaks it only because of the Corinth[ian]s' present necessity, who were then persecuted by the enemies of the Church, for which cause, and no other, he saith, 'Art thou loosed from a wife? Seek not a wife.', meaning whilst the time of these perturbations should continue in their heat; 'but if thou art bound, seek not to be loosed: if thou marriest, thou sinnest not', only increasest thy care: 'for the married careth for the things of this world, And I wish that you were without care, that ye might cleave fast unto the Lord without separation: For the time remaineth, that they which have wives be as though they had none' (1 Cor. 7): for the persecutors shall deprive you of them, either by imprisonment, banishment, or death; so that manifest it is, that the Apostle doth not hereby forbid marriage, but only adviseth the Corinth[ian]s to forbear a while, till God in mercy should curb the fury of their adversaries. For (as Eusebius writeth) Paul was afterward married himself, the which is very probable, being that interrogatively he saith, 'Have we not power to lead about a wife, being a sister, as well as the rest of the Apostles, and as the brethren of the Lord and Cephas?' (1 Cor. 9:5).

The fourth and last objection, is that of Solomon, 'I have found one man among a thousand, but a woman among them all have I not found' (Eccles. 7:30), for answer of which, if we look into the story of his life, we shall find therein a commentary upon this enigmatical sentence included. For it is there said that Solomon had seven hundred wives, and three hundred concubines, which number connexed make one thousand. These women turning his heart away from being perfect with the Lord his God (1 Kings 11:3), sufficient cause had he to say, that among the said thousand women found he not one upright. He saith not, that among a thousand women never any man found one worthy of commendation, but speaks in the first person singularly 'I have not found', meaning in his own experience: for this assertion is to beholden a part of the confession of his former follies, and no otherwise, his repentance being the intended drift of *Ecclesiastes*.

Thus having (by God's assistance) removed those stones, whereat some have stumbled, others broken their shins, I will proceed toward the period of my intended task, which is to decipher the excellency of women, of whose creation I will, for order's sake, observe. First, the efficient cause, which was God; secondly, the material cause, or that whereof she was made; thirdly, the formal cause, or fashion, and proportion of her feature; fourthly and lastly, the final cause, the end or purpose for which she was made. To begin with the first.

The efficient cause of woman's creation was Jehovah the Eternal; the truth of which is manifest in Moses his narration of the six days' works, where he saith, 'God created them male and female' (Gen. 1:28). And

David exhorting all the earth to sing unto the Lord, meaning, by a metonymy, earth, all creatures that live on the earth, of what nation or sex soever, gives this reason: 'For the Lord hath made us' (Psal. 100:3). That work then cannot choose but be good, yea very good, which is wrought by so excellent a workman as the Lord, for he being a glorious Creator, must needs effect a worthy creature. Bitter water can not proceed from a pleasant sweet fountain (Psal. 100:4), nor bad work from that workman which is perfectly good and in propriety (Math. 19:17), none but he.

Secondly, the material cause, or matter whereof woman was made, was of a refined mould, if I may so speak. For man was created of the dust of the earth (Gen. 2:7), but woman was made of a part of man, after that he was a living soul. Yet was she not produced from Adam's foot, to be his too low inferior, nor from his head to be his superior, but from his side, near his heart, to be his equal, that where he is Lord, she may be Lady. And therefore saith God concerning man and woman jointly, 'Let them rule over the fish of the sea, and over the fowls of the Heaven, and over every beast that moveth upon the earth' (Gen. 1:26). By which words, he makes their authority equal, and all creatures to be in subjection unto them both. This being rightly considered, doth teach men to make such account of their wives, as Adam did of Eve, 'This is bone of my bone, and flesh of my flesh' (Gen. 2:23), as also, that they neither do or wish any more hurt unto them, than unto their own bodies. For men ought to love their wives as themselves, because he that loves his wife, loves himself (Ephes. 5:28). And never man hated his own flesh (which the woman is) unless a monster in nature.

Thirdly, the formal cause, fashion, and proportion of woman was excellent, for she was neither like the beasts of the earth, fowls of the air, fishes of the sea, or any other inferior creature, but man was the only object, which she did resemble. For as God gave man a lofty countenance, that he might look up toward Heaven, so did he likewise give unto woman. And as the temperature of man's body is excellent, so is woman's. For whereas other creatures, by reason of their gross humours, have excrements for their habit, as fowls, their feathers, beasts, their hair, fishes, their scales, man and woman only, have their skin clear and smooth (Gen. 1:26). And (that more is) in the image of God were they both created; yea and to be brief, all the parts of their bodies, both external and internal, were correspondent and meet each for other.

Fourthly and lastly, the final cause, or end, for which woman was made, was to glorify God, and to be a collateral companion for man to glorify God, in using her body, and all the parts, powers, and faculties thereof, as instruments for his honour. As with her voice to sound forth his praises, like Miriam, and the rest of her company (Exod. 15:20); with her tongue not to utter words of strife, but to give good counsel unto her husband, the which he must not despise. For Abraham was bidden to give ear to Sarah his wife (Gen. 21:12); Pilate was willed by his wife not to have any hand in the condemning of Christ (Math. 27:19); and a sin it was in him, that he listened not to her; Leah and Rachel counselled Jacob to do according to the word of the Lord (Gen. 31:16); and the Shunamite put her husband in mind of harbouring the Prophet Elisha (1 Kings 4:9). Her hands should be open according to her ability, in contributing towards God's service, and distressed servants, like to that poor widow, which cast two mites into the treasury (Luke 8); and as Mary Magdalene, Susanna, and Joanna the wife of Herod's steward, with many other, which of their substance ministered unto Christ [Luke 24:1–10]. Her heart should be a receptacle for God's Word, like Mary that treasured up the sayings of Christ in her heart (Luke 1:51). Her feet should be swift in going to seek the Lord in his sanctuary, as Mary Magdalene made haste to seek Christ at his sepulchre (John 20:1). Finally, no power external or internal ought woman to keep idle, but to employ it in some service of God, to the glory of her Creator, and comfort of her own soul.

The other end for which woman was made, was to be a companion and helper for man; and if she must be an helper, and but an helper, then are those husbands to be blamed, which lay the whole burthen of domestical affairs and maintenance on the shoulders of their wives. For, as yoke-fellows they are to sustain part of each other's cares, griefs, and calamities, but as if two oxen be put in one yoke, the one being bigger than the other, the greater bears most weight, so the husband being the stronger vessel is to bear a greater burthen than his wife. And therefore the Lord said to Adam, 'In the sweat of thy face shalt thou eat thy bread, till thou return to the dust' (Gen. 3:19). And Saint Paul saith, 'That he that provideth not for his household is worse than an infidel' (1 Tim. 5:8).

1621

10. Lady Mary Wroth

Pamphilia to Amphilanthus

1

When night's black mantle could most darkness prove,
And sleep, death's image, did my senses hire
From knowledge of myself, then thoughts did move
Swifter than those, most swiftness need require.

In sleep, a chariot drawn by winged desire
I saw, where sat bright Venus, Queen of Love,
And at her feet her son, still adding fire
To burning hearts, which she did hold above;

But one heart flaming more than all the rest
The goddess held, and put it to my breast.
'Dear son, now shoot,' said she, 'thus must we win.'

He her obeyed, and martyred my poor heart.
I, waking, hoped as dreams it would depart;
Yet since, O me, a lover I have been.

2

Dear eyes, how well, indeed, you do adorn
That blessèd sphere which gazing souls hold dear,
The lovèd place of sought-for triumphs, near
The court of glory, where love's force was born.

How may they term you April's sweetest morn,
When pleasing looks from those bright lights appear,
A sunshine day; from clouds and mists still clear,
Kind nursing fires for wishes yet unborn.

Two stars of heaven, sent down to grace the earth,
Placed in that throne which gives all joys their birth,
Shining and burning, pleasing yet their charms,

Which, wounding, ev'n in hurts are deemed delights,
So pleasant is their force, so great their mights
As, happy, they can triumph in their harms.

3
Yet is there hope. Then, Love, but play thy part,
Remember well thyself, and think on me;
Shine in those eyes which conquered have my heart,
And see if mine be slack to answer thee.

Lodge in that breast, and pity moving see
For flames which in mine burn in truest smart,
Exiling thoughts that touch inconstancy,
Or those which waste not in the constant art.

Watch but my sleep, if I take any rest
For thought of you, my spirit so distressed
As, pale and famished, I for mercy cry.

Will you your servant leave? Think but on this:
Who wears love's crown must not do so amiss,
But seek their good, who on thy force do lie.

4
Forbear, dark night, my joys now bud again,
Lately grown dead, while cold aspects did chill
The root at heart, and my chief hope quite kill,
And thunders struck me in my pleasure's wane.

Then I, alas, with bitter sobs and pain
Privately groaned my fortune's present ill;
All light of comfort dimmed, woes in pride's fill,
With strange increase of grief I grieved in vain.

And most, as when a memory to good
Molested me, which still as witness stood
Of these best days in former times I knew,

Late gone, as wonders past, like the great snow,
Melted and wasted, with what change must know:
Now back the life comes where as once it grew.

5
Can pleasing sight misfortune ever bring?
Can firm desire a painful torment try?
Can winning eyes prove to the heart a sting?
Or can sweet lips in treason hidden lie?

The sun, most pleasing, blinds the strongest eye
If too much looked on, breaking the sight's string;
Desires still crossed must unto mischief hie,
And as despair a luckless chance may fling.

Eyes, having won, rejecting proves a sting,
Killing the bud before the tree doth spring;
Sweet lips, not loving, do as poison prove.

Desire, sight, eyes, lips, seek, see, prove and find,
You love may win, but curses if unkind:
Then show you harms dislike, and joy in love.

6
O strive not still to heap disdain on me,
Nor pleasure take, your cruelty to show
On hapless me, on whom all sorrows flow,
And biding make, as given and lost by thee.

Alas, ev'n grief is grown to pity me;
Scorn cries out 'gainst itself such ill to show,
And would give place for joy's delights to flow;
Yet wretched I all tortures bear from thee.

Long have I suffered, and esteemed it dear,
Since such thy will, yet grew my pain more near.
Wish you my end? Say so, you shall it have,

For all the depth of my heart-held despair
Is that for you I feel not death for care;
But now I'll seek it, since you will not save.

Song 1
'The spring now come at last
To trees, fields, to flowers
And meadows makes to taste
His pride, while sad showers
Which from mine eyes do flow,
Makes known with cruel pains
Cold winter yet remains,
No sign of spring we know.

The sun which to the earth
Gives heat, light and pleasure,
Joys in spring, hateth dearth,
Plenty makes his treasure.
His heat to me is cold,
His light all darkness is,
Since I am barred of bliss
I heat nor light behold.'

A shepherdess thus said,
Who was with grief oppressed,
For truest love betrayed
Barred her from quiet rest;
And weeping, thus said she:
'My end approacheth near,
Now willow must I wear,
My fortune so will be.

With branches of this tree
I'll dress my hapless head,
Which shall my witness be
My hopes in love are dead;
My clothes embroidered all
Shall be with garlands round,
Some scattered, others bound,
Some tied, some like to fall.

The bark my book shall be,
Where daily I will write
This tale of hapless me,
True slave to fortune's spite;

The root shall be my bed,
Where nightly I will lie
Wailing inconstancy,
Since all true love is dead.

And these lines I will leave,
If some such lover come
Who may them right conceive,
And place them on my tomb:
"She who still constant loved,
Now dead with cruel care,
Killed with unkind despair
And change, her end here proved."'

❀ ❀ ❀ ❀

7

Love, leave to urge, thou know'st thou hast the hand;
'Tis cowardice to strive where none resist;
Pray thee leave off, I yield unto thy band;
Do not thus still in thine own power persist.

Behold, I yield; let forces be dismissed;
I am thy subject, conquered, bound to stand;
Never thy foe, but did thy claim assist,
Seeking thy due of those who did withstand.

But now, it seems, thou wouldst I should thee love.
I do confess, 'twas thy will made me choose,
And thy fair shows made me a lover prove,
When I my freedom did for pain refuse.

Yet this, Sir God, your boyship I despise;
Your charms I obey, but love not want of eyes.

❀ ❀ ❀ ❀

8

Led by the pow'r of grief, to wailings brought
By false conceit of change fall'n on my part,
I seek for some small ease by lines which, bought,
Increase the pain; grief is not cured by art.

Ah! how unkindness moves within the heart
Which still is true and free from changing thought;
What unknown woe it breeds, what endless smart,
With ceaseless tears which causelessly are wrought.

It makes me now to shun all shining light,
And seek for blackest clouds me light to give,
Which to all others only darkness drive;
They on me shine, for sun disdains my sight.

Yet though I dark do live, I triumph may:
Unkindness nor this wrong shall love allay.

❀ ❀ ❀ ❀

9
Be you all pleased? Your pleasures grieve not me.
Do you delight? I envy not your joy.
Have you content? Contentment with you be.
Hope you for bliss? Hope still, and still enjoy.

Let sad misfortune hapless me destroy,
Leave crosses to rule me, and still rule free,
While all delights their contraries employ
To keep good back, and I but torments see.

Joys are bereaved, harms do only tarry,
Despair takes place, disdain hath got the hand;
Yet firm love holds my senses in such band
As, since despisèd, I with sorrow marry.

Then if with grief I now must coupled be,
Sorrow I'll wed; despair thus governs me.

❀ ❀ ❀ ❀

10
The weary traveller who, tired, sought
In places distant far, yet found no end
Of pain or labour, nor his state to mend,
At last with joy is to his home back brought,

Finds not more ease, though he with joy be fraught,
When past is fear, content like souls ascend,
Than I, on whom new pleasures do descend,
Which now as high as first-born bliss is wrought.

He, tired with his pains, I with my mind;
He all content receives by ease of limbs,
I, greatest happiness that I do find
Belief for faith, while hope in pleasure swims.

Truth saith, ' 'Twas wrong conceit bred my despite,
Which, once acknowledged, brings my heart's delight.'

❀ ❀ ❀ ❀

11
You endless torments that my rest oppress,
How long will you delight in my sad pain?
Will never love your favour more express?
Shall I still live, and ever feel disdain?

Alas, now stay, and let my grief obtain
Some end; feed not my heart with sharp distress;
Let me once see my cruel fortunes gain
At least release, and long-felt woes redress.

Let not the blame of cruelty disgrace
The honoured title of your godhead, Love;
Give not just cause for me to say, a place
Is found for rage alone on me to move.

O quickly end, and do not long debate
My needful aid, lest help do come too late.

❀ ❀ ❀ ❀

12
Cloyed with the torments of a tedious night,
I wish for day; which come, I hope for joy;
When cross I find new tortures to destroy
My woe-killed heart, first hurt by mischief's might;

Then cry for night, and once more day takes flight.
And brightness gone, what rest should here enjoy
Usurpèd is: hate will her force employ;
Night cannot grief entomb, though black as spite.

My thoughts are sad, her face as sad doth seem;
My pains are long, her hours tedious are;
My grief is great, and endless is my care;
Her face, her force, and all of woes esteem.

Then welcome night, and farewell flatt'ring day,
Which all hopes breed, and yet our joys delay.

❀ ❀ ❀ ❀

Song 2
All night I weep, all day I cry, ay me,
I still do wish, though yet deny, ay me;
I sigh, I mourn, I say that still
I only am the store for ill, ay me.

In coldest hopes I freeze, yet burn, ay me,
From flames I strive to fly, yet turn, ay me;
From grief I haste, but sorrows hie,
And on my heart all woes do lie, ay me.

From contraries I seek to run, ay me,
But contraries I cannot shun, ay me:
For they delight their force to try,
And to despair my thoughts do tie, ay me.

Whither, alas, then shall I go, ay me,
When as despair all hopes outgo, ay me?
If to the forest, Cupid hies,
And my poor soul to his laws ties, ay me.

To the court? O no, he cries, ay me,
There no true love you shall espy, ay me,
Leave that place to falsest lovers,
Your true love all truth discovers, ay me.

Then quiet rest, and no more prove, ay me;
All places are alike to love, ay me;
And constant be in this begun,
Yet say, till life with love be done, ay me.

❀ ❀ ❀ ❀

13
Dear, famish not what you yourself gave food,
Destroy not what your glory is to save,
Kill not that soul to which you spirit gave:
In pity, not disdain, your triumph stood.

An easy thing it is to shed the blood
Of one who, at your will, yields to the grave,
But more you may true worth by mercy crave
When you preserve, not spoil but nourish good.

Your sight is all the food I do desire;
Then sacrifice me not in hidden fire,
Or stop the breath which did your praises move.

Think but how easy 'tis a sight to give,
Nay, ev'n desert, since by it I do live;
I but chameleon-like would live, and love.

❀ ❀ ❀ ❀

14
Am I thus conquered? Have I lost the powers
That to withstand, which joys to ruin me?
Must I be still, while it my strength devours,
And captive leads me prisoner, bound, unfree?

Love first shall leave men's fancies to them free,
Desire shall quench love's flames, spring hate sweet showers,
Love shall lose all his darts, have sight, and see
His shame and wishings hinder happy hours.

Why should we not love's purblind charms resist?
Must we be servile, doing what he list?
No, seek some host to harbour thee: I fly

Thy babish tricks, and freedom do profess.
But O, my hurt makes my lost heart confess:
I love, and must; so, farewell liberty.

❀ ❀ ❀ ❀

15
Truly, poor Night, thou welcome art to me,
I love thee better in this sad attire
Than that which raiseth some men's fancies higher,
Like painted outsides, which foul inward be.

I love thy grave and saddest looks to see,
Which seems my soul and dying heart entire,
Like to the ashes of some happy fire
That flamed in joy, but quenched in misery.

I love thy count'nance, and thy sober pace
Which evenly goes, and as of loving grace
To us, and me amongst the rest oppressed,

Gives quiet peace to my poor self alone,
And freely grants day leave, when thou art gone,
To give clear light to see all ill redressed.

❀ ❀ ❀ ❀

16
Sleep, fie, possess me not, nor do not fright
Me with thy heavy, and thy deathlike might:
For counterfeiting's viler than death's sight,
And such deluding more my thoughts do spite.

Thou suff'rest falsest shapes my soul t'affright,
Sometimes in likeness of a hopeful sprite,
And oft times like my love, as in despite,
Joying thou canst with malice kill delight,

When I (a poor fool made by thee) think joy
Doth flow, when thy fond shadows do destroy
My that-while senseless self, left free to thee.

But now do well, let me forever sleep,
And so forever that dear image keep,
Or still wake, that my senses may be free.

❀ ❀ ❀ ❀

17
Sweet shades, why do you seek to give delight
To me, who deem delight in this vile place
But torment, sorrow, and mine own disgrace
To taste of joy, or your vain pleasing sight?

Show them your pleasures who saw never night
Of grief, where joying's fawning, smiling face
Appears as day, where grief found never space
Yet for a sigh, a groan, or envy's spite.

But O, on me a world of woes do lie,
Or else on me all harms strive to rely,
And to attend like servants bound to me.

Heat in desire, while frosts of care I prove,
Wanting my love, yet surfeit do with love,
Burn, and yet freeze: better in hell to be.

❀ ❀ ❀ ❀

18
Which should I better like of, day or night?
Since all the day I live in bitter woe,
Enjoying light more clear, my wrongs to know,
And yet most sad, feeling in it all spite.

In night, when darkness doth forbid all light
Yet see I grief apparent to the show,
Followed by jealousy, whose fond tricks flow,
And on unconstant waves of doubt alight.

I can behold rage cowardly to feed
Upon foul error, which these humours breed,
Shame, doubt and fear, yet boldly will think ill.

All these in both I feel; then which is best,
Dark to joy by day, light in night oppressed?
Leave both, and end: these but each other spill.
❀ ❀ ❀ ❀

Song 3
Stay, my thoughts, do not aspire
To vain hopes of high desire;
See you not all means bereft
To enjoy? No joy is left,
Yet still methinks my thoughts do say,
Some hopes do live amid dismay.

Hope, then once more, hope for joy,
Bury fear which joys destroy;
Thought hath yet some comfort giv'n,
Which despair hath from us driv'n;
Therefore dearly my thoughts cherish,
Never let such thinking perish.

'Tis an idle thing to plain,
Odder far to die for pain;
Think, and see how thoughts do rise,
Winning where there no hope lies,
Which alone is lovers' treasure,
For by thoughts we love do measure.

Then, kind thought, my fancy guide,
Let me never hapless slide;
Still maintain thy force in me,
Let me thinking still be free,
Nor leave thy might until my death,
But let me thinking yield up breath.
❀ ❀ ❀ ❀

19
Come darkest night, becoming sorrow best,
Light, leave thy light, fit for a lightsome soul:
Darkness doth truly suit with me oppressed,
Whom absence power doth from mirth control.

The very trees with hanging heads condole
Sweet summer's parting, and, of leaves distressed
In dying colours make a grief-full role,
So much, alas, to sorrow are they pressed.

Thus of dead leaves her farewell carpet's made;
Their fall, their branches, all their mournings prove,
With leafless, naked bodies, whose hues vade
From hopeful green, to wither in their love.

If trees and leaves, for absence, mourners be,
No marvel that I grieve, who like want see.
❀ ❀ ❀ ❀

20
The sun which glads the earth at his bright sight,
When in the morn he shows his golden face,
And takes the place from tedious drowsy night,
Making the world still happy in his grace,

Shows happiness remains not in one place,
Nor may the heavens alone to us give light,
But hide that cheerful face, though no long space,
Yet long enough for trial of their might.

But never sunset could be so obscure,
No desert ever had a shade so sad,
Nor could black darkness ever prove so bad
As pains which absence makes me now endure.

The missing of the sun awhile makes night,
But absence of my joy sees never light.
❀ ❀ ❀ ❀

21
When last I saw thee, I did not thee see,
It was thine image, which in my thoughts lay
So lively figured, as no time's delay
Could suffer me in heart to parted be;

And sleep so favourable is to me,
As not to let thy loved remembrance stray,
Lest that I, waking, might have cause to say,
There was one minute found to forget thee.

Then since my faith is such, so kind my sleep
That gladly thee presents into my thought,
And still true-lover-like thy face doth keep,
So as some pleasure shadow-like is wrought:

Pity my loving, nay, of conscience, give
Reward to me, in whom thyself doth live.
❋ ❋ ❋ ❋

22
Like to the Indians scorchèd with the sun
The sun which they do as their god adore:
So am I used by love, for evermore
I worship him, less favours have I won.

Better are they who thus to blackness run,
And so can only whiteness want deplore:
Than I who pale and white am with grief's store,
Nor can have hope, but to see hopes undone.

Besides their sacrifice received in sight
Of their chosen saint, mine hid as worthless rite,
Grant me to see where I my offerings give.

Then let me wear the mark of Cupid's might,
In heart, as they in skin of Phoebus' light,
Not ceasing offerings to love while I live.
❋ ❋ ❋ ❋

23
When everyone to pleasing pastime hies,
Some hunt, some hawk, some play, while some delight
In sweet discourse, and music shows joy's might;
Yet I my thoughts do far above these prize.

The joy which I take is, that free from eyes
I sit, and wonder at this day-like night,

So to dispose themselves, as void of right,
And leave true pleasure for poor vanities.

If hawk, my mind at wishèd end doth fly;
Discourse, I with my spirit talk, and cry
While others music choose as greatest grace.

O God, say I, can these fond pleasures move,
Or music be but in sweet thoughts of love?
❋ ❋ ❋ ❋

24
Once did I hear an agèd father say
Unto his son, who with attention hears
What age and wise experience ever clears
From doubts of fear or reason to betray,

'My son,' said he, 'behold thy father grey;
I once had, as thou hast, fresh tender years,
And like thee sported, destitute of fears;
But my young faults made me too soon decay.

'Love once I did, and like thee feared my love,
Led by the hateful thread of jealousy:
Striving to keep, I lost my liberty,
And gained my grief, which still my sorrows move.

'In time shun this; to love is no offence,
But doubt in youth, in age breeds penitence.'
❋ ❋ ❋ ❋

Song 4
Sweetest love return again,
Make not too long stay
Killing mirth and forcing pain,
Sorrow leading way:
Let us not thus parted be,
Love and absence ne'er agree.

But since you must needs depart,
And me hapless leave,

In your journey take my heart,
Which will not deceive:
Yours it is, to you it flies,
Joying in those lovèd eyes.

So in part we shall not part,
Though we absent be;
Time nor place nor greatest smart
Shall my bands make free:
Tied I am, yet think it gain;
In such knots I feel no pain.

But can I live, having lost
Chiefest part of me?
Heart is fled, and sight is crossed:
These my fortunes be.
Yet dear heart go, soon return:
As good there, as here to burn.

❋ ❋ ❋ ❋

25
Poor eyes be blind, the light behold no more,
Since that is gone which is your dear delight,
Ravished from you by greater pow'r and might,
Making your loss a gain to others' store.

O'erflow and drown, till sight to you restore
That blessèd star, and, as in hateful spite,
Send forth your tears in floods, to kill all sight
And looks, that lost wherein you joyed before.

Bury these beams which in some kindled fires,
And conquered have, their love-burnt hearts' desires
Losing, and yet no gain by you esteemed;

Till that bright star do once again appear,
Brighter than Mars when he doth shine most clear,
See not then by his might be you redeemed.

❋ ❋ ❋ ❋

26

Dear, cherish this, I and with it my soul's will,
Nor for it ran away do it abuse:
Alas, it left poor me, your breast to choose,
As the blessed shrine where it would harbour still.

Then favour show, and not unkindly kill
The heart which fled to you, but do excuse
That which for better, did the worse refuse,
And pleased I'll be, though heartless my life spill.

But if you will be kind, and just indeed,
Send me your heart, which in mine's place shall feed
On faithful love to your devotion bound;

There shall it see the sacrifices made
Of pure and spotless love which shall not vade
While soul and body are together found.

❀ ❀ ❀ ❀

27

Fie, tedious hope, why do you still rebel?
Is it not yet enough you flattered me,
But cunningly you seek to use a spell
How to betray; must these your trophies be?

I looked from you far sweeter fruit to see,
But blasted were your blossoms when they fell,
And those delights expected from hands free,
Withered and dead, and what seemed bliss proves hell.

No town was won by a more plotted sleight
Than I by you, who may my fortune write
In embers of that fire which ruined me:

Thus, hope, your falsehood calls you to be tried.
You're loth, I see, the trial to abide;
Prove true at last, and gain your liberty.

❀ ❀ ❀ ❀

28

Grief, killing grief, have not my torments been
Already great and strong enough, but still
Thou dost increase, nay glory in, my ill,
And woes new past, afresh new woes begin?

Am I the only purchase thou canst win?
Was I ordained to give despair her fill,
Or fittest I should mount misfortune's hill,
Who in the plain of joy cannot live in?

If it be so, grief come as welcome guest,
Since I must suffer for another's rest;
Yet this, good grief, let me entreat of thee:

Use still thy force, but not from those I love
Let me all pains and lasting torments prove;
So I miss these, lay all thy weights on me.

❀ ❀ ❀

29

Fly hence, O joy, no longer here abide:
Too great thy pleasures are for my despair
To look on; losses now must prove my fare
Who, not long since, on better fare relied.

But fool, how oft had I heav'n's changing spied
Before of mine own fate I could have care,
Yet now, past time I can too late beware,
When nothing's left but sorrows faster tied.

While I enjoyed that sun whose sight did lend
Me joy, I thought that day could have no end:
But soon a night came clothed in absence dark,

Absence more sad, more bitter than is gall,
Or death when on true lovers it doth fall,
Whose fires of love, disdain rest's poorer spark.

❀ ❀ ❀

30
You blessèd shades, which give me silent rest,
Witness but this when death hath closed mine eyes,
And separated me from earthly ties,
Being from hence to higher place addressed,

How oft in you I have lain here oppressed,
And have my miseries in woeful cries
Delivered forth, mounting up to the skies
Yet helpless back returned to wound my breast,

Which wounds did but strive how to breed more harm
To me, who can be cured by no one charm
But that of love, which yet may me relieve;

If not, let death my former pains redeem,
My trusty friends, my faith untouched esteem,
And witness I could love, who so could grieve.
❀ ❀ ❀ ❀

Song 5
Time, only cause of my unrest,
By whom I hoped once to be blessed,
How cruel art thou turned,
That first gav'st life unto my love,
And still a pleasure not to move
Or change, though ever burned;

Have I thee slacked, or left undone
One loving rite, and so have won
Thy rage or bitter changing,
That now no minutes I shall see
Wherein I may least happy be,
Thy favours so estranging?

Blame thyself and not my folly,
Time gave time but to be holy;
True love such ends best loveth.
Unworthy love doth seek for ends,
A worthy love but worth pretends,
Nor other thoughts it proveth.

Then stay thy swiftness, cruel Time,
And let me once more blessèd climb
To joy, that I may praise thee:
Let me, pleasure sweetly tasting,
Joy in love, and faith not wasting,
And on fame's wings I'll raise thee;

Never shall thy glory dying
Be until thine own untying,
That time no longer liveth;
'Tis a gain such time to lend,
Since so thy fame shall never end,
But joy for what she giveth.
❀ ❀ ❀ ❀

31
After long trouble in a tedious way
Of love's unrest, laid down to ease my pain,
Hoping for rest, new torments I did gain,
Possessing me, as if I ought t'obey,

When Fortune came, though blinded, yet did stay,
And in her blessèd arms did me enchain;
I, cold with grief, thought no warmth to obtain,
Or to dissolve that ice of joy's decay,

Till, 'Rise,' said she, 'Reward to thee doth send
By me, the servant of true lovers, joy;
Banish all clouds of doubt, all fears destroy,
And now on fortune, and on love depend.'

I her obeyed, and rising felt that love
Indeed was best, when I did least it move.
❀ ❀ ❀ ❀

32
How fast thou fliest, O time, on love's swift wings,
To hopes of joy, that flatters our desire,
Which to a lover still contentment brings;
Yet, when we should enjoy, thou dost retire.

Thou stay'st thy pace, false time, from our desire,
When to our ill thou hast'st with eagle's wings,
Slow only to make us see thy retire
Was for despair and harm, which sorrow brings.

O slack thy pace, and milder pass to love,
Be like the bee, whose wings she doth but use
To bring home profit, master's good to prove,
Laden and weary, yet again pursues.

So lade thyself with honey of sweet joy,
And do not me (the hive of love) destroy.

❀ ❀ ❀ ❀

33
How many eyes (poor Love) hast thou to guard
Thee from thy most desirèd wish and end?
Is it because some say thou'rt blind that, barred
From sight, thou shouldst no happiness attend?

Who blame thee so, small justice can pretend,
Since 'twixt thee and the sun no question hard
Can be, his sight but outward, thou canst bend
The heart, and guide it freely; thus, unbarred

Art thou, while we, both blind and bold, oft dare
Accuse thee of the harms ourselves should find:
Who, led with folly and by rashness blind,
Thy sacred pow'r do with a child's compare.

Yet Love, this boldness pardon: for admire
Thee sure we must, or be born without fire.

❀ ❀ ❀ ❀

34
Take heed mine eyes, how you your looks do cast,
Lest they betray my heart's most secret thought:
Be true unto yourselves, for nothing's bought
More dear than doubt, which brings a lover's fast.

Catch you all watching eyes, ere they be past,
Or take yours, fixed where your best love hath sought
The pride of your desires; let them be taught
Their faults, for shame they could no truer last.

Then look, and look with joy, for conquest won
Of those that searched your hurt in double kind;
So you kept safe, let them themselves look blind,
Watch, gaze, and mark, till they to madness run;

While you, mine eyes, enjoy full sight of love,
Contented that such happinesses move.

❀ ❀ ❀ ❀

35
False hope, which feeds but to destroy, and spill
What it first breeds; unnatural to the birth
Of thine own womb, conceiving but to kill,
And plenty gives to make the greater dearth.

So tyrants do who, falsely ruling earth,
Outwardly grace them, and with profit's fill
Advance those who appointed are to death,
To make their greater fall to please their will.

Thus shadow they their wicked vile intent,
Colouring evil with a show of good,
While in fair shows their malice so is spent:
Hope kills the heart, and tyrants shed the blood.

For hope deluding brings us to the pride
Of our desires, the farther down to slide.

❀ ❀ ❀ ❀

36
How well, poor heart, thou witness canst I love,
How oft my grief hath made thee shed for tears,
Drops of thy dearest blood, and how oft fears
Borne, testimony of the pains I prove;

What torments hast thou suffered, while above
Joy thou tortured wert with racks which longing bears;
Pinched with desires which yet but wishing rears,
Firm in my faith, in constancy to move.

Yet is it said, that sure love cannot be
Where so small show of passion is descried,
When thy chief pain is, that I must it hide
From all save only one, who should it see.

For know, more passion in my heart doth move,
Than in a million that make show of love.

❈ ❈ ❈ ❈

Song 6
You happy blessèd eyes,
Which in that ruling place
Have force both to delight, and to disgrace,
Whose light allures and ties
All hearts to your command:
O, look on me, who do at mercy stand.

'Tis you that rule my life,
'Tis you my comforts give,
Then let not scorn to me my ending drive;
Nor let the frowns of strife
Have might to hurt those lights
Which while they shine they are true love's delights.

See but when night appears,
And sun has lost his force,
How his loss doth all joy from us divorce;
And when he shines, and clears
The heav'ns from clouds of night,
How happy then is made our gazing sight.

But more than sun's fair light
Your beams do seem to me,
Whose sweetest looks do tie and yet make free;
Why should you then so spite
Poor me, as to destroy
The only pleasure that I taste of joy?

Shine then, O dearest lights,
With favour and with love,
And let no cause your cause of frownings move;
But as the soul's delights
So bless my then-blessed eyes,
Which unto you their true affection ties.

Then shall the sun give place
As to your greater might,
Yielding that you do show more perfect light.
O then but grant this grace
Unto your love-tied slave,
To shine on me, who to you all faith gave.

And when you please to frown,
Use your most killing eyes
On them who in untruth and falsehood lies,
But, dear, on me cast down
Sweet looks, for true desire,
That banish do all thoughts of feignèd fire.

❀ ❀ ❀

37

Night, welcome art thou to my mind distressed,
Dark, heavy, sad, yet not more sad than I:
Never couldst thou find fitter company
For thine own humour than I, thus oppressed.

If thou beest dark, my wrongs still unredressed
Saw never light, nor smallest bliss can spy;
If heavy, joy from me too fast doth hie,
And care outgoes my hope of quiet rest.

Then now in friendship join with hapless me,
Who am as sad and dark as thou canst be,
Hating all pleasure or delight of life;

Silence, and grief, with thee I best do love,
And from you three I know I cannot move:
Then let us live companions without strife.

❀ ❀ ❀

38
What pleasure can a banished creature have
In all the pastimes that invented are
By wit or learning, absence making war
Against all peace that may a biding crave?

Can we delight but in a welcome grave
Where we may bury pains, and so be far   ♪
From loathèd company, who always jar
Upon the string of mirth that pastime gave?

The knowing part of joy is deemed the heart;
If that be gone, what joy can joy impart,
When senseless is the feeler of our mirth?

No, I am banished, and no good shall find,
But all my fortunes must with mischief bind,
Who but for misery did gain a birth.
❋ ❋ ❋ ❋

39
If I were giv'n to mirth, 'twould be more cross
Thus to be robbed of my chiefest joy,
But silently I bear my greatest loss;
Who's used to sorrow, grief will not destroy.

Nor can I, as those pleasant wits, enjoy
My own framed words, which I account the dross
Of purer thoughts, or reckon them as moss,
While they, wit-sick, themselves to breathe employ.

Alas, think I, your plenty shows your want,
For where most feeling is, words are more scant.
Yet pardon me, live, and your pleasure take;

Grudge not if I, neglected, envy show;
'Tis not to you that I dislike do owe,
But, crossed myself, wish some like me to make.
❋ ❋ ❋ ❋

40
It is not love which you poor fools do deem,
That doth appear by fond and outward shows
Of kissing, toying, or by swearing's gloze:
O no, these are far off from love's esteem.

Alas, they are not such that can redeem
Love lost, or winning, keep those chosen blows;
Though oft with face and looks love overthrows,
Yet so slight conquest doth not him beseem.

'Tis not a show of sighs or tears can prove
Who loves indeed, which blasts of feignèd love
Increase or die, as favours from them slide;

But in the soul true love in safety lies,
Guarded by faith, which to desert still hies;
And yet kind looks do many blessings hide.
✳ ✳ ✳ ✳

41
You blessèd stars which do heav'n's glory show,
And at your brightness make our eyes admire:
Yet envy not, though I on earth below
Enjoy a sight which moves in me more fire.

I do confess such beauty breeds desire,
You shine, and clearest light on us bestow,
Yet doth a sight on earth more warmth inspire
Into my loving soul, his grace to know.

Clear, bright and shining as you are, is this
Light of my joy, fixed steadfast, nor will move
His light from me, nor I change from his love,
But still increase, as th'height of all my bliss.

His sight gives life unto my love-ruled eyes,
My love content, because in his, love lies.
✳ ✳ ✳ ✳

42

If ever love had force in human breast,
If ever he could move in pensive heart,
Or if that he such pow'r could but impart
To breed those flames whose heat brings joy's unrest.

Then look on me: I am to these addressed,
I am the soul that feels the greatest smart,
I am that heartless trunk of heart's depart,
And I that one by love and grief oppressed.

None ever felt the truth of love's great miss
Of eyes, till I deprivèd was of bliss;
For had he seen, he must have pity showed;

I should not have been made this stage of woe,
Where sad disasters have their open show:
O no, more pity he had sure bestowed.

❋ ❋ ❋ ❋

Song 7

Sorrow, I yield, and grieve that I did miss:
Will not thy rage be satisfied with this?
As sad a devil as thee,
Made me unhappy be;
Wilt thou not yet consent to leave, but still
Strive how to show thy cursèd, dev'lish skill?

I mourn, and dying am; what would you more?
My soul attends, to leave this cursèd shore
Where harms do only flow,
Which teach me but to know
The saddest hours of my life's unrest,
And tired minutes with grief's hand oppressed.

Yet all this will not pacify thy spite:
No, nothing can bring ease but my last night.
Then quickly let it be,
While I unhappy see
That time, so sparing to grant lovers bliss,
Will see, for time lost, there shall no grief miss.

Nor let me ever cease from lasting grief,
But endless let it be, without relief,
To win again of love
The favour I did prove,
And with my end please him, since, dying, I
Have him offended, yet unwillingly.

❀ ❀ ❀ ❀

43

O dearest eyes, the lights and guides of love,
The joys of Cupid who, himself born blind,
To your bright shining doth his triumphs bind,
For in your seeing doth his glory move.

How happy are those places where you prove
Your heav'nly beams, which makes the sun to find
Envy and grudging, he so long hath shined,
For your clear lights to match his beams above.

But now, alas, your sight is here forbid,
And darkness must these poor lost rooms possess,
So be all blessèd lights from henceforth hid,
That this black deed of darkness have excess.

For why should heaven afford least light to those
Who for my misery such darkness chose?

❀ ❀ ❀ ❀

44

How fast thou hast'st, O Spring, with sweetest speed
To catch thy waters which before are run,
And of the greater rivers welcome won,
Ere these thy new-born streams these places feed.

Yet you do well, lest staying here might breed
Dangerous floods, your sweetest banks t'o'errun,
And yet much better my distress to shun,
Which makes my tears your swiftest course succeed;

But best you do when with so hasty flight
You fly my ills, which now myself outgo,

Whose broken heart can testify such woe
That, so o'ercharged, my life blood wasteth quite.

Sweet Spring, then keep your way, be never spent,
And my ill days, or griefs, asunder rent.
❈ ❈ ❈ ❈

45
Good now, be still, and do not me torment
With multitudes of questions, be at rest,
And only let me quarrel with my breast,
Which still lets in new storms my soul to rent.

Fie, will you still my mischiefs more augment?
You say I answer cross, I that confessed
Long since; yet must I ever be oppressed
With your tongue-torture which will ne'er be spent?

Well then, I see no way but this will fright
That devil speech: alas, I am possessed,
And mad folks senseless are of wisdom's right;

The hellish spirit, Absence, doth arrest
All my poor senses to his cruel might:
Spare me then till I am myself and blessed.
❈ ❈ ❈ ❈

46
Love, thou hast all, for now thou hast me made
So thine, as if for thee I were ordained;
Then take thy conquest, nor let me be pained
More in thy sun, when I do seek thy shade.

No place for help have I left to invade,
That showed a face where least ease might be gained;
Yet found I pain increase, and but obtained
That this no way was to have love allayed,

When hot and thirsty, to a well I came,
Trusting by that to quench part of my flame,
But there I was by love afresh embraced;

Drink I could not, but in it I did see
Myself a living glass as well as she,
For love to see himself in, truly placed.

❀ ❀ ❀

47

O stay, mine eyes, shed not these fruitless tears,
Since hope is past to win you back again
That treasure which, being lost, breeds all your pain;
Cease from this poor betraying of your fears.

Think this too childish is, for where grief rears
So high a pow'r for such a wretched gain,
Sighs nor laments should thus be spent in vain:
True sorrow never outward wailing bears.

Be ruled by me, keep all the rest in store,
Till no room is that may contain one more,
Then in that sea of tears drown hapless me,

And I'll provide such store of sighs, as part
Shall be enough to break the strongest heart;
This done, we shall from torments freed be.

❀ ❀ ❀

48

How like a fire doth love increase in me,
The longer that it lasts, the stronger still,
The greater, purer, brighter, and doth fill
No eye with wonder more; then hopes still be

Bred in my breast, when fires of love are free
To use that part to their best pleasing will,
And now impossible it is to kill
The heat so great, where love his strength doth see.

Mine eyes can scarce sustain the flames, my heart
Doth trust in them my passions to impart,
And languishingly strive to show my love;

My breath not able is to breathe least part
Of that increasing fuel of my smart;
Yet love I will, till I but ashes prove.

❋ ❋ ❋ ❋

Sonnet

Let grief as far be from your dearest breast
As I do wish, or in my hands to ease;
Then should it banished be, and sweetest rest
Be placed to give content by love to please.

Let those disdains which on your heart do seize
Doubly return to bring her soul's unrest,
Since true love will not that beloved displease,
Or let least smart to their minds be addressed;

But oftentimes mistakings be in love.
Be they as far from false accusing right,
And still truth govern with a constant might,
So shall you only wishèd pleasures prove.

And as for me, she that shows you least scorn,
With all despite and hate, be her heart torn.

❋ ❋ ❋ ❋

Song

O me, the time is come to part,
And with it my life-killing smart:
Fond hope leave me, my dear must go
To meet more joy, and I more woe.

Where still of mirth enjoy thy fill,
One is enough to suffer ill:
My heart so well to sorrow used
Can better be by new griefs bruised.

Thou whom the heav'ns themselves like made
Should never sit in mourning shade:
No, I alone must mourn and end,
Who have a life in grief to spend.

My swiftest pace, to wailings bent,
Shows joy had but a short time lent
To bide in me, where woes must dwell,
And charm me with their cruel spell.

And yet when they their witchcrafts try,
They only make me wish to die:
But ere my faith in love they change,
In horrid darkness will I range.

❀ ❀ ❀ ❀

Song
Say Venus how long have I loved, and served you here,
Yet all my passions scorned or doubted, although clear?
Alas, think love deserveth love, and you have loved:
Look on my pains, and see if you the like have proved.
Remember then you are the goddess of desire,
And that your sacred pow'r hath touched and felt this fire.

Persuade these flames in me to cease, or them redress
In me, poor me, who storms of love have in excess.
My restless nights may show for me, how much I love,
My sighs unfeigned can witness what my heart doth prove,
My saddest looks do show the grief my soul endures,
Yet all these torments from your hands no help procures.

Command that wayward child your son to grant your right,
And that his bow and shafts he yield to your fair sight,
To you who have the eyes of joy, the heart of love,
And then new hopes may spring, that I may pity move:
Let him not triumph that he can both hurt and save,
And more, brag that to you yourself a wound he gave.

Rule him, or what shall I expect of good to see,
Since he that hurt you, he alas may murder me?

❀ ❀ ❀ ❀

Song
I, that am of all most crossed,
Having, and that had, have lost,
May with reason thus complain,
Since love breeds love, and love's pain.

That which I did most desire
To allay my loving fire,
I may have, yet now must miss,
Since another ruler is.

Would that I no ruler had,
Or the service not so bad,
Then might I with bliss enjoy
That which now my hopes destroy.

And that wicked pleasure got,
Brings with it the sweetest lot:
I, that must not taste the best,
Fed, must starve, and restless rest.
* * * *

Song
Love as well can make a biding
In a faithful shepherd's breast
As in princes', whose thoughts sliding
Like swift rivers never rest.

Change, to their minds, is best feeding,
To a shepherd all his care,
Who, when his love is exceeding,
Thinks his faith his richest fare;

Beauty, but a slight inviting,
Cannot stir his heart to change;
Constancy, his chief delighting,
Strives to flee from fancies strange;

Fairness to him is no pleasure,
If in other than his love;
Nor can esteem that a treasure
Which in her smiles doth not move.

This a shepherd once confessed,
Who loved well but was not loved;
Though with scorn and grief oppressed,
Could not yet to change be moved.

But himself he thus contented,
While in love he was accursed:
This hard hap he not repented,
Since best lovers speed the worst.
❀ ❀ ❀

Song
Dearest, if I, by my deserving,
May maintain in your thoughts my love,
Let me it still enjoy,
Nor faith destroy,
But pity love where it doth move.

Let no other new love invite you
To leave me who so long have served,
Nor let your pow'r decline,
But purely shine
On me, who have all truth preserved;

Or had you once found my heart straying,
Then would I not accuse your change,
But being constant still,
It needs must kill
One whose soul knows not how to range.

Yet may you love's sweet smiles recover,
Since all love is not yet quite lost,
But tempt not love too long,
Lest so great wrong
Make him think he is too much crossed.
❀ ❀ ❀

Song
Fairest and still truest eyes,
Can you the lights be, and the spies
Of my desires?
Can you shine clear for love's,
And yet the breeders be of spite
And jealous fires?

Mark what looks you do behold
Such as by jealousy are told
They want your love;
See how they sparkle in distrust
Which by a heat of thoughts unjust
In them do move.

Learn to guide your course by art,
Change your eyes into your heart
And patient be,
Till fruitless jealousy gives leave
By safest absence to receive
What you would see;

Then let love his triumph have
And suspicion such a grave
As not to move,
While wished freedom brings that bliss,
That you enjoy what all joy is,
Happy to love.

❀ ❀ ❀ ❀

Sonnet 1
In night yet may we see some kind of light,
When as the moon doth please to show her face
And in the sun's room yields her light and grace,
Which otherwise must suffer dullest night.

So are my fortunes, barred from true delight,
Cold and uncertain, like to this strange place,
Decreasing, changing in an instant space,
And even at full of joy turned to despite.

Justly on Fortune was bestowed the wheel,
Whose favours fickle and unconstant reel,
Drunk with delight of change and sudden pain;

Where pleasure hath no settled place of stay,
But turning still, for our best hopes decay,
And this, alas, we lovers often gain.

❀ ❀ ❀ ❀

2
Love like a juggler comes to play his prize,
And all minds draw his wonders to admire,
To see how cunningly he, wanting eyes,
Can yet deceive the best sight of desire.

The wanton child, how he can feign his fire
So prettily, as none sees his disguise,
How finely do his tricks, while we fools hire
The badge and office of tyrannies!

For in the end, such juggling he doth make,
As he our hearts instead of eyes doth take;
For men can only by their sleights abuse

The sight with nimble and delightful skill;
But if he play, his gain is our lost will;
Yet childlike, we cannot his sports refuse.
❈ ❈ ❈ ❈

3
Most blessèd night, the happy time for love,
The shade for lovers, and their love's delight,
The reign of love for servants free from spite,
The hopeful season for joy's sports to move:

Now hast thou made thy glory higher prove
Than did the god whose pleasant reed did smite
All Argus' eyes into a deathlike night,
Till they were safe, that none could love reprove;

Now thou hast closed those eyes from prying sight,
That nourish jealousy more than joys right,
While vain suspicion fosters their mistrust,

Making sweet sleep to master all suspect,
Which else their private fears would not neglect,
But would embrace both blinded, and unjust.
❈ ❈ ❈ ❈

4

Cruel suspicion, O! be now at rest,
Let daily torments bring to thee some stay;
Alas, make not my ill thy easeful prey,
Nor give loose reins to rage, when love's oppressed.

I am by care sufficiently distressed;
No rack can stretch my heart more, nor a way
Can I find out for least content to lay
One happy foot of joy, one step that's blessed.

But to my end thou fliest with greedy eye,
Seeking to bring grief by base jealousy;
O, in how strange a cage am I kept in!

No little sign of favour can I prove
But must be weighed, and turned to wronging love,
And with each humour must my state begin.

❄ ❄ ❄ ❄

5

How many nights have I with pain endured,
Which as so many ages I esteemed,
Since my misfortune, yet no whit redeemed
But rather faster tied, to grief assured?

How many hours have my sad thoughts endured
Of killing pains? Yet is it not esteemed
By cruel Love, who might have these redeemed,
And all these years of hours to joy assured:

But, fond child, had he had a care to save
As first to conquer, this my pleasure's grave
Had not been now to testify my woe;

I might have been an image of delight,
As now a tomb for sad misfortune's spite,
Which Love unkindly for reward doth show.

❄ ❄ ❄ ❄

6

My pain, still smothered in my grievèd breast,
Seeks for some ease, yet cannot passage find
To be discharged of this unwelcome guest;
When most I strive, more fast his burdens bind.

Like to a ship on Goodwins' cast by wind,
The more she strives, more deep in sand is pressed,
Till she be lost, so am I, in this kind,
Sunk, and devoured, and swallowed by unrest,

Lost, shipwrecked, spoiled, debarred of smallest hope,
Nothing of pleasure left; save thoughts have scope,
Which wander may. Go then, my thoughts, and cry

Hope's perished, Love tempest-beaten, Joy lost.
Killing Despair hath all these blessings crossed,
Yet Faith still cries, Love will not falsify.
❀ ❀ ❀ ❀

7

An end, fond jealousy: alas, I know
Thy hiddenest and thy most secret art;
Thou canst no new invention frame, but part
I have already seen, and felt with woe.

All thy dissemblings which by feignèd show
Won my belief, while truth did rule my heart,
I with glad mind embraced, and deemed my smart
The spring of joy, whose streams with bliss should flow

I thought excuses had been reasons true,
And that no falsehood could of thee ensue,
So soon belief in honest minds is wrought;

But now I find thy flattery and skill,
Which idly made me to observe thy will:
Thus is my learning by my bondage bought.
❀ ❀ ❀ ❀

8

Poor Love in chains and fetters, like a thief,
I met led forth, as chaste Diana's gain,
Vowing the untaught lad should no relief
From her receive, who gloried in fond pain.

She called him thief; with vows he did maintain
He never stole, but some sad slight of grief
Had giv'n to those who did his pow'r disdain,
In which revenge, his honour, was the chief.

She said he murdered, and therefore must die;
He, that he caused but love, did harms deny.
But while she thus discoursing with him stood,

The nymphs untied him, and his chains took off,
Thinking him safe; but he, loose, made a scoff,
Smiling, and scorning them, flew to the wood.
❀ ❀ ❀ ❀

9

Pray do not use these words, 'I must be gone'.
Alas, do not foretell mine ills to come,
Let not my care be to my joys a tomb,
But rather find my loss with loss alone.

Cause me not thus a more distressèd one,
Not feeling bliss because of this sad doom
Of present cross, for thinking will o'ercome
And lose all pleasure, since grief breedeth none.

Let the misfortune come at once to me,
Nor suffer me with grief to punished be;
Let me be ignorant of mine own ill,

Than with the fore-knowledge quite to lose
That which, with so much care and pains, love chose
For his reward: but joy now, then mirth kill.
❀ ❀ ❀ ❀

10
Folly would needs make me a lover be,
When I did little think of loving thought,
Or ever to be tied, while she told me
That none can live but to these bands are brought.

I, ignorant, did grant, and so was bought,
And sold again to lovers' slavery;
The duty to that vanity once taught,
Such band is, as we will not seek to free.

Yet when I well did understand his might,
How he inflamed, and forced one to affect,
I loved and smarted, counting it delight
So still to waste, which reason did reject.

When love came blindfold, and did challenge me:
Indeed I loved, but, wanton boy, not he.
❀ ❀ ❀ ❀

Song
The springing time of my first loving
Finds yet no winter of removing,
Nor frosts to make my hopes decrease,
But with the summer still increase.

The trees may teach us love's remaining,
Who suffer change with little paining:
Though winter make their leaves decrease,
Yet with the summer they increase.

As birds by silence show their mourning
In cold, yet sing at spring's returning,
So may love, nipped awhile, decrease,
But as the summer soon increase.

Those that do love but for a season,
Do falsify both love and reason,
For reason wills, if love decrease,
It like the summer should increase.

❀ ❀ ❀ ❀

Song
Though love sometimes may be mistaken,
The truth yet ought not to be shaken,
Or though the heat awhile decrease,
It with the summer may increase.

And since the spring time of my loving
Found never winter of removing,
Nor frosts to make my hopes decrease,
Shall as the summer still increase.

Love, a child, is ever crying,
Please him, and he straight is flying,
Give him, he the more is craving,
Never satisfied with having.

His desires have no measure,
Endless folly is his treasure,
What he promiseth he breaketh,
Trust not one word that he speaketh.

He vows nothing but false matter,
And to cozen you he'll flatter,
Let him gain the hand, he'll leave you,
And still glory to deceive you.

He will triumph in your wailing,
And yet cause be of your failing:
These his virtues are, and slighter
Are his gifts, his favours lighter.

Feathers are as firm in staying,
Wolves no fiercer in their preying.
As a child then leave him crying,
Nor seek him, so giv'n to flying.

Being past the pains of love,
Freedom gladly seeks to move,
Says that love's delights were pretty,
But to dwell in them 'twere pity;

And yet truly says that love
Must of force in all hearts move,
But though his delights are pretty,
To dwell in them were a pity.

Let love slightly pass like love,
Never let it too deep move,
For though love's delights are pretty,
To dwell in them were great pity.

Love no pity hath of love,
Rather griefs than pleasures move,
So though his delights are pretty,
To dwell in them would be pity.

Those that like the smart of love,
In them let it freely move,
Else, though his delights are pretty,
Do not dwell in them, for pity.

O pardon, Cupid, I confess my fault:
Then mercy grant me in so just a kind,
For treason never lodgèd in my mind
Against thy might, so much as in a thought.

And now my folly have I dearly bought,
Nor could my soul least rest or quiet find
Since rashness did my thoughts to error bind,
Which now thy fury, and my harm, hath wrought.

I curse that thought and hand which that first framed
For which by thee I am most justly blamed;
But now that hand shall guided be aright,

And give a crown unto thy endless praise,
Which shall thy glory, and thy greatness raise
More than these poor things could thy honour spite.

❀ ❀ ❀ ❀

A Crown of Sonnets Dedicated to Love

In this strange labyrinth how shall I turn?
Ways are on all sides, while the way I miss:
If to the right hand, there in love I burn;
Let me go forward, therein danger is.

If to the left, suspicion hinders bliss;
Let me turn back, shame cries I ought return,
Nor faint, though crosses with my fortune kiss;
Stand still is harder, although sure to mourn.

Thus let me take the right, or left hand way,
Go forward, or stand still, or back retire:
I must these doubts endure without allay
Or help, but travail find for my best hire.

Yet that which most my troubled sense doth move,
Is to leave all, and take the thread of Love.
❀ ❀ ❀ ❀

2
Is to leave all, and take the thread of Love,
Which line straight leads unto the soul's content,
Where choice delights with pleasure's wings do move,
And idle fancy never room had lent.

When chaste thoughts guide us, then our minds are bent
To take that good which ills from us remove:
Light of true love brings fruit which none repent,
But constant lovers seek, and wish to prove.

Love is the shining star of blessing's light,
The fervent fire of zeal, the root of peace,
The lasting lamp, fed with the oil of right,
Image of faith, and womb for joy's increase.

Love is true virtue, and his ends delight;
His flames are joys, his bands true lovers' might.
❀ ❀ ❀ ❀

3

His flames are joys, his bands true lovers' might,
No stain is there, but pure, as purest white,
Where no cloud can appear to dim his light,
Nor spot defile, but shame will soon requite.

Here are affections tried by Love's just might,
As gold by fire, and black discerned by white,
Error by truth, and darkness known by light,
Where faith is valued for Love to requite.

Please him, and serve him, glory in his might,
And firm he'll be, as innocency white,
Clear as th'air, warm as sun's beams, as day light,
Just as truth, constant as fate, joyed to requite.

Then Love obey, strive to observe his might,
And be in his brave court a glorious light.
❀ ❀ ❀ ❀

4

And be in his brave court a glorious light:
Shine in the eyes of faith and constancy,
Maintain the fires of Love still burning bright,
Not slightly sparkling, but light flaming be,

Never to slack till earth no stars can see,
Till sun and moon do leave us to dark night,
And second chaos once again do free
Us and the world from all division's spite.

Till then, affections, which his followers are,
Govern our hearts, and prove his power's gain
To taste this pleasing sting, seek with all care,
For happy smarting is it, with small pain;

Such as, although it pierce your tender heart
And burn, yet burning you will love the smart.
❀ ❀ ❀ ❀

5

And burn, yet burning you will love the smart,
When you shall feel the weight of true desire,
So pleasing, as you would not wish your part
Of burden should be missing from that fire;

But faithful and unfeignèd heat aspire,
Which sin abolisheth, and doth impart
Salves to all fear, with virtues which inspire
Souls with divine love, which shows his chaste art,

And guide he is to joyings; open eyes
He hath to happiness, and best can learn
Us means how to deserve: this he descries,
Who, blind, yet doth our hiddenest thoughts discern.

Thus we may gain, since living in blessed Love,
He may our prophet and our tutor prove.
❋ ❋ ❋ ❋

6

He may our prophet and our tutor prove,
In whom alone we do this power find,
To join two hearts as in one frame to move,
Two bodies, but one soul to move the mind,

Eyes, which must care to one dear object bind,
Ears to each other's speech, as if above
All else they sweet and learnèd were; this kind
Content of lovers witnesseth true Love:

It doth enrich the wits, and make you see
That in yourself which you knew not before,
Forcing you to admire such gifts should be
Hid from your knowledge, yet in you the store.

Millions of these adorn the throne of Love,
How blessed be they then, who his favours prove.
❋ ❋ ❋ ❋

7

How blessèd be they then, who his favours prove,
A life whereof the birth is just desire,
Breeding sweet flame, which hearts invite to move
In these loved eyes which kindle Cupid's fire,

And nurse his longings with his thoughts entire,
Fixed on the heat of wishes formed by Love;
Yet whereas fire destroys, this doth aspire,
Increase, and foster all delights above.

Love will a painter make you, such as you
Shall able be to draw your only dear
More lively, perfect, lasting and more true
Than rarest workman, and to you more near.

These be the least, then all must needs confess,
He that shuns love doth love himself the less.
❀ ❀ ❀ ❀

8

He that shuns love doth love himself the less,
And cursèd he whose spirit not admires
The worth of love, where endless blessedness
Reigns, and commands, maintained by heav'nly fires

Made of virtue, joined by truth, blown by desires,
Strengthened by worth, renewed by carefulness,
Flaming in never-changing thoughts: briars
Of jealousy shall here miss welcomeness,

Nor coldly pass in the pursuits of love,
Like one long frozen in a sea of ice;
And yet but chastely let your passions move,
Nor thought from virtuous love your minds entice.

Never to other ends your fancies place,
But where they may return with honour's grace.
❀ ❀ ❀ ❀

9
But where they may return with honour's grace,
Where Venus' follies can no harbour win,
But chasèd are, as worthless of the face
Or style of Love, who hath lascivious been.

Our hearts are subject to her son, where sin
Never did dwell, or rest one minute's space;
What faults he hath, in her did still begin,
And from her breast he sucked his fleeting pace.

If lust be counted love, 'tis falsely named
By wickedness, a fairer gloss to set
Upon that vice which else makes men ashamed
In the own phrase to warrant, but beget

This child for love, who ought, like monster born,
Be from the court of Love and Reason torn.
❋ ❋ ❋ ❋

10
Be from the court of Love and Reason torn,
For Love in Reason now doth put his trust,
Desert and liking are together born
Children of Love and Reason, parents just.

Reason adviser is, Love ruler must
Be of the state, which crown he long hath worn,
Yet so, as neither will in least mistrust
The government where no fear is born of scorn.

Then reverence both their mights thus made of one,
But wantonness and all those errors shun,
Which wrongers be, impostures, and alone
Maintainers of all follies ill begun:

Fruit of a sour, and unwholesome ground,
Unprofitably pleasing, and unsound.
❋ ❋ ❋ ❋

11
Unprofitably pleasing, and unsound,
When heaven gave liberty to frail dull earth
To bring forth plenty that in ills abound,
Which ripest yet do bring a certain dearth.

A timeless and unseasonable birth,
Planted in ill, in worse time springing found,
Which hemlock-like might feed a sick-wit's mirth,
Where unruled vapours swim in endless round.

Then joy we not in what we ought to shun,
Where shady pleasures show, but true-born fires
Are quite quenched out, or by poor ashes won
Awhile to keep those cool and wan desires.

O no, let Love his glory have, and might
Be given to him, who triumphs in his right.
❀ ❀ ❀ ❀

12
Be given to him, who triumphs in his right,
Nor fading be, but like those blossoms fair
Which fall for good, and lose their colours bright,
Yet die not, but with fruit their loss repair.

So may Love make you pale with loving care,
When sweet enjoying shall restore that light
More clear in beauty than we can compare,
If not to Venus in her chosen night.

And who so give themselves in this dear kind,
These happinesses shall attend them, still
To be supplied with joys, enriched in mind,
With treasures of content, and pleasure's fill.

Thus Love to be divine doth here appear,
Free from all fogs, but shining fair and clear.
❀ ❀ ❀ ❀

13
Free from all fogs, but shining fair and clear,
Wise in all good, and innocent in ill,
Where holy friendship is esteemèd dear,
With truth in Love, and justice in our will.

In Love these titles only have their fill
Of happy life-maintainer, and the mere
Defence of right, the punisher of skill
And fraud; from whence directions doth appear.

To thee then, Lord commander of all hearts,
Ruler of our affections, kind and just,
Great King of Love, my soul from feignèd smarts
Or thought of change I offer to your trust.

This crown, myself, and all that I have more,
Except my heart, which you bestowed before.
❀ ❀ ❀ ❀

14
Except my heart, which you bestowed before,
And for a sign of conquest gave away
As worthless to be kept in your choice store,
Yet one more spotless with you doth not stay.

The tribute which my heart doth truly pay
Is faith untouched, pure thoughts discharge the score
Of debts for me, where constancy bears sway,
And rules as lord, unharmed by envy's sore.

Yet other mischiefs fail not to attend,
As enemies to you, my foes must be:
Cursed jealousy doth all her forces bend
To my undoing; thus my harms I see.

So though in love I fervently do burn,
In this strange labyrinth how shall I turn?
❀ ❀ ❀ ❀

Song 1
Sweet, let me enjoy thy sight
More clear, more bright than morning sun,
Which in spring-time gives delight
And by which summer's pride is won.
Present sight doth pleasures move,
Which in sad absence we must miss,
But when met again in love,
Then twice redoubled is our bliss.

Yet this comfort absence gives,
And only faithful loving tries,
That, though parted, love's force lives
As just in heart as in our eyes.
But such comfort banish quite,
Far sweeter is it, still to find
Favour in thy lovèd sight,
Which present smiles with joys combined.

Eyes of gladness, lips of love,
And hearts from passions not to turn,
But in sweet affections move
In flames of faith to live, and burn.
Dearest, then this kindness give,
And grant me life, which is your sight,
Wherein I more blessèd live,
Than gracèd with the sun's fair light.
❀ ❀ ❀ ❀

2
Sweet Silvia in a shady wood,
With her fair nymphs laid down,
Saw not far off where Cupid stood,
The monarch of love's crown,
All naked, playing with his wings,
Within a myrtle tree,
Which sight a sudden laughter brings,
His godhead so to see.

And fondly they began to jest,
With scoffing and delight,

Not knowing he did breed unrest,
And that his will's his right.
When he perceiving of their scorn,
Grew in such desp'rate rage,
Who, but for honour first was born,
Could not his rage assuage,

Till shooting of his murd'ring dart,
Which not long 'lighting was,
Knowing the next way to the heart,
Did through a poor nymph pass.
This shot, the others made to bow,
Besides all those to blame,
Who scorners be, or not allow
Of pow'rful Cupid's name.

Take heed then, nor do idly smile,
Nor love's commands despise,
For soon will he your strength beguile,
Although he want his eyes.

❀ ❀ ❀ ❀

3
Come, merry spring, delight us,
For winter long did spite us,
In pleasure still persever,
Thy beauties ending never:
Spring, and grow
Lasting so,
With joys increasing ever.

Let cold from hence be banished,
Till hopes from me be vanished,
But bless thy dainties, growing
In fullness freely flowing:
Sweet birds sing
For the spring
All mirth is now bestowing.

Philomel in this arbour
Makes now her loving harbour,

Yet of her state complaining,
Her notes in mildness straining,
Which, though sweet,
Yet do meet
Her former luckless paining.

❀ ❀ ❀

4
Lovers, learn to speak but truth,
Swear not, and your oaths forgo,
Give your age a constant youth,
Vow no more than what you'll do.

Think it sacrilege to break
What you promise shall in love,
And in tears what you do speak,
Forget not, when the ends you prove.

Do not think it glory is
To entice and then deceive,
Your chief honours lie in this:
By worth what won is, not to leave.

'Tis not for your fame to try
What we, weak, not oft refuse,
In our bounty our faults lie,
When you to do a fault will choose.

Fie, leave this, a greater gain
'Tis to keep when you have won,
Than what purchased is with pain,
Soon after in all scorn to shun.

For if worthless to be prized,
Why at first will you it move,
And if worthy, why despised?
You cannot swear, and lie, and love.

Love, alas, you cannot like,
'Tis but for a fashion moved,
None can choose and then dislike,
Unless it be by falsehood proved.

But your choice is, and your love,
How most number to deceive,
As if honour's claim did move
Like Popish law, none safe to leave.

Fly this folly, and return
Unto truth in love, and try,
None but martyrs happy burn,
More shameful ends they have that lie.

❊ ❊ ❊ ❊

1
My heart is lost, what can I now expect:
An ev'ning fair, after a drowsy day?
Alas, fond fancy, this is not the way
To cure a mourning heart, or salve neglect.

They who should help, do me and help reject,
Embracing loose desires and wanton play,
While wanton base delights do bear the sway,
And impudency reigns without respect.

O Cupid, let your mother know her shame,
'Tis time for her to leave this youthful flame
Which doth dishonour her, is age's blame,
And takes away the greatness of thy name.

Thou god of love, she only queen of lust,
Yet strives by weak'ning thee, to be unjust.

❊ ❊ ❊ ❊

2
Late in the forest I did Cupid see
Cold, wet and crying; he had lost his way,
And, being blind, was farther like to stray,
Which sight a kind compassion bred in me.

I kindly took and dried him, while that he,
Poor child, complained he starvèd was with stay,
And pined for want of his accustomed prey,
For none in that wild place his host would be.

I glad was of his finding, thinking sure
This service should my freedom still procure,
And in my arms I took him then unharmed,

Carrying him safe unto a myrtle bower,
But in the way he made me feel his pow'r,
Burning my heart, who had him kindly warmed.

✽ ✽ ✽ ✽

3
Juno, still jealous of her husband Jove,
Descended from above, on earth to try
Whether she there could find his chosen love,
Which made him from the heavens so often fly.

Close by the place where I for shade did lie
She chasing came, but when she saw me move,
'Have you not seen this way,' said she, 'to hie
One, in whom virtue never ground did prove?

'He, in whom love doth breed to stir more hate,
Courting a wanton nymph for his delight?
His name is Jupiter, my lord by fate,
Who for her leaves me, heav'n, his throne and light.'

'I saw him not,' said I, 'although here are
Many, in whose hearts love hath made like war.'

✽ ✽ ✽ ✽

4
When I beheld the image of my dear,
With greedy looks mine eyes would that way bend,
Fear and Desire did inwardly contend,
Fear to be marked, Desire to draw still near;

And in my soul a Spirit would appear,
Which boldness warranted, and did pretend
To be my Genius, yet I durst not lend
My eyes in trust, where others seemed so clear.

Then did I search from whence this danger rose,
If such unworthiness in me did rest,
As my starved eyes must not with sight be blessed,
When Jealousy her poison did disclose.

Yet in my heart, unseen of jealous eye,
The truer image shall in triumph lie.
❀ ❀ ❀

5
Like to huge clouds of smoke which well may hide
The face of fairest day, though for a while,
So wrong may shadow me, till truth do smile,
And justice, sun-like, hath those vapours tied.

O doting Time, canst thou for shame let slide
So many minutes, while ills do beguile
Thy age and worth, and falsehoods thus defile
Thy ancient good, where now but crosses bide?

Look but once up, and leave thy toiling pace,
And on my miseries thy dim eye place;
Go not so fast, but give my care some end,

Turn not thy glass, alas, unto my ill,
Since thou with sand it canst not so far fill,
But to each one my sorrows will extend.
❀ ❀ ❀

6
O! that no day would ever more appear,
But cloudy night to govern this sad place,
Nor light from heav'n these hapless rooms to grace,
Since that light's shadowed which my love holds dear.

Let thickest mists in envy master here,
And sun-born day for malice show no face,
Disdaining light, where Cupid and the race
Of lovers are despised, and shame shines clear.

Let me be dark, since barred of my chief light,
And wounding Jealousy commands by might,
But stage-play-like disguisèd pleasures give:

To me it seems, as ancient fictions make
The stars all fashions and all shapes partake,
While in my thoughts true form of love shall live.

❈ ❈ ❈ ❈

7

No time, no room, no thought or writing can
Give rest or quiet to my loving heart.
Or can my memory or fancy scan
The measure of my still renewing smart.

Yet would I not, dear Love, thou shouldst depart,
But let my passions, as they first began,
Rule, wound and please: it is thy choicest art
To give disquiet which seems ease to man.

When all alone, I think upon thy pain,
How thou dost travail our best selves to gain:
Then hourly thy lessons I do learn,

Think on thy glory, which shall still ascend
Until the world come to a final end,
And then shall we thy lasting pow'r discern.

❈ ❈ ❈ ❈

8

How glow-worm-like the sun doth now appear:
Cold beams do from his glorious face descend,
Which shows his days and force draw to an end,
Or that to leave-taking his time grows near.

This day his face did seem but pale, though clear;
The reason is, he to the north must lend
His light, and warmth must to that climate bend,
Whose frozen parts could not love's heat hold dear.

Alas, if thou, bright sun, to part from hence
Grieve so, what must I, hapless, who from thence,
Where thou dost go, my blessing shall attend?

Thou shalt enjoy that sight for which I die,
And in my heart thy fortunes do envy;
Yet grieve; I'll love thee, for this state may end.
❀ ❀ ❀ ❀

9
My muse, now happy, lay thyself to rest,
Sleep in the quiet of a faithful love,
Write you no more, but let the fancies move
Some other hearts; wake not to new unrest.

But if you study, be those thoughts addressed
To truth, which shall eternal goodness prove,
Enjoying of true joy, the most and best,
The endless gain which never will remove.

Leave the discourse of Venus and her son
To young beginners, and their brains inspire
With stories of great love, and from that fire
Get heat to write the fortunes they have won.

And thus leave off, what's past shows you can love,
Now let your constancy your honour prove.

1630

11. Diana Primrose

from *A Chain of Pearl, or A Memorial of the Peerless Graces,
and Heroic Virtues of Queen Elizabeth, of Glorious Memory.*

The first pearl: Religion
The goodliest pearl in fair Eliza's chain;
Is true Religion, which did chiefly gain

A royal lustre to the rest, and tied
The hearts of all to her when Mary died.
And though she found the realm infected much
With superstition, and abuses, such
As (in all humane judgement) could not be
Reformed without domestic mutiny,
And great hostility from Spain and France;
Yet she undaunted, bravely did advance
Christ's glorious ensign, maugre all the fears
Or dangers which appeared: and for ten years
She swayed the sceptre with a lady's hand,
Not urging any Romist in the land,
By sharp edicts the temple to frequent,
Or to partake the Holy Sacrament.
But factious Romanists not thus content,
Their agents to their Holy Father sent,
Desiring him, by solemn Bull, proclaim
Elizabeth an heretic, and name
Some other sovereign, which might erect
Their masking Mass, and hence forthwith eject
The Evangelical profession,
Which flourished under her protection.
The Pope to this petition condescends,
And soon his leaden Bull to England sends,
Which by one Felton, on the Bishop's Gate
Of London was affixed; but the state
For that high treason punished him with death,
That would dethrone his Queen, Elizabeth.
Yet was this ball of wildfire working still,
In many Romanists which had a will,
The present State and Government to change;
That they in all idolatry might range.
And hence it came that great Northumberland,
Associate with Earl of Westmoreland,
And many moe, their banners did display
In open field; hoping to win the day.
Against these rebels, noble Sussex went;
And soon their bloody purpose did prevent.
Westmoreland fled, Northumberland did die,
For that foul crime, and deep disloyalty;
Having engaged thousands in that cause.

After which time, the Queen made stricter laws.
Against recusants, and with lion's heart,
She banged the Pope, and took the gospel's part.
The Pope perceiving that his Bull was baited
In such rude sort, and all his hopes defeated,
Cries out to Spain for help; who takes occasion
Thereby t'attempt the conquest of this nation.
But such sage counsellors Eliza had;
As, though both Spain and Rome were almost mad
For grief and anger, yet they still did fail,
And against England never could prevail.

The fourth pearl: Temperance
The golden bridle of Bellerephon
Is Temperance, by which our passion,
And appetite we conquer and subdue
To reason's regiment: else may we rue
Our yielding to men's Siren-blandishments,
Which are attended with so foul events.
This pearl in her was so conspicuous,
As that the King her brother still did use,
To style her his 'sweet sister Temperance';
By which her much admired self-governance,
Her passions still she checked, and still she made
The world astonished, that so undismayed
She did with equal tenor still proceed
In one fair course, not shaken as a reed:
But built upon the rock of Temperance:
Not dazed with fear, not 'mazed with any chance;
Not with vain hope (as with an empty spoon)
Fed or allured to cast beyond the moon:
Not with rash anger to precipitate,
Not fond to love, nor too, too prone to hate:
Not charmed with parasites, or Siren's songs,
Whose hearts are poisoned, though their sugared tongues
Swear, vow, and promise all fidelity,
When they are brewing deepest villainy.
Not led to vain or too profuse expense,
Pretending thereby state magnificence:

Not spending on these momentany pleasures
Her precious time: but deeming her best treasures
Her subjects' love, which she so well preserved,
By sweet and mild demeanour, as it served
To guard her surer, than an army royal;
So true their loves were to her, and so loyal:
O Golden Age! O blessed and happy years!
O music sweeter than that of the spheres!
When prince and people mutually agree
In sacred concord, and sweet symphony!

The seventh pearl: Fortitude
This goodly pearl, is that rare Fortitude,
Wherewith this sacred princess was endued.
Witness her brave undaunted look, when Parry
Was fully bent she should by him miscarry:
The wretch confessed, that her great Majesty
With strange amazement did him terrify.
So heavenly-graceful, and so full of awe,
Was that Majestic Queen, which when some saw,
They thought an angel did appear: she shone
So bright, as none else could her paragon.
But that which doth beyond all admiration
Illustrate her, and in her, this whole nation;
Is that heroic march of hers and speech
At Tilbury, where she did all beseech
Bravely to fight for England, telling them
That what their fortune was, should hers be then.
And that with full resolve she thither came,
Ready to win, or quite to lose the game.
Which words delivered in most princely sort,
Did animate the army, and report
To all the world her magnanimity,
Whose haughty courage nought could terrify.
Well did she show, great Henry was her sire,
Whom Europe did for valour most admire,
'Mongst all the warlike princes which were then
Enthronised with regal diadem.

1642

12. Anne Stagg, et al.

*A True Copy of the Petition of the Gentlewomen, and
Tradesmen's wives, in and about the City of London. Delivered, to the
Honourable, the Knights, Citizens and Burgesses, of the House of
Commons in Parliament, the 4th of February, 1641.
Together with their several reasons why their sex ought thus to petition,
as well as the men; and the manner how both their petition and
reasons was delivered. Likewise the answer which
the Honourable Assembly sent to them by Mr Pym, as they stood
at the House door.*

To the Honourable knights, citizens and burgesses, of the House of Commons assembled in Parliament. The most humble petition of the gentlewomen, tradesmen's wives, and many others of the female sex, all inhabitants of the city of London, and the suburbs thereof.

With lowest submission, showing that we also with all thankful humility acknowledging the unwearied pains, care and great charge, besides hazard of health and life, which you the noble worthies of this honourable and renowned Assembly have undergone, for the safety both of Church and Commonwealth, for a long time already past; for which not only we your humble petitioners, and all well affected in this kingdom, but also all other good Christians are bound now and at all times to acknowledge; yet notwithstanding that many worthy deeds have been done by you, great danger and fear do still attend us, and will, as long as popish lords and superstitious bishops are suffered to have their voice in the House of Peers, and that accursed and abominable idol of the Mass suffered in the kingdom, and that arch-enemy of our prosperity and reformation lieth in the tower, yet not receiving his deserved punishment.

All these under correction, gives us great cause to suspect, that God is angry with us, and to be the chief causes why your pious endeavours for a further reformation proceedeth not with that success as you desire, and is most earnestly prayed for of all that wish well to true religion, and the flourishing estate both of King and kingdom; the insolencies of the papists and their abettors raiseth a just fear and suspicion of sowing sedition, and breaking out into bloody persecution in this kingdom, as they have done in Ireland, the thoughts of which sad and barbarous events maketh our tender hearts to melt within us, forcing us humbly to petition to this honourable Assembly, to make safe provision for yourselves and us, before it be too late.

And whereas we, whose hearts have joined cheerfully with all those petitions which have been exhibited unto you in the behalf of the purity of religion, and the liberty of our husbands, persons, and estates, recounting ourselves to have an interest in the common privileges with them, do with the same confidence assure ourselves to find the same gracious acceptance with you, for easing of those grievances, which in regard of our frail condition, do more nearly concern us, and do deeply terrify our souls: our domestical dangers with which this kingdom is so much distracted, especially growing on us from those treacherous and wicked attempts already are such, as we find ourselves to have as deep a share as any other.

We cannot but tremble at the very thoughts of the horrid and hideous facts which modesty forbids us now to name, occasioned by the bloody wars in Germany, his Majesty's late Northern Army, how often did it affright our hearts, whilst their violence began to break out so furiously upon the persons of those, whose husbands or parents were not able to rescue: we wish we had no cause to speak of those insolencies, and savage usage and unheard of rapes, exercised upon our sex in Ireland, and have we not just cause to fear they will prove the forerunners of our ruin, except Almighty God by the wisdom and care of this Parliament be pleased to succour us, our husbands and children, which are as dear and tender unto us, as the lives and blood of our hearts, to see them murthered and mangled and cut in pieces before our eyes, to see our children dashed against the stones, and the mother's milk mingled with the infant's blood, running down the streets; to see our houses on flaming fire over our heads: oh how dreadful would this be! We thought it misery enough (though nothing to that we have just cause to fear) but few years since for some of our sex, by unjust divisions from their bosom comforts, to be rendered in a manner widows, and the children fatherless, husbands were imprisoned from the society of their wives, even against the laws of God and Nature; and little infants suffered in their fathers banishments: thousands of our dearest friends have been compelled to fly from Episcopal persecutions into desert places amongst wild beasts, there finding more favour than in their native soil, and in the midst of all their sorrows, such hath the pity of the prelates been, that our cries could never enter into their ears or hearts, nor yet through multitudes of obstructions could never have access or come nigh to those Royal mercies of our most gracious Sovereign, which we confidently hope, would have relieved us: but after all these pressures ended, we humbly signify, that our present fears are, that unless the blood-thirsty faction of the papists and prelates be hindered in their designs, ourselves here in England, as well as they in Ireland, shall be exposed to that misery which is more intolerable than that which is already past, as namely to the rage not of men alone, but of devils incarnate, (as we may so say) besides the thraldom of our souls and consciences in matters concerning God, which of all things are most dear unto us.

Now the remembrance of all these fearful accidents aforementioned, do strongly move us from the example of the woman of Tekoah [2 Sam. 14:1–21] to fall submissively at the feet of his Majesty, our dread Sovereign, and cry help O King, help O ye the noble worthies now sitting in Parliament: And we humbly beseech you, that you will be a means to his Majesty and the House of Peers, that they will be pleased to take our heart breaking grievances into timely consideration, and to add strength and encouragement to your noble endeavours, and further that you would move his Majesty with our humble requests, that he would be graciously pleased according to the example of the good King Asa, to purge both the court and kingdom of that great idolatrous service of the Mass, which is tolerated in the Queen's court, this sin (as we conceive) is able to draw down a greater curse upon the whole kingdom, than all your noble and pious endeavours can prevent, which was the cause that the good and pious King Asa would not suffer idolatry in his own mother [1 Kings 15:11–13], whose example if it shall please his Majesty's gracious goodness to follow, in putting down popery and idolatry both in great and small, in court and in the kingdom throughout, to subdue the papists and their abettors, and by taking away the power of the prelates, whose government by long and woeful experience we have found to be against the liberty of our conscience and the freedom of the Gospel, and the sincere profession and practice thereof, then shall our fears be removed, and we may expect that God will pour down his blessings in abundance both upon his Majesty, and upon this Honourable Assembly, and upon the whole Land.

For which your new petitioners shall pray affectionately.

The Reasons follow.

It may be thought strange, and unbeseeming our sex to show ourselves by way of petition to this Honourable Assembly: but the matter being rightly considered, of the right and interest we have in the common and public cause of the Church, it will, as we conceive (under correction) be found a duty commanded and required.

First, because Christ hath purchased us at as dear a rate as he hath done men, and therefore requireth the like obedience for the same mercy as of men.

Secondly, because in the free enjoying of Christ in his own laws, and a flourishing estate of the Church and Commonwealth, consisteth the happiness of women as well as men.

Thirdly, because women are sharers in the common calamities that accompany both Church and Commonwealth, when oppression is exercised over the Church or kingdom wherein they live; and an unlimited power have been given to prelates to exercise authority over the consciences of women, as well as men; witness Newgate, Smithfield, and other places of persecution, wherein women as well as men have felt the smart of their fury.

Neither are we left without example in Scripture, for when the state of the Church, in the time of King Ahasuerus was by the bloody enemies thereof sought to be utterly destroyed, we find that Esther the Queen and her maids fasted and prayed [Esther 4:16], and that Esther petitioned to the King in the behalf of the Church: and though she enterprised this duty with the hazard of her own life, being contrary to the law to appear before the King before she were sent for [Esther 5 and 7–8], yet her love to the Church carried her thorow all difficulties, to the performance of that duty.

On which grounds we were emboldened to present our humble petition into this Honourable Assembly, not weighing the reproaches which may and are by many cast upon us, who (not well weighing the premises) scoff and deride our good intent. We do it not out of any self conceit, or pride of heart, as seeking to equal ourselves with men, either in authority or wisdom: but according to our places to discharge that duty we owe to God, and the cause of the Church, as far as lieth in us, following herein the example of the men, which have gone in this duty before us.

A relation of the manner how it was delivered,
with their answer, sent by Mr Pym.

This petition, with their reasons, was delivered the 4th of February 1641 by Mistress Anne Stagg, a gentlewoman and brewer's wife, and many others with her of like rank and quality, which when they had delivered it, after some time spent in reading of it, the Honourable Assembly sent them an answer by Mr Pym, which was performed in this manner.

Mr Pym came to the Commons' door, and called for the women, and spake unto them in these words: 'Good women, your petition and the reasons have been read in the House; and is very thankfully accepted of, and is come in a seasonable time: You shall (God willing) receive from us all the satisfaction which we can possibly give to your just and lawful desires. We entreat you to repair to your houses, and turn your petition which you have delivered here, into prayers at home for us; for we have been, are, and shall be (to our utmost power) ready to believe you, your husbands, and children, and to perform the trust committed unto us, towards God, our King and country, as becometh faithful Christians and loyal subjects.'

1648

13. Elizabeth Poole

A Vision: Wherein is Manifested the Disease and Cure of the Kingdom. Being the sum of what was lately delivered to the council of War, by E.P. touching the death of the King, &c.

'Sirs,

I have been (by the pleasure of the most High) made sensible of the distresses of this land, and also a sympathiser with you in your labours: for having sometimes read your *Remonstrance*, I was for many days made a sad mourner for her; the pangs of a travailing woman was upon me, and the pangs of death oft-times panging me, being a member in her body, of whose dying state I was made purely sensible. And after many days mourning, a vision was set before me, to show her cure, and the manner of it, by this similitude: a man who is a member of the Army, having sometimes much bewailed her state, saying, he could gladly be a sacrifice for her, and was set before me, presenting the body of the Army, and on the other hand, a woman crooked, sick, weak and imperfect in body, to present unto me, the weak and imperfect state of the kingdom. I having the gift of faith upon me for her cure was thus to appeal to the person, on the other hand, that he should improve his faithfulness to the kingdom, by using diligence for the cure of this woman, as I by the gift of faith on me should direct him. Nevertheless it is not the gift of faith in me, say I, nor the act of diligence in you but in dependence on the divine will, which calls me to believe, and you to act. Wherefore I being called to believe ought not to stagger, neither you being called to act should be slack. For look how far you come short of acting (as before the Lord for her cure) not according to the former rule by men prescribed for cure, but according to the direction of the gift of faith in me, so far shall you come short of her consolation; and look how far you shall act, as before the Lord, with diligence for her cure, you shall be made partakers of her consolation.'

She being after demanded, whether she had any direction to give the Council, she answered, no: for the present, for she was in this case presented to herself as the Church, which spirit is in you, and shall guide you.

'I am therefore to signify unto you, that there is but one step between you and restoration, the which whosoever taketh not warily shall stumble, and fall, and be taken, and that is this, you are to stand as in the presence of the Lord, to be dead unto all your own interests, lives, liberties, freedoms, or whatsoever you might call yours: yet pleading for them still with men, speaking to everyone in his own language, for they are your due with them; but except you are as ready to resign them up to the will of the eternal pleasure, as to plead them with men, you shall surely lose them: For he that will save his life shall lose it, and he that will lose it shall save it [Mark 8:35; Luke 9:24].

'The Lord hath a controversy with the great and mighty men of the Earth, with the Captains, and rulers, and Governors: You may be great and mighty upon the Earth, and maintain his controversy, but against the mighty men of the Earth is his controversy held, for as you are the potsherd of the Earth, he will surely break you to pieces, till there be not a shred left to carry coals on. The kingly power is undoubtedly fallen into your hands; therefore my advice is that you take heed to improve it for the Lord. You have justly blamed those who have gone before you, for betraying their trust therein. I speak not this as you are soldiers, but as the spirit of judgement and justice is most lively appearing in you, this is therefore the great work which lieth upon you, to become dead to every pleasant picture, which might present itself for your delight, that you perfectly dying in the will of the Lord, you might find your resurrection in him.'

She being afterwards asked by some of the Chief Officers whether she conceived they were called to deliver up the trust to them committed either to Parliament or people, she answered,

'No, for this reason, it being committed to their care and trust, it should certainly be required at their hands, but take them with you as younger brethren who may be helpful to you. Nevertheless know you are in the place of watchmen, wherefore slack not your watch over them: for the account of the Stewardship shall be required at your hands [Luke 16:2].

It was further said unto her,

'How then shall we be free from the aspersions of the people, who will be ready to judge that we improve this interest for our own ends?'

She answered,

'Set yourselves, as before the Lord, to discharge the trust committed to you, and trust him with your reward: I speak not this that you should be exalted above your brethren, but that you might stand in faithfulness to discharge your duty: For he that will save his life will lose it, and he that will lose it shall save it. You have been noblemen, behaving yourselves with much valour and courage (as amongst men) now therefore lose not your reward, for this will be the greatest piece of courage that ever you were made the examples of, if you shall be as well content to lose house, land, wife and children, or whatever you might call yours in divine will, as ever you were to lay down your lives in the field.'

'Dear sirs,

I have considered the agreement of the people that is before you, and I am very jealous lest you should betray your trust in it (inasmuch as the kingly power is fallen into your hands) in giving it up to the people; for thereby you give up the trust committed to you, and in so doing you will prove yourselves more treacherous than they that went before you, they being no ways able to improve it without you. You justly blame the King for betraying his trust, and the Parliament for betraying theirs: This is the great thing I have to say to you, "Betray not your trust."

'I have yet another message to show you, I know not what acceptance it made find with you, yet I am content, here it is, let it find what acceptance it may, I leave it with you.

'The Message is as followeth:

"Dear Sirs,

Having already found so free admission into your presences it hath given me the greater encouragement (though more peculiarly, the truth persuading me thereunto) to present you with my thoughts in these following lines. I am in divine pleasure made sensible of the might of the affairs which lie upon you; and the spirit of sympathy abiding in me, constraineth me to groan with you in your pains. You may remember I told you the kingly power is undoubtedly fallen into your hands, which power is to punish evil doers, and to praise them that do well. Now therefore my humble advice to you is, that you stand as in the awful presence of the most high Father, acting your parts before God and man, you stand in the place of interpreters, for many hard sayings present themselves to you, and will do, look for it. Wherefore, see that you give unto men the things that are theirs, and unto God the things that are His. It is true indeed, as unto men (I know I appeal by the gift of God upon me) the King is your father and husband, which you were and are to obey in the Lord, and no other way, for when he forgot his subordination to divine faithhood and headship, thinking he had begotten you a generation to his own pleasure, and taking you a wife for his own lusts, thereby is the yoke taken from your necks (I mean the neck of the spirit and law, which is the bond of your union, that the holy life in it might not be profaned, it being free and cannot be bound. For the law of the Spirit of life in Christ Jesus, hath freed us from the law of sin and of death [Rom. 8:2], for the letter of the law which speaketh to the flesh killeth, therefore you must suffer of men in the flesh, for the Lord's sake, that so dying to your own bodies (that is to all self interest in divine will) you might also receive your resurrection, for you must die before you can rise, you must lose your lives, interests, liberties, and all (before you can save them) casting your crown at the feet of the Lamb, who only is worthy, yet still pleading for them with men, for they are your due with them, a share they may not deny you. Blessed are the dead which die in the Lord: for they rest from their labours, and their works do follow them [Rev. 14:13].

'From your own labours, I wish you rest in the Lord, that the fruit of your labours, which is the life of your faith may follow you to prison, and to death. Know this, that true liberty either is not bound to anything, nor from anything, for it is subject to this or that (neither this nor that in divine will) nevertheless as from the Lord you have all that you have, and are so to the Lord, you owe all that you have, and are for his name sake. So from the King in subordination.

'You have all that you have and are, and also in subordination you owe him all that you have and are, and although he would not be your father and husband, subordinate, but absolute, yet know that you are for the Lord's sake to honour his person. For he is the father and husband of your bodies, as unto men, and therefore your right cannot be without him, as unto men. I know and am very sensible, that no small strait lieth upon you in respect of securing his person (for the manifold conceived inconveniences following, and necessities of evil event) in respect of raising more wars, and also other things well known to you which will present themselves unpossible for you to avoid, nevertheless, this is my humble and hearty prayer to the everlasting Father (which I present to you in words, that you may be edified thereby). Remember I said, everlasting Father, for so we shall best know him for our consolation; that it might please him of his infinite, eternal life and goodness to grant you a sure and certain knowledge of this, that all things which are impossible with men (at the utmost extent of impossibility) are possible with him, who only saith it, and it cometh to pass, the Lord of hosts, the God of the whole earth, who commandeth all hosts of men, Angels and Devils, whose eyes run to and fro throughout the face of the whole earth, to show himself strong in the behalf of all those that trust in him. Wherefore put your swords into his hands for your defence, and fear not to act the part of Abigail, seeing Nabal hath refused it (by appropriating his goods to himself) in relieving David and his men in their distress [1 Sam. 25]; it was to her praise, it shall be to yours, fear it not:

'Only consider that as she lifted not her hand against her husband to take his life, no more do ye against yours. For as the Lord revenged his own cause on him, he shall do on yours. For vengeance is mine, I will repay it, saith the Lord [Rom. 12:19], who made him the Saviour of your body, though he hath profaned his Saviourship. Stretch not forth the hand against him. For know this, the conquest was not without divine displeasure, whereby kings came to reign, though through lust they tyrannised: which God excuseth not, but judgeth; and his judgements are fallen heavy, as you see, upon Charles your Lord. Forget not your pity towards him, for you were given him an helper in the body of the people, which people are they that agreed with him to subject unto the punishment of evil doers, and the praise of them that do well, which law is the spirit of your union. And although this bond be broken on his part, you never heard that a wife might put away her husband, as he is the head of her body, but for the Lord's sake suffereth his terror to her flesh, though she be free in the spirit to the Lord; and he being incapable to act as her husband, she acteth in his stead; and having the spirit of union abiding in her, she considereth him in his temptations, as tempted with him. And if he will usurp over her, she appealeth to the Fatherhood for her offence, which is the spirit of justice, and is in you. For I know no power in England to whom it is committed, save yourselves (and the present Parliament) which are to act in the Church of Christ, as she by the gift of faith upon her, shall be your guide for the cure of her body, that you might therefore commit an unsound member to Satan (though the head) as it is flesh; that the spirit might be saved in the day of the Lord (I believe). And accordingly you may hold the hands of your husband, that he pierce not your bowels with a knife or sword to take your life. Neither may you take his, I speak unto you as men, fathers, and brethren in the Lord (who are to walk by this rule). Whatsoever you would that men should do unto you, do ye the same unto them [Matt. 7:12]. I know it would affright you to be cut off in your iniquity; but O, how fame would you have your iniquity taken away. Consider also others in their amazement; I know you have said it, and I believe, that if you could see suitable sorrow for so great offence, you should embrace it. I beseech you in the bowels of love, for there it is I plead with you, look upon the patience of God towards you, and see if it will not constrain you to forbearance for his sake. I know the spirit of sanctity is in you; and I know as well the spirit of bondage holdeth you oft-times, that you cannot but groan for deliverance. Wherefore I beseech you for the Lord's sake, whose I am, and whom I serve in the spirit, that you let not go the Vision which I showed you concerning the cure of England, as it was presented to me, wherein the party acting, being first required to stand, as in the

awful presence of God, and to act for her cure, according to the direction
which he should receive from the Church, by the gift of faith upon her: (act
he must) but not after any former rule by men prescribed for cure, but after
the rule of the gift of faith) which I humbly beseech the Almighty Lord to
establish in you.

'I rest,

'Your servant in the Church and Kingdom of Christ.

Elizabeth Poole.'

After the delivery of this, she was asked, whether she spake against the
bringing of him to trial, or against their taking of his life. She answered,

'Bring him to his trial, that he may be convicted in his conscience, but
touch not his person.'

1654

14. Anna Trapnel

*Strange and Wonderful News From Whitehall: or the Mighty Visions
proceeding from Mistress Anna Trapnel to diverse Colonels, Ladies and
gentlewomen, concerning the government of the commonwealth of
England, Scotland, and Ireland; and her revelations touching his
highness the Lord Protector, and the army. With her Declaration
touching the state affairs of Great Britain; even from the death of the
late King Charles, to the dissolution of the last Parliament.
And the manner how she lay eleven days, and twelve nights in a trance,
without once taking any sustenance, except a cup of small beer once
in 24 hours; during which time, she uttered many things herein
mentioned, relating to the governors, churches, ministry, universities,
and all the three nations; full of wonder and admiration,
for all that shall read and peruse the same.*

Upon the seventh day of the eleventh month called January, being the sixth
day of the week, or Friday, Mr Powel, Minister of the Gospel in Wales,
being brought before the Council at Whitehall, to give an account of some
things by him delivered in his public exercises. Among many other friends
who came to see what would be done with him, there came a maid, Mrs
Anna Trapnel by name, who waiting in a little room near the Council door,
where there was a fire. Amongst many others she stayed for Mr Powel's

coming forth, and then intending to return home, she was beyond her own thoughts or intentions, having much trouble in her thoughts; and being as it were seized by the Lord, she was carried forth in a spirit of prayer and singing from noon till night, and went down into Mr Robert's lodging, who kept the ordinary in Whitehall, and finding her natural strength going from her, she took her bed about eleven of the clock in the night, where she lay from that day being the seventh day of the month, to the nineteenth day of the same month, in all twelve days together. The first five days she neither eat nor drank, and the rest of the time, once in twenty-four hours; sometimes a very little toast in small beers; sometimes only chewed it, and took down the moisture; sometimes she drank of the small beer, and sometimes only washed her mouth therewith, and then cast it forth, lying in bed with her eyes shut, and her hands seldom seen to move. She delivered in that time many and various things, speaking every day three or four hours, and sometimes praying both night and day, and singing spiritual songs; which many eminent persons hearing of, amongst the rest, came Colonel Sydenham (a member of the Council) Colonel West, Colonel Bennet, with his wife, Colonel Bingham, the Lady Dercy, the Lady Vermuden, and diverse others; who heard her declare as followeth, to wit:

'That seven years since she being sick of a fever, and given over by all her friends as one not like to live, the Lord then gave her faith to believe from that Scripture, after two days I will revive thee, and the thirtieth day I will raise thee up, and thou shalt live in my sight. Which two days I understood to be two weeks that I should lie in that fever; and at that very time and hour that it took her, that very hour it left her; and accordingly from which time, the Lord make use of her for refreshing of afflicted ones, and such as were under temptation. And when that time was ended, she being in her chamber, desired of the Lord to know whether she had done that which was of, and from himself, reply was made to her, that she should approve her heart to God, and for that she had been faithful in a little, she should be made an instrument of much more, for particular souls shall not only have benefit by her, but the universality of Saints shall have discoveries of God through her. Whereupon she prayed that she might be led by the still waters, and honour God secretly, being conscious to herself of the deceitfulness of her own heart, looking upon herself as the worst amongst God's flock. Whereupon the Lord told her that out of the mouths of babes and sucklings he would perfect his praise [Psalms 8:2]. After which she had many visions and revelations touching the Government of the Nation, the Parliament, Army, and Ministry, and having fasted nine days, nothing coming within her lips, she had a most strange vision of horns [Dan. 7]. She saw four horns which were four powers. The first was that of the Bishops, which first horn she saw broken in two, and thrown aside. Then appeared the second horn, and joined to it an head, and although it seemed to be more white than the first, yet it endeavouring to get aloft it was suddenly pulled down and broken to pieces. The third horn had many splinters joined to it like to the scales of a fish, and this was presented to a Parliament consisting of many men, having very fair and plausible pretences of love. Yet this horn she saw broken to pieces, and so scattered that not so much as one bit remained. Then she saw the fourth horn, and that was very short, but very sharp, and full of variety of colours sparkling red and white, and it was said to her, that this last horn was different from the other three, because of great proud and swelling words, and great promises of kindness should go forth to it from all people, like unto that of Absolom, speaking good words to the people in the gate to draw their affections away from honest David [2 Sam. 15:1–13]. After this she had a vision, wherein she saw many oaks, with spreading branches full of leaves. And presently she saw a very goodly tree for stature and completeness every way, before which great tree the rest of the oaks crumbled to dust, which she perceiving, desired Scripture to make known to her the vision. Whereupon reply was made in the first of Isaiah: They shall be confounded in the oaks which they have chosen [Isaiah 1:29].

Another vision she had two nights before the Lord Protector was proclaimed, at which time she saw a glorious throne with winged Angels flying before the throne, and crying, 'Holy, holy, holy, unto the Lord; the great one is coming down with terror to the enemies, and glory and deliverance to the sincere, and them that are upright in the earth.' In another vision she saw a great company of little children walking on the earth, and a light shining round about them, and a very glorious person in the midst of them, with a crown on his head, speaking these words: 'These will I honour with my reigning presence in the midst of them, and the oppressor shall die in the wilderness.'

When she was at Whitehall she saw as it were great darkness on the earth, and a marvellous dust like unto a thick mist, or smoke, ascending upward from the earth; and at a little distance a great company of cattle, some like bulls, some like oxen, and some lesser cattle, their faces and heads like men, having on either side their heads a horn. For the foremost, his countenance was perfectly like unto —'s and on a sudden there was a great shout of those that followed him, he being singled out alone, and the foremost and he looking back they bowed themselves unto him, and leaped up from the earth and showed much joy that he was become their Supreme. And immediately they fawning upon him, he seemed to run at her; and as he was near to her breast with his horn, an hand and arm grasped her ground, and a voice said to her, 'I will be thy safety'; and then he ran at many precious saints that stood in his way, and that durst look boldly in his face, he gave them many pushes, scratching them with his horns, and driving them into several houses. He ran along still; at length there was a great silence, and suddenly there broke forth great fury in the earth, and they were presently scattered, their horns broken, and so tumbled into graves. With that she broke forth, and sang praise, and the Lord said to her, 'Mark that Scripture, three horns shall arise, and a fourth shall come out different from the former, which shall be more terrible to the saints than others that went before [Dan. 8:8–14]: though like a Lamb, as is spoken in the Revelations, in appearance a Lamb; but pushing with his horns, like a beast: being not only one, but many, and much strength joined together [Rev. 13:11–18].'

Upon the tenth of February or eleventh month, the relator came into the chamber where she lay, where he heard her making melody with a spiritual song, and after she had done singing, she broke forth into these and the like words: 'It is not all the force in the world that can strike one stroke against thine, but thou sufferest them to come forth to try thine. Oh that thine could believe thee for the breaking of thine enemies as well as for the binding up of thine own people, all things under the sun, all things before, in or round about you, shall work for your good, when you come to know more of the mystery and life of the Scriptures, how will you praise his Highness? The enemy is strong, Satan is strong, instruments are strong, temptations are strong. But what strengths are against thy flock, they cannot be without the lion, and lion-like creatures. But oh! If thy servants suffer, let them not suffer through passion, or rash words, but as lambs. There is a zeal which is but from nature, that a man's own spirit may prompt him to but the zeal of God is accompanied with meekness, humility, grief for Christ. And seeing thou hast taken thine handmaid into the mount, who can keep in the rushing wind? Who can rule the influences of the heavenly orison? Yea, who can stop thy Spirit? It is good to be in the territories, in the regions, where thou walkst before thy servant. O how glittering, how glorious are they. What sparklings are there if Thou hast yet a great gust to come upon the earth, a great wind that shall shake the trees that now appear upon the Earth, that are full of the leaves of profession; but they have nothing but outward beauty an outward flourish; but thy trees, oh Lord, are full of sap. A great number of people have said, 'O let our oaks stand, let them not be cut down.' But says the Lord, 'I will make you ashamed in the oaks that ye have chosen, and because ye will have those, I will now give you other oaks; and what are they? A first, a second, and a third power, and they are broken one after another. But oh thine own have had a great hand in these things: thine have said, 'We will have oaks and gardens, how have they run to and fro?' saith the Lord. 'And now I will give you gardens, but they shall have no springs in them; but they shall be as dry chopped ground; yea, as fallow-ground. What loveliness is there, to walk upon fallow ground? You may have stumbling walkings upon them: you shall have no green grass in these gardens. What have all the gardens of the Earth been? They have been as stumbling blocks to thine. But oh, thou wilt by these strange ways, draw up thine into thy upper and nether springs: thou hast deceived thy saints once more about these gardens. Let them now run after them no more, but be ashamed and abashed, we have hankered from mountain to hill. We have said 'Salvation is in this hill, and in that mountain' but let us not say so any longer. When we shall be drawn up to thee, then we shall prosper; and thou wilt give us a vineyard, and gardens, and fruitful trees of thine own, which shall abide.'

And after some repose she sang diverse hymns, or spiritual songs; and among other things spake as followeth:

'Lord, let it be founded in their ears, and let them mark, it will be as great superfluity as ever, as great lust, as great wickedness, as great enmity as ever; yea, and greater than before. Oh, they are all for themselves; and doth not Satan appear in their feasts, and in their garments, and in their locks. Yea, O Gideon, when in thine own family there are those that are naked and wanton, oh let not this be found in thy family. David had not such in his family; and if thou must rule the nation, then be sure to look into thine own family, and rule that. But perhaps thou mayst say thou canst not rule them. O then remember, what God said to Eli of old, because of his sons [1 Sam. 27–36]. How can any go and cry out to King Jesus, if he have him not in his own bosom? But oh, he is a sealed one, then how beautiful will his walks be; and if the spirit of Christ reign in his soul, then he may reign for Christ; otherwise not. Therefore, you doubting Christians, have a care that you have courage given into your hearts, before you go out to plead against Antichrist, the Devil and wickedness, and come, you Army-men, and acquaint yourselves with the Lord Jehovah, for if you have not acquaintance with him, then all you have is nothing. Oh do justice, and do it for justice' sake, and not for by-ends or respects: And then, oh Gideon, who art in the highest place, thou art not only to do justice thyself, but thou art to see justice done in all places, courts, or councils, and committees, that they may not feed upon the poor. Thou art not only to receive pleasures at home, but to establish righteousness abroad. Oh by your diligence make it manifest that you love justice and mercy, as you seem to do. Oh remember Absolom, who was of a fair and gentle courage, and of a lovely nature, but it was to steal away the hearts of the people from his father David. But God forbid your Honour should be stained with the least guilt thereof.'

And thus soon after she ended in prayer and singing, having lain in bed eleven days and twelve nights together. After which time, she rose up in the morning, and the same day travelled on foot from Whitehall to Hackney; and from thence back to Mark Lane in London in health and strength.

1663

15. Mary Carleton

The Case of Madam Mary Carleton lately styled
'The German Princess', truly stated: with an historical relation
of her birth, education, and fortunes; in an appeal to
His Illustrious Highness Prince Rupert.

To His Most Illustrious Highness Prince Rupert, Count Palatine of the Rhine, And Duke of Cumberland, & c.

Great Prince,

To whom should the injured innocence of a foreign and desolate woman address itself but to your noble and merciful protection, who with the majestical glories of your relation to this crown, have most condescending compassions to the distressed and low estate of the afflicted.

For when I considered the general report of this your generosity and clemency even in the greatest incitements of passion, amidst the victorious progress of your arms, I could not but presume your Highness would open your ears to the complaints of an abused woman, in a case wherein the laws are altogether as silent, as in the loudest and clamorous noise of the war.

Besides, the different necessity of my cause, and the vindication of it, did inevitably put me upon your Highness's patronage. I am traduced and calumniated as an impostor (and the scandal continues after all the umbrages of it are vanished) and that I am not a German, nor so well descended there as I have alleged, and do and will maintain. Therefore to your Highness as the sacred and fittest sanctuary of this truth I have betook myself; whose excellent purity I do so revere and honour, that I would not soil it with the least tincture of a pretence, or paint of falsehood for a world.

Your Highness drew your first princely breath, which hath since filled the trump of fame, within the limits of that circle of the Rhine, where I was born. And within the confines of your paternal dominions, my infant cries were to be heard; and therefore with all alacrity I submit my cause, and my stronger cries for justice to your Highness, who partakes equally of this and my country.

Notwithstanding, I should not have been so bold as to have given your Highness this trouble, but that I have been informed you have been graciously pleased to pity my ruins, and to express your resentment of those incivilities I have suffered. And indeed that with the just indignation of other noble persons, who are pleased to honour my desertion and privacy with their company, is the only support I have against those miseries I endure, the more unsupportable because irremediable by the laws of this kingdom made against *femes covert*.

I take not upon me to dispute the equity thereof, but in all submiss obedience do cast myself and my cause at your Highness's feet, most humbly requesting and beseeching your grace and favour in some extraordinary redress to be vouchsafed to

Your Highness's most obedient and most devoted servant, Mary Carleton.

❊ ❊ ❊ ❊

It will suffice, that I was liberally and honourably educated, and such principles laid, that I wonder at the superstructure of my fortune. I knew not what belonged to vulgar and plebeian customs or conditions, and they that idly tax my discourses and behaviour with mimic pedantry, know not the generous emanations of a right born soul. And so, that which probably makes me obnoxious to the censures of the multitude, as it hath to the hatred of my new relations, is the low spiritedness, and pitiful ignorance of such mechanic and base people.

I would not be thought to boast of any accomplishments, which some persons (who favour my distressed estate, and they are of honour also) do please to acknowledge in me, all the use I can make of them, shall serve only for an argument against that vile and impertinent falsehood, that I am of a most sordid and base extraction in this kingdom, no better than the daughter of a fiddler at Canterbury.

That blasphemous lie was first broached in an anonymous libel, entitled *The Lawyer's Clerk Trappanned by the Crafty Whore of Canterbury*, but at whose instigation I could never tell, nor did I make enquiry, but at last spontaneously the roguery discovered itself at my being in custody near Newgate, where I understood the Devil and necessity with the writer, and undertaker, were as instrumental as the Devil and covetousness, in the occasioner of that report. But that fellow is of so lewd and miserable an infamy, for such defamatory pamphlets, that his name will poison the eyes of the reader, and fester even my charity in forgiving him, to proceed.

The time of my deliberated departure being come, and other intervening accidents having confirmed me to the pursuance of that journey, some piece-meal rumours whereof have been scattered up and down, not far distant from the truth – namely constraint and awe of an unliked and unsuitable match, which the freedom of my soul most highly abominated and resented – I privately by night withdrew from my governess, and by the way of Utrecht, where I stayed a while incognito, thence passed to Amsterdam, and so to Rotterdam, I came to the Brill, and there took shipping for England, the Elysium of my wishes and expectations being in hope to find it a land of angels, but I perceive it now to be, as to me, a place of torments.

I am not single, or the first woman, that hath put herself upon such hazards, or pilgrimages, the stories of all times abound with such examples, enough to make up a volume. I might as well have given lustre to a romance as any of those supposed heroines: and since it is the method of those pieces, and the art of that way of writing to perplex and intricate the commencement and progress of such adventures, with unexpected and various difficulties and troubles, and at last bring them to the long desired fruition of their dear bought content, I am not altogether out of heart, but that Providence may have some tender and more courteous consideration of me. For I protest I know not what crime, offence or demerit of mine hath rendered her so averse and intractable as she hath proved to my designs.

Nor do the modern and very late times want examples of the like adventures. I could mention a princess, and great personage out of the North, who not long since came into my country, and hath passed two or three times between Italy and France, and keeps her design yet undiscovered, and is the only lady errant in the world. I could mention another of a far worse consequence in this country, a she-general, who followed the camp to the other world in America, & c. and was the occasion of the loss of the design. Mine compared with those are mere puny stories, and inconsiderable, I neither concerned my travail in negotiating peace, or carrying war, but was merely my own free agent.

Nor can I be blamed for this course, for besides the necessity and enforcements of forsaking my country, without running into a more unsupportable condition of marriage than this I am now in, (for my patience and suffering, and continence I have; I trust in my own power, and shall endeavour to keep them undisturbed and uncorrupted, whatever temptations or occasions, by reason of this unjust separation, now are, or shall be put upon me hereafter. But my life is not in my disposal or preservation, which I had certainly endangered at home, if I had been bedded to him whom my heart abhorred): and besides other reasons, which I cannot in prudence yet render to the world, the very civility and purity of my design, without any lustful or vicious appurtenant, would fairly excuse me.

What harm have I done in pretending to great titles? Ambition and affection of greatness to good and just purposes was always esteemed and accounted laudable and praiseworthy, and the sign and character of a virtuous mind, nor do I think it an unjust purpose in me to contrive my own advancement by such illustrious pretences as they say I made use of, to grant the question, that I am not so honourably descended as I insinuated to the catch-dolt my father-in-law, (which yet by their favour they shall first better and more evidently disprove than as yet they have done, before I relinquish my just claim to my honour) I think I do rather deserve commendation than reproach. If the best things are to be imitated, I had a good precept and warrant for my assumption of such a personage as they were willing to believe me to be. If indeed by any misbecoming act unhandsome and unbefitting such a person, I had profaned that quality, and bewrayed and discovered any inconsistent meanness therewith (as it was very difficult to personate greatness for so long a time without slips or mistakes) I had deserved to be severely punished and abominated by all gentlemen. Whereas after all these loads of imputations which my enemies have heaped upon me, I do with my acknowledgements to them for it, enjoy, and am happy in many of their loves and good estimation.

And I will yet continue the same respects, and make the world to know that there is no possibility of such perfections, without a more intent care and elegancy of learning, to which I have by great labour and industry attained. I need not therefore engage further in this preliminary part of my defence, only as an irrefragable confutation of the poorness of my birth, and in this kingdom, I would have my adversaries know, as some of them do, though they don't well understand, that the several languages I have ready and at my command, as the Greek, Latin, French, Italian, Spanish, English, and something of the Oriental tongues, all which I pronounce with a Dutch dialect and idiom, are not common and ordinary endowments of an English spinster, no not of the best rank of the city. And since I must praise myself, in short, I came not here to learn anything for use or ornament of a woman, but only the ways to a better fortune.

I come now to the matter of fact, the first place I touched at was Gravesend, where I arrived towards the end of March, and without any stay took a tide-boat, came to London in company with a parson or minister, who officiously, but I suppose out of design, gave me the trouble of his service and attendance to the Exchange Tavern right against the Stock, betwixt the Poultry and Cornhill, the house of one Mr King, not having any knowledge of the master or his acquaintance, and free, God knows, from any design, for I would have entered any other house if I had found the doors open, or could have raised the folks nearer to my landing, for I was distempered with the night's passage; but it was so early in the morning, five o'clock, that there was nobody stirring elsewhere, only here by mishap Mr King himself was up and standing at the bar, telling of brass farthings, whom the parson desired to fill a pint of wine, which he readily performed, and brought to a room behind the bar. While the wine was a drinking, (which was Rhenish wine, the compliment being put upon me by the parson as the fruit of my own happy country) Sir John very rudely began to accost me, and to offer some incivilities to me, which I found no other way to avoid, than by pretending want of rest to the master of the house, and acquainting him with my charge of jewels, and that I was, as I do justify myself to be, a person of quality. Hereupon a room was provided for me to repose myself in, and the clergyman took his leave with a troublesome promise of waiting upon me another day to give me a visit, which I was forced to admit, and to tell him, I would leave word wherever I went; but he considering as I suppose of the unfeasibleness of his desires, and the publicness of the place, neglected his promise and troubled me no more.

❋ ❋ ❋ ❋

So on Easter morning, with three coaches, in which with the bride and bridegroom were all the kindred that were privy to the business, and pretended a licence, they carried me to Clothfair by Smithfield, and in the Church of Great St Bartholomew's, married me by one Mr Smith, who was well paid for his pains. And now they thought themselves possessed of their hopes, but because they would prevent the noise and fame of their good fortune from public discourse, that no sinister accident might intervene before Mr Carleton had bedded me, offence being likely to be taken at Court, (as they whispered to themselves) that a private subject had married a foreign princess, they had before determined to go to Barnet, and thither immediately after the celebration of the marriage we were driven in the coaches, where we had a handsome treatment, and there we stayed Sunday and Monday, both which nights Mr Carleton lay with me, and on Tuesday morning we were married again, a licence being then obtained to make the match more fast and sure, at their instance with me to consent to it.

This being done, and their fears over, they resolved to put me in a garb befitting the estate and dignity they fancied I had; and they were so far possessed with a belief of it, that they gave out, I was worth no less than 80000li. *per annum*, and my husband, as I must now style him, published so much in a coffee-house; adding withal, to the extolling of his good hap, that there was a further estate but that it was my modesty or design to conceal it, and that he could not attribute his great fortune to anything but the Fates, for he had not anything to balance with the least of my estate and merits. So do conceited heights of sudden prosperity and greatness dazzle the eyes and judgement of the most, nor could this young man be much blamed for his vainglorious mistake.

My clothes being made at the charge of my father-in-law, and other fineries of the mode and fashion sent me by some of his kindred and friends – who prided themselves in this happy affinity, and who had an eye upon some advantages also, and therefore gave me this early bribe, as testimonies of their early respect – and as for jewels I had of mine own of all sorts, for necklaces, pendants and bracelets, of admirable splendour and brightness. I was in a prince-like attire, and a splendid equipage and retinue, accoutred for public view among all the great ladies of the court and the town on Mayday ensuing. At which time in my Lady Bludworth's coach, which the same friends procured for my greater accommodation, and accompanied with the same lady with footmen and pages, I rode to Hyde Park, in open view of that celebrious cavalcade and assembly, much gazed upon by them all, the eximiousness of my fortune drawing their eyes upon me; particularly that noble lady gave me precedence, and the right hand, and a neat treatment after our divertissement of turning up and down the park.

I was altogether ignorant of what estate my husband was, and therefore made no nicety to take those places his friends gave me, and if I be taxed for incivility herein, it was his fault that he instructed me no better in my quality, for I conceited still that he was some landed, honourable and wealthy man.

Things yet went fairly on, the same observances and distances continued, and lodgings befitting a person of quality taken for me in Durham Yard, at one Mr Green's, where my husband and I enjoyed one another with mutual complacency, till the return of the moneys out of Germany failing the day and their rich hopes, old Mr Carleton began to suspect he was deceived in his expectation, and that all was not gold that glistered. But to remove such a prejudice from himself, as if he were the author of those scandals that were now prepared against my innocence, a letter is produced, and sent from some then unknown hand, which reflected much upon my honour and reputation; and thereupon on the fifth or sixth of May ensuing, I was by a warrant dragged forth of my new lodgings, with all the disgrace and contumely that could be cast upon the vilest offender in the world, at the instigation of old Mr Carleton, who was the prosecutor, and by him and his agents divested and stripped of all my clothes, and plundered of all my jewels, and my money, my very bodice, and a pair of silk stockings, being also pulled from me, and in a strange array carried before a Justice.

❋ ❋ ❋ ❋

The fashions and customs here are much different from those of our country, where the wife shares an equal portion with her husband in all things of weal and woe, and can *liber intentare*, begin and commence, and finish a suit in her own name. They buy and sell, and keep accounts, manage the affairs of household, and the trade, and do all things relating to their several stations and degrees. I have heard and did believe the proverb, that England was a heaven for women, but I never saw that heaven described in its proper terms, for as to as much as I see of it, 'tis a very long prospect, and almost disappears to view. It is to be enjoyed but at second hand, and all by the husband's title. Quite contrary to the custom of the Russians, where it is a piece of their divinity; that because it's said that the Bishop must be the husband of one wife, they put out of orders, and from all ecclesiastical function such clergymen, who by the Canon being bound to be married, are by death deprived of their wives; so that their tenure to their livings and preferments clearly depends upon the welfare and long life of their yoke-fellows, in whose choice, as of such moment to their well-being, they are very curious, as they are afterwards in their care and preservation of them.

I could instance in many other customs of nearer nations, in respect to female right and propriety in their own dowers, as well as in their husbands' estates: but *cum fueris Romae, Romano vivite more*. I will not quarrel the English laws, which I question not are calculated and well accommodated to the genius and temper of the people.

While I mention these customs, I cannot forbear to complain of a very great rudeness and incivility to which the mass and generality of the English vulgar are most pronely inclined, that is, to hoot and hallow, and pursue strangers with their multitudes through the streets, pressing upon them even to the danger of their lives; and when once a cry, or some scandalous humour is bruited among them, they become brutes indeed. A barbarity I thought could not possibly be in this nation, whom I heard famed for so much civility and urbanity. This I experimented the other day in Fanchurch Street, as I was passing through it upon some occasion, which being noised and scattered among the prentices, I was forced to bethink of some shift and stratagem to avoid them: which was by putting my maid into a coach, that by good hap was at hand, and stepping into an adjoining tavern, which, the herd mistaking my maid for me and following the coach as supposing me there for the convenience thereof, gave me the opportunity of escaping from them. A regulation of this kind of uproar by some severe penalties, would much conduce not only to the honour of the government of the city, but the whole nation in general; having heard the French very much complain of the like injuries and affronts. But those to me I may justly place to my husband's account, who hath exposed me to the undeserved wonder, and to be a May-game to the town.

And to his debility and meanness of spirit, I am likewise beholding for some other scandalous libels and pasquils divulged upon this occasion of our marriage; chiefly for the ribaldry of some pitiful poetry, entitled, *A Westminster-wedding*, which equally reflects as much upon himself as me. This tameness of his doth hugely incense me; and I swear, were it not for the modesty of my sex, the bonds of which I will not be provoked to transgress, I would get satisfaction myself of those pitiful fellows, who by this impudent and saucy scribbling, do almost every day bespatter my honour. At least, I wonder my husband doth not vindicate himself, and assert his own individual reputation, having threatened so much in print against a civil person that formerly and first of all endeavoured to clear and justify mine.

But when I consider how apt his kindred are to return to their vomit of slandering me, and reckoning the nine days' wonder of their great cheat discovered is over, are like those that have eat shame and drank after it, I did the less wonder at his stupidity and senselessness of those indignities done him. And commonly those that have no regard to another's honour, have as little respect for their own; as he is master of another man's life, that is a contemner of his own.

I shall therefore omit all the subsequent sneaking lies, raised by the same kindred, when they saw their more mighty and potent accusations helped forward with such prejudices, noise and ostentation, were at once disappointed and blown to nothing. Such are those chimeras of their framing and fancying, that I was seen in man's apparel, with a sword and feather, in design to do mischief to somebody; and that I have used to do so (and so punctual are they in this lie, as to name both the time and place); that I resolved to set up a coffee-house; and at last to turn player or actor; with an hundred other slams to sully my name, and of a multitude of the like, to make one or other of those calumnies and reproaches to stick upon me.

Whereas on the contrary I do resolve, as soon as my cause is heard, and justice done me by the supreme power, if I cannot otherwise attain it, to retire and return back, though not immediately to my own home, yet to make such approaches at necessary distance for the present, that I might be in readiness and view of all transactions there, as soon as this bluster shall be so laid here, that I shall not fear the tail of this hurricane pursuing me. Yet shall I always have my heart and my arms open to Mr Carleton, as a person whom for his person and naturals I do and shall ever affect, as his wife and my husband, maugre all those practices (as for my part) of rendering us mutually hateful and suspect to each other.

1667

16. Katherine Philips

from *Poems*

*Upon the double murther of King Charles I,
in answer to a libellous copy of rhymes by
Vavasor Powell.*

I think not on the State, nor am concerned
Which way soever the great helm is turned:
But as that son whose father's danger nigh
Did force his native dumbness, and untie
The fettered organs; so this is a cause
That will excuse the breach of Nature's laws.
Silence were now a sin, nay passion now
Wise men themselves for merit would allow.
What noble eye could see (and careless pass)
The dying lion kicked by every ass?
Has Charles so broke God's Laws, he must not have
A quiet crown, nor yet a quiet grave?
Tombs have been sanctuaries; thieves lie there
Secure from all their penalty and fear.
Great Charles his double misery was this,
Unfaithful friends, ignoble enemies.
Had any heathen been this Prince's foe,
He would have wept to see him injured so.
His title was his crime, they'd reason good

To quarrel at the right they had withstood.
He broke God's laws, and therefore he must die;
And what shall then become of thee and I?
Slander must follow treason; but yet stay,
Take not our reason with our King away.
Though you have seized upon all our defence,
Yet do not sequester our common sense.
But I admire not this new supply:
No bounds will hold those who at sceptres fly.
Christ will be King, but I ne'er understood
His subjects built his kingdom up with blood,
Except their own; or that he would dispense
With his commands, though for his own defence.
Oh to what height of horror are they come
Who dare pull down a crown, tear up a tomb?

*To her Royal Highness the Duchess of York, on her
commanding me to send her some things that
I had written.*

To you whose dignity strikes us with awe,
And whose far greater judgement gives us law,
(Your mind being more transcendent than your state,
For while but knees to this, hearts bow to that),
These humble papers never durst come near,
Had not your pow'rful word bid them appear;
In which such majesty, such sweetness dwells,
As in one act obliges, and compels.
None can dispute commands vouchsafed by you.
What shall my fears then and confusion do?
They must resign, and by their just pretence
Some value set on my obedience.
For in religious duties, 'tis confessed,
The most implicit are accepted best.
If on that score Your Highness will excuse
This blushing tribute of an artless muse,
She may (encouraged by your least regard,
Which first can worth create, and then reward)
At modest distance with improvèd strains
That mercy celebrate which now she gains.

But should you that severer justice use,
Which these too prompt approaches may produce,
As the swift hind which hath escapèd long,
Believes a vulgar shot would be a wrong;
But wounded by a Prince falls without shame,
And what in life she loses, gains in fame:
So if a ray from you chance to be sent,
Which to consume, and not to warm, is meant;
My trembling muse at least more nobly dies,
And falls by that a truer sacrifice.

On the Death of the Queen of Bohemia.
Although the most do with officious heat
Only adore the living and the great;
Yet this Queen's merits fame so far hath spread,
That she rules still, though dispossessed and dead.
For losing one, two other crowns remained;
Over all hearts and her own griefs she reigned.
Two thrones so splendid, as to none are less
But to that third which she does now possess.
Her heart and birth Fortune so well did know,
That seeking her own fame in such a foe,
She dressed the spacious theatre for the fight,
And the admiring world called to the sight:
An army then of mighty sorrows brought,
Who all against this single virtue fought;
And sometimes stratagems, and sometimes blows,
To her heroic soul they did oppose:
But at her feet their vain attempts did fall,
And she discovered and subdued them all.
Till Fortune weary of her malice grew,
Became her captive and her trophy too:
And by too late a tribute begged t'have been
Admitted subject to so brave a Queen.
But as some hero who a field hath won,
Viewing the things he had so greatly done;
When by his spirit's flight he finds that he
With his own life must buy his victory,
He makes the slaughtered heap that next him lies

His funeral pile, and then in triumph dies:
So fell this royal dame, with conquering spent,
And left in every breast her monument;
Wherein so high an epitaph is writ,
As I must never dare to copy it.
But that bright angel which did on her wait,
In fifty years' contention with her fate,
And in that office did with wonder see
How great her troubles, how much greater she;
How she maintained her best prerogative,
In keeping still the power to forgive:
How high she did in her devotion go,
And how her condescension stooped as low;
With how much glory she had ever been
A daughter, sister, mother, wife, and queen;
Will sure employ some deathless muse to tell
Our children this instructive miracle,
Who may her sad illustrious life recite,
And after all her wrongs may do her right.

To Mr Henry Lawes

Nature, which is the vast creation's soul,
That steady curious agent in the whole,
The art of heaven, the order of this frame,
Is only number in another name.
For as some king conqu'ring what was his own,
Hath choice of several titles to his crown;
So harmony on this score now, that then,
Yet still is all that takes and governs men.
Beauty is but composure, and we find
Content is but the concord of the mind,
Friendship the unison of well-tuned hearts,
Honour the chorus of the noblest parts,
And all the world on which we can reflect
Music to th' ear, or to the intellect.
If then each man a little world must be,
How many worlds are copied out in thee,
Who art so richly formed, so complete

T'epitomize all that is good and great;
Whose stars this brave advantage did impart,
Thy nature's as harmonious as thy art?
Thou dost above the poets' praises live,
Who fetch from thee th' eternity they give.
And as true reason triumphs over sense,
Yet is subjected to intelligence:
So poets on the lower world look down,
But Lawes on them; his height is all his own.
For, like divinity itself, his lyre
Rewards the wit it did at first inspire.
And thus by double right poets allow
His and their laurel should adorn his brow.
Live then, great soul of nature, to assuage
The savage dullness of this sullen age.
Charm us to sense; for though experience fail
And reason too, thy numbers may prevail.
Then, like those ancients, strike, and so command
All nature to obey thy gen'rous hand.
None will resist but such who needs will be
More stupid than a stone, a fish, a tree.
Be it thy care our age to new-create:
What built a world may sure repair a State.

Friendship's Mystery; to my dearest Lucasia

1
Come, my Lucasia, since we see
   That miracles men's faith do move,
By wonder and by prodigy
   To the dull angry world let's prove
   There's a religion in our love.

2
For though we were designed t'agree,
   That Fate no liberty destroys,
But our election is as free
   As angels, who with greedy choice
   Are yet determined to their joys.

3

Our hearts are doubled by the loss,
    Here mixture is addition grown;
We both diffuse, and both engross:
    And we whose minds are so much one,
    Never, yet ever are alone.

4

We court our own captivity
    Than thrones more great and innocent:
'Twere banishment to be set free,
    Since we wear fetters whose intent
    Not bondage is, but ornament.

5

Divided joys are tedious found,
    And griefs united easier grow:
We are ourselves but by rebound,
    And all our titles shuffled so,
    Both princes, and both subjects too.

6

Our hearts are mutual victims laid,
    While they (such power in friendship lies)
Are altars, priests, and off'rings made:
    And each heart which thus kindly dies,
    Grows deathless by the sacrifice.

Content, To my dearest Lucasia.
1

    Content, the false world's best disguise,
    The search and faction of the wise,
    Is so abstruse and hid in night,
    That, like that fairy Red-cross Knight,
Who treacherous falsehood for clear truth had got,
Men think they have it when they have it not.

2

    For courts Content would gladly own,
    But she ne'er dwelt about a throne:
    And to be flattered, rich, and great,
    Are things which do men's senses cheat.
But grave experience long since this did see,
Ambition and Content would ne'er agree.

3

    Some vainer would Content expect
    From what their bright outsides reflect:
    But sure Content is more divine
    Than to be digged from rock or mine:
And they that know her beauties will confess,
She needs no lustre from a glittering dress.

4

    In mirth some place her, but she scorns
    Th'assistance of such crackling thorns,
    Nor owes herself to such thin sport,
    That is so sharp and yet so short:
And painters tell us they the same strokes place,
To make a laughing and a weeping face.

5

    Others there are that place Content
    In liberty from government:
    But whomsoe'er Passion deprave,
    Though free from shackles, he's a slave.
Content and bondage differ only then,
When we are chained by vices, not by men.

6

    Some think the camp Content does know,
    And that she fits o'th' victor's brow:
    But in his laurel there is seen
    Often a cypress-bough between.
Nor will Content herself in that place give,
Where noise and tumult and destruction live.

7

> But yet the most discreet believe,
> The schools this jewel do receive,
> And thus far's true without dispute,
> Knowledge is still the sweetest fruit.

But whilst men seek for truth they lose their peace;
And who heaps knowledge, sorrow doth increase.

8

> But now some sullen hermit smiles,
> And thinks he all the world beguiles,
> And that his cell and dish contain
> What all mankind wish for in vain.

But yet his pleasure's followed with a groan,
For man was never born to be alone.

9

> Content herself best comprehends
> Betwixt two souls, and they two friends,
> Whose either joys in both are fixed,
> And multiplied by being mixed:

Whose minds and interests are so the same;
Their griefs, when once imparted, lose that name.

10

> These far removed from all bold noise,
> And (what is worse) all hollow joys,
> Who never had a mean design,
> Whose flame is serious and divine,

And calm, and even, must contented be,
For they've both union and society.

11

> Then, my Lucasia, we who have
> Whatever love can give or crave;
> Who can with pitying scorn survey
> The trifles which the most betray;

With innocence and perfect friendship fired
By virtue joined, and by our choice retired.

12
    Whose mirrors are the crystal brooks,
    Or else each others' hearts and looks;
    Who cannot wish for other things
    Than privacy and friendship brings:
Whose thoughts and persons changed and mixed are one,
Enjoy Content, or else the world hath none.

A Dialogue of Absence 'twixt Lucasia and Orinda,
set by Mr Henry Lawes

Lucasia Say, my Orinda, why so sad?
Orinda Absence from thee doth tear my heart;
Which, since with thine it union had,
Each parting splits. **Lucasia** And can we part?
Orinda Our bodies must. **Lucasia** But never we:
Our souls, without the help of sense,
By ways more noble and more free
Can meet, and hold intelligence.
Orinda And yet those souls, when first they met,
Looked out at windows through the eyes.
Lucasia But soon did such acquaintance get,
Not Fate nor Time can them surprise.
Orinda Absence will rob us of that bliss
To which this friendship title brings:
Love's fruits and joys are made by this
Useless as crowns to captived kings.
Lucasia Friendship's a science, and we know
There contemplation's most employed.
Orinda Religion's so, but practick too,
And both by niceties destroyed.
Lucasia But who ne'er parts can never meet,
And so that happiness were lost.
Orinda Thus pain and death are sadly sweet,
Since health and heav'n such price must cost.
Chorus But we shall come where no rude hand shall sever,
And there we'll meet and part no more forever.

To the Excellent Mrs Anne Owen, upon her receiving the
name of Lucasia, and adoption into our Society,
December 28, 1651.

We are complete, and Fate hath now
No greater blessing to bestow:
Nay the dull world must now confess
We have all worth, all happiness.
Annals of State are trifles to our fame,
Now 'tis made sacred by Lucasia's name.

But as though through a burning-glass
The Sun more vigorous doth pass,
Yet still with general freedom shines;
For that contracts, but not confines:
So though by this her beams are fixèd here,
Yet she diffuses glory everywhere.

Her mind is so entirely bright,
The splendour would but wound our sight,
And must to some disguise submit,
Or we could never worship it.
And we by this relation are allowed
Lustre enough to be Lucasia's cloud.

Nations will own us now to be
A temple of divinity;
And pilgrims shall ten ages hence
Approach our tombs with reverence.
May then that time which did such bliss convey
Be kept by us perpetual Holy-day.

———

Wiston Vault

And why this vault and tomb? alike we must
Put off distinction, and put on our dust.
Nor can the stateliest fabric help to save
From the corruptions of a common grave;
Nor for the resurrection more prepare,
Than if the dust were scattered into air.
What then? Th'ambition's just, say some, that we

May thus perpetuate our memory.
Ah false vain task of art! Ah poor weak man!
Whose monument does more than's merit can:
Who by his friends' best care and love's abused,
And in his very epitaph accused:
For did they not suspect his name would fall,
There would not need an epitaph at all.
But after death too I would be alive,
And shall, if my Lucasia do, survive.
I quit these pomps of death, and am content,
Having her heart to be my monument:
Though ne'er stone to me, 'twill stone for me prove,
By the peculiar miracles of love.
There I'll inscription have which no tomb gives,
Not, 'Here Orinda lies', but 'Here she lives'.

Friendship in Emblem, or the Seal.
To my dearest Lucasia.

1
The hearts thus intermixèd speak
A love that no bold shock can break;
For joined and growing both in one,
Neither can be disturbed alone.

2
That means a mutual knowledge too;
For what is't either heart can do,
Which by its panting sentinel
It does not to the other tell?

3
That friendship hearts so much refines,
It nothing but itself designs:
The hearts are free from lower ends,
For each point to the other tends.

4
They flame, 'tis true, and several ways,
But still those flames do so much raise,

That while to either they incline
They yet are noble and divine.

5

From smoke or hurt those flames are free,
From grossness or mortality:
The heart (like Moses' bush presumed)
Warmed and enlightened, not consumed.

6

The compasses that stand above
Express this great immortal love;
For friends, like them, can prove this true,
They are, and yet they are not, two.

7

And in their posture is expressed
Friendship's exalted interest:
Each follows where the other leans,
And what each does, this other means.

8

And as when one foot does stand fast,
And t'other circles seeks to cast,
The steady part does regulate
And make the wand'rer's motion straight:

9

So friends are only two in this,
T'reclaim each other when they miss:
For whosoe'er will grossly fall,
Can never be a friend at all.

10

And as that useful instrument
For even lines was ever meant;
So friendship from good angels springs,
To teach the world heroic things.

11

As these are found out in design

To rule and measure every line;
So friendship governs actions best,
Prescribing unto all the rest.

12
And as in nature nothing's set
So just as lines in number met;
So compasses for these being made,
Do friendship's harmony persuade.

13
And like to them, so friends may own
Extension, not division:
Their points, like bodies, separate;
But head, like souls, knows no such fate.

14
And as each part so well is knit,
That their embraces ever fit:
So friends are such by destiny,
And no third can the place supply.

15
There needs no motto to the seal:
But that we may the mind reveal
To the dull eye, it was thought fit
That friendship only should be writ.

16
But as there are degrees of bliss,
So there's no friendship meant by this,
But such as will transmit to fame
Lucasia and Orinda's name.

To my Lucasia.
Let dull philosophers enquire no more
In nature's womb, or causes strive t'explore,
By what strange harmony and course of things
Each body to the whole a tribute brings;

What secret unions secret neighbourings make,
And of each other how they do partake.
These are but low experiments: but he
That nature's harmony entire would see,
Must search agreeing souls, sit down and view
How sweet the mixture is, how full, how true;
By what soft touches spirits greet and kiss,
And in each other can complete their bliss.
A wonder so sublime, it will admit
No rude spectator to contemplate it.
The object will refine, and he that can
Friendship revere, must be a noble man.
How much above the common rate of things
Must they then be from whom this union springs?
But what's all this to me, who live to be
Disprover of my own morality?
And he that knew my unimprovèd soul,
Would say I meant all friendship to control.
But bodies move in time, and so must minds;
And though th'attempt no easy progress finds,
Yet quit me not, lest I should desp'rate grow,
And to such friendship add some patience now.
O may good heav'n but so much virtue lend,
To make me fit to be Lucasia's friend!
But I'll forsake myself, and seek a new
Self in her breast that's far more rich and true.
Thus the poor bee unmarked doth hum and fly,
And droned with age would unregarded die,
Unless some lucky drop of precious gum
Do bless the insect with an amber tomb.
Then glorious in its funeral the bee
Gets eminence, and gets eternity.

To Mrs Mary Aubrey

Soul of my soul, my joy, my crown, my friend,
A name which all the rest doth comprehend;
how happy are we now, whose souls are grown
By an incomparable mixture one:
Whose well-acquainted minds are now as near
As love, or vows, or friendship can endear?

I have no thought but what's to thee revealed,
Nor thou desire that is from me concealed.
Thy heart locks up my secrets richly set,
And my breast is thy private cabinet.
Thou shed'st no tear but what my moisture lent,
And if I sigh, it is thy breath is spent.
United thus, what horror can appear
Worthy our sorrow, anger, or our fear?
Let the dull world alone to talk and fight,
And with their vast ambitions nature fright;
Let them despise so innocent a flame,
While envy, pride, and faction play their game:
But we by love sublimed so high shall rise,
To pity kings, and conquerors despise,
Since we that sacred union have engrossed
Which they and all the factious world have lost.

To Mrs M.A. at parting

1
I have examined and do find,
    Of all that favour me
There's none I grieve to leave behind
    But only only thee.
To part with thee I needs must die,
Could parting sep'rate thee and I.

2
But neither chance nor compliment
    Did element our love;
'Twas sacred sympathy was lent
    Us from the choir above.
That friendship Fortune did create,
Still fears a wound from Time or Fate.

3
Our changed and mingled souls are grown
    To such acquaintance now,
That if each would resume their own,
    Alas! We know not how.

We have each other so engrossed,
That each is in the union lost.

4

And thus we can no absence know,
    Nor shall we be confined;
Our active souls will daily go
    To learn each other's mind.
Nay, should we never meet to sense,
Our souls would hold intelligence.

5

Inspirèd with a flame divine
    I scorn to court a stay;
For from that noble soul of thine
    I ne'er can be away.
But I shall weep when thou dost grieve;
Nor can I die whilst thou dost live.

6

By my own temper I shall guess
    At thy felicity,
And only like my happiness
    Because it pleaseth thee.
Our hearts at any time will tell
If thou, or I, be sick, or well.

7

All honour sure I must pretend,
    All that is good or great;
She that would be Rosania's friend,
    Must be at least complete.
If I have any bravery,
'Tis cause I have so much of thee.

8

Thy leiger soul in me shall lie,
    And all thy thoughts reveal;
Then back again with mine shall fly,
    And thence to me shall steal.
Thus still to one another tend;
Such is the sacred name of friend.

9
Thus our twin-souls in one shall grow,
    And teach the world new love,
Redeem the age and sex, and show
    A flame fate dares not move:
And courting death to be our friend,
Our lives together too shall end.

10
A dew shall dwell upon our tomb
    Of such a quality,
That fighting armies, thither come,
    Shall reconcilèd be.
We'll ask no epitaph, but say
'Orinda and Rosania'.

To my dearest Antenor, on his parting.
Though it be just to grieve when I must part
With him that is the guardian of my heart;
Yet by an happy change the loss of mine
Is with advantage paid in having thine.
And I (by that dear guest instructed) find
Absence can do no hurt to souls combined.
As we were born to love, brought to agree
By the impressions of divine decree:
So when united nearer we became,
It did not weaken, but increase, our flame.
Unlike to those who distant joys admire,
But slight them when possessed of their desire.
Each of our souls did its own temper fit,
And in the other's mould so fashioned it,
That now our inclinations both are grown,
Like to our interests and persons, one;
And souls whom such an union fortifies,
Passion can ne'er destroy, nor fate surprise.
Now as in watches, though we do not know
When the hand moves, we find it still doth go:
So I, by secret sympathy inclined,
Will absent meet, and understand thy mind;

And thou at thy return shalt find thy heart
Still safe, with all the love thou didst impart.
For though that treasure I have ne'er deserved,
It shall with strong religion be preserved.
And besides this thou shalt in me survey
Thyself reflected while thou art away.
For what some forward arts do undertake,
The images of absent friends to make,
And represent their actions in a glass,
Friendship itself can only bring to pass,
That magic which both fate and time beguiles,
And in a moment runs a thousand miles.
So in my breast thy picture drawn shall be,
My guide, life, object, friend, and destiny:
And none shall know, though they employ their wit,
Which is the right Antenor, thou, or it.

To my Lucasia, in defence of declared Friendship

1

O my Lucasia, let us speak our love,
   And think not that impertinent can be,
Which to us both doth such assurance prove,
   And whence we find how justly we agree.

2

Before we knew the treasures of our love,
   Our noble aims our joys did entertain;
And shall enjoyment nothing then improve?
   'Twere best for us then to begin again.

3

Now we have gained, we must not stop, and sleep
   Out all the rest of our mysterious reign:
It is as hard and glorious to keep
   A victory, as it is to obtain.

4

Nay to what end did we once barter minds,
   Only to know and to neglect the claim?

Or (like some wantons) our pride pleasure finds
  To throw away the thing at which we aim.

5

If this be all our friendship does design,
  We covet not enjoyment then, but power:
To our opinion we our bliss confine,
  And love to have, but not to smell, the flower.

6

Ah then let misers bury thus their gold,
  Who though they starve no farthing will produce:
But we loved to enjoy and to behold,
  And sure we cannot spend our stock by use.

7

Think not 'tis needless to repeat desires;
  The fervent turtles always court and bill,
And yet their spotless passion never tires,
  But does increase by repetition still.

8

Although we know we love, yet while our soul
  Is thus imprisoned by the flesh we wear,
There's no way left that bondage to control,
  But to convey transactions through the ear.

9

Nay, though we read our passions in the eye,
  It will oblige and please to tell them too:
Such joys as these by motion multiply,
  Were't but to find that our souls told us true.

10

Believe not then, that being now secure
  Of either's heart, we have no more to do:
The spheres themselves by motion do endure,
  And they move on by circulation too.

11

And as a river, when it once hath paid
  The tribute which it to the ocean owes,

Stops not, but turns, and having curled and played
   On its own waves, the shore it overflows.

12

So the soul's motion does not end in bliss,
   But on herself she scatters and dilates,
And on the object doubles, till by this
   She finds new joys which that reflux creates.

13

But then because it cannot all contain,
   It seeks a vent by telling the glad news,
First to the heart which did its joys obtain,
   Then to the heart which did those joys produce.

14

When my soul then doth such excursions make,
   Unless thy soul delight to meet it too,
What satisfaction can it give or take,
   Thou being absent at the interview?

15

'Tis not distrust; for were that plea allowed,
   Letters and visits all would useless grow:
Love's whole expression then would be its cloud,
   And it would be refined to nothing so.

16

If I distrust, 'tis my own worth for thee,
   'Tis my own fitness for a love like thine;
And therefore still new evidence would see,
   T'assure my wonder that thou canst be mine.

17

But as the morning-sun to drooping flowers,
   As weary travellers a shade do find,
As to the parchèd violet evening-showers;
   Such is from thee to me a look that's kind.

18

But when that look is dressed in words, 'tis like
   The mystic pow'r of music's unison;

Which when the finger doth one viol strike,
   The other's string heaves to reflection.

19
Be kind to me, and just then to our love,
   To which we owe our free and dear converse;
And let not tract of time wear or remove
   It from the privilege of that commerce.

20
Tyrants do banish what they can't requite:
   But let us never know such mean desires;
But to be grateful to that love delight
   Which all our joys and noble thoughts inspires.

A Country-life
How sacred and how innocent
   A country-life appears,
How free from tumult, discontent,
   From flattery or fears!
This was the first and happiest life,
   When man enjoyed himself;
Till pride exchangèd peace for strife,
   And happiness for pelf.
'Twas here the poets were inspired,
   Here taught the multitude;
The brave they here with honour fired,
   And civilised the rude.
That Golden Age did entertain
   No passion but of love;
The thoughts of ruling and of gain
   Did ne'er their fancies move.
None then did envy neighbour's wealth,
   Nor plot to wrong his bed:
Happy in friendship and in health,
   On roots, not beasts, they fed.
They knew no law nor physic then,
   Nature was all their wit.
And if there yet remain to men

Content, sure this is it.
What blessings doth this world afford
　　To tempt or bribe desire?
Her courtship is all fire and sword,
　　Who would not then retire?
Then welcome dearest solitude,
　　My great felicity;
Though some are pleased to call thee rude,
　　Thou art not so, but we.
Them that do covet only rest,
　　A cottage will suffice:
It is not brave to be possessed
　　Of earth, but to despise.
Opinion is the rate of things,
　　From hence our peace doth flow;
I have a better fate than kings,
　　Because I think it so.
When all the stormy world doth roar
　　How unconcerned am I?
I cannot fear to tumble lower
　　Who never could be high.
Secure in these unenvied walls
　　I think not on the state,
And pity no man's case that falls
　　From his ambition's height.
Silence and innocence are safe;
　　A heart that's nobly true
At all these little arts can laugh
　　That do the world subdue.
While others revel it in state,
　　Here I'll contented sit,
And think I have as good a fate
　　As wealth and pomp admit.
Let some in courtship take delight,
　　And to th' exchange resort;
Then revel out a winter's night,
　　Not making love, but sport.
These never know a noble flame,
　　'Tis lust, scorn, or design:
While vanity plays all their game,
　　Let peace and honour mine.

When the inviting spring appears,
    To Hyde Park let them go,
And hasting thence be full of fears
    To lose Spring-Garden show.
Let others (nobler) seek to gain
    In knowledge happy fate,
And others busy them in vain
    To study ways of state.
But I, resolvèd from within,
    Confirmèd from without,
In privacy intend to spin
    My future minutes out.
And from this hermitage of mine
    I banish all wild toys,
And nothing that is not divine
    Shall dare to tempt my joys.
There are below but two things good,
    Friendship and honesty,
And only those of all I would
    Ask for felicity.
In this retired and humble seat
    Free from both war and strife,
I am not forced to make retreat
    But choose to spend my life.

On Rosania's Apostacy, and Lucasia's Friendship
Great soul of friendship whither art thou fled,
Where dost thou now choose to repose thy head?
Or art thou nothing but voice, air and name,
Found out to put souls in pursuit of fame?
Thy flames being thought immortal, we may doubt
Whether they e'er did burn that see them out.

Go wearied soul find out thy wonted rest,
In the safe harbour of Orinda's breast,
There all unknown adventures thou hast found
In thy late transmigrations expound;
That so Rosania's darkness may be known
To be her want of lustre, not thy own.

Then to the great Lucasia have recourse,
There gather up new excellence and force,
Till by a free unbiased clear commerce,
Endearments which no tongue can e'er rehearse,
Lucasia and Orinda shall thee give
Eternity, and make even friendship live.

Hail great Lucasia, thou shalt doubly shine,
What was Rosania's own is now twice thine;
Thou saw'st Rosania's chariot and her flight,
And so the double portion is thy right:
Though 'twas Rosania's spirit be content,
Since 'twas at first from thy Orinda sent.

The World

We falsely think it due unto our friends,
That we should grieve for their untimely ends.
He that surveys the world with serious eyes,
And strips her from her gross and weak disguise,
Shall find 'tis injury to mourn their fate;
He only dies untimely who dies late.
For if 'twere told to children in the womb,
To what a stage of mischiefs they must come;
Could they foresee with how much toil and sweat
Men court that gilded nothing, being great;
What pains they take not to be what they seem,
Rating their bliss by others' false esteem,
And sacrificing their content, to be
Guilty of grave and serious vanity;
How each condition hath its proper thorns,
And what one man admires, another scorns;
How frequently their happiness they miss,
So far even from agreeing what it is,
That the same person we can hardly find,
Who is an hour together in one mind:
Sure they would beg a period of their breath,
And what we call their birth would count their death.
Mankind is mad; for none can live alone,
Because their joys stand by comparison:

And yet they quarrel at society,
And strive to kill they know not whom, nor why.
We all live by mistake, delight in dreams,
Lost to ourselves, and dwelling in extremes;
Rejecting what we have, though ne'er so good,
And prizing what we never understood.
Compared t' our boisterous inconstancy
Tempests are calm, and discords harmony.
Hence we reverse the world, and yet do find
The God that made can hardly please our mind.
We live by chance, and slip into events;
Have all of beasts except their innocence.
The soul, which no man's pow'r can reach, a thing
That makes each woman man, each man a king,
Doth so much lose, and from its height so fall,
That some contend to have no soul at all.
'Tis either not observed, or at the best
By passion fought withal, by sin depressed.
Freedom of will (God's image) is forgot;
And if we know it, we improve it not.
Our thoughts, though nothing can be more our own,
Are still unguided, very seldom known.
Time 'scapes our hands as water in a sieve,
We come to die e'er we begin to live.
Truth, the most suitable and noble prize,
Food of our spirits, yet neglected lies.
Error and shadows are our choice, and we
Owe our perdition to our own decree.
If we search truth, we make it more obscure;
And when it shines, cannot the light endure.
For most men now, who plod, and eat, and drink,
Have nothing less their bus'ness than to think.
And those few that enquire, how small a share
Of truth they find, how dark their notions are!
That serious evenness that calms the breast,
And in a tempest can bestow a rest,
We either not attempt, or else decline,
By ev'ry trifle snatched from our design.
(Others he must in his deceits involve,
Who is not true unto his own resolve.)
We govern not ourselves, but loose the reins,

Counting our bondage to a thousand chains;
And with as many slaveries content
As there are tyrants ready to torment,
We live upon a rack extended still
To one extreme or both, but always ill.
For since our fortune is not understood,
We suffer less from bad than from the good.
The sting is better dressed and longer lasts,
As surfeits are more dangerous than fasts.
And to complete the misery to us,
We see extremes are still contiguous.
And as we run so fast from what we hate,
Like squibs on ropes, to know no middle state;
So outward storms strengthened by us, we find
Our fortune as disordered as our mind.
But that's excused by this, it doth its part;
A treach'rous world befits a treach'rous heart.
All ill's our own, the outward storms we loath
Receive from us their birth, their sting, or both.
And that our vanity be past a doubt,
'Tis one new vanity to find it out.
Happy are they to whom God gives a grave,
And from themselves as from his wrath doth save.
'Tis good not to be born; but if we must,
The next good is, soon to return to dust.
When th' uncaged soul fled to eternity
Shall rest, and live, and sing, and love, and see.
Here we but crawl and grovel, play and cry;
Are first our own, then others', enemy:
But there shall be defaced both stain and score,
For time, and death, and sin shall be no more.

An Epitaph on my Honoured mother-in-law
Mrs Philips of Portheynon in Cardiganshire,
who died January 1, Anno 1662/3

Reader stay, it is but just;
Thou dost not tread on common dust.
For underneath this stone does lie
One whose name can never die:

Who from an honoured linage sprung,
Was to another matchèd young;
Whose happiness she ever sought;
One blessing was, and many brought.
And to her spouse her faith did prove
By fifteen pledges of their love.
But when by death of him deprived,
An honourable widow lived
Full four and twenty years, wherein
Though she had much afflicted been,
Saw many of her children fall,
And public ruin threaten all.
Yet from above assisted, she
Both did and suffered worthily.
She to the Crown, and Church adhered,
And in their sorrows them revered,
With piety which knew no strife,
But was as sober as her life.
A furnished table, open door,
That for her friends, this for the poor
She kept; yet did her fortune find,
Too narrow for her nobler mind;
Which seeking objects to relieve,
Did food to many orphans give,
Who in her life no want did know,
But all the poor are orphans now.
Yet hold, her fame is much too safe,
To need a written epitaph.
Her fame was so confessed, that she
Can never here forgotten be,
Till Cardigan itself become,
To its own ruined heaps a tomb.

---

*Lucasia, Rosania and Orinda parting at a
fountain July 1663*

1

Here, here are our enjoyments done,
   And since the love and grief we wear
   Forbids us either word or tear,

And art wants here expression,
See nature furnish us with one.

2

The kind and mournful nymph which here
   Inhabits in her humble cells,
   No longer her own sorrow tells,
Nor for it now concerned appears,
But for our parting sheds these tears.

3

Unless she may afflicted be,
   Lest we should doubt her innocence;
   Since she hath lost her best pretence
Unto a matchless purity;
Our love being clearer far than she.

4

Cold as the streams that from her flow
   Or (if her privater recess
   A greater coldness can express)
Then cold as those dark beds of snow
Our hearts are at this parting blow.

5

But time that has both wings and feet,
   Our suffering minutes being spent,
   Will visit us with new content.
And sure, if kindness be so sweet,
'Tis harder to forget than meet.

6

Then though the sad adieu we say,
   Yet as the wine we hither bring,
   Revives, and then exalts the spring;
So let our hopes to meet allay,
The fears and sorrows of this day.

Epitaph. On her son H. P. at St Syth's Church
where her body also lies interred.

What on earth deserves our trust?
Youth and beauty both are dust.
Long we gathering are with pain,
What one moment calls again.
Seven years childless, marriage past,
A son, a son is born at last:
So exactly limbed and fair,
Full of good spirits, mien, and air,
As a long life promisèd,
Yet, in less than six weeks dead.
Too promising, too great a mind
In so small room to be confined:
Therefore, as fit in heav'n to dwell,
He quickly broke the prison shell.
So the subtle alchemist,
Can't with Hermes' seal resist
The powerful spirit's subtler flight,
But 'twill bid him long good night.
And so the sun if it arise
Half so glorious as his eyes,
Like this infant, takes a shroud,
Buried in a morning cloud.

Orinda to Lucasia parting October 1661 at London.

Adieu dear object of my love's excess,
And with thee all my hopes of happiness,
With the same fervent and unchangèd heart
Which did its whole self once to thee impart,
(And which though fortune has so sorely bruised,
Would suffer more, to be from this excused)
I to resign thy dear converse submit,
Since I can neither keep, nor merit it.
Thou hast too long to me confinèd been,
Who ruin am without, passion within.
My mind is sunk below thy tenderness,
And my condition does deserve it less;
I'm so entangled and so lost a thing

By all the shocks my daily sorrow bring,
That wouldst thou for thy old Orinda call
Thou hardly couldst unravel her at all.
And should I thy clear fortunes interline
With the incessant miseries of mine?
No, no, I never loved at such a rate
To tie thee to the rigours of my fate,
As from my obligations thou art free,
Sure thou shalt be so from my injury,
Though every other worthiness I miss,
Yet I'll at least be generous in this.
I'd rather perish without sigh or groan,
Than thou shouldst be condemned to give me one;
Nay in my soul I rather could allow
Friendship should be a sufferer, than thou;
Go then, since my sad heart has set thee free,
Let all the loads and chains remain on me.
Though I be left the prey of sea and wind,
Thou being happy wilt in that be kind;
Nor shall I my undoing much deplore,
Since thou art safe, whom I must value more.
Oh mayst thou ever be so, and as free
From all ills else, as from my company,
And may the torments thou hast had from it
Be all that heaven will to thy life permit.
And that they may thy virtue service do,
Mayest thou be able to forgive them too:
But though I must this sharp submission learn,
I cannot yet unwish thy dear concern.
Not one new comfort I expect to see,
I quit my joy, hope, life, and all but thee;
Nor seek I thence aught that may discompose
That mind where so serene a goodness grows.
I ask no inconvenient kindness now,
To move thy passion, or to cloud thy brow;
And thou wilt satisfy my boldest plea
By some few soft remembrances of me,
Which may present thee with this candid thought,
I meant not all the troubles that I brought.
Own not what passion rules, and fate does crush,
But wish thou couldst have done't without a blush,
And that I had been, ere it was too late,

Either more worthy, or more fortunate.
Ah who can love the thing they cannot prize?
But thou mayst pity though thou dost despise.
Yet I should think that pity bought too dear,
If it should cost those precious eyes a tear.
Oh may no minutes' trouble thee possess,
But to endear the next hour's happiness;
And mayst thou when thou art from me removed,
Be better pleased, but never worse beloved:
Oh pardon me for pouring out my woes
In rhyme now, that I dare not do't in prose.
For I must lose whatever is called dear,
And thy assistance all that loss to bear,
    And have more cause than ere I had before,
    To fear that I shall never see thee more.

Orinda upon little Hector Philips

1
Twice forty months of wedlock I did stay,
Then had my vows crowned with a lovely boy,
And yet in forty days he dropped away,
O swift vicissitude of human joy.

2
I did but see him and he disappeared,
I did but pluck the rosebud and it fell,
A sorrow unforeseen and scarcely feared,
For ill can mortals their afflictions spell.

3
And now (sweet babe) what can my trembling heart
Suggest to right my doleful fate or thee,
Tears are my muse and sorrow all my art,
So piercing groans must be thy elegy.

4
Thus whilst no eye is witness of my moan,
I grieve thy loss (Ah boy too dear to live)
And let the unconcernèd world alone,
Who neither will, nor can refreshment give.

5

An off'ring too for thy sad tomb I have,
Too just a tribute to thy early hearse,
Receive these gasping numbers to thy grave,
The last of thy unhappy mother's verse.

⸺

Orinda to Lucasia

1

Observe the weary birds e'er night be done,
How they would fain call up the tardy sun,
   With feathers hung with dew,
   And trembling voices too.
They court their glorious planet to appear,
   That they may find recruits of spirits there.
   The drooping flowers hang their heads,
And languish down into their beds:
While brooks more bold and fierce than they,
   Wanting those beams, from whence
   All things drink influence,
Openly murmur and demand the day.

Thou my Lucasia art far more to me,
Than he to all the underworld can be;
   From thee I've heat and light,
   Thy absence makes my night.
But ah! my friend, it now grows very long,
The sadness weighty, and the darkness strong:
   My tears (its dew) dwell on my cheeks,
   And still my heart thy dawning seeks,
And to the mournfully it cries,
   That if too long I wait,
   E'vn thou mayst come too late,
And not restore my life, but close my eyes.

⸺

1668

17. Margaret Cavendish, Duchess of Newcastle

The Convent of Pleasure

The actor's names

Three Gentlemen
Lady Happy
Madame Mediator
Monsieur Take-Pleasure, and Dick, his Man
Monsieur Facil
Monsieur Adviser
Monsieur Courtly
Lady Amorous
Lady Vertue
The Princess
Two Mean Women
A Lady, and her Maid
Two Ladies
A Distracted Lady, and her Maid
A Citizen's Wife   } [Played by the ladies of the convent]
Two Ancient Ladies
A Gentleman and a Young Lady
A Shepherd
Sea-Nymphs
An Ambassador
Mimick

I.i

Enter three gentlemen

1 Gentleman Tom, where have you been, you look so sadly of it?
2 Gentleman I have been at the funeral of the Lord Fortunate; who has left his daughter, the Lady Happy, very rich, having no other daughter but her.
1 Gentleman If she be so rich, it will make us all young men, spend all our wealth in fine clothes, coaches, and lackeys, to set out our wooing hopes.
3 Gentleman If all her wooers be younger brothers, as most of us gallants are, we shall undo ourselves upon bare hopes, without probability. But is she handsome, Tom?

2 Gentleman Yes, she is extreme handsome, young, rich, and virtuous.

1 Gentleman Faith, that is too much for one woman to possess.

2 Gentleman Not if you were to have her.

1 Gentleman No, not for me; but in my opinion too much for any other man.

Exeunt

I.ii

Enter the Lady Happy, and one of her attendants

Servant Madame, you being young, handsome, rich, and virtuous, I hope you will not cast away those gifts of Nature, Fortune, and Heaven, upon a person which cannot merit you?

Lady Happy Let me tell you, that riches ought to be bestowed on such as are poor, and want means to maintain themselves; and youth, on those that are old; beauty, on those that are ill-favoured; and virtue, on those that are vicious. So that if I should place my gifts rightly, I must marry one that's poor, old, ill favoured, and debauched.

Servant Heaven forbid.

Lady Happy Nay, Heaven doth not only allow of it, but commands it; for we are commanded to give to those that want.

Enter Madame Mediator to the Lady Happy.

Madame Mediator Surely, madame, you do but talk, and intend not to go where you say.

Lady Happy Yes, truly, my words and intentions go even together.

Madame Mediator But surely you will not encloister yourself, as you say.

Lady Happy Why, what is there in the public world that should invite me to live in it?

Madame Mediator More than if you should banish yourself from it.

Lady Happy Put the case I should marry the best of men, if any best there be; yet would a married life have more crosses and sorrows than pleasure, freedom, or happiness: nay marriage to those that are virtuous is a greater restraint than a monastery. Or, should I take delight in admirers? They might gaze on my beauty, and praise my wit, and I receive nothing from their eyes, nor lips. For words vanish as soon as spoken, and sights are not substantial. Besides, I should lose more of my reputation by their visits, than gain by their praises. Or, should I quit reputation and turn courtesan, there would be more lost in my health, than gained by my lovers, I should find more pain than pleasure. Besides, the troubles and frights I should be put to, with the quarrels and brouilleries that jealous rivals make, would be a torment to me; and 'tis only for the sake of men, when women retire not: And since there is so much folly, vanity and falsehood in men, why should women trouble and vex themselves for their sake; for retiredness bars the life from nothing else but men.

Madame Mediator O yes, for those that encloister themselves, bar themselves from all other worldly pleasures.

Lady Happy The more fools they.

Madame Mediator Will you call those fools that do it for the Gods' sake?

Lady Happy No madame, it is not for the Gods' sake, but for opinion's sake. For, can any rational creature think or believe the Gods take delight in the creature's uneasy life? Or, did they command or give leave to Nature to make senses for no use; or to cross, vex and pain them? For, what profit or pleasure can it be to the Gods to have men or women wear coarse linen or rough woollen, or to flay their skin with hair-cloth, or to eat or saw through their flesh with cords? Or, what profit or pleasure can it be to the Gods to have men eat more fish than flesh, or to fast? Unless the Gods did feed on such meat themselves; for then, for fear the Gods should want it, it were fit for men to abstain from it. The like for garments, for fear the Gods should want fine clothes to adorn themselves, it were fit men should not wear them. Or, what profit or pleasure can it be to the Gods to have men to lie uneasily on the hard ground, unless the Gods and Nature were at variance, strife and wars; as if what is displeasing unto Nature, were pleasing to the Gods, and to be enemies to her, were to be friends to them.

Madame Mediator But being done for the Gods' sake, it makes that which in Nature seems to be bad, in divinity to be good.

Lady Happy It cannot be good, if it be neither pleasure, nor profit to the Gods; neither do men anything for the Gods but their own sake.

Madame Mediator But when the mind is not employed with vanities, nor the senses with luxury; the mind is more free, to offer its adorations, prayers and praises to the Gods.

Lady Happy I believe the Gods are better pleased with praises than fasting. But when the senses are dulled with abstinency, the body weakened with fasting, the spirits tired with watching, the life made uneasy with pain, the soul can have but little will to worship. Only the imagination doth frighten it into active zeal, which devotion is rather forced than voluntary; so that their prayers rather flow out of their mouth, than spring from their heart, like rainwater that runs through gutters, or like water that's forced up a hill by artificial pipes and cisterns. But those that pray not unto the Gods, or praise them more in prosperity than adversity, more in pleasures than pains, more in liberty than restraint, deserve neither the happiness of ease, peace, freedom, plenty and tranquillity in this world, nor the glory and blessedness of the next. And if the Gods should take pleasure in nothing but in the torments of their creatures, and would not prefer those prayers that are offered with ease and delight, I should believe the Gods were cruel. And, what creature, that had reason or rational understanding, would serve cruel masters, when they might serve a kind mistress, or would forsake the service of their kind mistress, to serve cruel masters? Wherefore, if the Gods be cruel, I will serve Nature; but the Gods are bountiful, and give all that's good, and bid us freely please ourselves in that which is best for us: and that is best, what is most temperately used, and longest may be enjoyed, for excess doth waste itself, and all it feeds upon.

Madame Mediator In my opinion your doctrine, and your intention do not agree together.

Lady Happy Why?

Madame Mediator You intend to live encloistered and retired from the world.

Lady Happy 'Tis true, but not from pleasures; for, I intend to encloister myself from the world, to enjoy pleasure, and not to bury myself from it; but to encloister myself from the encumbered cares and vexations, troubles and perturbance of the world.

Madame Mediator But if you encloister yourself, how will you enjoy the company of men, whose conversation is thought the greatest pleasure?

Lady Happy Men are the only troublers of women; for they only cross and oppose their sweet delights, and peaceable life; they cause their pains, but not their pleasures. Wherefore those women that are poor, and have not means to buy delights, and maintain pleasures, are only fit for men; for having not means to please themselves, they must serve only to please others. But those women, where Fortune, Nature, and the Gods are joined to make them happy, were mad to live with men, who make the female sex their slaves. But I will not be so enslaved, but will live retired from their company. Wherefore, in order thereto, I will take so many noble persons of my own sex, as my estate will plentifully maintain, such whose births are greater than their fortunes, and are resolved to live a single life, and vow virginity. With these I mean to live encloistered with all the delights and pleasures that are allowable and lawful. My cloister shall not be a cloister of restraint, but a place for freedom, not to vex the senses but to please them.

> For every sense shall pleasure take,
> And all our lives shall merry make:
> Our minds in full delight shall joy,
> Not vexed with every idle toy:

Each season shall our caterers be,
To search the land, and fish the sea;
To gather fruit and reap the corn,
That's brought to us in Plenty's Horn;
With which we'll feast and please our taste,
But not luxurious make a waste.
We'll clothe ourselves with softest silk,
And linen fine as white as milk.
We'll please our sight with pictures rare;
Our nostrils with perfumed air.
Our ears with sweet melodious sound,
Whose substance can be nowhere found;
Our taste with sweet delicious meat,
And savoury sauces we will eat:
Variety each sense shall feed,
And change in them new appetites breed.
Thus will in pleasure's convent I
Live with delight, and with it die.

Exeunt

II.i

Enter Monsieur Take-pleasure, and his man Dick

Monsieur Take-Pleasure Dick, am I fine today?

Dick Yes, sir, as fine as feathers, ribbons, gold, and silver can make you.

Monsieur Take-Pleasure Dost thou think I shall get the Lady Happy?

Dick Not if it be her fortune to continue in that name.

Monsieur Take-Pleasure Why?

Dick Because if she marry Your Worship she must change her name; for the wife takes the name of her husband, and quits her own.

Monsieur Take-Pleasure Faith, Dick, if I had her wealth I should be happy.

Dick It would be according as Your Worship would use it; but, on my conscience, you would be more happy with the lady's wealth, than the lady would be with Your Worship.

Monsieur Take-Pleasure Why should you think so?

Dick Because women never think themselves happy in marriage.

Monsieur Take-Pleasure You are mistaken; for women never think themselves happy until they be married.

Dick The truth is, sir, that women are always unhappy in their thoughts, both before and after marriage; for, before marriage they think themselves unhappy for want of a husband; and after they are married, they think themselves unhappy for having a husband.

Monsieur Take-Pleasure Indeed women's thoughts are restless.

Enter Monsieur Facil, and Monsieur Adviser, to Monsieur Take-pleasure; all in their wooing accoutrements

Monsieur Take-Pleasure Gentlemen, I perceive you are all prepared to woo.

Monsieur Facil Yes faith, we are all prepared to be wooers. But whom shall we get to present us to the Lady Happy?

Monsieur Adviser We must set on bold faces, and present ourselves.

Monsieur Take-Pleasure Faith, I would not give my hopes for an indifferent portion.

Monsieur Facil Nor I.

Monsieur Adviser The truth is, we are all stuffed with hopes, as cushions are with feathers.

Enter Monsieur Courtly

Monsieur Courtly O gentlemen, gentlemen, we are all utterly undone.

Monsieur Adviser Why, what's the matter?

Monsieur Courtly Why, the Lady Happy hath encloistered herself, with twenty ladies more.

Monsieur Adviser The Devil she hath?

Monsieur Facil The Gods forbid.

Monsieur Courtly Whether it was the Devil or the Gods that have persuaded her to it, I cannot tell; but gone in she is.

Monsieur Take-Pleasure I hope it is but a blast of devotion, which will soon flame out.

Enter Madame Mediator

Monsieur Take-Pleasure O Madame Mediator, we are all undone, the Lady Happy is encloistered.

Madame Mediator Yes, gentlemen, the more is the pity.

Monsieur Adviser Is there no hopes?

Madame Mediator Faith, little.

Monsieur Facil Let us fee the clergy to persuade her out, for the good of the Commonwealth.

Madame Mediator Alas gentlemen! They can do no good, for she is not a vot'ress to the Gods but to Nature.

Monsieur Courtly If she be a vot'ress to Nature, you are the only person fit to be Lady Prioress; and so by your power and authority you may give us leave to visit your nuns sometimes.

Madame Mediator Not but at a grate, unless in time of building, or when they are sick; but howsoever, the Lady Happy is Lady Prioress herself, and will admit none of the masculine sex, not so much as to a grate, for she will suffer no grates about the cloister. She has also women-physicians, surgeons and apothecaries, and she is the chief confessor herself, and gives what indulgences or absolutions she pleaseth. Also, her house, where she hath made her Convent, is so big and convenient, and so strong, as it needs no addition or repair. Besides, she has so much compass of ground within her walls, as there is not only room and place enough for gardens, orchards, walks, groves, bowers, arbours, ponds, fountains, springs and the like; but also conveniency for much provision, and hath women for every office and employment. For though she hath not above twenty ladies with her, yet she hath a numerous company of female servants, so as there is no occasion for men.

Monsieur Take-Pleasure If there be so many women, there will be the more use for men. But pray Madame Mediator, give me leave, rightly to understand you, by being more clearly informed. You say the Lady Happy is become a vot'ress to Nature; and if she be a vot'ress to Nature, she must be a mistress to men.

Madame Mediator By your favour, sir, she declares that she hath avoided the company of men, by retirement, merely, because she would enjoy the variety of pleasures which are in Nature; of which, she says, men are obstructers. For, instead of increasing pleasure, they produce pain; and, instead of giving content, they increase trouble; instead of making the female sex happy, they make them miserable; for which, she hath banished the masculine company forever.

Monsieur Adviser Her heretical opinions ought not to be suffered, nor her doctrine allowed; and she ought to be examined by a masculine synod, and punished with a severe husband, or tortured with a deboist husband.

Madame Mediator The best way, gentlemen, is to make your complaints, and put up a petition to the State, with your desires for a redress.

Monsieur Courtly Your counsel is good.

Monsieur Facil We will follow it, and go presently about it.

Exeunt

II.ii

Enter the Lady Happy, with her ladies; as also Madame Mediator

Lady Happy Ladies, give me leave to desire your confession, whether or no you repent your retirement.

Ladies Most excellent lady, it were as probable a repentance could be in Heaven amongst angels as amongst us.

Lady Happy Now Madame Mediator, let me ask you, do you condemn my act of retirement?

Madame Mediator I approve of it with admiration and wonder, that one that is so young should be so wise.

Lady Happy Now give me leave to inform you, how I have ordered this our Convent of Pleasure. First, I have such things as are for our ease and conveniency; next for pleasure, and delight; as I have change of furniture, for my house; according to the four seasons of the year, especially our chambers. As in the Spring, our chambers are hung with silk-damask, and all other things suitable to it; and a great looking-glass in each chamber, that we may view ourselves and take pleasure in our own beauties, whilst they are fresh and young; also, I have in each chamber a cupboard of such plate, as is useful, and whatsoever is to be used is there ready to be employed; also, I have all the floor strewed with sweet flowers. In the Summer I have all our chambers hung with taffety, and all other things suitable to it, and a cupboard of porcelain, and of plate, and all the floor, strewed every day with green rushes or reaves, and cisterns placed near our bedheads, wherein water may run out of small pipes made for that purpose. To invite repose in the Autumn, all our chambers are hung with gilt leather, or franchipane; also, beds and all other things suitable; and the rooms matted with very fine mats. In the Winter our chambers must be hung with tapestry, and our beds of velvet, lined with satin, and all things suitable to it, and all the floor spread over with Turkey carpets, and a cupboard of gilt plate; and all the wood for firing to be cypress and juniper; and all the lights to be perfumed wax. Also, the bedding and pillows are ordered according to each season; viz. to be stuffed with feathers in the Spring and Autumn, and with down in the Winter, but in the Summer to be only quilts, either of silk, or fine holland; and our sheets, pillows, tablecloths and towels, to be of pure fine holland, and every day clean. Also, the rooms we eat in, and the vessels we feed withal, I have according to each season; and the linen we use to our meat, to be pure fine diaper, and damask, and to change it fresh every course of meat. As for our galleries, stair-cases, and passages, they shall be hung with various pictures; and, all along the wall of our gallery, as long as the Summer lasts, do stand, upon pedestals, flower-pots, with various flowers; and in the Winter orange-trees: and my gardens to be kept curiously, and flourish, in every season of all sorts of flowers, sweet herbs and fruits, and kept so as not to have a weed in it, and all the groves, wildernesses, bowers and arbours pruned, and kept free from dead boughs branches or leaves; and all the ponds, rivulets, fountains, and springs, kept clear, pure and fresh. Also, we will have the choicest meats every season doth afford, and that every day our meat, be dressed several ways, and our drink cooler or hotter according to the several seasons; and all our drinks fresh and pleasing. Change of garments are also provided, of the newest fashions for every season, and rich trimming; so as we may be accoutred properly, and according to our several pastimes: and our shifts shall be of the finest and purest linen that can be bought or spun.

Ladies None in this world can be happier.

Lady Happy Now ladies, let us go to our several pastimes, if you please.

Exeunt

II.iii

Enter two ladies

Lady Amorous Madame, how do you, since you were married?
Lady Vertue Very well, I thank you.
Lady Amorous I am not so well as I wish I were.

Enter Madame Mediator to them

Madame Mediator Ladies, do you hear the news?
Lady Vertue What news?
Madame Mediator Why there is a great foreign Princess arrived, hearing of the famous Convent of Pleasure, to be one of Nature's devotes.
Lady Amorous What manner of lady is she?
Madame Mediator She is a princely brave woman truly, of a masculine presence.
Lady Vertue But, Madame Mediator, do they live in such pleasure as you say? For they'll admit you, a widow, although not us, by reason we are wives.
Madame Mediator In so much pleasure, as Nature never knew, before this Convent was: and for my part, I had rather be one in the Convent of Pleasure, than Empress of the whole world. For every lady there enjoyeth as much pleasure as any absolute monarch can do, without the troubles

and cares, that wait on royalty; besides, none can enjoy those pleasures they have, unless they live such a retired or retreated life free from the world's vexations.

Lady Vertue Well, I wish I might see and know, what pleasures they enjoy.

Madame Mediator If you were there, you could not know all their pleasure in a short time, for their varieties will require a long time to know their several changes; besides, their pleasures and delights vary with the seasons; so that what with the several seasons, and the varieties of every season, it will take up a whole life's time.

Lady Vertue But I could judge of their changes by their single principles.

Madame Mediator But they have variety of one and the same kind.

Lady Vertue But I should see the way or manner of them.

Madame Mediator That you might.

Exeunt

II.iv

Enter Monsieur Adviser, Monsieur Courtly, Monsieur Take-pleasure, and Monsieur Facil

Monsieur Courtly Is there no hopes to get those ladies out of their Convent?

Monsieur Adviser No faith, unless we could set the Convent on fire.

Monsieur Take-Pleasure For Jupiter's sake, let us do it, let's every one carry a fire-brand to fire it.

Monsieur Courtly Yes, and smoke them out, as they do a swarm of bees.

Monsieur Facil Let's go presently about it.

Monsieur Adviser Stay, there is a great Princess there.

Monsieur Take-Pleasure 'Tis true, but when that Princess is gone, we will surely do it.

Monsieur Adviser Yes, and be punished for our villainy.

Monsieur Take-Pleasure It will not prove villainy, for we shall do Nature good service.

Monsieur Adviser Why, so we do Nature good service, when we get a wench with child, but yet the civil laws do punish us for it.

Monsieur Courtly They are not civil laws that punish lovers.

Monsieur Adviser But those are civil laws that punish adulterers.

Monsieur Courtly Those are barbarous laws that make love adultery.

Monsieur Adviser No, those are barbarous laws that make adultery love.

Monsieur Facil Well, leaving love and adultery, they are foolish women that vex us with their retirement.

Monsieur Adviser Well, gentlemen, although we rail at the Lady Happy for retiring, yet if I had such an estate as she, and would follow her example; I make no doubt but you would all be content to encloister yourselves with me upon the same conditions, as those ladies encloister themselves with her.

Monsieur Take-Pleasure Not unless you had women in your Convent.

Monsieur Adviser Nay, faith, since women can quit the pleasure of men, we men may well quit the trouble of women.

Monsieur Courtly But is there no place where we may peek into the Convent?

Monsieur Adviser No, there are no grates, but brick and stone walls.

Monsieur Facil Let us get out some of the bricks or stones.

Monsieur Adviser Alas! The walls are a yard thick.

Monsieur Facil But nothing is difficult to willing minds.

Monsieur Adviser My mind is willing; but my reason tells me, it is impossible; wherefore, I'll never go about it.

Monsieur Take-Pleasure Faith, let us resolve to put ourselves in women's apparel, and so by that means get into the Convent.

Monsieur Adviser We shall be discovered.

Monsieur Take-Pleasure Who will discover us?

Monsieur Adviser We shall discover ourselves.

Monsieur Take-Pleasure We are not such fools as to betray ourselves.

Monsieur Adviser We cannot avoid it, for, our very garb and behaviour; besides, our voices will discover us. For we are as untoward to make curtsies in petticoats, as women are to make legs in breeches; and it will be as great a difficulty to raise our voices to a treble-sound, as for women to press down their voices to a bass. Besides, we shall never frame our eyes and mouths to such coy, dissembling looks, and pretty simpering mopes and smiles, as they do.

Monsieur Courtly But we will go as strong lusty country wenches, that desire to serve them in inferior places, and offices, as cook-maids, laundry-maids, dairy-maids, and the like.

Monsieur Facil I do verily believe, I could make an indifferent cook-maid, but not a laundry-, nor a dairy-maid; for I cannot milk cows, nor starch gorgets, but I think I could make a pretty shift, to wash some of the ladies' night-linen.

Monsieur Take-Pleasure But they employ women in all places in their gardens; and for brewing, baking and making all sorts of things; besides, some keep their swine, and twenty suchlike offices and employments there are which we should be very proper for.

Monsieur Facil O yes, for keeping of swine belongs to men; remember the prodigal son.

Monsieur Adviser Faith, for our prodigality we might be all swine-herds.
Monsieur Courtly Also we shall be proper for gardens, for we can dig, and set, and sow.
Monsieur Take-Pleasure And we are proper for brewing.
Monsieur Adviser We are more proper for drinking, for I can drink good beer, or ale, when 'tis brewed; but I could not brew such beer, or ale, as any man could drink.
Monsieur Facil Come, come, we shall make a shift one way or other: besides, we shall be very willing to learn, and be very diligent in our services, which will give good and great content; wherefore, let us go and put these designs into execution.
Monsieur Courtly Content, content.
Monsieur Adviser Nay, faith, let us not trouble ourselves for it, 'tis in vain.

Exeunt

———

III.i

Enter the Princess, and the Lady Happy, with the rest of the ladies belonging to the Convent

Lady Happy Madame, Your Highness has done me much honour, to come from a splendid court to a retired convent.
Princess Sweet Lady Happy, there are many that have quit their crowns and power, for a cloister of restraint; then well may I quit a court of troubles for a Convent of Pleasure: but the greatest pleasure I could receive were to have your friendship.
Lady Happy I should be ungrateful, should I not be not only your friend, but humble servant.
Princess I desire you would be my mistress, and I your servant; and upon this agreement of friendship I desire you will grant me one request.
Lady Happy Anything that is in my power to grant.
Princess Why then, I observing in your several recreations, some of your ladies do accoutre themselves in masculine habits, and act lovers parts; I desire you will give me leave to be sometimes so accoutred and act the part of your loving servant.
Lady Happy I shall never desire to have any other loving servant than yourself.
Princess Nor I any other loving mistress than yourself.
Lady Happy More innocent lovers never can there be,
Than my most princely lover, that's a she.

Princess Nor never convent did such pleasures give,
Where lovers with their mistresses may live.

Enter a lady, asking whether they will see the play

Lady May it please Your Highness, the play is ready to be acted.

Masque Scene

*The Scene is opened, the Princess and Lady Happy sit down,
and the play is acted within the scene; the Princess and the Lady Happy
being spectators. Enter one dressed like a man that speaks the Prologue*

> Noble spectators, you shall see tonight
> A play, which though't be dull, yet's short to sight;
> For, since we cannot please your ears with wit,
> We will not tire your limbs, long here to sit.

III.ii

Enter two mean women

1 Woman O neighbour well met, where have you been?

2 Woman I have been with my neighbour the cobbler's wife to comfort her for the loss of her husband, who is run away with Goody Mettle the tinker's wife.

1 Woman I would to Heaven my husband would run away with Goody Shred the botcher's wife, for he lies all day drinking in an ale-house, like a drunken rogue as he is, and when he comes home, he beats me all black and blue, when I and my children are almost starved for want.

2 Woman Truly neighbour, so doth my husband; and spends not only what he gets, but what I earn with the sweat of my brows, the whilst my children cry for bread, and he drinks that away, that should feed my small children, which are too young to work for themselves.

1 Woman But I will go, and pull my husband out of the ale-house, or I'll break their lattice-windows down.

2 Woman Come, I'll go and help; for my husband is there too: but we shall be both beaten by them.

1 Woman I care not: for I will not suffer him to be drunk, and I and my children starve; I had better be dead.

Exeunt

III.iii

Enter a lady and her maid

Lady Oh, I am sick!
Maid You are breeding a child, madame .
Lady I have not one minute's time of health.

Exeunt

III.iv

Enter two ladies

1 Lady Why weep you, madame ?
2 Lady Have I not cause to weep when my husband hath played all his estate away at dice and cards, even to the clothes on his back?
1 Lady I have as much cause to weep then as you; for, though my husband hath not lost his estate at play, yet he hath spent it amongst his whores; and is not content to keep whores abroad, but in my house, under my roof, and they must rule as chief mistresses.
2 Lady But my husband hath not only lost his own estate, but also my portion; and hath forced me with threats, to yield up my jointure, so that I must beg for my living, for anything I know as yet.
1 Lady If all married women were as unhappy as I, marriage were a curse.
2 Lady No doubt of it.

Exeunt

III.v

Enter a lady, as almost distracted, running about the stage,
and her maid follows her

Lady Oh! My child is dead, my child is dead, what shall I do, what shall I do?
Maid You must have patience, madame.
Lady Who can have patience to lose their only child? Who can? Oh I shall run mad, for I have no patience.

Runs off the stage. Exit Maid after her

III.vi

Enter a citizen's wife, as into a tavern, where a bush is hung out,
and meets some gentlemen there

Citizen's Wife Pray gentlemen, is my husband, Mr Negligent here?
1 Gentleman He was, but he is gone some quarter of an hour since.
Citizen's Wife Could he go, gentlemen?
2 Gentleman Yes, with a supporter.
Citizen's Wife Out upon him! Must he be supported? Upon my credit gentlemen, he will undo himself and me too, with his drinking and carelessness, leaving his shop and all his commodities at sixes and sevens; and his prentices and journeymen are as careless and idle as he; besides, they cozen him of his wares. But, was it a he- or she-supporter, my husband was supported by?
1 Gentleman A she-supporter; for it was one of the maidservants, which belong to this tavern.
Citizen's Wife Out upon him knave, must he have a she-supporter, in the Devil's name? But I'll go and seek them both out with a vengeance.
2 Gentleman Pray, let us entreat your stay to drink a cup of wine with us.
Citizen's Wife I will take your kind offer; for wine may chance to abate choleric vapours, and pacify the spleen.
1 Gentleman That it will; for wine and good company are the only abaters of vapours.
2 Gentleman It doth not abate vapours so much as cure melancholy.
Citizen's Wife In truth, I find a cup of wine doth comfort me sometimes.
1 Gentleman It will cheer the heart.
2 Gentleman Yes, and enlighten the understanding.
Citizen's Wife Indeed, and my understanding requires enlightening.

Exeunt

III.vii

Enter a lady big with child, groaning as in labour,
and a company of women with her

Lady Oh my back, my back will break, Oh! Oh! Oh!
1 Woman Is the midwife sent for?
2 Woman Yes, but she is with another lady.
Lady Oh my back! Oh! Oh! Oh! Juno, give me some ease.

Exeunt

III.viii

Enter two ancient ladies

1 Lady I have brought my son into the world with great pains, bred him with tender care, much pains and great cost; and must he now be hanged for killing a man in a quarrel? When he should be a comfort and staff of my age, is he to be my age's affliction?

2 Lady I confess it is a great affliction; but I have had as great; having had but two daughters, and them fair ones, though I say it, and might have matched them well. But one of them was got with child to my great disgrace; th'other run away with my butler, not worth the droppings of his taps.

1 Lady Who would desire children, since they come to such misfortunes?

Exeunt

III.ix

Enter one woman meeting another

1 Woman Is the midwife come, for my lady is in a strong labour?

2 Woman No, she cannot come, for she hath been with a lady that hath been in strong labour these three days of a dead child, and 'tis thought she cannot be delivered.

Enter another woman

3 Woman Come away, the midwife is come.

1 Woman Is the lady delivered, she was with?

3 Woman Yes, of life; for she could not be delivered, and so she died.

2 Woman Pray tell not our lady so: for, the very fright of not being able to bring forth a child will kill her.

Exeunt

III.x

Enter a gentleman who meets a fair young lady

Gentleman Madame, my lord desires you to command whatsoever you please, and it shall be obeyed.

Lady I dare not command, but I humbly entreat, I may live quiet and free from his amours.

Gentleman He says he cannot live, and not love you.
Lady But he may live, and not lie with me.
Gentleman He cannot be happy, unless he enjoy you.
Lady And I must be unhappy, if he should.
Gentleman He commanded me to tell you that he will part from his lady for your sake.
Lady Heaven forbid, I should part man and wife.
Gentleman Lady, he will be divorced for your sake.
Lady Heaven forbid I should be the cause of a divorce between a noble pair.
Gentleman You had best consent; for, otherwise he will have you against your will.
Lady I will send his lordship an answer tomorrow; pray him to give me so much time.
Gentleman I shall, lady.

Exit gentleman. Lady sola

Lady I must prevent my own ruin, and the sweet virtuous lady's, by going into a nunnery; wherefore, I'll put myself into one tonight. There will I live, and serve the Gods on high, and leave this wicked world and vanity.

Exit

One enters and speaks the Epilogue

> Marriage is a curse we find,
> Especially to women kind:
> From the cobbler's wife we see,
> To ladies, they unhappy be.

Lady Happy [*to the Princess*] Pray servant, how do you like this play?
Princess My sweet mistress, I cannot in conscience approve of it; for though some few be unhappy in marriage, yet there are many more that are so happy as they would not change their condition.
Lady Happy O servant, I fear you will become an apostate.
Princess Not to you sweet mistress.

Exeunt

Enter the gentlemen

1 Gentleman There is no hopes of dissolving this Convent of Pleasure.
2 Gentleman Faith, not as I can perceive.

3 Gentleman We may be sure, this Convent will never be dissolved, by reason it is ennobled with the company of great Princesses, and glorified with a great fame; but the fear is, that all the rich heirs will make convents, and all the young beauties associate themselves in such convents.

1 Gentleman You speak reason; wherefore, let us endeavour to get wives, before they are encloistered.

Exeunt

IV.i

Enter Lady Happy dressed as a shepherdess; she walks very melancholy, then speaks as to herself

Lady Happy My name is happy, and so was my condition, before I saw this Princess; but now I am like to be the most unhappy maid alive. But why may not I love a woman with the same affection I could a man?

    No, no, Nature is Nature, and still will be

    The same she was from all eternity.

Enter the Princess in masculine shepherd's clothes

Princess My dearest mistress, do you shun my company? Is your servant become an offence to your sight?

Lady Happy No, servant! Your presence is more acceptable to me than the presence of our Goddess Nature, for which she, I fear, will punish me, for loving you more than I ought to love you.

Princess Can lovers love too much?

Lady Happy Yes, if they love not well.

Princess Can any love be more virtuous, innocent and harmless than ours?

Lady Happy I hope not.

Princess Then let us please ourselves, as harmless lovers use to do.

Lady Happy How can harmless lovers please themselves?

Princess Why very well, as, to discourse, embrace and kiss, so mingle souls together.

Lady Happy But innocent lovers do not use to kiss.

Princess Not any act more frequent amongst us women-kind; nay, it were a sin in friendship, should not we kiss: then let us not prove ourselves reprobates.

They embrace and kiss, and hold each other in their arms

Princess These my embraces though of female kind,
May be as fervent as a masculine mind.

The scene is opened, the Princess and Lady Happy go in

A pastoral within the scene

*The scene is changed into a green, or plain, where sheep
are feeding, and a Maypole in the middle.
Lady Happy as a shepherdess, and the Princess as a shepherd are
sitting there. Enter another shepherd, and woos the Lady Happy*

Shepherd Fair shepherdess do not my suit deny,
O grant my suit, let me not for love die:
Pity my flocks, oh save their shepherd's life;
Grant you my suit, be you their shepherd's wife.
Lady Happy How can I grant to everyone's request?
Each shepherd's suit lets me not be at rest;
For which I wish, the winds might blow them far,
That no love-suit might enter to my ear.

*Enter Madame Mediator in a shepherdess dress,
and another shepherd*

Shepherd Good dame unto your daughter speak for me.
Persuade her I your son-in-law may be:
I'll serve your swine, your cows bring home to milk;
Attend your sheep, whose wool's as soft as silk;
I'll plough your grounds, corn I'll in Winter sow,
Then reap your harvest, and your grass I'll mow;
Gather your fruits in Autumn from the tree.
All this and more I'll do, if y'speak for me.
Shepherdess My daughter vows a single life,
And swears, she ne'er will be a wife;
But live a maid, and flocks will keep,
And her chief company shall be sheep.

The Princess as a shepherd, speaks to the Lady Happy

Princess My shepherdess, your wit flies high,
Up to the sky,

And views the gates of Heaven,
Which are the planets seven;
Sees how fixed stars are placed,
And how the meteors waste;
What makes the snow so white,
And how the sun makes light;
What makes the biting cold
On everything take hold;
And hail a mixed degree,
'Twixt snow and ice you see
From whence the winds do blow;
What thunder is, you know,
And what makes lightning flow
Like liquid streams, you show.
From sky you come to th'Earth,
And view each creature's birth;
Sink to the centre deep,
Where all dead bodies sleep;
And there observe to know,
What makes the minerals grow;
How vegetables sprout,
And how the plants come out;
Take notice of all seed,
And what the Earth doth breed;
Then view the springs below,
And mark how waters flow;
What makes the tides to rise
Up proudly to the skies,
And shrinking back descend,
As fearing to offend.
Also your wit doth view
The vapour and the dew,
In Summer's heat, that wet
Doth seem like the Earth's sweat;
In Winter-time, that dew
Like paint's white to the view,
Cold makes that thick, white, dry;
As cerusse it doth lie
On th' Earth's black face, so fair
As painted ladies are;
But, when a heat is felt,

That frosty paint doth melt.
　　Thus Heav'n and Earth you view,
And see what's old, what's new;
How bodies transmigrate,
Lives are predestinate.
Thus doth your wit reveal
What Nature would conceal.
Lady Happy My shepherd,
All those that live do know it,
That you are born a poet,
Your wit doth search mankind,
In body and in mind;
The appetites you measure,
And weigh each several pleasure;
Do figure every passion,
And every humour's fashion;
See how the fancy's wrought,
And what makes every thought;
Fathom conceptions low,
From whence opinions flow;
Observe the memory's length,
And understanding's strength
Your wit doth reason find,
The centre of the mind,
Wherein the rational soul
Doth govern and control,
There doth she sit in state,
Predestinate by fate,
And by the Gods' decree,
That Sovereign she should be.
　　And thus your wit can tell,
How souls in bodies dwell;
As that the mind dwells in the brain,
And in the mind the soul doth reign,
And in the soul the life doth last,
For with the body it doth not waste;
Nor shall wit like the body die,
But live in the world's memory.
Princess May I live in your favour, and be possessed with your love and person, is the height of my ambitions.
Lady Happy I can neither deny you my love nor person.

Princess In amorous pastoral verse we did not woo.
As other pastoral lovers use to do.
Lady Happy Which doth express, we shall more constant be,
And in a married life better agree.
Princess We shall agree, for we true love inherit,
Join as one body and soul, or Heav'nly spirit.

Here come rural sports, as country dances about the Maypole:
that pair which dances best is crowned King and Queen of the shepherds
that year; which happens to the Princess, and the Lady Happy

Lady Happy [*to the Princess*] Let me tell you, servant, that our custom is
to dance about this Maypole, and that pair which dances best is crowned
King and Queen of all the shepherds and shepherdesses this year: which
sport if it please you we will begin.
Princess Nothing, sweetest mistress, that pleases you, can displease me.

They dance; after the dancing the Princess and Lady Happy
are crowned with a garland of flowers. A shepherd speaks.
(Written by my Lord Duke)

> You've won the prize; and justly; so we all
> Acknowledge it with joy, and offer here
> Our hatchments up, our sheep-hooks as your due,
> And scrips of corduant, and oaten pipe;
> So all our pastoral ornaments we lay
> Here at your feet, with homage to obey
> All your commands, and all these things we bring
> In honour of our dancing Queen and King;
> For dancing heretofore has got more riches
> Than we can find in all our shepherds' breeches;
> Witness rich Holmby: long then may you live,
> And for your dancing what we have we give.

A wassail is carried about and syllabubs. Another shepherd speaks,
or sings this that follows (by my Lord Duke)

> The jolly wassail now do bring,
> With apples drowned in stronger ale,
> And fresher syllabubs, and sing;
> Then each to tell their love-sick tale:

So home by couples, and thus draw
Ourselves by holy Hymen's Law.

*The scene vanishes. Enter the Princess sola, and walks a turn
or two in a musing posture, then views herself, and speaks.*

Princess What, have I on a petticoat? Oh Mars! Thou God of War, pardon
my sloth; but yet remember thou art a lover, and so am I. But you will say,
my kingdom wants me, not only to rule, and govern it, but to defend it. But
what is a kingdom in comparison of a beautiful mistress? Base thoughts fly
off, for I will not go; did not only a kingdom, but the world want me.

Exit

*Enter the Lady Happy sola, and melancholy, and after
a short musing speaks*

Lady Happy O Nature, O you Gods above,
Suffer me not to fall in love;
O strike me dead here in this place
Rather than fall into disgrace.

Enter Madame Mediator

Madame Mediator What, Lady Happy, solitary alone! And musing like a
disconsolate lover!
Lady Happy No, I was meditating of holy things.
Madame Mediator Holy things! What holy things?
Lady Happy Why, such holy things as the Gods are.
Madame Mediator By my truth, whether your contemplation be of Gods
or of men, you are become lean and pale since I was in the Convent last.

Enter the Princess

Princess Come my sweet mistress, shall we go to our sports and recreations?
Madame Mediator Beshrew me, Your Highness hath sported too much I
fear.
Princess Why, Madame Mediator, say you so?
Madame Mediator Because the Lady Happy looks not well, she is become
pale and lean.
Princess Madame Mediator, your eyes are become dim with time; for my
sweet mistress appears with greater splendour than the God of Light.

Madame Mediator For all you are a great Princess, give me leave to tell you,

   I am not so old, nor yet so blind,
   But that I see you are too kind.

Princess Well, Madame Mediator, when we return from our recreations, I will ask your pardon, for saying, your eyes are dim, conditionally you will ask pardon for saying my mistress looks not well.

Exeunt

The Scene is opened, and there is presented a rock as in the sea,
whereupon sits the Princess and the Lady Happy; the Princess as
the Sea-God Neptune, the Lady Happy as a Sea-Goddess:
the rest of the ladies sit somewhat lower, dressed like Water-Nymphs;
the Princess begins to speak a speech in verse, and after her the
Lady Happy makes her speech.

Princess I am the King of all the seas,
All wat'ry creatures do me please,
Obey my power and command,
And bring me presents from the land;
The waters open their flood-gates,
Where ships do pass, sent by the Fates;
Which Fates do yearly, as May-dew,
Send me a tribute from Peru,
From other nations besides,
Brought by their servants, winds and tides,
Ships fraught and men to me they bring;
My watery kingdom lays them in.
Thus from the Earth a tribute I
Receive, which shows my power thereby:
Besides, my kingdom's richer far
Than all the Earth and every star.

Lady Happy I feed the sun, which gives them light,
And makes them shine in darkest night,
Moist vapour from my breast I give,
Which he sucks forth, and makes him live,
Or else his fire would soon go out,
Grow dark, or burn the world throughout.

Princess What Earthly creature's like to me,
That hath such power and majesty?
My palaces are rocks of stone,

And built by Nature's hand alone;
No base, dissembling, coz'ning art
Do I employ in any part,
In all my kingdom large and wide,
Nature directs and doth provide
Me all provisions which I need,
And cooks my meat on which I feed.
Lady Happy My cabinets are oyster-shells,
In which I keep my orient-pearls,
To open them I use the tide,
As keys to locks, which opens wide,
The oyster-shells then out I take;
Those, orient-pearls and crowns do make;
And modest coral I do wear,
Which blushes when it touches air.
On silver waves I sit and sing,
And then the fish lie listening:
Then sitting on a rocky stone,
I comb my hair with fish's bone;
The whil'st Apollo, with his beams,
Doth dry my hair from wat'ry streams.
His light doth glaze the water's face,
Make the large sea my looking-glass;
So when I swim on waters high,
I see myself as I glide by:
But when the sun begins to burn,
I back into my waters turn,
And dive unto the bottom low:
Then on my head the waters flow,
In curled waves and circles round;
And thus with waters am I crowned.
Princess Besides, within the waters deep,
In hollow rocks my court I keep;
Of ambergris my bed is made,
Whereon my softer limbs are laid,
There take I rest; and whilst I sleep,
The sea doth guard, and safe me keep
From danger; and, when I awake,
A present of a ship doth make.
No Prince on Earth hath more resort,
Nor keeps more servants in his court;

Of Mermaids you're waited on,
And Mermen do attend upon
My person; some are counsellors,
Which order all my great affairs;
Within my wat'ry kingdom wide,
They help to rule, and so to guide
The Commonwealth; and are by me
Preferred unto an high degree.
Some Judges are, and Magistrates,
Decide each cause, and end debates;
Others, commanders in the war;
And some to Governments prefer;
Others are Neptune's Priests which pray
And preach when is a holy-day.
And thus with method order I,
And govern all with Majesty;
I am sole monarch of the sea,
And all therein belongs to me.

A Sea-Nymph sings this following song

1
We watery nymphs rejoice and sing
About God Neptune our sea's King;
In sea-green habits, for to move
His Godhead, for to fall in love.

2
That with his trident he doth stay
Rough foaming billows which obey:
And when in triumph he doth stride
His managed dolphin for to ride.

3
All his sea-people to his wish,
From whale to herring subject fish,
With acclamations do attend him,
And pray's more riches still to send him.

Exeunt. The scene vanishes

V.i

*Enter the Princess and the Lady Happy; the Princess is in a man's
apparel as going to dance; they whisper sometime; then the Lady Happy
takes a ribbon from her arm, and gives it to the Princess, who gives her
another instead of that, and kisses her hand. They go in and come
presently out again with all the company to dance, the music plays;
and after they have danced a little while, in comes Madame Mediator
wringing her hands, and spreading her arms; and full of passion
cries out*

Madame Mediator O ladies, ladies! You're all betrayed, undone, undone;
for there is a man disguised in the Convent, search and you'll find it.

*They all skip from each other, as afraid of each other; only
the Princess and the Lady Happy stand still together*

Princess You may make the search, Madame Mediator; but you will quit
me, I am sure.
Madame Mediator By my faith but I will not, for you are most to be
suspected.
Princess But you say the man is disguised like a woman, and I am accoutred like a man.
Madame Mediator Fidle, fadle, that is nothing to the purpose.

*Enter an ambassador to the Prince; the ambassador kneels,
the Prince bids him rise*

Prince What came you here for?
Ambassador May it please Your Highness, the Lords of your Council sent
me to inform Your Highness, that your subjects are so discontented at your
absence, that if Your Highness do not return into your kingdom soon,
they'll enter this kingdom by reason they hear you are here; and some
report as if Your Highness were restrained as prisoner.
Prince So I am, but not by the State, but by this fair lady, who must be
your Sovereigness.

The ambassador kneels and kisses her hand

Prince But since I am discovered, go from me to the Councillors of this
State, and inform them of my being here, as also the reason, and that I ask

their leave I may marry this lady; otherwise, tell them I will have her by force of arms.

Exit ambassador

Madame Mediator O the Lord! I hope you will not bring an army, to take away all the women, will you?

Prince No, Madame Mediator, we will leave you behind us.

Exeunt

V.ii

Enter Madame Mediator lamenting and crying with a handkerchief in her hand

Madame Mediator O gentlemen, that I never had been born, we're all undone and lost!

Monsieur Adviser Why, what's the matter?

Madame Mediator Matter? Nay, I doubt, there's too much matter.

Monsieur Adviser How?

Madame Mediator How, never such a mistake! Why we have taken a man for a woman.

Monsieur Adviser Why, a man is for a woman.

Madame Mediator Fidle, fadle, I know that as well as you can tell me; but there was a young man dressed in woman's apparel, and entered our Convent, and the Gods know what he hath done. He is mighty handsome, and that's a great temptation to virtue; but I hope all is well. But this wicked world will lay aspersion upon anything or nothing; and therefore I doubt, all my sweet young birds are undone, the Gods comfort them.

Monsieur Courtly But could you never discover it? Nor have no hint he was a man?

Madame Mediator No truly, only once I saw him kiss the Lady Happy; and you know women's kisses are unnatural, and methought they kissed with more alacrity than women use, a kind of titillation, and more vigorous.

Monsieur Adviser Why, did you not then examine it?

Madame Mediator Why, they would have said I was but an old jealous fool, and laughed at me; but experience is a great matter. If the Gods had not been merciful to me, he might have fallen upon me.

Monsieur Courtly Why, what if he had?

Madame Mediator Nay, if he had I care not, for I defy the flesh as much as I renounce the Devil, and the pomp of this wicked world. But if I could but have saved my young sweet virgins, I would willingly have sacrificed my body for them; for we are not born for ourselves but for others.

Monsieur Adviser 'Tis piously said, truly, lovingly and kindly.

Madame Mediator Nay, I have read *The Practice of Piety*. But further they say, he is a foreign Prince; and they say, they're very hot.

Monsieur Courtly Why, you are Madame Mediator, you must mediate and make a friendship.

Madame Mediator Od's body what do you talk of mediation, I doubt they are too good friends. Well, this will be news for court, town and country, in private letters, in the Gazette, and in abominable ballets, before it be long, and jeered to death by the pretending wits. But, good gentlemen, keep this as a secret, and let not me be the author, for you will hear abundantly of it before it be long.

Monsieur Adviser But, Madame Mediator, this is no secret, it is known all the town over, and the State is preparing to entertain the Prince.

Madame Mediator Lord! To see how ill news will fly so soon abroad.

Monsieur Courtly Ill news indeed for us wooers.

Monsieur Adviser We only wooed in imagination but not in reality.

Madame Mediator But you all had hopes.

Monsieur Adviser We had so; but she only has the fruition: for it is said, the Prince and she are agreed to marry; and the State is so willing, as they account it an honour, and hope shall reap much advantage by the match.

Madame Mediator Yes, yes; but there is an old and true saying, 'There's much between the cup and the lip'.

Exeunt

V.iii

*Enter the Prince as bridegroom, and the Lady Happy as bride,
hand in hand under a canopy borne over their heads by men;
the Magistrates march before, then the hautboys; and then the bridal
guests, as coming from the church, where they were married.
All the company bids them joy. They thank them*

Madame Mediator Although Your Highness will not stay to feast with your guests, pray dance before you go.

Prince We will both dance and feast before we go; come madame let us dance, to please Madame Mediator.

The Prince and Princess dance

Prince Now, noble friends, dance you; and the Princess, and I, will rest ourselves.

After they have danced, the Lady Happy, as now Princess,
speaks to the Lady Vertue

Lady Happy [*to Lady Vertue*] Lady Vertue, I perceive you keep Mimick
still. [*to the Prince*] Sir this is the Mimick I told you of. [*to Mimick*]
Mimick, will you leave your lady and go with me?
Mimick I am a married man, and have married my lady's maid Nan, and
she will keep me at home do what I can; but you've now a mimick of your
own, for the Prince has imitated a woman.
Lady Happy What you rogue, do you call me a fool?
Mimick Not I, please Your Highness, unless all women be fools.
Prince Is your wife a fool?
Mimick Man and wife, 'tis said, makes but one fool. [*He kneels to the*
Prince.] I have an humble petition to Your Highness.
Prince Rise; what petition is that?
Mimick That Your Highness would be pleased to divide the Convent in
two equal parts; one for fools, and th' other for married men, as madmen.
Prince I'll divide it for virgins and widows.
Mimick That will prove a Convent of Pleasure indeed; but they will never
agree, especially if there be some disguised Prince amongst them. But you
had better bestow it on old decrepit and bed-rid matrons, and then it may
be called the Convent of Charity, if it cannot possibly be named the
Convent of Chastity.
Prince Well, to show my charity, and to keep your wife's chastity, I'll
bestow my bounty in a present, on the condition you speak the Epilogue.
Come, noble friends, let us feast before we part.

Exeunt

Mimick solus

Mimick An Epilogue says he, the Devil an Epilogue have I: let me study.
[*He questions and answers himself.*] I have it, I have it; No faith, I have it
not; I lie, I have it, I say, I have it not; fie Mimick, will you lie? Yes, Mimick,
I will lie, if it be my pleasure: But I say, it is gone. What is gone? The
Epilogue. When had you it? I never had it; then you did not lose it; that is
all one, but I must speak it, although I never had it. How can you speak it,
and never had it? I, marry, that's the question; but words are nothing, and
then an Epilogue is nothing, and so I may speak nothing. Then nothing be
my speech.

Epilogue

Noble spectators by this candlelight,
I know not what to say, but bid goodnight:
I dare not beg applause, our poetess then
Will be enraged, and kill me with her pen;
For she is careless, and is void of fear;
If you dislike her play she doth not care.
But I shall weep, my inward grief shall show
Through floods of tears, that through my eyes will flow.
And so poor Mimick he for sorrow die.
And then through pity you may chance to cry:
But if you please, you may a cordial give,
Made up with praise, and so he long may live.

1673

18. Bathsua Makin

from *An Essay to Revive the Ancient Education
of Gentlewomen*

*To all ingenious and virtuous ladies, more especially to
her Highness the Lady Mary, eldest daughter to his Royal Highness
the Duke of York.*

Custom, when it is inveterate, has a mighty influence: it has the force of
nature itself. The barbarous custom to breed women low is grown general
amongst us, and hath prevailed so far, that it is verily believed (especially
amongst a sort of debauched sots) that women are not endued with such
reason, as men; nor capable of improvement by education, as they are. It is
looked upon as a monstrous thing, to pretend the contrary. A learned
woman is thought to be a comet that bodes mischief whenever it appears.
To offer to the world the liberal education of women is to deface the image
of God in man, it will make women so high, and men so low, like fire in the
house-top, it will set the whole world in a flame.

These things, and worse than these, are commonly talked of, and verily
believed by many, who think themselves wise men: to contradict these is a
bold attempt, where the attempter must expect to meet with much opposition.

Therefore, ladies, I beg the candid opinion of your sex, whose interest I assert. More especially I implore the favour of Your Royal Highness, a person most eminent amongst them, whose patronage alone will be sufficient protection. What I have written is not out of humour to show how much may be said of a trivial thing to little purpose. I verily think, women were formerly educated in the knowledge of arts and tongues, and by their education, many did rise to a great height in learning. Were women thus educated now, I am confident the advantage would be very great. The women would have honour and pleasure, their relations profit, and the whole nation advantage. I am very sensible it is an ill time to set on foot this design: wherein not only learning but virtue itself is scorned and neglected, as pedantic things, fit only for the vulgar. I know no better way to reform these exorbitancies, than to persuade women to scorn those toys and trifles they now spend their time about, and to attempt higher things, here offered. This will either reclaim the men; or make them ashamed to claim the sovereignty over such as are more wise and virtuous than themselves. Were a competent number of schools erected to educate ladies ingenuously, methinks I see how ashamed men would be of their ignorance, and how industrious the next generation would be to wipe off their reproach.

I expect to meet with many scoffs and taunts from inconsiderate and illiterate men, that prize their own lusts and pleasure more than your profit and content. I shall be the less concerned at these, so long as I am in your favour; and this discourse may be a weapon in your hands to defend yourselves, whilst you endeavour to polish your souls, that you may glorify God, and answer the end of your creation, to be meet helps to your husbands. Let not your ladyships be offended, that I do not (as some have wittily done) plead for female pre-eminence. To ask too much is the way to be denied all. God has made the man the head, if you be educated and instructed, as I propose, I am sure you will acknowledge it, and be satisfied that you are helps, that your husbands do consult and advise with you (which if you be wise they will be glad of) and that your husbands have the casting voice, in whose determinations you will acquiesce. That this may be the effect of this education in all ladies that shall attempt it, is the desire of

> Your servant.

❀ ❀ ❀ ❀

Women have formerly been educated in arts and tongues
Little is recorded concerning the manner, how women were educated formerly. You can expect my proof to be only topical and by circumstances. It does appear out of sacred writ, that women were employed in most of

the great transactions that happened in the world, even in reference to religion. Miriam seems to be next to Moses and Aaron, she was a great poet, and philosopher [Exod. 16:20–21]: for both learning, and religion were generally in former times wrapped up in verse. The women met David, singing triumphant songs [1 Sam. 18:6–7], composed (it's like by themselves) a great specimen of liberal education. Deborah, the deliverer of Israel, was without all doubt a learned woman that understood the law [Judges 4–5]. Huldah, the prophetesses, dwelt in a college, (we may suppose) where women were trained up in good literature. We may be sure she was a very wise woman. For King Josiah sends Hilkiah the priest, and the nobles of his court, in a case of difficulty and danger, to consult with her. (2 Chron. 34:20, 21 etc.)

In the New Testament we find Anna, a prophetess [Luke 2:36–8]. Paul, (Romans 16: 1) commends unto them Phebe, who was not only a servant of Christ, but a servant of the Church at Cencrea. Verse 12 he tells us Triphena, Thiphosa and Persis laboured much in the Lord. Priscilla instructed Apollos.

Timothy's grandmother called Lois, and his Mother Eunice were not only gracious women, but learned women; for from a child they instructed him in the Holy Scriptures. (2 Timothy 1:5 compared with chapter 3:15). The children of the Elect Lady, found walking in the truth, were instructed by her [2 John]. Philip's four daughters were prophetesses (Acts 21). Though women may not speak in the church, yet those extraordinary enabled, to whom Paul speaks (1 Corinthians 11:5), might. For Paul directs them they should not pray nor prophesy with their heads uncovered, which supposes they might do the things. I shall not dispute these texts what this praying and prophesying was; it serves my turn, that women extraordinarily enabled were publicly employed.

We may infer from the stories of the Muses, that this way of education was very ancient. All conclude the heroes were men famous in their generation, therefore canonized after their deaths. We may with like reason conclude, Minerva and the nine Muses were women famous for learning whilst they lived, and therefore thus adored when dead.

❋ ❋ ❋ ❋

It may now be demanded, by those studious of antiquity, why the virtues, the disciplines, the nine Muses, the devisers, and the patrons of all good arts, the three Graces, should rather be represented under the feminine sex, and their pictures be drawn to the portraitures of damsels, and not have masculine denominations, and the effigies of men? Yea, why Christians themselves, in all their books and writings which they commit to posterity, still continue the same practice? Why Wisdom is said to be the daughter of the highest, and not the son? Why Faith, Hope, and Charity, her daughters, are represented as women? Why should the seven Liberal Arts be expressed in women's shapes? Doubtless this is one reason; women were the inventors of many of these arts, and the promoters of them, and since have studied them, and attained to an excellency in them. And being, thus adorned and beautified with these arts, as a testimony of our gratitude for their invention, and as a token of honour for their proficiency; we make women the emblems of these things, having no fitter hieroglyphics to express them by. I shall add this one thing, worthy observation, to the great honour and commendation of the feminine sex.

The parts of the world have their denomination from women, Asia is so called from the nymph Asia, the mother of Japethus and Prometheus. Europe, from Europa the daughter of Agenor. Lybia (which is Africa) from Libia the daughter of Epaphus. America (lately discovered) bears the same female figure.

It is usual for men to pride and boast themselves in the wisdom, valour, and riches of their ancestors; what wise men their forefathers have been, what great things they have done, and what large possessions they have had, when they themselves are degenerated and become ignorant, cowardly, beggarly, debauched sots.

I hope women will make another use of what I have said; instead of claiming honour from what women have formerly been, they will labour to imitate them in learning those arts their sex has invented, in studying those tongues they have understood, and in practising those virtues shadowed under their shapes; the knowledge of art and tongues, the exercise of virtue and piety, will certainly (let men say what they will) make them honourable.

Care ought to be taken by us to educate women in learning.

That I may be more distinct in what I intend, I shall distinguish of women,

Women are of two sorts, { RICH – of good natural parts

POOR – of low parts.

I do not mean, that it is necessary to the *esse*, to the substance, or to the salvation of women, to be thus educated. Those that are mean in the world, have not an opportunity for this education. Those that are of low parts, though they have opportunity, cannot reach this; *Ex quovis liguo non fit Minerva*. My meaning is, persons that God has blessed with the things of this world, that have competent natural parts, ought to be educated in knowledge. That is, it is much better they should spend the time of their youth, to be competently instructed in those things usually taught to gentlewomen at schools, and the overplus of their time to be spent in gaining arts, and tongues, and useful knowledge, rather than to trifle away so many precious minutes merely to polish their hands and feet, to curl their locks, to dress and trim their bodies; and in the meantime to neglect their souls, and not at all, or very little to endeavour to know God, Jesus Christ, themselves, and the things of nature, arts, and tongues, subservient to these. I do not deny but women ought to be brought up to a comely and decent carriage, to their needs, to neatness, to understand all those things that do particularly belong to their sex. But when these things are competently cared for, and where there are endowments of nature and leisure, then higher things ought to be endeavoured after. Merely to teach gentlewomen to frisk and dance, to paint their faces, to curl their hair, to put on a whisk, to wear gay clothes, is not truly to adorn, but to adulterate their bodies; yea, (what is worse) to defile their souls. This (like Circe's cup) turns them to beasts; whilst their belly is their God, they become swine; whilst lust they become goats; and whilst pride is their God, they become devils. Doubtless this under-breeding of women began among heathen and barbarous people; it continues with the Indians, where they make their women mere slaves, and wear them out in drudgery. It is practised amongst degenerate and apostate Christians, upon the same score and now is a part of their religion; it would therefore be a piece of reformation to correct it; and it would notably countermine them who fight against us, as Satan against Adam, by seducing our women, who then easily seduce their husbands.

Had God intended women only as a finer sort of cattle, he would not have made them reasonable. Brutes, a few degrees higher than drils or monkeys, (which the Indians use to do many offices) might have better fitted some men's lust, pride, and pleasure; especially those that desire to keep them ignorant to be tyrannised over.

God intended woman as a helpmeet to man, in his constant conversation, and in the concerns of his family and estate, when he should most need, in sickness, weakness, absence, death, etc. Whilst we neglect to fit them for those things, we renounce God's blessing, he has appointed women for, are ungrateful to him, cruel to them, and injurious to ourselves.

❀ ❀ ❀

I hope I shall by this discourse persuade some parents to be more careful for the future of the breeding of their daughters. You cark and care to get great portions for them, which sometimes occasions their ruin. Here is a sure portion, an easy way to make them excellent. How many born to good fortunes, when their wealth has been wasted, have supported themselves and families too by their wisdom?

I hope some of these considerations will at least move some of this abused sex to set a right value upon themselves, according to the dignity of their creation, that they might, with an honest pride and magnanimity, scorn to be bowed down and made to stoop to such follies and vanities, trifles and nothings, so far below them, and unproportionable to their noble souls, nothing inferior to those of men, and equally precious to God in Christ, in whom there is neither male nor female.

Let a generous resolution possess your minds, seeing men in this age have invaded women's vices, in a noble revenge, reassume those virtues, which men sometimes unjustly usurped to themselves, but ought to have left them in common to both sexes.

Postscript

If any enquire where this education may be performed, such may be informed, that a school is lately erected for gentlewomen at Tottenham-high-cross, within four miles of London, in the road to Ware, where Mrs Makin is Governess, who was sometimes tutoress to the Princess Elisabeth, daughter to King Charles the First; where, by the blessing of God, gentlewomen may be instructed in the principles of religion; and in all manner of sober and virtuous education. More particularly, in all things ordinarily taught in other schools:

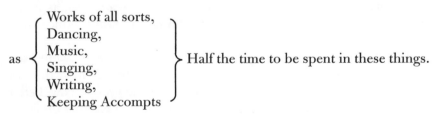

as $\left\{\begin{array}{l}\text{Works of all sorts,}\\ \text{Dancing,}\\ \text{Music,}\\ \text{Singing,}\\ \text{Writing,}\\ \text{Keeping Accompts}\end{array}\right\}$ Half the time to be spent in these things.

The other half to be employed in gaining the Latin and French tongues; and those that please, may learn Greek and Hebrew, the Italian and Spanish. In all which this gentlewoman has a competent knowledge.

Gentlewomen of eight or nine years old, that can read well, may be instructed in a year or two (according to their parts) in the Latin and French tongues; by such plain and short rules, accommodated to the grammar of the English tongue, that they may easily keep what they have learned, and recover what they shall lose, as those that learn music by notes.

Those that will bestow longer time, may learn the other languages, aforementioned, as they please.

Repositories also for visibles shall be prepared; by which, from behold-ing the things, gentlewomen may learn the names, natures, values, and life of herbs, shrubs, trees, mineral juices, metals and stones.

Those that please, may learn limning, preserving, pastry, and cookery.

Those that will allow longer time, may attain some general knowledge in astronomy, geography; but especially in arithmetic and history.

Those that think one language enough for a woman, may forbear the languages, and learn only experimental philosophy; and more, or fewer of the other things aforementioned, as they incline.

The rate certain shall be 20 *l. per annum*. But if a competent improve-ment be made in the tongues, and the other things aforementioned, as shall be agreed upon, then something more will be expected. But the parents shall judge what shall be deserved by the undertaker.

Those that think these things improbable or impracticable, may have further account every Tuesday at Mr Mason's coffee house in Cornhill, near the Royal Exchange; and Thursdays at the Bolt and Tun in Fleet Street, between the hours of three and six in the afternoons, by some person whom Mrs Makin shall appoint.

1678

19. Anne Bradstreet
from *Several Poems*

The Prologue.

1

To sing of wars, of captains, and of kings,
Of cities founded, of commonwealths begun,
For my mean pen, are too superior things,
And how they all, or each, their dates have run:
Let poets and historians set these forth,
My obscure verse, shall not so dim their worth.

2

But when my wond'ring eyes and envious heart,
Great Bartas' sugared lines do but read o'er;

Fool, I do grudge, the Muses did not part
'Twixt him and me, that over-fluent store;
A Bartas can do, what a Bartas will,
But simple I, according to my skill.

3

From schoolboy's tongue, no rhethoric we expect,
Nor yet a sweet consort, from broken strings,
Nor perfect beauty, where's a main defect,
My foolish, broken, blemished Muse so sings;
And this to mend, alas, no art is able,
'Cause nature made it so irreparable.

4

Nor can I, like that fluent, sweet-tongued Greek
Who lisped at first, speak afterwards more plain
By art, he gladly found what he did seek,
A full requital of his striving pain:
Art can do much, but this maxim's most sure,
A weak or wounded brain admits no cure.

5

I am obnoxious to each carping tongue,
Who says, my hand a needle better fits,
A poet's pen, all scorn, I should thus wrong;
For such despite they cast on female wits:
If what I do prove well, it won't advance,
They'll say it's stol'n, or else, it was by chance.

6

But sure the antic Greeks were far more mild,
Else of our sex, why feigned they those nine,
And poesy made, Calliope's own child,
So 'mongst the rest, they placed the arts divine:
But this weak knot they will full soon untie,
The Greeks did nought, but play the fool and lie.

7

Let Greeks be Greeks, and women what they are,
Men have precedency, and still excel,
It is but vain, unjustly to wage war,

Men can do best, and women know it well;
Pre-eminence in each, and all is yours,
Yet grant some small acknowledgement of ours.

8
And oh, ye high flown quills, that soar the skies,
And ever with your prey, still catch your praise,
If e'er you deign these lowly lines your eyes
Give thyme or parsley wreath, I ask no bays:
This mean and unrefined ore of mine,
Will make your glistering gold but more to shine.

The Four Ages of Man
Lo! Now four other acts upon the stage,
Childhood, and Youth, the Manly, and Old Age.
The first: son unto phlegm, grandchild to water,
Unstable, supple, moist, and cold's his nature.
The second, frolic, claims his pedigree,
From blood air, for hot, and moist is he.
The third, of fire, and choler is composed,
Vindicative, and quarrelsome disposed.
The last, of earth, and heavy melancholy,
Solid, hating all lightness, and all folly.
Childhood was clothed in white, and given to show,
His spring was intermixed with some snow.
Upon his head a garland nature set:
Of primrose, daisy, and the violet.
Such cold mean flowers the spring puts forth betime,
Before the sun hath throughly heat the clime.
His hobby striding, did not ride, but run,
And in his hand an hour-glass new begun,
In dangers every moment of a fall,
And when 'tis broke, then ends his life and all.
But if he hold, till it have run its last,
Then may he live, till threescore years or past.
Next, Youth came up, in gorgeous attire;
(As that fond age, doth most of all desire.)
His suit of crimson, and his scarf of green:
His pride in's countenance, quickly seen.
Garland of roses, pinks, and gillyflowers,

Seemed on's head to grow bedewed with showers:
His face as fresh, as is Aurora fair,
When blushing, she first 'gins to light the air.
No wooden horse, but one of metal tried:
He seems to fly, or swim, and not to ride.
Then prancing on the stage, about he wheels;
But as he went, death waited at his heels.
The next came up, in a more graver sort,
As one that cared for a good report.
His sword by's side, and choler in his eyes;
But neither used as yet, for he was wise.
Of Autumn fruits a basket on his arm.
His golden god in's purse, which was his charm.
And last of all, to act upon this stage;
Leaning upon his staff, comes up Old Age.
Under his arm a sheaf of wheat he bore,
A harvest of the best, what needs he more?
In's other hand a glass, ev'n almost run,
Thus writ about: 'This out, then I am done.'
His hoary hairs, and grave aspect made way;
And all gave care, to what he had to say.
These being met, each in his equipage,
Intend to speak, according to their age:
But wise Old Age, did with all gravity,
To childish Childhood, give precedency.
And to the rest, his reason mildly told;
That he was young, before he grew so old.
To do as he, each one full soon assents,
Their method was, that of the elements,
That each should tell, what of himself he knew;
Both good and bad, but yet no more than's true:
With heed now stood, three ages of frail man,
To hear the child, who crying, thus began.

Childhood

Ah me! conceived in sin, and born with sorrow,
A nothing, here today, and gone tomorrow.
Whose mean beginning, blushing can't reveal,
But night and darkness, must with shame conceal.
My mother's breeding sickness, I will spare;

Her nine months weary burthen not declare.
To show her bearing pains, I should do wrong,
To tell those pangs, which can't be told by tongue;
With tears into this world I did arrive;
My mother still did waste, as I did thrive:
Who yet with love, and all alacrity,
Spending was willing, to be spent for me;
With wayward cries, I did disturb her rest;
Who sought still to appease me, with the breast,
With weary arms, she danced, and 'By, by' sung,
When wretched I (ingrate) had done the wrong.
When infancy was past, my childishness,
Did act all folly, that it could express.
My silliness did only take delight,
In that which riper age did scorn, and slight:
In rattles, baubles, and such toyish stuff.
My then ambitious thoughts, were low enough.
My highborn soul, so straitly was confined:
That its own worth, it did not know, nor mind.
This little house of flesh, did spacious count:
Through ignorance, all troubles did surmount.
Yet this advantage, had mine ignorance,
Freedom from envy, and from arrogance.
How to be rich, or great, I did not cark;
A baron or a duke, ne'er made my mark.
Nor studious was, kings' favours how to buy,
With costly presence, or base flattery.
No office coveted, wherein I might
Make strong myself, and turn aside weak right.
No malice bear, to this, or that great peer,
Nor unto buzzing whisperers, gave ear.
I gave no hand, nor vote, for death, or life:
I'd nought to do, 'twixt king and people's strife.
No statist I: nor marti'list i' th' field;
Where'er I went, mine innocence was shield.
My quarrels, not for diadems did rise;
But for an apple, plum, or some such prize,
My strokes did cause no blood, no wounds, or scars.
My little wrath did end soon as my wars.
My duel was no challenge, nor did seek.
My foe should weltering, in his bowels reek.

I had no suits at law, neighbours to vex.
Nor evidence for lands, did me perplex.
I feared no storms, nor all the winds that blows,
I had no ships at sea, no freights to lose.
I feared no drought, nor wet, I had no crop,
Nor yet on future things did set my hope.
This was mine innocence, but ah the seeds,
Lay rakèd up; of all the cursèd weeds,
Which sprouted forth, in my ensuing age,
As he can tell, that next comes on the stage.
But yet let me relate, before I go,
The sins, and dangers I am subject to.
From birth, stained with Adam's sinful fact;
Thence I began to sin, as soon as act.
A perverse will, a love to what's forbid:
A serpent's sting in pleasing face lay hid.
A lying tongue as soon as it could speak,
And fifth commandment do daily break.
Oft stubborn, peevish, sullen, pout, and cry:
Then nought can please, and yet I know not why.
As many are my sins, so dangers too:
For sin brings sorrow, sickness, death, and woe.
And though I miss, the tossings of the mind:
Yet griefs, in my frail flesh, I still do find.
What gripes of wind, mine infancy did pain?
What tortures I, in breeding teeth sustain?
What crudities my cold stomach hath bred?
Whence vomits, flux, and worms have issuèd?
What breaches, knocks, and falls I daily have?
And some perhaps, I carry to my grave.
Sometimes in fire, sometimes in water fall:
Strangely preserved, yet mind it not at all.
At home, abroad, my danger's manifold.
That wonder 'tis, my glass till now doth hold.
I've done, unto my elders I give way.
For 'tis but little, that a child can say.

Youth

My goodly clothing, and my beauteous skin,
Declare some greater riches are within;

But what is best I'll first present to view,
And then the worst, in a more ugly hue;
For thus to do, we on this stage assemble,
Then let not him, which hath most craft dissemble;
Mine education, and my learning's such,
As might myself, and others, profit much:
With nurture trainèd up in virtue's schools,
Of science, arts, and tongues, I know the rules,
The manners of the court, I also know,
And so likewise what they in th' country do;
The brave attempts of valiant knights I prize,
That dare scale walls and forts, reared to the skies;
The snorting horse, the trumpet, drum I like,
The glitt'ring sword, the pistol and the pike;
I cannot lie entrenched, before a town,
Nor wait till good success our hopes do crown;
I scorn the heavy corslet, musket-proof,
I fly to catch the bullet that's aloof;
Though thus in field, at home, to all most kind;
So affable that I can suit each mind;
I can insinuate into the breast,
And by my mirth can raise the heart depressed;
Sweet music 'raps my brave harmonious soul,
My high thoughts elevate beyond the pole.
My wit, my bounty, and my courtesy,
Make all to place their future hopes on me.
This is my best, but Youth is known alas!
To be as wild as is the snuffing ass,
As vain as froth, or vanity can be,
That who would see vain man, may look on me:
My gifts abused, my education lost,
My woeful parents' longing hopes are crossed,
My wit, evaporates in merriment:
My valour, in some beastly quarrel's spent;
My lust doth hurry me, to all that's ill,
I know no law, nor reason, but my will;
Sometimes lay wait to take a wealthy purse,
Or stab the man, in's own defence (that's worse),
Sometimes I cheat (unkind) a female heir,
Of all at once, who not so wise, as fair,
Trusteth my loving looks, and glozing tongue,

Until her friends, treasure, and honour's gone.
Sometimes I sit carousing others' health,
Until mine own be gone, my wit, and wealth;
From pipe to pot, from pot to words, and blows,
For he that loveth wine, wanteth no woes;
Whole nights, with ruffins, roarers, fiddlers spend,
To all obscenity, mine ears I lend.
All counsel hate, which tends to make me wise,
And dearest friends count for mine enemies;
If any care I take, 'tis to be fine,
For sure my suit more than my virtues shine;
If time from lewd companions I can spare,
'Tis spent to curl and pounce my new-bought hair;
Some new Adonis I do strive to be,
Sardanapalus, now survives in me:
Cards, dice, and oaths, concomitant, I love;
To plays, to masques, to taverns still I move;
And in a word, if what I am you'd hear,
Seek out a British, brutish Cavalier;
Such wretch, such monster am I; but yet more,
I have no heart at all, this to deplore.
Remembering not the dreadful day of doom,
Nor yet that heavy reckoning soon to come;
Though dangers do attend me every hour,
And ghastly death oft threats me with her power:
Sometimes by wounds in idle combats taken,
Sometimes by agues all my body shaken;
Sometimes by fevers, all my moisture drinking,
My heart lies frying, and my eyes are sinking;
Sometimes the quinsy, painful pleurisy,
With sad affrights of death, doth menace me;
Sometimes the two-fold pox, my face be-mars
With outward marks and inward loathsome scars;
Sometimes the frenzy, strangely mads my brain,
That oft for it, in Bedlam I remain.
Too many's my diseases to recite,
That wonder 'tis I yet behold the light,
That yet my bed in darkness is not made,
And I in black oblivion's den now laid;
Of aches full my bones, of woe my heart,
Clapped in that prison, never thence to start

Thus I have said, and what I've been you see,
Childhood and Youth are vain, yea vanity.

Middle Age

Childhood and Youth, forgot, sometimes I've seen,
And now am grown more staid, that have been green,
What they have done, the same was done by me,
As was their praise, or shame, so mine must be.
Now age is more, more good you may expect;
But more mine age, the more is my defect.
When my wild oats, were sown, and ripe, and mown,
I then received a harvest of mine own.
My reason, then bad judge, how little hope,
My empty seed should yield a better crop.
Then with both hands, I grasped the world together,
Thus out of one extreme, into another.
But yet laid hold, on virtue seemingly,
Who climbs without hold, climbs dangerously.
Be my condition mean, I then take pains;
My family to keep, but not for gains.
A father I, then for children must provide:
But if none, then for kindred near allied.
If rich, I'm urged then to gather more.
To bear a part i' th' world, and feed the poor,
 If noble, then mine honour to maintain.
If not riches, nobility can gain.
For time, for place, likewise for each relation,
I wanted not my ready allegation.
Yet all my powers, for self-ends are not spent,
For hundreds bless me, for my bounty lent.
Whose backs I've clothed, and bellies I have fed;
With mine own fleece, and with my household bread.
Yea justice I have done, was I in place;
To cheer the good, and wicked to deface.
The proud I crushed, th' oppressèd I set free,
The liars curbed but nourished verity.
Was I a pastor, I my flock did feed:
And gently led the lambs, as they had need,
A captain I, with skill I trained my band;
And showed them how, in face of foes to stand.

If a soldier, with speed I did obey,
As readily as could my leader say:
Was I a labourer, I wrought all day,
As cheerfully as e'er I took my pay.
Thus hath mine age (in all) sometimes done well.
Sometimes again mine age been worse then hell.
In meanness, greatness, riches, poverty;
Did toil, did broil; oppressed, did steal and lie.
Was I as poor, as poverty could be,
Then baseness was companion unto me.
Such scum, as hedges, and highways do yield,
As neither sow, nor reap, nor plant, nor build.
If to agriculture, I was ordained,
Great labours, sorrows, crosses I sustained.
The early cock, did summon but in vain
My wakeful thoughts, up to my painful gain.
My weary beast, rest from his toil can find;
But if I rest, the more distressed my mind.
If happiness my sordidness hath found,
'Twas in the crop of my manurèd ground:
My thriving cattle and my new milch cow,
My fleecèd sheep, and fruitful farrowing sow.
To greater things, I never did aspire,
My dunghill thoughts, or hopes, could reach no higher.
If to be rich, or great, it was my fate;
How was I broiled with envy, and with hate?
Greater, than was the great'st, was my desire,
And greater still, did set my heart on fire.
And by ambition's sails, I was so carried;
That over flats, and sands, and rocks I hurried,
Oppressed, and sunk, and staved, all in my way;
That did oppose me, to my longèd bay:
My thirst was higher, than nobility,
And oft longed sore, to taste on royalty.
Then kings must be deposed or put to flight
I might possess the throne which was their right.
There set, I rid myself straight out of hand
Of such competitors as might in time withstand.
Then thought my state firm founded, sure to last
But in a trice 'tis ruined by a blast,
Though cemented with more than noble blood

The bottom nought, and so no longer stood.
Sometimes vainglory is the only bait,
Whereby my empty soul, is lured and caught.
Be I of wit, of learning, and of parts;
I judge, I should have room, in all men's hearts.
And envy gnaws, if any do surmount.
I hate not to be held in high'st account.
If bias like, I'm stripped unto my skin,
I glory in my wealth, I have within.
Thus good, and bad, and what I am, you see,
Now in a word, what my diseases be.
The vexing stone, in bladder and in reines,
The strangury torments me with sore pains;
The windy colic oft my bowels rend,
To break the darksome prison, where it's penned;
The cramp and gout doth sadly torture me,
And the restraining lame sciatica;
The asthma, megrim, palsy, lethargy,
The quartan ague, dropsy, lunacy,
Subject to all distempers, that's the truth,
Though some more incident to Age, or Youth:
And to conclude, I may not tedious be,
Man at his best estate is vanity.

Old Age
What you have been, ev'n such have I before,
And all you say, say I, and somewhat more;
Babe's innocence, Youth's wildness I have seen,
And in perplexèd Middle Age have been,
Sickness, dangers, and anxieties have passed,
And on this stage am come to act my last:
I have been young, and strong, and wise as you,
But now, *bis pueri senes*, is too true;
In every age I've found much vanity,
An end of all perfection now I see.
It's not my valour, honour, nor my gold,
My ruined house, now falling can uphold;
It's not my learning, rhetoric, wit so large,
Now hath the power, death's warfare, to discharge;
It's not my goodly state, nor bed of down,

That can refresh, or ease, if conscience frown;
Nor from alliance can I now have hope,
But what I have done well, that is my prop;
He that in youth is godly, wise, and sage,
Provides a staff for to support his age.
Mutations great, some joyful, and some sad,
In this short pilgrimage I oft have had;
Sometimes the heavens with plenty smiled on me,
Sometimes again, rained all adversity;
Sometimes in honour, sometimes in disgrace,
Sometime an abject, then again in place,
Such private changes oft mine eyes have seen,
In various times of state I've also been.
I've seen a kingdom flourish like a tree,
When it was ruled by that celestial she;
And like a cedar, others so surmount,
That but for shrubs they did themselves account;
Then saw I France, and Holland saved, Calais won,
And Philip, and Albertus, half undone;
I saw all peace at home, terror to foes,
But ah, I saw at last those eyes to close:
And then, me thought, the day at noon grew dark,
When it had lost that radiant sun-like spark,
In midst of griefs, I saw our hopes revive,
(For 'twas our hopes then kept our hearts alive)
We changed our Queen for King under whose rays
We joyed in many blessed and prosperous days.
I've seen a prince, the glory of our land,
In prime of youth seized by heaven's angry hand,
Which filled our hearts with fears, with tears our eyes,
Wailing his fate and our own destinies.
I've seen from Rome, an execrable thing,
A plot to blow up nobles, and their King;
But saw the horrid act soon disappointed
And land and nobles saved with their anointed.
I've princes seen, to live on others' lands,
A royal one, by gifts from strangers' hands.
I've seen designs at Rhè, and Cadiz crossed,
And poor Palatinate forever lost;
I've seen unworthy men, advancèd high,
And better ones, suffer extremity:

But neither favour, riches, title, state
Could length their days or once reverse their fate.
I've seen one stabbed, some to lose their heads;
And others fly, struck both with guilt and dread.
I've seen, and so have you, for 'tis but late,
The desolation, of a goodly state.
Plotted and acted, so that none can tell,
Who gave the counsel, but the Prince of Hell.
Three hundred thousand slaughtered innocents
By bloody Popish hellish miscreants:
Oh may you live, and so you will I trust,
To see them swill in blood until they burst.
I've seen a king by force thrust from his throne
And an usurper subtly mount thereon,
I've seen a land unmoulded rent in twain.
But yet may live, to see't made up again:
I've seen it plundered, taxed and soaked in blood,
But out of evil, ye may see much good.
What are my thoughts this is no time to say
Men may more freely speak another day.
These are no old wives' tales, but this is truth;
We old men love to tell, what's done in youth.
But I return, from whence I stepped awry,
My memory is bad, and brain is dry.
My almond-tree grey hairs do flourish now,
And back, once straight, begins apace to bow.
My grinders now are few, my sight doth fail
My skin is wrinkled, and my cheeks are pale.
No more rejoice, at music's pleasing noise,
But waking glad to hear the cock's shrill voice.
I cannot scent, savours of pleasant meat,
Nor savours find, in what I drink or eat.
My hands and arms, once strong, have lost their might,
I cannot labour, much less can I:
My comely legs, as nimble as the roe,
Now stiff and numb, can hardly creep or go.
My heart sometimes as fierce, as lion bold,
Now trembling, is all fearful, sad, and cold;
My golden bowl, and silver cord, e'er long,
Shall both be broke, by racking death so strong;
I then shall go, whence I shall come no more,

Sons, nephews, leave, my farewell to deplore;
In pleasures, and in labours, I have found,
That earth can give no consolation sound.
To great, to rich, to poor, to young, to old,
To mean, to noble, fearful, or to bold:
From king to beggar, all degrees shall find
But vanity, vexation of the mind;
Yea knowing much, the pleasant'st life of all,
Hath yet amongst those sweets, some bitter gall.
Though reading others' works, doth much refresh,
Yet studying much, brings weariness to th' flesh;
My studies, labours, readings, all are done,
And my last period now ev'n almost run;
Corruption, my father, I do call,
Mother, and sisters both; the worms, that crawl,
In my dark house, such kindred I have store,
There, I shall rest, 'til heavens shall be no more;
And when this flesh shall rot, and be consumed,
This body, by this soul, shall be assumed;
And I shall see, with these same very eyes,
My strong Redeemer, coming in the skies;
Triumph I shall, o'er sin, o'er death, o'er hell,
And in that hope, I bid you all farewell.

A Dialogue between Old England and New, concerning their present troubles, Anno 1642

New England

Alas, dear mother, fairest Queen, and best,
With honour, wealth, and peace, happy and blessed;
What ails thee hang thy head, and cross thine arms?
And sit i' th' dust, to sigh these sad alarms?
What deluge of new woes thus overwhelm
The glories of thy ever famous realm?
What means this wailing tone, this mournful guise?
Ah, tell thy daughter, she may sympathise.

Old England

Art ignorant indeed of these my woes?
Or must my forcèd tongue these griefs disclose?

And must myself dissect my tattered state,
Which 'mazed Christendom stands wond'ring at?
And thou a child, a limb, and dost not feel
My fainting weakened body now to reel?
This physic-purging potion I have taken,
Will bring consumption, or an ague quaking,
Unless some cordial thou fetch from high,
Which present help may ease my malady.
If I decease, dost think thou shalt survive?
Or by my wasting state, dost think to thrive?
Then weigh our case, if 't be not justly sad,
Let me lament alone, while thou art glad.

New England

And thus, alas, your state you much deplore,
In general terms, but will not say wherefore:
What med'cine shall I seek to cure this woe,
If th' wound's so dangerous I may not know?
But you perhaps would have me guess it out.
What, hath some Hengist, like that Saxon stout,
By fraud, and force, usurped thy flow'ring crown,
Or by tempestuous wars thy fields trod down?
Or hath Canutus, that brave valiant Dane,
The regal, peaceful sceptre from thee ta'en?
Or is't a Norman, whose victorious hand
With English blood bedews thy conquered land?
Or is't intestine wars that thus offend?
Do Maud and Stephen for the crown contend?
Do barons rise, and side against their King?
And call in foreign aid, to help the thing?
Must Edward be deposed, or is't the hour
That second Richard must be clapped i' th' Tower?
Or is the fatal jar again begun,
That from the red, white pricking roses sprung?
Must Richmond's aid, the nobles now implore,
To come, and break the tushes of the Boar?
If none of these, dear mother, what's your woe?
Pray, do not fear Spain's bragging Armado?
Doth your ally, fair France, conspire your wrack?
Or, doth the Scots play false behind your back?
Doth Holland quit you ill, for all your love?

Whence is this storm, from earth, or heaven above?
Is't drought, is't famine, or is't pestilence?
Dost feel the smart, or fear the consequence?
Your humble child entreats you, show your grief,
Though arms, nor purse she hath, for your relief:
Such is her poverty, yet shall be found
A suppliant for your help, as she is bound.

Old England

I must confess, some of those sores you name,
My beauteous body at this present maim;
But foreign foe, nor feignèd friend I fear,
For they have work enough (thou knowst) elsewhere;
Nor is it Alcie's son, and Henry's daughter,
Whose proud contention cause this slaughter;
Nor nobles siding, to make John no King
French Lewis unjustly to the crown to bring;
No Edward, Richard, to lose rule, and life,
Nor no Lancastrians, to renew old strife;
No Duke of York, nor Earl of March, to soil
Their hands in kindred's blood, whom they did foil:
No crafty tyrant now usurps the seat,
Who nephews slew, that so he might be great.
No need of Tudor, roses to unite,
None knows which is the red, or which the white:
Spain's braving fleet a second time is sunk,
France knows, how oft my fury she hath drunk;
By Edward third, and Henry fifth of fame,
Her lilies in mine arms avouch the same.
My sister Scotland hurts me now no more,
Though she hath been injurious heretofore.
What Holland is, I am in some suspense,
But trust not much unto his excellence;
For wants, sure some I feel, but more I fear,
And for the pestilence, who knows how near?
Famine, and plague, two sisters of the sword,
Destruction to a land doth soon afford;
They're for my punishments ordained on high,
Unless our tears prevent it speedily.
But yet, I answer not what you demand,
To show the grievance of my troubled land;

Before I tell the effect, I'll show the cause,
Which are my sins, the breach of sacred laws;
Idolatry, supplanter of a nation,
Which foolish superstitious adoration;
Are liked and countenanced by men of might,
The Gospel trodden down, and hath no right;
Church Offices were sold, and bought, for gain,
That Pope had hope, to find Rome here again;
For oaths, and blasphemies, did ever ear
From Beelzebub himself, such language hear?
What scorning of the saints of the most high,
What injuries did daily on them lie;
What false reports, what nicknames did they take,
Not for their own, but for their master's sake;
And thou, poor soul, wert jeered among the rest,
Thy flying for the truth was made a jest;
For sabbath-breaking, and for drunkenness,
Did ever land profaneness more express?
From crying bloods, yet cleansèd am not I,
Martyrs, and others, dying causelessly:
How many princely heads on blocks laid down,
For nought, but title to a fading crown?
'Mongst all the cruelties by great ones done,
Oh, Edward's babes, and Clarence' hapless son,
O Jane, why didst thou die in flow'ring prime,
Because of royal stem, that was thy crime:
For bribery, adultery, and lies,
Where is the nation, I can't paralize;
With usury, extortion, and oppression,
These be the Hydras of my stout transgression;
These be the bitter fountains, heads, and roots,
Whence flowed the source, the sprigs, the boughs, and fruits;
Of more than thou canst hear, or I relate,
That with high hand I still did perpetrate;
For these, were threatenèd the woeful day,
I mocked the preachers, put it far away;
The sermons yet upon record do stand,
That cried, destruction to my wicked land:
I then believed not, now I feel and see
The plague of stubborn incredulity.
Some lost their livings, some in prison pent,

Some fined, from house and friends to exile went:
Their silent tongues to heaven did vengeance cry,
Who saw their wrongs and hath judged righteously,
And will repay it sevenfold in my lap,
This is forerunner of my after-clap.
Nor took I warning by my neighbours' falls,
I saw sad Germany's dismantled walls.
I saw her people famished, nobles slain,
Her fruitful land, a barren heath remain.
I saw (unmoved) her armies foiled and fled,
Wives forced, babes tossed, her houses calcinèd,
I saw strong Rochelle yielded to her foe,
Thousands of starvèd Christians there also.
I saw poor Ireland bleeding out her last,
Such cruelties as all reports have passed.
My heart obdurate, stood not yet aghast.
Now sip I of that cup, and just 't may be,
The bottom dregs reservèd are for me.

New England

To all you've said, sad mother, I assent
Your fearful sins, great cause there's to lament,
My guilty hands (in part) hold up with you,
A sharer in your punishment's my due,
But all you say, amounts to this effect,
Not what you feel, but what you do expect.
Pray in plain terms, what is your present grief,
Then let's join heads, and hearts for your relief.

Old England

Well, to the matter then, there's grown of late,
'Twixt King and peers a question of state,
Which is the chief, the law, or else the King,
One said it's he, the other no such thing.
'Tis said my better part in Parliament,
To ease my groaning land showed their intent,
To crush the proud, and right to each man deal.
To help the Church, and stay the commonweal,
So many obstacles come in their way,
As puts me to a stand what I should say,
Old customs, new prerogatives stood on,

Had they not held law fast, all had been gone,
Which by their prudence stood them in such stead,
They took high Strafford lower by the head,
And to their Laud be 't spoke, they held i' th' Tower,
All England's metropolitan that hour,
This done, an Act they would have passèd fain,
No prelate should his Bishopric retain;
Here tugged they hard indeed, for all men saw,
This must be done by Gospel, not by law.
Next the militia they urgèd fore,
This was denied, I need not say wherefore.
The King displeased, at York himself absents,
They humbly beg return, show their intents,
The writing, printing, posting to and fro,
Shows all was done, I'll therefore let it go.
But now I come to speak of my disaster,
Contention's grown 'twixt subjects and their master:
They worded it so long, they fell to blows,
That thousands lay on heaps, here bleeds my woes.
I that no wars, so many years have known,
Am now destroyed, and slaughtered by mine own,
But could the field alone this cause decide,
One battle, two or three I might abide,
But these may be beginnings of more woe,
Who knows, but this may be my overthrow.
Oh pity me, in this sad perturbation,
My plundered towns, my houses' devastation,
My weeping virgins, and my young men slain,
My wealthy trading fallen, my dearth of grain,
The seed time's come, but ploughman hath no hope,
Because he knows not, who shall in his crop:
The poor they want their pay, their children bread,
Their woeful mothers' tears unpitièd.
If any pity in thy heart remain,
Or any childlike love thou dost retain,
For my relief do what there lies in thee
And recompense that good I've done to thee.

New England
Dear mother cease complaints, and wipe your eyes,
Shake off your dust, cheer up, and now arise,

You are my mother, nurse, and I your flesh,
Your sunken bowels gladly would refresh:
Your griefs I pity, but soon hope to see,
Out of your troubles much good fruit to be.
To see these latter days of hoped for good,
Though now be clouded all with tears and blood;
After dark popery the day did clear,
But now the sun in's brightness shall appear,
Blessed be the nobles of thy noble land,
With ventured lives for truth's defence that stand,
Blessed be thy Commons, who for common good,
And thine infringèd laws have boldly stood.
Blessed be thy counties who did aid thee still
With hearts and states, to testify their will.
Blessed be thy preachers, who do cheer thee on,
O cry: the sword of God, and Gideon:
And shall I not on those wish Mero's curse,
That help thee not with prayers, arms, and purse,
And for myself, let miseries abound,
If mindless of thy state I e'er be found.
These are the days, the Church's foes to crush,
To root out Popelings, head, tail, branch, and rush.
Let's bring Baal's vestments forth to make a fire,
Their mitres, surplices, and all their tire,
Copes, rochets, crosiers, and such empty trash,
And let their names consume, but let the flash
Light Christendom, and all the world to see,
We hate Rome's whore, with all her trumpery.
Go on brave Essex, with a loyal heart,
Not false to king nor to thy better part,
But those that hurt his people and his crown,
As duty binds, expel, and tread them down:
And ye brave nobles, chase away all fear,
And to this hopeful cause closely adhere
O mother, can you weep, and have such peers.
When they are gone, then drown yourself in tears.
If now you weep so much, that then no more,
The briny ocean will o'erflow your shore,
These, these, are they (I trust) with Charles our King
Out of all mists, such glorious days shall bring,
That dazzled eyes beholding much shall wonder

At that thy settled peace, thy wealth and splendour,
Thy Church and Weal, established in such manner,
That all shall joy that thou displayedst thy banner,
And discipline erected, so I trust,
That nursing kings shall come and lick thy dust:
Then justice shall in all thy courts take place,
Without respect of persons, or of case,
Then bribes shall cease, and suits shall not stick long,
Patience, and purse of clients oft to wrong:
Then high commissions shall fall to decay,
And pursevants and catchpoles want their pay,
So shall thy happy nation ever flourish,
When truth and righteousness they thus shall nourish.
When thus in peace, thine armies brave send out,
To sack proud Rome, and all her vassals rout:
There let thy name, thy fame, thy valour shine,
As did thine ancestors in Palestine,
And let her spoils, full pay, with int'rest be,
Of what unjustly once she polled from thee,
Of all the woes thou canst let her be sped,
Execute to th' full the vengeance threatenèd.
Bring forth the beast that ruled the world with's beak,
And tear his flesh, and set your feet on's neck,
And make his filthy den so desolate,
To th' stonishment of all that knew his state.
This done, with brandished swords, to Turkey go,
(For then what is't, but English blades dare do?)
And lay her waste, for so's the sacred doom,
And do to Gog, as thou hast done to Rome.
Oh Abraham's seed lift up your heads on high,
For sure the day of your redemption's nigh;
The scales shall fall from your long-blinded eyes,
And him you shall adore, who now despise,
Then fullness of the nations in shall flow,
And Jew and Gentile, to one worship go,
Then follows days of happiness and rest,
Whose lot doth fall to live therein is blessed:
No Canaanite shall then be found i' th' land,
And holiness, n horses bells shall stand,
If this make way thereto, then sigh no more,
But if at all, thou didst not see't before.

Farewell dear mother, rightest cause prevail,
And in a while you'll tell another tale.

———

The Author to her Book
Thou ill-formed offspring of my feeble brain,
Who after birth didst by my side remain,
Till snatched from thence by friends, less wise than true
Who thee abroad exposed to public view,
Made thee in rags, halting to th'press to trudge,
Where errors were not lessened (all may judge).
At thy return my blushing was not small,
My rambling brat (in print) should mother call,
I cast thee by as one unfit for light
Thy visage was so irksome to my sight;
Yet being mine own at length affection would
Thy blemishes amend if so I could:
I washed thy face, but more defects I saw,
And rubbing off a spot, still made a flaw.
I stretched by joints to make thee even feet,
Yet still thou run'st more hobbling than is meet;
In better dress to trim thee was my mind,
But nought save some home-spun cloth, i' th'house I find
In this array, 'mongst vulgars mayst thou roam;
In critics' hands, beware thou dost not come;
And take thy way where yet thou art not known,
If for thy father asked, say thou hadst none:
And for thy mother, she alas is poor,
Which caused her thus to send thee out of door.

———

1688

20. Aphra Behn

Oroonoko, or The Royal Slave. A True History

I do not pretend, in giving you the history of this royal slave, to entertain
my reader with adventures of a feigned hero, whose life and fortunes fancy
may manage at the poet's pleasure; nor in relating the truth, design to

adorn it with any accidents but such as arrived in earnest to him. And it shall come simply into the world, recommended by its own proper merits and natural intrigues; there being enough of reality to support it, and to render it diverting, without the addition of invention.

I was myself an eye-witness to a great part of what you will find here set down; and what I could not be witness of, I received from the mouth of the chief actor in this history, the hero himself, who gave us the whole transactions of his youth; and though I shall omit, for brevity's sake, a thousand little accidents of his life, which, however pleasant to us, where history was scarce, and adventures very rare, yet might prove tedious and heavy to my reader, in a world where he finds diversions for every minute, new and strange. But we, who were perfectly charmed with the character of this great man, were curious to gather every circumstance of his life.

The scene of the last part of his adventures lies in a colony in America, called Surinam, in the West Indies.

But before I give you the story of this gallant slave, 'tis fit I tell you the manner of bringing them to these new colonies; for those they make use of there not being natives of the place; for those we live with in perfect amity without daring to command 'em; but, on the contrary, caress 'em with all the brotherly and friendly affection in the world; trading with them for their fish, venison, buffalos' skins, and little rarities; as marmosets, a sort of monkey, as big as a rat or weasel, but of marvellous and delicate shape, and has face and hands like a human creature; and cousheries, a little beast in the form and fashion of a lion, as big as a kitten, but so exactly made in all parts like that noble beast that it is it in miniature. Then for little parakeetoes, great parrots, macaws, and a thousand other birds and beasts of wonderful and surprising forms, shapes, and colours. For skins of prodigious snakes, of which there are some threescore yards in length; as is the skin of one that may be seen at his Majesty's Antiquary's. Where are also some rare flies, of amazing forms and colours, presented to 'em by myself; some as big as my fist, some less; and all of various excellencies, such as art cannot imitate. Then we trade for feathers, which they order into all shapes, make themselves little short habits of 'em, and glorious wreaths for their heads, necks, arms, and legs, whose tinctures are unconceivable. I had a set of these presented to me, and I gave 'em to the King's Theatre, and it was the dress of the Indian Queen, infinitely admired by persons of quality; and were unimitable. Besides these, a thousand little knacks and rarities in nature, and some of art; as their baskets, weapons, aprons, etc. We dealt with 'em with beads of all colours, knives, axes, pins, and needles; which they used only as tools to drill holes with in their ears, noses, and lips, where they hang a great many little things; as long beads, bits of tin, brass or silver, beat thin, and any shining trinket. The beads they weave into aprons about a quarter of an ell long, and of the same breadth; working them very prettily in flowers of several colours of beads; which apron they wear just before 'em, as Adam and Eve did the fig leaves; the men wearing a long strip of linen, which they deal with us for. They thread these beads also on long cotton threads, and make girdles to tie their aprons to, which come twenty times, or more, about the waist; and then cross, like a shoulder-belt, both ways, and round their necks, arms, and legs. This adornment, with their long black hair, and the face painted in little specks or flowers here and there, makes 'em a wonderful figure to behold. Some of the beauties, which indeed are finely shaped, as almost all are, and who have pretty features, are very charming and novel; for they have all that is called beauty, except the colour, which is a reddish yellow; or after a new oiling, which they often use to themselves, they are of the colour of a new brick, but smooth, soft, and sleek. They are extreme modest and bashful, very shy, and nice of being touched. And though they are all thus naked, if one lives forever among 'em, there is not to be seen an indecent action, or glance; and being continually used to see one another so unadorned, so like our first parents before the Fall, it seems as if they had no wishes; there being nothing to heighten curiosity, but all you can see, you see at once, and every moment see; and where there is no novelty, there can be no curiosity. Not but I have seen a handsome young Indian, dying for love of a very beautiful young Indian maid; but all his courtship was, to fold his arms, pursue her with his eyes, and sighs were all his language. While she, as if no such lover were present; or rather as if she desired none such, carefully guarded her eyes from beholding him; and never approached him, but she looked down with all the blushing modesty I have seen in the most severe and cautious of our world. And these people represented to me an absolute idea of the first state of innocence, before man knew how to sin. And 'tis most evident and plain, that simple Nature is the most harmless, inoffensive, and virtuous mistress. 'Tis she alone, if she were permitted, that better instructs the world, than all the inventions of man. Religion would here but destroy that tranquillity, they possess by ignorance; and laws would but teach 'em to know offence, of which now they have no notion. They once made mourning and fasting for the death of the English Governor, who had given his hand to come on such a day to 'em, and neither came nor sent; believing, when once a man's word was passed, nothing but death could or should prevent his keeping it. And when they saw he was not dead, they asked him, what name they had for a man who promised a thing he did not do? The Governor told them, such a man was a liar, which was a word of infamy to a gentleman. Then one of 'em replied, 'Governor, you are a liar, and guilty of that infamy.' They have a native justice, which knows no fraud; and they understand no vice, or cunning, but when they are taught by the white men. They have plurality of wives, which, when they grow old, serve those that succeed 'em, who are young; but with a servitude easy and respected; and unless they take slaves in war, they have no other attendants.

Those on that continent where I was had no king; but the oldest war-captain was obeyed with great resignation.

A war-captain is a man who has led them on to battle with conduct and success; of whom I shall have occasion to speak more hereafter, and of some other of their customs and manners, as they fall in my way.

With these people, as I said, we live in perfect tranquillity and good understanding, as it behoves us to do; they knowing all the places where to seek the best food of the country, and the means of getting it; and for very small and unvaluable trifles, supply us with that 'tis impossible for us to get; for they do not only in the wood, and over the savannahs, in hunting, supply the parts of hounds, by swiftly scouring through those almost impassable places; and by the mere activity of their feet run down the nimblest deer, and other eatable beasts. But in the water, one would think they were gods of the rivers, or fellow-citizens of the deep; so rare an art they have in swimming, diving, and almost living in water; by which they command the less swift inhabitants of the floods. And then for shooting; what they cannot take, or reach with their hands, they do with arrows; and have so admirable an aim, that they will split almost a hair; and at any distance that an arrow can reach: they will shoot down oranges, and other fruit, and only touch the stalk with the darts' points, that they may not hurt the fruit. So that they being, on all occasions, very useful to us, we find it absolutely necessary to caress 'em as friends, and not to treat 'em as slaves; nor dare we do other, their numbers so far surpassing ours in that continent.

Those, then, whom we make use of to work in our plantations of sugar, are Negroes, black slaves altogether, which are transported thither in this manner.

Those who want slaves make a bargain with a master, or captain of a ship, and contract to pay him so much apiece, a matter of twenty pound a head for as many as he agrees for, and to pay for 'em when they shall be delivered on such a plantation. So that when there arrives a ship laden with slaves, they who have so contracted go aboard, and receive their number by lot; and perhaps in one lot that may be for ten, there may happen to be three or four men; the rest women and children. Or be there more or less of either sex, you are obliged to be contented with your lot.

Coramantien, a country of blacks so called, was one of those places in which they found the most advantageous trading for these slaves; and thither most of our great traders in that merchandise trafficked; for that nation is very warlike and brave; and having a continual campaign, being always in hostility with one neighbouring prince or other, they had the fortune to take a great many captives: for all they took in battle, were sold as slaves; at least, those common men who could not ransom themselves. Of these slaves so taken, the general only has all the profit; and of these generals, our captains and masters of ships buy all their freights.

The King of Coramantien was himself a man of a hundred and odd years old, and had no son, though he had many beautiful black wives; for most certainly there are beauties that can charm of that colour. In his younger years he had had many gallant men to his sons, thirteen of which died in battle, conquering when they fell; and he had only left him for his successor one grandchild, son to one of these dead victors; who, as soon as he could bear a bow in his hand, and a quiver at his back, was sent into the field, to be trained up, by one of the oldest generals, to war; where, from his natural inclination to arms, and the occasions given him, with the good conduct of the old general, he became, at the age of seventeen, one of the most expert captains and bravest soldiers that ever saw the field of Mars. So that he was adored as the wonder of all that world, and the darling of the soldiers. Besides, he was adorned with a native beauty so transcending all those of his gloomy race, that he struck an awe and reverence, even into those that knew not his quality; as he did into me, who beheld him with surprise and wonder, when afterwards he arrived in our world.

He had scarce arrived at his seventeenth year, when fighting by his side, the general was killed with an arrow in his eye, which the Prince Oroonoko (for so was this gallant Moor called) very narrowly avoided; nor had he, if the general who saw the arrow shot, and perceiving it aimed at the prince, had not bowed his head between, on purpose to receive it in his own body rather than it should touch that of the prince, and so saved him.

'Twas then, afflicted as Oroonoko was, that he was proclaimed general in the old man's place; and then it was, at the finishing of that war, which had continued for two years, that the prince came to court, where he had hardly been a month together, from the time of his fifth year, to that of seventeen; and 'twas amazing to imagine where it was he learned so much humanity: or, to give his accomplishments a juster name, where 'twas he got that real greatness of soul, those refined notions of true honour, that absolute generosity, and that softness that was capable of the highest passions of love and gallantry, whose objects were almost continually fighting men, or those mangled, or dead; who heard no sounds but those of war and groans. Some part of it we may attribute to the care of a Frenchman of wit and learning; who, finding it turn to very good account to be a sort of royal tutor to this young black, and perceiving him very ready, apt, and quick of apprehension, took a great pleasure to teach him morals, language, and science; and was for it extremely beloved and valued by him. Another reason was he loved, when he came from war, to see all the English gentlemen that traded thither; and did not only learn their language, but that of the Spaniards also, with whom he traded afterwards for slaves.

I have often seen and conversed with this great man, and been a witness to many of his mighty actions; and do assure my reader, the most illustrious courts could not have produced a braver man, both for greatness of courage and mind, a judgement more solid, a wit more quick, and a conversation more sweet and diverting. He knew almost as much as if he had read much. He had heard of and admired the Romans; he had heard of the late Civil Wars in England, and the deplorable death of our great monarch; and would discourse of it with all the sense, and abhorrence of the injustice imaginable. He had an extreme good and graceful mien, and all the civility of a well-bred great man. He had nothing of barbarity in his nature, but in all points addressed himself, as if his education had been in some European court.

This great and just character of Oroonoko gave me an extreme curiosity to see him, especially when I knew he spoke French and English, and that I could talk with him. But though I had heard so much of him, I was as greatly surprised when I saw him as if I had heard nothing of him; so beyond all report I found him. He came into the room, and addressed himself to me, and some other women, with the best grace in the world. He was pretty tall, but of a shape the most exact that can be fancied. The most famous statuary could not form the figure of a man more admirably turned from head to foot. His face was not of that brown, rusty black which most of that nation are, but of perfect ebony, or polished jet. His eyes were the most awful that could be seen, and very piercing; the white of 'em being like snow, as were his teeth. His nose was rising and Roman, instead of African and flat. His mouth, the finest shaped that could be seen; far from those great turned lips, which are so natural to the rest of the Negroes. The whole proportion and air of his face was so noble, and exactly formed, that, bating his colour, there could be nothing in nature more beautiful, agreeable, and handsome. There was no one grace wanting, that bears the standard of true beauty. His hair came down to his shoulders, by the aids of art; which was by pulling it out with a quill, and keeping it combed; of which he took particular care. Nor did the perfections of his mind come short of those of his person; for his discourse was admirable upon almost any subject; and whoever had heard him speak would have been convinced of their errors, that all fine wit is confined to the white men, especially to those of Christendom; and would have confessed that Oroonoko was as capable even of reigning well, and of governing as wisely, had as great a soul, as politic maxims, and was as sensible of power, as any prince civilized in the most refined schools of humanity and learning, or the most illustrious courts.

This prince, such as I have described him, whose soul and body were so admirably adorned, was (while yet he was in the court of his grandfather) as I said, as capable of love, as 'twas possible for a brave and gallant man to be; and in saying that, I have named the highest degree of love; for sure, great souls are most capable of that passion.

I have already said, the old general was killed by the shot of an arrow, by the side of this prince, in battle; and that Oroonoko was made general. This old dead hero had one only daughter left of his race; a beauty, that to describe her truly, one need say only, she was female to the noble male; the beautiful black Venus, to our young Mars; as charming in her person as he, and of delicate virtues. I have seen a hundred white men sighing after her, and making a thousand vows at her feet, all in vain, and unsuccessful. And she was, indeed too great for any, but a prince of her own nation to adore.

Oroonoko coming from the wars, (which were now ended) after he had made his court to his grandfather, he thought in honour he ought to make a visit to Imoinda, the daughter of his foster-father, the dead general; and to make some excuses to her, because his preservation was the occasion of her father's death; and to present her with those slaves that had been taken in this last battle, as the trophies of her father's victories. When he came, attended by all the young soldiers of any merit, he was infinitely surprised at the beauty of this fair Queen of Night, whose face and person was so exceeding all he had ever beheld, that lovely modesty with which she received him, that softness in her look, and sighs, upon the melancholy occasion of this honour that was done by so great a man as Oroonoko, and a prince of whom she had heard such admirable things; the awfulness wherewith she received him, and the sweetness of her words and behaviour while he stayed, gained a perfect conquest over his fierce heart, and made him feel the victor could be subdued. So that having made his first compliments, and presented her a hundred and fifty slaves in fetters, he told her, with his eyes, that he was not insensible of her charms; while Imoinda, who wished for nothing more than so glorious a conquest, was pleased to believe, she understood that silent language of new-born love; and from that moment, put on all her additions to beauty.

The prince returned to court with quite another humour than before; and though he did not speak much of the fair Imoinda, he had the pleasure to hear all his followers speak of nothing but the charms of that maid; insomuch that, even in the presence of the old King, they were extolling her, and heightening, if possible, the beauties they had found in her; so that nothing else was talked of, no other sound was heard in every corner where there were whisperers, but 'Imoinda! Imoinda!'.

'Twill be imagined Oroonoko stayed not long before he made his second visit; nor, considering his quality, not much longer before he told her he adored her. I have often heard him say, that he admired by what strange inspiration he came to talk things so soft, and so passionate, who never knew love, nor was used to the conversation of women; but (to use his own words) he said, most happily, some new, and till then unknown, power instructed his heart and tongue in the language of love, and at the same time, in favour of him, inspired Imoinda with a sense of his passion. She was touched with what he said, and returned it all in such answers as went to his very heart, with a pleasure unknown before. Nor did he use those obligations ill, that love had done him; but turned all his happy moments to the best advantage; and as he knew no vice, his flame aimed at nothing but honour, if such a distinction may be made in love; and especially in that country, where men take to themselves as many as they can maintain; and where the only crime and sin with woman is to turn her off, to abandon her to want, shame and misery. Such ill morals are only practised in Christian countries, where they prefer the bare name of religion; and, without virtue or morality, think that's sufficient. But Oroonoko was none of those professors; but as he had right notions of honour, so he made her such propositions as were not only and barely such; but, contrary to the custom of his country, he made her vows, she should be the only woman he would possess while he lived; that no age or wrinkles should incline him to change; for her soul would be always fine, and always young; and he should have an eternal idea in his mind of the charms she now bore, and should look into his heart for that idea, when he could find it no longer in her face.

After a thousand assurances of his lasting flame, and her eternal empire over him, she condescended to receive him for her husband; or rather, received him as the greatest honour the gods could do her.

There is a certain ceremony in these cases to be observed, which I forgot to ask how 'twas performed; but 'twas concluded on both sides, that in obedience to him, the grandfather was to be first made acquainted with the design: for they pay a most absolute resignation to the monarch, especially when he is a parent also.

On the other side, the old King, who had many wives and many concubines, wanted not court-flatterers to insinuate in his heart a thousand tender thoughts for this young beauty; and who represented her to his fancy, as the most charming he had ever possessed in all the long race of his numerous years. At this character his old heart, like an extinguished brand, most apt to take fire, felt new sparks of love, and began to kindle; and now grown to his second childhood, longed with impatience to behold this gay thing, with whom, alas! he could but innocently play. But how he should be confirmed she was this wonder, before he used his power to call her to court (where maidens never came, unless for the King's private use) he was next to consider; and while he was so doing, he had intelligence brought him, that Imoinda was most certainly mistress to the Prince Oroonoko. This gave him some chagrin: however, it gave him also an opportunity, one day, when the prince was a-hunting, to wait on a man of quality, as his slave and attendant, who should go and make a present to Imoinda, as from the prince; he should then, unknown, see this fair maid, and have an opportunity to hear what message she would return the prince for his present; and from thence gather the state of her heart, and degree of her inclination. This was put in execution, and the old monarch saw, and burned. He found her all he had heard, and would not delay his happiness, but found he should have some obstacle to overcome her heart; for she expressed her sense of the present the prince had sent her, in terms so sweet, so soft and pretty, with an air of love and joy that could not be dissembled; insomuch that 'twas past doubt whether she loved Oroonoko entirely. This gave the old King some affliction; but he salved it with this, that the obedience the people pay their king, was not at all inferior to what they paid their gods. And what love would not oblige Imoinda to do, duty would compel her to.

He was therefore no sooner got to his apartment, but he sent the royal veil to Imoinda; that is, the ceremony of invitation; he sends the lady, he has a mind to honour with his bed, a veil, with which she is covered, and secured for the King's use; and 'tis death to disobey; besides, held a most impious disobedience.

'Tis not to be imagined the surprise and grief that seized this lovely maid at this news and sight. However, as delays in these cases are dangerous, and pleading worse than treason; trembling, and almost fainting, she was obliged to suffer herself to be covered and led away.

They brought her thus to court; and the King, who had caused a very rich bath to be prepared, was led into it, where he sat under a canopy, in state, to receive this longed-for virgin, whom he having commanded should be brought to him. They (after disrobing her) led her to the bath, and making fast the doors, left her to descend. The King, without more courtship, bade her throw off her mantle, and come to his arms. But Imoinda, all in tears, threw herself on the marble, on the brink of the bath, and besought him to hear her. She told him, as she was a maid, how proud of the divine glory she should have been, of having it in her power to oblige her king; but as by the laws he could not, and from his royal goodness would not, take from any man his wedded wife: so she believed she should be the occasion of making him commit a great sin, if she did not reveal her state and condition, and tell him she was another's, and could not be so happy to be his.

The King, enraged at this delay, hastily demanded the name of the bold man, that had married a woman of her degree without his consent. Imoinda, seeing his eyes fierce, and his hands tremble (whether with age or anger, I know not; but she fancied the last), almost repented she had said so much, for now she feared the storm would fall on the prince; she therefore said a thousand things to appease the raging of his flame, and to prepare him to hear who it was with calmness; but before she spoke, he imagined who she meant, but would not seem to do so, but commanded her to lay aside her mantle, and suffer herself to receive his caresses; or, by his gods he swore, that happy man whom she was going to name should die, though it were even Oroonoko himself. 'Therefore,' said he, 'deny this marriage, and swear thyself a maid.' 'That,' replied Imoinda, 'by all our powers I do; for I am not yet known to my husband.' ''Tis enough,' said the King, ''tis enough both to satisfy my conscience and my heart.' And rising from his seat, he went and led her into the bath; it being in vain for her to resist.

In this time, the prince, who was returned from hunting, went to visit his Imoinda, but found her gone; and not only so, but heard she had received the royal veil. This raised him to a storm; and in his madness, they had much ado to save him from laying violent hands on himself. Force first prevailed, and then reason. They urged all to him that might oppose his rage; but nothing weighed so greatly with him as the King's old age, uncapable of injuring him with Imoinda. He would give way to that hope, because it pleased him most, and flattered best his heart. Yet this served not altogether to make him cease his different passions, which sometimes raged within him, and sometimes softened into showers. 'Twas not enough to appease him, to tell him his grandfather was old, and could not that way injure him, while he retained that awful duty which the young men are used there to pay to their grave relations. He could not be convinced he had no cause to sigh and mourn for the loss of a mistress he could not with all his strength and courage retrieve. And he would often cry, 'O, my friends! were she in walled cities, or confined from me in fortifications of the greatest strength; did enchantments or monsters detain her from me; I would venture through any hazard to free her. But here, in the arms of a feeble old man, my youth, my violent love, my trade in arms, and all my vast desire of glory, avail me nothing. Imoinda is as irrecoverably lost to me as if she were snatched by the cold arms of death. Oh! she is never to be retrieved. If I would wait tedious years, till fate should bow the old King to his grave; even that would not leave me Imoinda free; but still that custom that makes it so vile a crime for a son to marry his father's wives or mistresses would hinder my happiness; unless I would either ignobly set an ill precedent to my successors, or abandon my country, and fly with her to some unknown world who never heard our story.'

But it was objected to him, that his case was not the same; for Imoinda being his lawful wife, by solemn contract, 'twas he was the injured man, and might, if he so pleased, take Imoinda back, the breach of the law being on his grandfather's side; and that if he could circumvent him, and redeem her from the otan, which is the palace of the King's women, a sort of seraglio, it was both just and lawful for him so to do.

This reasoning had some force upon him, and he should have been entirely comforted, but for the thought that she was possessed by his grandfather. However, he loved so well, that he was resolved to believe what most favoured his hope; and to endeavour to learn from Imoinda's own mouth, what only she could satisfy him in; whether she was robbed of that blessing which was only due to his faith and love. But as it was very hard to get a sight of the women (for no men ever entered into the otan but when the King went to entertain himself with some one of his wives, or mistresses; and 'twas death at any other time, for any other to go in), so he knew not how to contrive to get a sight of her.

While Oroonoko felt all the agonies of love, and suffered under a torment the most painful in the world, the old King was not exempted from his share of affliction. He was troubled for having been forced by an irresistible passion, to rob his [grand]son of a treasure, he knew, could not but be extremely dear to him, since she was the most beautiful that ever had been seen; and had besides all the sweetness and innocence of youth and modesty, with a charm of wit surpassing all. He found that, however she was forced to expose her lovely person to his withered arms, she could only sigh and weep there, and think of Oroonoko; and oftentimes could not forbear speaking of him, though her life were, by custom, forfeited by owning her passion. But she spoke not of a lover only, but of a prince dear to him, to whom she spoke; and of the praises of a man who, till now, filled the old man's soul with joy at every recital of his bravery, or even his name. And 'twas this dotage on our young hero, that gave Imoinda a thousand privileges to speak of him, without offending; and this condescension in the old King, that made her take the satisfaction of speaking of him so very often.

Besides, he many times inquired how the prince bore himself; and those of whom he asked, being entirely slaves to the merits and virtues of the prince, still answered what they thought conduced best to his service; which was, to make the old King fancy that the prince had no more interest in Imoinda, and had resigned her willingly to the pleasure of the King; that he diverted himself with his mathematicians, his fortifications, his officers, and his hunting.

This pleased the old lover, who failed not to report these things again to Imoinda, that she might, by the example of her young lover, withdraw her heart, and rest better contented in his arms. But however she was forced to receive this unwelcome news, in all appearance, with unconcern and content, her heart was bursting within, and she was only happy when she could get alone, to vent her griefs and moans with sighs and tears.

What reports of the prince's conduct were made to the King, he thought good to justify as far as possibly he could by his actions; and when he appeared in the presence of the King, he showed a face not at all betraying his heart. So that in a little time, the old man, being entirely convinced that he was no longer a lover of Imoinda, he carried him with him, in his train, to the otan, often to banquet with his mistress. But as soon as he entered, one day, into the apartment of Imoinda, with the King, at the first glance from her eyes, notwithstanding all his determined resolution, he was ready to sink in the place where he stood; and had certainly done so, but for the support of Aboan, a young man, who was next to him; which, with his change of countenance, had betrayed him, had the King chanced to look that way. And I have observed, 'tis a very great error in those, who laugh when one says, 'A Negro can change colour'; for I have seen 'em as frequently blush, and look pale, and that as visibly as ever I saw in the most beautiful white. And 'tis certain that both these changes were evident, this day, in both these lovers. And Imoinda, who saw with some joy the change in the prince's face, and found it in her own, strove to divert the King from beholding either, by a forced caress, with which she met him; which was a new wound in the heart of the poor dying prince. But as soon as the King was busied in looking on some fine thing of Imoinda's making, she had time to tell the prince, with her angry, but love-darting eyes, that she resented his coldness, and bemoaned her own miserable captivity. Nor were his eyes silent, but answered hers again, as much as eyes could do, instructed by the most tender, and most passionate heart that ever loved. And they spoke so well, and so effectually, as Imoinda no longer doubted, but she was the only delight, and darling of that soul she found pleading in 'em its right of love, which none was more willing to resign than she. And 'twas this powerful language alone that in an instant conveyed all the thoughts of their souls to each other; that they both found there wanted but opportunity to make them both entirely happy. But when he saw another door opened by Onahal (a former old wife of the King's, who now had charge of Imoinda), and saw the prospect of a bed of state made ready, with sweets and flowers for the dalliance of the King; who immediately led the trembling victim from his sight, into that prepared repose. What rage! What wild frenzies seized his heart! Which forcing to keep within bounds, and to suffer without noise, it became the more insupportable, and rent his soul with ten thousand pains. He was forced to retire, to vent his groans, where he fell down on a carpet, and lay struggling a long time, and only breathing now and then, 'O Imoinda!'. When Onahal had finished her necessary affair within, shutting the door, she came forth, to wait till the King called; and hearing someone sighing in the other room, she passed on, and found the prince in that deplorable condition, which she thought needed her aid. She gave him cordials, but all in vain; till finding the nature of his disease, by his sighs, and naming Imoinda. She told him, he had not so much cause as he imagined to afflict himself; for if he knew the King so well as she did, he would not lose a moment in jealousy, and that she was confident that Imoinda bore, at this moment, part in his affliction. Aboan was of the same opinion; and both together persuaded him to reassume his courage; and all sitting down on the carpet, the prince said so many obliging things to Onahal, that he half-persuaded her to be of his party. And she promised him she would thus far comply with his just desires, that she would let Imoinda know how faithful he was, what he suffered, and what he said.

This discourse lasted till the King called, which gave Oroonoko a certain satisfaction; and with the hope Onahal had made him conceive, he assumed a look as gay as 'twas possible a man in his circumstances could do; and presently after, he was called in with the rest who waited without. The King commanded music to be brought, and several of his young wives and mistresses came all together, by his command, to dance before him; where Imoinda performed her part with an air and grace so passing all the rest, as her beauty was above 'em, and received the present, ordained as a prize. The prince was every moment more charmed with the new beauties and graces he beheld in this fair one. And while he gazed, and she danced, Onahal was retired to a window with Aboan.

This Onahal, as I said, was one of the cast-mistresses of the old King;

and 'twas these (now past their beauty) that were made guardians, or governants to the new and the young ones; and whose business it was, to teach them all those wanton arts of love, with which they prevailed and charmed heretofore in their turn; and who now treated the triumphing happy ones with all the severity, as to liberty and freedom, that was possible, in revenge of their honours they rob them of; envying them those satisfactions, those gallantries and presents, that were once made to themselves, while youth and beauty lasted, and which they now saw pass regardless by, and were paid only to the bloomings. And certainly, nothing is more afflicting to a decayed beauty, than to behold in itself declining charms, that were once adored; and to find those caresses paid to new beauties, to which once she laid a claim; to hear 'em whisper, as she passes by, 'That once was a delicate woman.' These abandoned ladies therefore endeavour to revenge all the despites, and decays of time, on these flourishing happy ones. And 'twas this severity, that gave Oroonoko a thousand fears he should never prevail with Onahal, to see Imoinda. But as I said, she was now retired to a window with Aboan.

This young man was not only one of the best quality, but a man extremely well made, and beautiful; and coming often to attend the King to the otan, he had subdued the heart of the antiquated Onahal, which had not forgot how pleasant it was to be in love. And though she had some decays in her face, she had none in her sense and wit; she was there agreeable still, even to Aboan's youth; so that he took pleasure in entertaining her with discourses of love. He knew also, that to make his court to these she-favourites was the way to be great; these being the persons that do all affairs and business at court. He had also observed that she had given him glances more tender and inviting, than she had done to others of his quality. And now, when he saw that her favour could so absolutely oblige the prince, he failed not to sigh in her ear, and to look with eyes all soft upon her, and give her hope that she had made some impressions on his heart. He found her pleased at this, and making a thousand advances to him; but the ceremony ending, and the King departing, broke up the company for that day, and his conversation.

Aboan failed not that night to tell the prince of his success, and how advantageous the service of Onahal might be to his amour with Imoinda. The prince was overjoyed with this good news, and besought him, if it were possible to caress her, so as to engage her entirely; which he could not fail to do, if he complied with her desires. 'For then,' said the prince, 'her life lying at your mercy, she must grant you the request you make in my behalf.' Aboan understood him, and assured him, he would make love so effectually, that he would defy the most expert mistress of the art, to find out whether he dissembled it, or had it really. And 'twas with impatience they waited the next opportunity of going to the otan.

The wars came on, the time of taking the field approached, and 'twas impossible for the prince to delay his going at the head of his army, to encounter the enemy. So that every day seemed a tedious year, till he saw his Imoinda; for he believed he could not live, if he were forced away without being so happy. 'Twas with impatience therefore, that he expected the next visit the King would make; and according to his wish, it was not long.

The parley of the eyes of these two lovers had not passed so secretly, but an old jealous lover could spy it; or rather, he wanted not flatterers, who told him they observed it. So that the prince was hastened to the camp, and this was the last visit he found he should make to the otan; he therefore urged Aboan to make the best of this last effort, and to explain himself so to Onahal, that she, deferring her enjoyment of her young lover no longer, might make way for the prince to speak to Imoinda.

The whole affair being agreed on between the prince and Aboan, they attended the King, as the custom was, to the otan; where, while the whole company was taken up in beholding the dancing and antic postures the women-royal made, to divert the king, Onahal singled out Aboan, whom she found most pliable to her wish. When she had him where she believed she could not be heard, she sighed to him, and softly cried, 'Ah, Aboan! When will you be sensible of my passion? I confess it with my mouth, because I would not give my eyes the lie; and you have but too much already perceived they have confessed my flame. Nor would I have you believe, that because I am the abandoned mistress of a king, I esteem myself altogether divested of charms. No, Aboan; I have still a rest of beauty enough engaging, and have learned to please too well, not to be desirable. I can have lovers still, but will have none but Aboan.' 'Madam,' replied the half-feigning youth, 'you have already, by my eyes, found, you can still conquer; and I believe 'tis in pity of me, you condescend to this kind confession. But, madam, words are used to be so small a part of our country-courtship, that 'tis rare one can get so happy an opportunity as to tell one's heart; and those few minutes we have are forced to be snatched for more certain proofs of love, than speaking and sighing; and such I languish for.'

He spoke this with such a tone, that she hoped it true, and could not forbear believing it; and being wholly transported with joy, for having subdued the finest of all the King's subjects to her desires, she took from her ears two large pearls, and commanded him to wear 'em in his. He would have refused 'em, crying, 'Madam, these are not the proofs of your love that I expect; 'tis opportunity, 'tis a lone hour only, that can make me happy.' But forcing the pearls into his hand, she whispered softly to him, 'Oh! do not fear a woman's invention, when love sets her a-thinking.' And pressing his hand, she cried, 'This night you shall be happy. Come to the gate of the orange-groves, behind the otan; and I will be ready, about midnight, to receive you.' 'Twas thus agreed, and she left him, that no notice might be taken of their speaking together.

The ladies were still dancing, and the King, laid on a carpet, with a great deal of pleasure, was beholding them, especially Imoinda, who that day appeared more lovely than ever, being enlivened with the good tidings Onahal had brought her of the constant passion the prince had for her. The prince was laid on another carpet, at the other end of the room, with his eyes fixed on the object of his soul; and as she turned, or moved, so did they; and she alone gave his eyes and soul their motions. Nor did Imoinda employ her eyes to any other use, than in beholding with infinite pleasure the joy she produced in those of the prince. But while she was more regarding him, than the steps she took, she chanced to fall; and so near him, as that leaping with extreme force from the carpet, he caught her in his arms as she fell; and 'twas visible to the whole presence, the joy wherewith he received her. He clasped her close to his bosom, and quite forgot that reverence that was due to the mistress of a king, and that punishment that is the reward of a boldness of this nature; and had not the presence of mind of Imoinda (fonder of his safety, than her own) befriended him, in making her spring from his arms, and fall into her dance again, he had, at that instant met his death; for the old King, jealous to the last degree, rose up in rage, broke all the diversion, and led Imoinda to her apartment, and sent out word to the prince, to go immediately to the camp; and that if he were found another night in court, he should suffer the death ordained for disobedient offenders.

You may imagine how welcome this news was to Oroonoko, whose unseasonable transport and caress of Imoinda was blamed by all men that loved him; and now he perceived his fault, yet cried, that for such another moment he would be content to die.

All the otan was in disorder about this accident; and Onahal was particularly concerned, because on the prince's stay depended her happiness; for she could no longer expect that of Aboan. So that ere they departed, they contrived it so, that the prince and he should both come that night to the grove of the otan, which was all of oranges and citrons, and that there they would wait her orders.

They parted thus, with grief enough, till night, leaving the King in

possession of the lovely maid. But nothing could appease the jealousy of
the old lover. He would not be imposed on, but would have it that Imoinda
made a false step on purpose to fall into Oroonoko's bosom, and that all
things looked like a design on both sides, and 'twas in vain she protested
her innocence. He was old and obstinate, and left her more than half
assured that his fear was true.

The King, going to his apartment, sent to know where the prince was,
and if he intended to obey his command. The messenger returned, and
told him, he found the prince pensive, and altogether unprepared for the
campaign; that he lay negligently on the ground, and answered very little.
This confirmed the jealousy of the King, and he commanded that they
should very narrowly and privately watch his motions; and that he should
not stir from his apartment, but one spy or other should be employed to
watch him. So that the hour approaching, wherein he was to go to the
citron grove; and taking only Aboan along with him, he leaves his apartment,
and was watched to the very gate of the otan; where he was seen to enter,
and where they left him, to carry back the tidings to the King.

Oroonoko and Aboan were no sooner entered, but Onahal led the
prince to the apartment of Imoinda; who, not knowing anything of her
happiness, was laid in bed. But Onahal only left him in her chamber, to
make the best of his opportunity, and took her dear Aboan to her own;
where he showed the height of complaisance for his prince, when, to give
him an opportunity, he suffered himself to be caressed in bed by Onahal.

The prince softly wakened Imoinda, who was not a little surprised with
joy to find him there; and yet she trembled with a thousand fears. I believe
he omitted saying nothing to this young maid, that might persuade her to
suffer him to seize his own, and take the rights of love; and I believe she
was not long resisting those arms, where she so longed to be; and having
opportunity, night and silence, youth, love, and desire, he soon prevailed;
and ravished in a moment, what his old grandfather had been endeavouring
for so many months.

'Tis not to be imagined the satisfaction of these two young lovers; nor
the vows she made him, that she remained a spotless maid, till that night,
and that what she did with his grandfather, had robbed him of no part of
her virgin-honour, the gods, in mercy and justice, having reserved that for
her plighted lord, to whom of right it belonged. And 'tis impossible to
express the transports he suffered, while he listened to a discourse so charming, from her loved lips; and clasped that body in his arms, for whom he
had so long languished; and nothing now afflicted him, but his sudden
departure from her; for he told her the necessity, and his commands; but
should depart satisfied in this: that since the old King had hitherto not

been able to deprive him of those enjoyments which only belonged to him, he believed for the future he would be less able to injure him; so that, abating the scandal of the veil, which was no otherwise so, than that she was wife to another. He believed her safe, even in the arms of the King, and innocent; yet would he have ventured at the conquest of the world, and have given it all, to have had her avoided that honour of receiving the royal veil. 'Twas thus, between a thousand caresses, that both bemoaned the hard fate of youth and beauty, so liable to that cruel promotion. 'Twas a glory that could well have been spared here, though desired and aimed at by all the young females of that kingdom.

But while they were thus fondly employed, forgetting how time ran on, and that the dawn must conduct him far away from his only happiness, they heard a great noise in the otan, and unusual voices of men; at which the prince, starting from the arms of the frighted Imoinda, ran to a little battleaxe he used to wear by his side; and having not so much leisure, as to put on his habit, he opposed himself against some who were already opening the door; which they did with so much violence, that Oroonoko was not able to defend it; but was forced to cry out with a commanding voice, 'Whoever ye are that have the boldness to attempt to approach this apartment thus rudely, know, that I, the Prince Oroonoko, will revenge it with the certain death of him that first enters. Therefore, stand back, and know, this place is sacred to love, and me this night; to-morrow 'tis the King's.'

This he spoke with a voice so resolved and assured, that they soon retired from the door, but cried, ''Tis by the King's command we are come; and being satisfied by thy voice, O Prince, as much as if we had entered, we can report to the King the truth of all his fears, and leave thee to provide for thy own safety, as thou art advised by thy friends.'

At these words they departed, and left the prince to take a short and sad leave of his Imoinda; who, trusting in the strength of her charms, believed she should appease the fury of a jealous king, by saying, she was surprised, and that it was by force of arms he got into her apartment. All her concern now was for his life, and therefore she hastened him to the camp; and with much ado prevailed on him to go. Nor was it she alone that prevailed; Aboan and Onahal both pleaded, and both assured him of a lie that should be well enough contrived to secure Imoinda. So that, at last, with a heart sad as death, dying eyes, and sighing soul, Oroonoko departed, and took his way to the camp.

It was not long after the King in person came to the otan; where, beholding Imoinda with rage in his eyes, he upbraided her wickedness and perfidy, and threatening her royal lover, she fell on her face at his feet, bedewing the floor with her tears, and imploring his pardon for a fault which she had not with her will committed; as Onahal, who was also prostrate with her, could testify: that, unknown to her, he had broke into her apartment, and ravished her. She spoke this much against her conscience; but to save her own life, 'twas absolutely necessary she should feign this falsity. She knew it could not injure the prince, he being fled to an army that would stand by him, against any injuries that should assault him. However, this last thought of Imoinda's being ravished, changed the measures of his revenge; and whereas before he designed to be himself her executioner, he now resolved she should not die. But as it is the greatest crime in nature amongst 'em to touch a woman, after having been possessed by a son, a father, or a brother; so now he looked on Imoinda as a polluted thing, wholly unfit for his embrace; nor would he resign her to his grandson, because she had received the royal veil. He therefore removes her from the otan, with Onahal; whom he put into safe hands, with order they should be both sold off as slaves to another country, either Christian, or heathen; 'twas no matter where.

This cruel sentence, worse than death, they implored, might be reversed; but their prayers were vain, and it was put in execution accordingly, and that with so much secrecy, that none, either without, or within the otan, knew anything of their absence or their destiny.

The old King, nevertheless executed this with a great deal of reluctancy; but he believed he had made a very great conquest over himself, when he had once resolved, and had performed what he resolved. He believed now, that his love had been unjust; and that he could not expect the gods, or Captain of the Clouds (as they call the unknown Power), would suffer a better consequence from so ill a cause. He now begins to hold Oroonoko excused; and to say, he had reason for what he did. And now everybody could assure the King, how passionately Imoinda was beloved by the prince; even those confessed it now, who said the contrary before his flame was not abated. So that the King being old, and not able to defend himself in war, and having no sons of all his race remaining alive, but only this, to maintain him on his throne; and looking on this as a man disobliged, first by the rape of his mistress, or rather, wife; and now by depriving him wholly of her, he feared, might make him desperate, and do some cruel thing, either to himself or his old grandfather, the offender; he began to repent him extremely of the contempt he had, in his rage, put on Imoinda. Besides, he considered he ought in honour to have killed her, for this offence, if it had been one. He ought to have had so much value and consideration for a maid of her quality, as to have nobly put her to death; and not to have sold her like a common slave, the greatest revenge, and the most disgraceful of any; and to which they a thousand times prefer death, and implore it; as Imoinda did, but could not obtain that honour. Seeing therefore it was certain that Oroonoko would highly resent this affront, he thought good to make some excuse for his rashness to him; and to that end he sent a messenger to the camp, with orders to treat with him about the matter, to gain his pardon, and to endeavour to mitigate his grief; but that by no means he should tell him, she was sold, but secretly put to death; for he knew he should never obtain his pardon for the other.

When the messenger came, he found the prince upon the point of engaging with the enemy; but as soon as he heard of the arrival of the messenger, he commanded him to his tent, where he embraced him, and received him with joy; which was soon abated, by the downcast looks of the messenger, who was instantly demanded the cause by Oroonoko, who, impatient of delay, asked a thousand questions in a breath; and all concerning Imoinda. But there needed little return, for he could almost answer himself of all he demanded, from his sighs and eyes. At last, the messenger casting himself at the prince's feet, and kissing them, with all the submission of a man that had something to implore which he dreaded to utter, he besought him to hear with calmness what he had to deliver to him, and to call up all his noble and heroic courage, to encounter with his words, and defend himself against the ungrateful things he must relate. Oroonoko replied, with a deep sigh, and a languishing voice, 'I am armed against their worst efforts – for I know they will tell me, Imoinda is no more – and after that, you may spare the rest.' Then, commanding him to rise, he laid himself on a carpet, under a rich pavilion, and remained a good while silent, and was hardly heard to sigh. When he was come a little to himself, the messenger asked him leave to deliver that part of his embassy, which the prince had not yet divined. And the prince cried, 'I permit thee.' Then he told him the affliction the old King was in, for the rashness he had committed in his cruelty to Imoinda; and how he deigned to ask pardon for his offence, and to implore the prince would not suffer that loss to touch his heart too sensibly, which now all the gods could not restore him, but might recompense him in glory, which he begged he would pursue; and that death, that common revenger of all injuries, would soon even the account between him, and a feeble old man.

Oroonoko bade him return his duty to his lord and master; and to assure him, there was no account of revenge to be adjusted between them; if there were, 'twas he was the aggressor, and that death would be just, and, maugre his age, would see him righted; and he was contented to leave his share of glory to youths more fortunate, and worthy of that favour from the gods. That henceforth he would never lift a weapon, or draw a bow; but abandon the small remains of his life to sighs and tears, and the continual thoughts of what his lord and grandfather had thought good to send out of the world, with all that youth, that innocence, and beauty.

After having spoken this, whatever his greatest officers, and men of the best rank could do, they could not raise him from the carpet, or persuade him to action, and resolutions of life; but commanding all to retire, he shut himself into his pavilion all that day, while the enemy was ready to engage; and wondering at the delay, the whole body of the chief of the army then addressed themselves to him, and to whom they had much ado to get admittance. They fell on their faces at the foot of his carpet, where they lay, and besought him with earnest prayers and tears, to lead them forth to battle, and not let the enemy take advantages of them; and implored him to have regard to his glory, and to the world, that depended on his courage and conduct. But he made no other reply to all their supplications but this, that he had now no more business for glory; and for the world, it was a trifle not worth his care: 'Go,' continued he, sighing, 'and divide it amongst you; and reap with joy what you so vainly prize, and leave me to my more welcome destiny.'

They then demanded what they should do, and whom he would constitute in his room, that the confusion of ambitious youth and power might not ruin their order, and make them a prey to the enemy. He replied, he would not give himself the trouble – but wished 'em to choose the bravest man amongst 'em, let his quality or birth be what it would. 'For, O my friends!' said he, 'it is not titles make men brave or good; or birth that bestows courage and generosity, or makes the owner happy. Believe this, when you behold Oroonoko the most wretched, and abandoned by Fortune, of all the creation of the gods.' So turning himself about, he would make no more reply to all they could urge or implore.

The army beholding their officers return unsuccessful, with sad faces, and ominous looks, that presaged no good luck, suffered a thousand fears to take possession of their hearts, and the enemy to come even upon them, before they would provide for their safety, by any defence; and though they were assured by some, who had a mind to animate them, that they should be immediately headed by the prince, and that in the meantime Aboan had orders to command as general; yet they were so dismayed for want of that great example of bravery, that they could make but a very feeble resistance; and at last, downright, fled before the enemy, who pursued 'em to the very tents, killing 'em. Nor could all Aboan's courage, which that day gained him immortal glory, shame 'em into a manly defence of themselves. The guards that were left behind, about the prince's tent, seeing the soldiers flee before the enemy, and scatter themselves all over the plain, in great disorder, made such outcries as roused the prince from his amorous slumber, in which he had remained buried for two days, without permitting any sustenance to approach him. But, in spite of all his resolutions, he had not the constancy of grief, to that degree, as to make him insensible of the danger of his army; and in that instant he leaped from his couch, and cried, 'Come, if we must die, let us meet death the noblest way; and 'twill be more like Oroonoko to encounter him at an army's head, opposing the torrent of a conquering foe, than lazily, on a couch, to wait his lingering pleasure, and die every moment by a thousand wrecking thoughts; or be tamely taken by an enemy, and led a whining, lovesick slave, to adorn the triumphs of Jamoan, that young victor, who already is entered beyond the limits I had prescribed him.'

While he was speaking, he suffered his people to dress him for the field; and sallying out of his pavilion, with more life and vigour in his countenance than ever he showed, he appeared like some divine power descended to save his country from destruction; and his people had purposely put on him all things that might make him shine with most splendour, to strike a reverend awe into the beholders. He flew into the thickest of those that were pursuing his men; and being animated with despair, he fought as if he came on purpose to die, and did such things as will not be believed that human strength could perform; and such as soon inspired all the rest with new courage and new order. And now it was, that they began to fight indeed; and so, as if they would not be outdone, even by their adored hero, who turning the tide of the victory, changing absolutely the fate of the day, gained an entire conquest; and Oroonoko having the good fortune to single out Jamoan, he took him prisoner with his own hand, having wounded him almost to death.

This Jamoan afterwards became very dear to him, being a man very gallant, and of excellent graces, and fine parts; so that he never put him amongst the rank of captives, as they used to do, without distinction, for the common sale, or market; but kept him in his own court, where he retained nothing of the prisoner but the name, and returned no more into his own country, so great an affection he took for Oroonoko; and by a thousand tales and adventures of love and gallantry, flattered his disease of melancholy and languishment; which I have often heard him say, had certainly killed him, but for the conversation of this prince and Aboan, and the French governor he had from his childhood, of whom I have spoken before, and who was a man of admirable wit, great ingenuity, and learning; all which he had infused into his young pupil. This Frenchman was banished out of his own country, for some heretical notions he held; and though he was a man of very little religion, he had admirable morals, and a brave soul.

After the total defeat of Jamoan's army, which all fled, or were left dead upon the place, they spent some time in the camp; Oroonoko choosing rather to remain a while there in his tents, than to enter into a place, or live in a court where he had so lately suffered so great a loss. The officers, therefore, who saw and knew his cause of discontent, invented all sorts of diversions and sports, to entertain their prince. So that what with those amusements abroad, and others at home, that is, within their tents, with the persuasions, arguments, and care of his friends and servants that he more peculiarly prized, he wore off in time a great part of that chagrin, and torture of death of despair, which the first effects of Imoinda's death had given him. Insomuch as having received a thousand kind embassies from the King, and invitations to return to court, he obeyed, though with no little reluctancy; and when he did so, there was a visible change in him, and for a long time he was much more melancholy than before. But time lessens all extremes, and reduces 'em to mediums and unconcern; but no motives of beauties, though all endeavoured it, could engage him in any sort of amour, though he had all the invitations to it, both from his own youth, and others' ambitions and designs.

Oroonoko was no sooner returned from this last conquest, and received at court with all the joy and magnificence that could be expressed to a young victor, who was not only returned triumphant, but beloved like a deity, when there arrived in the port an English ship.

This person had often before been in these countries, and was very well known to Oroonoko, with whom he had trafficked for slaves, and had used to do the same with his predecessors.

This commander was a man of a finer sort of address, and conversation, better bred, and more engaging, than most of that sort of men are; so that he seemed rather never to have been bred out of a court, than almost all his life at sea. This captain therefore was always better received at court than most of the traders to those countries were; and especially by Oroonoko, who was more civilized, according to the European mode, than any other had been, and took more delight in the white nations; and, above all, men of parts and wit. To this captain he sold abundance of his slaves; and for the favour and esteem he had for him, made him many presents, and obliged him to stay at court as long as possibly he could. Which the captain seemed to take as a very great honour done him, entertaining the prince every day with globes and maps, and mathematical discourses and instruments; eating, drinking, hunting, and living with him with so much familiarity, that it was not to be doubted but he had gained very greatly upon the heart of this gallant young man. And the captain in return of all these mighty favours, besought the prince to honour his vessel with his presence, some day or other, to dinner, before he should set sail: which he condescended to accept, and appointed his day. The captain, on his part, failed not to have all things in a readiness, in the most magnificent order he could possibly. And the day being come, the captain, in his boat, richly adorned with carpets and velvet cushions, rowed to the shore to receive the Prince (with another long-boat, where was placed all his music and trumpets, with which Oroonoko was extremely delighted), who met him on the shore, attended by his French governor, Jamoan, Aboan, and about a hundred of the noblest of the youths of the court. And after they had first carried the prince on board, the boats fetched the rest off; where they found a very splendid treat, with all sorts of fine wines; and were as well entertained as 'twas possible in such a place to be.

The prince having drunk hard of punch, and several sorts of wine, as did all the rest (for great care was taken, they should want nothing of that part of the entertainment), was very merry, and in great admiration of the ship, for he had never been in one before; so that he was curious of beholding every place, where he decently might descend. The rest, no less curious, who were not quite overcome with drinking, rambled at their pleasure fore and aft, as their fancies guided 'em. So that the captain, who had well laid his design before, gave the word, and seized on all his guests; they clapping great irons suddenly on the prince, when he was leaped down into the hold, to view that part of the vessel; and locking him fast down, secured him. The same treachery was used to all the rest; and all in one instant, in several places of the ship, were lashed fast in irons, and betrayed to slavery. That great design over, they set all hands to work to hoist sail; and with as treacherous and fair a wind, they made from the shore with this innocent and glorious prize, who thought of nothing less than such an entertainment.

Some have commended this act, as brave, in the captain; but I will spare my sense of it, and leave it to my reader, to judge as he pleases.

It may be easily guessed, in what manner the prince resented this indignity, who may be best resembled to a lion taken in a toil; so he raged, so he struggled for liberty, but all in vain; and they had so wisely managed his fetters, that he could not use a hand in his defence to quit himself of a life that would by no means endure slavery; nor could he move from the place, where he was tied, to any solid part of the ship, against which he might have beat his head, and have finished his disgrace that way. So that being deprived of all other means, he resolved to perish for want of food. And pleased at last with that thought, and toiled and tired by rage and indignation, he laid himself down, and sullenly resolved upon dying, and refused all things that were brought him.

This did not a little vex the captain, and the more so, because, he found almost all of 'em of the same humour; so that the loss of so many brave slaves, so tall and goodly to behold, would have been very considerable. He therefore ordered one to go from him (for he would not be seen himself) to Oroonoko, and to assure him he was afflicted for having rashly done so unhospitable a deed, and which could not be now remedied, since they were far from shore; but since he resented it in so high a nature, he assured him he would revoke his resolution, and set both him and his friends ashore on the next land they should touch at; and of this the messenger gave him his oath, provided he would resolve to live. And Oroonoko, whose honour was such as he never had violated a word in his life himself, much less a solemn asseveration, believed in an instant what this man said; but replied, he expected for a confirmation of this, to have his shameful fetters dismissed. This demand was carried to the captain, who returned him answer that the offence had been so great which he had put upon the prince, that he durst not trust him with liberty while he remained in the ship, for fear lest by a valour natural to him, and a revenge that would animate that valour, he might commit some outrage fatal to himself and the King his master, to whom this vessel did belong. To this Oroonoko replied, he would engage his honour to behave himself in all friendly order and manner, and obey the command of the captain, as he was Lord of the King's vessel, and general of those men under his command.

This was delivered to the still doubting captain, who could not resolve to trust a heathen he said, upon his parole, a man that had no sense or notion of the God that he worshipped. Oroonoko then replied, he was very sorry to hear that the captain pretended to the knowledge and worship of any gods, who had taught him no better principles, than not to credit as he would be credited; but they told him, the difference of their faith occasioned that distrust. For the captain had protested to him upon the word of a Christian, and sworn in the name of a great God; which if he should violate, he would expect eternal torment in the world to come. 'Is that all the obligation he has to be just to his oath?' replied Oroonoko. 'Let him know, I swear by my honour, which to violate, would not only render me contemptible and despised by all brave and honest men, and so give myself perpetual pain, but it would be eternally offending and displeasing all mankind, harming, betraying, circumventing, and outraging all men. But punishments hereafter are suffered by oneself; and the world

takes no cognisance whether this God have revenged 'em, or not, 'tis done
so secretly, and deferred so long. While the man of no honour, suffers every
moment the scorn and contempt of the honester world, and dies every day
ignominiously in his fame, which is more valuable than life. I speak not this
to move belief, but to show you how you mistake, when you imagine, that
he who will violate his honour will keep his word with his gods.' So, turning from him with a disdainful smile, he refused to answer him, when he
urged him to know what answer he should carry back to his captain; so
that he departed without saying any more.

The captain pondering and consulting what to do, it was concluded
that nothing but Oroonoko's liberty would encourage any of the rest to
eat, except the Frenchman, whom the captain could not pretend to keep
prisoner, but only told him he was secured because he might act something in favour of the prince, but that he should be freed as soon as they
came to land. So that they concluded it wholly necessary to free the prince
from his irons, that he might show himself to the rest; that they might have
an eye upon him, and that they could not fear a single man.

This being resolved, to make the obligation the greater, the captain himself went to Oroonoko; where, after many compliments, and assurances of
what he had already promised, he receiving from the prince his parole, and
his hand, for his good behaviour, dismissed his irons, and brought him
to his own cabin; where, after having treated and reposed him a while (for
he had neither eat nor slept in four days before), he besought him to visit
those obstinate people in chains, who refused all manner of sustenance;
and entreated him oblige 'em to eat, and assure 'em of that liberty the
first opportunity.

Oroonoko, who was too generous, not to give credit to his words, showed
himself to his people, who were transported with excess of joy at the sight
of their darling prince; falling at his feet, and kissing and embracing 'em;
believing, as some divine oracle, all he assured 'em. But he besought 'em
to bear their chains with that bravery that became those whom he had
seen act so nobly in arms; and that they could not give him greater proofs
of their love and friendship, since 'twas all the security the captain (his
friend) could have, against the revenge, he said, they might possibly justly
take, for the injuries sustained by him. And they all, with one accord,
assured him, they could not suffer enough, when it was for his repose and
safety.

After this they no longer refused to eat, but took what was brought 'em,
and were pleased with their captivity, since by it they hoped to redeem the
prince, who, all the rest of the voyage, was treated with all the respect due
to his birth, though nothing could divert his melancholy; and he would

often sigh for Imoinda, and think this a punishment due to his misfortune, in having left that noble maid behind him, that fatal night, in the otan, when he fled to the camp.

Possessed with a thousand thoughts of past joys with this fair young person, and a thousand griefs for her eternal loss, he endured a tedious voyage, and at last arrived at the mouth of the river of Surinam, a colony belonging to the King of England, and where they were to deliver some part of their slaves. There the merchants and gentlemen of the country going on board, to demand those lots of slaves they had already agreed on; and, amongst those, the overseers of those plantations where I then chanced to be, the captain, who had given the word, ordered his men to bring up those noble slaves in fetters, whom I have spoken of; and having put 'em, some in one, and some in other lots, with women and children (which they call pickaninnies), they sold 'em off, as slaves, to several merchants and gentlemen; not putting any two in one lot, because they would separate 'em far from each other; not daring to trust 'em together, lest rage and courage should put 'em upon contriving some great action, to the ruin of the colony.

Oroonoko was first seized on, and sold to our overseer, who had the first lot, with seventeen more of all sorts and sizes, but not one of quality with him. When he saw this, he found what they meant; for, as I said, he understood English pretty well; and being wholly unarmed and defenceless, so as it was in vain to make any resistance, he only beheld the captain with a look all fierce and disdainful, upbraiding him with eyes, that forced blushes on his guilty cheeks, he only cried, in passing over the side of the ship, 'Farewell, sir. 'Tis worth my suffering, to gain so true a knowledge both of you, and of your gods by whom you swear.' And desiring those that held him to forbear their pains, and telling 'em he would make no resistance, he cried, 'Come, my fellow-slaves; let us descend, and see if we can meet with more honour and honesty in the next world we shall touch upon.' So he nimbly leaped into the boat, and showing no more concern, suffered himself to be rowed up the river, with his seventeen companions.

The gentleman that bought him was a young Cornish gentleman, whose name was Trefry; a man of great wit, and fine learning, and was carried into those parts by the Lord-Governor, to manage all his affairs. He, reflecting on the last words of Oroonoko to the captain, and beholding the richness of his vest, no sooner came into the boat, but he fixed his eyes on him; and finding something so extraordinary in his face, his shape and mien, a greatness of look, and haughtiness in his air, and finding he spoke English, had a great mind to be inquiring into his quality and fortune; which, though Oroonoko endeavoured to hide, by only confessing he was above the rank of common slaves, Trefry soon found he was yet something greater than he confessed; and from that moment began to conceive so vast an esteem for him, that he ever after loved him as his dearest brother, and showed him all the civilities due to so great a man.

Trefry was a very good mathematician, and a linguist; could speak French and Spanish; and in the three days they remained in the boat (for so long were they going from the ship, to the plantation) he entertained Oroonoko so agreeably with his art and discourse, that he was no less pleased with Trefry, than he was with the prince; and he thought himself, at least, fortunate in this, that since he was a slave, as long as he would suffer himself to remain so, he had a man of so excellent wit and parts for a master. So that before they had finished their voyage up the river, he made no scruple of declaring to Trefry all his fortunes, and most part of what I have here related, and put himself wholly into the hands of his new friend, whom he found resenting all the injuries were done him, and was charmed with all the greatnesses of his actions; which were recited with that modesty, and delicate sense, as wholly vanquished him, and subdued him to his interest. And he promised him on his word and honour, he would find the means to re-conduct him to his own country again: assuring him, he had a perfect abhorrence of so dishonourable an action; and that he would sooner have died, than have been the author of such a perfidy. He found the prince was very much concerned to know what became of his friends, and how they took their slavery; and Trefry promised to take care about the inquiring after their condition, and that he should have an account of 'em.

Though, as Oroonoko afterwards said, he had little reason to credit the words of a Backearary, yet he knew not why; but he saw a kind of sincerity, and awful truth in the face of Trefry; he saw an honesty in his eyes, and he found him wise and witty enough to understand honour. For it was one of his maxims, 'A man of wit could not be a knave or villain.'

In their passage up the river, they put in at several houses for refreshment; and ever when they landed, numbers of people would flock to behold this man; not but their eyes were daily entertained with the sight of slaves, but the fame of Oroonoko was gone before him, and all people were in admiration of his beauty. Besides, he had a rich habit on, in which he was taken, so different from the rest, and which the captain could not strip him of, because he was forced to surprise his person in the minute he sold him. When he found his habit made him liable, as he thought, to be gazed at the more, he begged Trefry to give him something more befitting a slave, which he did, and took off his robes. Nevertheless he shone through all, and his osenbrigs (a sort of brown holland suit he had on) could not conceal the graces of his looks and mien; and he had no less admirers, than when he had his dazzling habit on. The royal youth appeared in spite of the slave, and people could not help treating him after a different manner, without designing it. As soon as they approached him, they venerated and esteemed him; his eyes insensibly commanded respect, and his behaviour insinuated it into every soul. So that there was nothing talked of but this young and gallant slave, even by those who yet knew not that he was a prince.

I ought to tell you that the Christians never buy any slaves but they give 'em some name of their own, their native ones being likely very barbarous, and hard to pronounce; so that Mr Trefry gave Oroonoko that of Caesar; which name will live in that country as long as that (scarce more) glorious one of the great Roman; for 'tis most evident he wanted no part of the personal courage of that Caesar, and acted things as memorable, had they been done in some part of the world replenished with people, and historians, that might have given him his due. But his misfortune was to fall in an obscure world, that afforded only a female pen to celebrate his fame; though I doubt not but it had lived from others' endeavours, if the Dutch, who immediately after his time, took that country, had not killed, banished, and dispersed all those that were capable of giving the world this great man's life, much better than I have done. And Mr Trefry, who designed it, died before he began it; and bemoaned himself for not having undertook it in time.

For the future, therefore, I must call Oroonoko, Caesar since by that name only he was known in our Western world, and by that name he was received on shore at Parham-House, where he was destined a slave. But if the King himself (God bless him) had come ashore, there could not have been greater expectations by all the whole plantation, and those neighbouring ones, than was on ours at that time; and he was received more like a governor, than a slave. Notwithstanding, as the custom was, they assigned him his portion of land, his house, and his business, up in the plantation. But as it was more for form, than any design, to put him to his task, he endured no more of the slave but the name, and remained some days in the house, receiving all visits that were made him, without stirring towards that part of the plantation where the Negroes were.

At last, he would needs go view his land, his house, and the business assigned him. But he no sooner came to the houses of the slaves, which are like a little town by itself, the Negroes all having left work, but they all came forth to behold him, and found he was that prince who had, at several times, sold most of 'em to these parts; and from a veneration they pay to great men, especially if they know 'em, and from the surprise and awe they had at the sight of him, they all cast themselves at his feet, crying out, in their language, 'Live, O King! Long live, O King!'. And kissing his feet, paid him even divine homage.

Several English gentlemen were with him; and what Mr. Trefry had told 'em was here confirmed; of which he himself before had no other witness than Caesar himself. But he was infinitely glad to find his grandeur confirmed by the adoration of all the slaves.

Caesar troubled with their over-joy, and over-ceremony, besought 'em to rise, and to receive him as their fellow-slave; assuring them, he was no better. At which they set up with one accord a most terrible and hideous mourning and condoling, which he and the English had much ado to appease; but at last they prevailed with 'em, and they prepared all their barbarous music, and everyone killed and dressed something of his own stock (for every family has their land apart, on which, at their leisure times, they breed all eatable things), and clubbing it together, made a most magnificent supper, inviting their Grandee Captain, their Prince, to honour it with his presence; which he did, and several English with him; where they all waited on him, some playing, others dancing before him all the time, according to the manners of their several nations; and with unwearied industry, endeavouring to please and delight him.

While they sat at meat, Mr Trefry told Caesar that most of these young slaves were undone in love with a fine she-slave, whom they had had about six months on their land; the prince, who never heard the name of love without a sigh, nor any mention of it without the curiosity of examining further into that tale, which of all discourses was most agreeable to him, asked, how they came to be so unhappy, as to be all undone for one fair slave? Trefry, who was naturally amorous, and loved to talk of love as well as anybody, proceeded to tell him they had the most charming black that ever was beheld on their plantation, about fifteen or sixteen years old, as he guessed; that, for his part, he had done nothing but sigh for her ever since she came; and that all the white beauties he had seen never charmed him so absolutely as this fine creature had done; and that no man, of any nation, ever beheld her, that did not fall in love with her; and that she had all the slaves perpetually at her feet; and the whole country resounded with the fame of Clemene. 'For so,' said he, 'we have christened her. But she denies us all with such a noble disdain, that 'tis a miracle to see, that she, who can give such eternal desires should herself be all ice and unconcern. She is adorned with the most graceful modesty that ever beautified youth; the softest sigher – that, if she were capable of love, one would swear she languished for some absent happy man; and so retired, as if she feared a rape even from the god of day; or that the breezes would steal kisses from her delicate mouth. Her task of work some sighing lover every day makes it his petition to perform for her, which she accepts blushing, and with reluctancy, for fear he will ask her a look for a recompense, which he dares not presume to hope; so great an awe she strikes into the hearts of her admirers. 'I do not wonder,' replied the prince, 'that Clemene should refuse slaves, being as you say, so beautiful, but wonder how she escapes those that can entertain her as you can do;or why, being your slave, you do not oblige her to yield.' 'I confess,' said Trefry, 'when I have, against her will, entertained her with love so long as to be transported with my passion; even above decency, I have been ready to make use of those advantages of strength and force nature has given me. But oh! she disarms me with that modesty and weeping so tender and so moving that I retire, and thank my stars she overcame me.' The company laughed at his civility to a slave, and Caesar only applauded the nobleness of his passion and nature; since that slave might be noble, or, what was better, have true notions of honour and virtue in her. Thus passed they this night, after having received from the slaves all imaginable respect and obedience.

The next day Trefry asked Caesar to walk, when the heat was allayed, and designedly carried him by the cottage of the fair slave; and told him, she whom he spoke of last night lived there, retired. 'But,' says he, 'I would not wish you to approach, for, I am sure, you will be in love as soon as you behold her.' Caesar assured him, he was proof against all the charms of that sex; and that if he imagined his heart could be so perfidious to love again, after Imoinda, he believed he should tear it from his bosom. They had no sooner spoke, but a little shock-dog, that Clemene had presented her, which she took great delight in, ran out; and she, not knowing anybody was there, ran to get it in again, and bolted out on those who were just speaking of her. When seeing them, she would have run in again; but Trefry caught her by the hand, and cried, 'Clemene, however you fly a lover, you ought to pay some respect to this stranger' (pointing to Caesar). But she, as if she had resolved never to raise her eyes to the face of a man again, bent 'em the more to the earth, when he spoke, and gave the Prince the leisure to look the more at her. There needed no long gazing, or consideration, to examine who this fair creature was; he soon saw Imoinda all over her; in a minute he saw her face, her shape, her air, her modesty, and all that called forth his soul with joy at his eyes, and left his body destitute of almost life; it stood without motion, and for a minute knew not that it had a being; and, I believe, he had never come to himself, so oppressed he was with over-joy, if he had not met with this allay, that he perceived Imoinda fall dead in the hands of Trefry. This awakened him, and he ran to her aid, and caught her in his arms, where, by degrees she came to herself;

and 'tis needless to tell with what transports, what ecstasies of joy, they both awhile beheld each other, without speaking; then snatched each other to their arms; then gazed again, as if they still doubted whether they possessed the blessing they grasped. But when they recovered their speech, 'tis not to be imagined, what tender things they expressed to each other; wondering what strange fate had brought them again together. They soon informed each other of their fortunes, and equally bewailed their fate; but, at the same time, they mutually protested, that even fetters and slavery were soft and easy; and would be supported with joy and pleasure, while they could be so happy to possess each other, and be able to make good their vows. Caesar swore he disdained the empire of the world, while he could behold his Imoinda; and she despised grandeur and pomp, those vanities of her sex, when she could gaze on Oroonoko. He adored the very cottage where she resided, and said that little inch of the world would give him more happiness than all the universe could do; and she vowed, it was a palace while adorned with the presence of Oroonoko.

Trefry was infinitely pleased with this novel, and found this Clemene was the fair mistress of whom Caesar had before spoke; and was not a little satisfied, that Heaven was so kind to the prince as to sweeten his misfortunes by so lucky an accident; and leaving the lovers to themselves, was impatient to come down to Parham-House (which was on the same plantation) to give me an account of what had happened. I was as impatient to make these lovers a visit, having already made a friendship with Caesar; and from his own mouth learned what I have related, which was confirmed by his Frenchman, who was set on shore to seek his fortunes; and of whom they could not make a slave, because a Christian; and he came daily to Parham-Hill to see and pay his respects to his pupil prince. So that concerning and interesting myself, in all that related to Caesar, whom I had assured of liberty, as soon as the Governor arrived, I hasted presently to the place where the lovers were, and was infinitely glad to find this beautiful young slave (who had already gained all our esteems, for her modesty and her extraordinary prettiness) to be the same I had heard Caesar speak so much of. One may imagine then, we paid her a treble respect; and though from her being carved in fine flowers and birds all over her body, we took her to be of quality before, yet, when we knew Clemene was Imoinda, we could not enough admire her.

I had forgot to tell you, that those who are nobly born of that country are so delicately cut and raced all over the fore-part of the trunk of their bodies that it looks as if it were japanned; the works being raised like high point round the edges of the flowers. Some are only carved with a little flower, or bird, at the sides of the temples, as was Caesar; and those who are so carved over the body resemble our ancient Picts, that are figured in the chronicles, but these carvings are more delicate.

From that happy day Caesar took Clemene for his wife, to the general joy of all people; and there was as much magnificence as the country would afford at the celebration of this wedding: and in a very short time after she conceived with child; which made Caesar even adore her, knowing he was the last of his great race. This new accident made him more impatient of liberty, and he was every day treating with Trefry for his and Clemene's liberty; and offered either gold, or a vast quantity of slaves, which should be paid before they let him go, provided he could have any security that he should go when his ransom was paid. They fed him from day to day with promises, and delayed him, till the Lord-Governor should come; so that he began to suspect them of falsehood, and that they would delay him till the time of his wife's delivery, and make a slave of that too. For all the breed is theirs to whom the parents belong. This thought made him very uneasy, and his sullenness gave them some jealousies of him; so that I was obliged, by some persons, who feared a mutiny (which is very fatal sometimes in those colonies, that abound so with slaves, that they exceed the whites in vast numbers), to discourse with Caesar, and to give him all the satisfaction I possibly could; they knew he and Clemene were scarce an hour in a day from my lodgings; that they eat with me, and that I obliged 'em in all things I was capable of. I entertained them with the *Lives of the Romans*, and great men, which charmed him to my company; and her, with teaching her all the pretty works that I was mistress of; and telling her stories of nuns, and endeavouring to bring her to the knowledge of the true God. But of all discourses, Caesar liked that the worst, and would never be reconciled to our notions of the Trinity, of which he ever made a jest; it was a riddle, he said, would turn his brain to conceive, and one could not make him understand what faith was. However, these conversations failed not altogether so well to divert him, that he liked the company of us women much above the men; for he could not drink, and he is but an ill companion in that country that cannot. So that obliging him to love us very well, we had all the liberty of speech with him, especially myself, whom he called his 'Great Mistress'; and indeed my word would go a great way with him. For these reasons, I had opportunity to take notice to him, that he was not well pleased of late, as he used to be; was more retired and thoughtful; and told him, I took it ill he should suspect we would break our words with him, and not permit both him and Clemene to return to his own kingdom, which was not so long a way but when he was once on his voyage he would quickly arrive there. He made me some answers that showed a doubt in him, which made me ask what advantage it would be to doubt? It would but give us a fear of him, and possibly compel us to treat him so as I should be very loth to behold: that is, it might occasion his confinement. Perhaps this was not so luckily spoke of me, for I perceived he resented that word, which I strove to soften again in vain. However, he assured me that, whatsoever resolutions he should take, he would act nothing upon the white people; and as for myself, and those upon that plantation where he was, he would sooner forfeit his eternal liberty, and life itself, than lift his hand against his greatest enemy on that place. He besought me to suffer no fears upon his account, for he could do nothing that honour should not dictate; but he accused himself for having suffered slavery so long; yet he charged that weakness on love alone, who was capable of making him neglect even glory itself; and, for which, now he reproaches himself every moment of the day. Much more to this effect he spoke, with an air impatient enough to make me know he would not be long in bondage; and though he suffered only the name of a slave, and had nothing of the toil and labour of one, yet that was sufficient to render him uneasy; and he had been too long idle, who used to be always in action, and in arms. He had a spirit all rough and fierce, and that could not be tamed to lazy rest; and though all endeavours were used to exercise himself in such actions and sports as this world afforded, as running, wrestling, pitching the bar, hunting and fishing, chasing and killing tigers of a monstrous size, which this continent affords in abundance; and wonderful snakes, such as Alexander is reported to have encountered at the River of Amazons, and which Caesar took great delight to overcome; yet these were not actions great enough for his large soul, which was still panting after more renowned action.

Before I parted that day with him, I got, with much ado, a promise from him to rest yet a little longer with patience, and wait the coming of the Lord-Governor, who was every day expected on our shore; he assured me he would, and this promise he desired me to know was given perfectly in complaisance to me, in whom he had an entire confidence.

After this, I neither thought it convenient to trust him much out of our view, nor did the country, who feared him; but with one accord it was advised to treat him fairly, and oblige him to remain within such a compass, and that he should be permitted, as seldom as could be, to go up to the plantations of the Negroes; or, if he did, to be accompanied by some that should be rather in appearance attendants than spies. This care was for some time taken, and Caesar looked upon it as a mark of extraordinary respect, and was glad his discontent had obliged 'em to be more observant to him; he received new assurance from the overseer, which was confirmed to him by the opinion of all the gentlemen of the country, who made their court to him. During this time that we had his company more frequently than hitherto we had had, it may not be unpleasant to relate to you the diversions we entertained him with, or rather he us.

My stay was to be short in that country, because my father died at sea, and never arrived to possess the honour designed him (which was Lieutenant-General of six and thirty islands, besides the Continent of Surinam), nor the advantages he hoped to reap by them; so that though we were obliged to continue on our voyage, we did not intend to stay upon the place. Though, in a word, I must say thus much of it, that certainly had his late Majesty, of sacred memory, but seen and known what a vast and charming world he had been master of in that continent, he would never have parted so easily with it to the Dutch. 'Tis a continent whose vast extent was never yet known, and may contain more noble earth than all the universe besides; for, they say, it reaches from east to west; one way as far as China, and another to Peru. It affords all things both for beauty and use; 'tis there eternal spring, always the very months of April, May, and June; the shades are perpetual, the trees bearing at once all degrees of leaves and fruit, from blooming buds to ripe autumn; groves of oranges, lemons, citrons, figs, nutmegs, and noble aromatics continually bearing their fragrances. The trees appearing all like nosegays adorned with flowers of different kinds; some are all white, some purple, some scarlet, some blue, some yellow; bearing at the same time, ripe fruit, and blooming young, or producing every day new. The very wood of all these trees have an intrinsic value above common timber; for they are, when cut, of different colours, glorious to behold; and bear a price considerable, to inlay withal. Besides this, they yield rich balm and gums; so that we make our candles of such an aromatic substance as does not only give a sufficient light, but, as they burn, they cast their perfumes all about. Cedar is the common firing, and all the houses are built with it. The very meat we eat, when set on the table, if it be native (I mean of the country) perfumes the whole room; especially a little beast called an armadillo, a thing which I can liken to nothing so well as a rhinoceros; 'tis all in white armour, so jointed that it moves as well in it, as if it had nothing on: this beast is about the bigness of a pig of six weeks old. But it were endless to give an account of all the diverse wonderful and strange things that country affords, and which we took a very great delight to go in search of; though those adventures are oftentimes fatal, and at least dangerous. But while we had Caesar in our company on these designs we feared no harm, nor suffered any.

As soon as I came into the country, the best house in it was presented me, called St John's Hill. It stood on a vast rock of white marble, at the foot of which the river ran a vast depth down, and not to be descended on that side; the little waves, still dashing and washing the foot of this rock, made the softest murmurs and purlings in the world; and the opposite bank was adorned with such vast quantities of different flowers eternally blowing, and every day and hour new, fenced behind 'em with lofty trees of a thousand rare forms and colours, that the prospect was the most ravishing that sands can create. On the edge of this white rock, towards the river, was a walk or grove of orange and lemon trees, about half the length of the Mall here; flowery and fruit-bearing branches met at the top, and hindered the sun, whose rays are very fierce there, from entering a beam into the grove; and the cool air that came from the river made it not only fit to entertain people in, at all the hottest hours of the day, but refreshed the sweet blossoms, and made it always sweet and charming; and sure, the whole globe of the world cannot show so delightful a place as this grove was. Not all the gardens of boasted Italy can produce a shade to outvie this, which nature had joined with art to render so exceeding fine; and 'tis a marvel to see how such vast trees, as big as English oaks, could take footing on so solid a rock, and in so little earth, as covered that rock: but all things by nature there are rare, delightful, and wonderful. But to our sports.

Sometimes we would go surprising, and in search of young tigers in their dens, watching when the old ones went forth to forage for prey; and oftentimes we have been in great danger, and have fled apace for our lives, when surprised by the dams. But once, above all other times, we went on this design, and Caesar was with us, who had no sooner stolen a young tiger from her nest, but going off, we encountered the dam, bearing a buttock of a cow, which she had torn off with her mighty paw, and going with it towards her den; we had only four women, Caesar, and an English gentleman, brother to Harry Martin, the great Oliverian; we found there was no escaping this enraged and ravenous beast. However, we women fled as fast as we could from it; but our heels had not saved our lives, if Caesar had not laid down his cub, when he found the tiger quit her prey to make more speed towards him; and taking Mr Martin's sword, desired to stand aside, or follow the ladies. He obeyed him, and Caesar met this monstrous beast of might, size, and vast limbs, who came with open jaws upon him; and fixing his awful stern eyes full upon those of the beast, and putting himself into a very steady and good aiming posture of defence, ran his sword quite through her breast down to her very heart, home to the hilt of the sword; the dying beast stretched forth her paw, and going to grasp his thigh, surprised with death in that very moment, did him no other harm than fixing her long nails in his flesh very deep, feebly wounded him, but could not grasp the flesh to tear off any. When he had done this, he hollowed to us to return; which, after some assurance of his victory, we did, and found him lunging out the sword from the bosom of the tiger, who was laid in her blood on the ground; he took up the cub, and with an unconcern that had nothing of the joy or gladness of a victory, he came and laid the whelp at my feet. We all extremely wondered at his daring, and at the bigness of the beast, which was about the height of a heifer, but of mighty, great, and strong limbs.

Another time, being in the woods, he killed a tiger, which had long infested that part, and borne away abundance of sheep and oxen, and other things, that were for the support of those to whom they belonged; abundance of people assailed this beast, some affirming they had shot her with several bullets quite through the body, at several times; and some swearing they shot her through the very heart, and they believed she was a devil rather than a mortal thing. Caesar, had often said, he had a mind to encounter this monster, and spoke with several gentlemen who had attempted her; one crying, 'I shot her with so many poisoned arrows', another with his gun in this part of her, and another in that; so that he, remarking all these places where she was shot, fancied still he should overcome her, by giving her another sort of a wound than any had yet done, and one day said (at the table), 'What trophies and garlands ladies will you make me, if I bring you home the heart of this ravenous beast, that eats up all your lambs and pigs?' We all promised he should be rewarded at all our hands. So taking a bow, which he chus'd out of a great many, he went up into the wood, with two gentlemen, where he imagined this devourer to be; they had not passed very far in it, but they heard her voice, growling and grumbling, as if she were pleased with something she was doing. When they came in view, they found her muzzling in the belly of a new-ravished sheep, which she had torn open; and seeing herself approached, she took fast hold of her prey, with her fore-paws, and set a very fierce raging look on Caesar, without offering to approach him, for fear, at the same time, of losing what she had in possession. So that Caesar remained a good while, only taking aim, and getting an opportunity to shoot her where he designed; 'twas some time before he could accomplish it and to wound her, and not kill her, would but have enraged her the more, and endangered him. He had a quiver of arrows at his side, so that if one failed, he could be supplied; at last, retiring a little, he gave her opportunity to eat, for he found she was ravenous, and fell to as soon as she saw him retire, being more eager of her prey than of doing new mischiefs. When he going softly to one side of her, and hiding his person behind certain herbage that grew high and thick, he took so good aim, that, as he intended, he shot her just into the eye, and the arrow was sent with so good a will, and so sure a hand, that it stuck in her brain, and made her caper, and become mad for a moment or two; but being seconded by another arrow, she fell dead upon the prey. Caesar cut her open with a knife, to see where those wounds were that had been reported to him, and why she did not die of 'em. But I shall now relate a thing that possibly will find no credit among men, because 'tis a notion commonly received with us, that nothing can receive a wound in the heart and live; but when the heart of this courageous animal was taken out, there were seven bullets of lead in it, the wounds seamed up with great scars, and she lived with the bullets a great while, for it was long since they were shot. This heart the conqueror brought up to us, and 'twas a very great curiosity, which all the country came to see; and which gave Caesar occasion of many fine discourses of accidents in war and strange escapes.

At other times he would go a-fishing; and discoursing on that diversion, he found we had in that country a very strange fish, called a numb eel (an eel of which I have eaten), that, while it is alive, it has a quality so cold, that those who are angling, though with a line of never so great a length, with a rod at the end of it, it shall, in the same minute the bait is touched by this eel, seize him or her that holds the rod with a numbness, that shall deprive 'em of sense, for a while; and some have fallen into the water, and others dropped as dead on the banks of the rivers where they stood, as soon as this fish touches the bait. Caesar used to laugh at this, and believed it impossible a man could lose his force at the touch of a fish; and could not understand that philosophy, that a cold quality should be of that nature. However, he had a great curiosity to try whether it would have the same effect on him it had on others, and often tried, but in vain; at last, the sought-for fish came to the bait, as he stood angling on the bank; and instead of throwing away the rod, or giving it a sudden twitch out of the water, whereby he might have caught both the eel, and have dismissed the rod, before it could have too much power over him; for experiment-sake, he grasped it but the harder, and fainting fell into the river; and being still possessed of the rod, the tide carried him, senseless as he was, a great way, till an Indian boat took him up; and perceived, when they touched him, a numbness seize them, and by that knew the rod was in his hand; which, with a paddle (that is, a short oar) they struck away, and snatched it into the boat, eel and all. If Caesar were almost dead, with the effect of this fish, he was more so with that of the water, where he had remained the space of going a league; and they found they had much ado to bring him back to life. But at last they did, and brought him home, where he was in a few hours well recovered and refreshed; and not a little ashamed to find he should be overcome by an eel, and that all the people, who heard his defiance, would laugh at him. But we cheered him up; and he being convinced, we had the eel at supper; which was a quarter of an ell about, and most delicate meat; and was of the more value, since it cost so dear, as almost the life of so gallant a man.

About this time we were in many mortal fears, about some disputes the English had with the Indians; so that we could scarce trust ourselves, without great numbers, to go to any Indian towns, or place, where they abode; for fear they should fall upon us, as they did immediately after my coming away; and that it was in the possession of the Dutch, who used 'em not so civilly as the English; so that they cut in pieces all they could take, getting into houses, and hanging up the mother, and all her children about her; and cut a footman, I left behind me, all in joints, and nailed him to trees.

This feud began while I was there; so that I lost half the satisfaction I proposed, in not seeing and visiting the Indian towns. But one day, bemoaning of our misfortunes upon this account, Caesar told us, we need not fear; for if we had a mind to go, he would undertake to be our guard. Some would, but most would not venture; about eighteen of us resolved, and took barge; and, after eight days, arrived near an Indian town. But approaching it, the hearts of some of our company failed, and they would not venture on shore; so we polled who would, and who would not. For my part, I said, if Caesar would, I would go; he resolved, so did my brother, and my woman, a maid of good courage. Now none of us speaking the language of the people, and imagining we should have a half diversion in gazing only; and not knowing what they said, we took a fisherman that lived at the mouth of the river, who had been a long inhabitant there, and obliged him to go with us. But because he was known to the Indians, as trading among 'em; and being, by long living there, become a perfect Indian in colour, we, who resolved to surprise 'em, by making 'em see something they never had seen (that is, white people), resolved only myself, my brother, and woman should go; so Caesar, the fisherman, and the rest, hiding behind some thick reeds and flowers, that grew in the banks, let us pass on towards the town, which was on the bank of the river all along. A little distant from the houses, or huts, we saw some dancing, others busied in fetching and carrying of water from the river. They had no sooner spied us, but they set up a loud cry, that frighted us at first; we thought it had been for those that should kill us, but it seems it was of wonder and amazement. They were all naked, and we were dressed, so as is most commode for the hot countries, very glittering and rich; so that we appeared extremely fine; my own hair was cut short, and I had a taffety cap, with black feathers, on my head; my brother was in a stuff-suit, with silver loops and button, and abundance of green ribbon; this was all infinitely surprising to them, and because we saw them stand still, till we approached 'em, we took heart and advanced; came up to 'em, and offered 'em our hands; which they took, and looked on us round about, calling still for more company; who came swarming out, all wondering, and crying out 'Tepeeme'; taking their hair up in their hands, and spreading it wide to those they called out to; as if they would say (as indeed it signified), 'Numberless wonders', or not to be recounted, no more than to number the hair of their heads. By degrees they grew more bold, and from gazing upon us round; they touched us, laying their hands upon all the features of our faces, feeling our breasts and arms, taking up one petticoat, then wondering to see another; admiring our shoes and stockings, but more our garters, which we gave 'em; and they tied about their legs, being laced with silver lace at the ends, for they much esteem any shining things. In fine, we suffered 'em to survey us as they pleased, and we thought they would never have done admiring us. When Caesar, and the rest, saw we were received with such wonder, they came up to us; and finding the Indian trader whom they knew (for 'tis by these fishermen, called Indian traders, we hold a commerce with 'em; for they love not to go far from home, and we never go to them), when they saw him therefore they set up a new joy, and cried in their language, 'Oh! here's our Tiguamy, and we shall now know whether those things can speak'. So advancing to him, some of 'em gave him their hands, and cried, 'Amora Tiguamy'; which is as much as, 'How do you do?' or, 'Welcome, friend', and all, with one din, began to gabble to him, and asked, if we had sense and wit? If we could talk of affairs of life, and war, as they could do? If we could hunt, swim, and do a thousand things they use? He answered 'em, we could. Then they invited us into their houses, and dressed venison and buffalo for us; and, going out, gathered a leaf of a tree, called a sarumbo leaf, of six yards long, and spread it on the ground for a table-cloth and cutting another in pieces instead of plates, setting us on little bow Indian stools, which they cut out of one entire piece of wood, and paint, in a sort of Japan-work. They serve everyone their mess on these pieces of leaves, and it was very good, but too high-seasoned with pepper. When we had eat, my brother and I took out our flutes, and played to 'em, which gave 'em new wonder; and I soon perceived, by an admiration, that is natural to these people; and by the extreme ignorance and simplicity of 'em, it were not difficult to establish any unknown or extravagant religion among them; and to impose any notions or fictions upon 'em. For seeing a kinsman of mine set some paper afire, with a burning-glass, a trick they had never before seen, they were like to have adored him for a god; and begged he would give 'em the characters or figures of his name, that they might oppose it against winds and storms; which he did, and they held it up in those seasons, and fancied it had a charm to conquer them; and kept it like a holy relic. They are very superstitious, and called him the great Peeie, that is, Prophet. They showed us their Indian Peeie, a youth of about sixteen years old, as handsome as Nature could make a man. They consecrate a beautiful youth from his infancy, and all arts are used to complete him in the finest manner, both in beauty and shape. He is bred to all the little arts and cunning they are capable of; to all the legerdemain tricks and sleight-of-hand, whereby he imposes upon the rabble; and is both a doctor in physic and divinity. And by these tricks makes the sick believe he sometimes eases their pains, by drawing from the afflicted part little serpents, or odd flies, or worms, or any strange thing; and though they have besides undoubted good remedies, for almost all their diseases, they cure the patient more by fancy than by medicines, and make themselves feared, loved, and reverenced. This young Peeie had a very young wife, who, seeing my brother kiss her, came running and kissed me; after this they kissed one another, and made it a very great jest, it being so novel; and new admiration and laughing went round the multitude, that they never will forget that ceremony, never before used or known. Caesar had a mind to see and talk with their war-captains, and we were conducted to one of their houses, where we beheld several of the great captains, who had been at council. But so frightful a vision it was to see 'em no fancy can create; no such dreams can represent so dreadful a spectacle. For my part, I took 'em for hobgoblins, or fiends, rather than men; but however their shapes appeared, their souls were very humane and noble; but some wanted their noses, some their lips, some both noses and lips, some their ears, and others cut through each cheek, with long slashes, through which their teeth appeared; they had several other formidable wounds and scars, or rather dismemberings; they had comitias, or little aprons before 'em; and girdles of cotton, with their knives naked stuck in it; a bow at their backs, and a quiver of arrows on their thighs; and most had feathers on their heads of diverse colours. They cried 'Amora Tiguamy' to us, at our entrance, and were pleased we said as much to 'em: they seated us, and gave us drink of the best sort; and wondered as much as the others had done before, to see us. Caesar was marvelling as much at their faces, wondering how they should all be so wounded in war; he was impatient to know how they all came by those frightful marks of rage or malice, rather than wounds got in noble battle. They told us, by our interpreter, that when any war was waging, two men, chosen out by some old captain, whose fighting was past, and who could only teach the theory of war, these two men were to stand in competition for the generalship, or great war-captain; and being brought before the old judges, now past labour, they are asked, what they dare do, to show they are worthy to lead an army? When he, who is first asked, making no reply, cuts off his nose, and throws it contemptibly on the ground; and the other does something to himself that he thinks surpasses him, and perhaps deprives himself of lips and an eye; so they slash on till one gives out, and many have died in this debate. And it's by a passive valour they show and prove their activity; a sort of courage too brutal to be applauded by our black hero; nevertheless, he expressed his esteem of 'em.

In this voyage Caesar begot so good an understanding between the Indians and the English, that there were no more fears, or heart-burnings during our stay; but we had a perfect, open, and free trade with 'em. Many things remarkable, and worth reciting, we met with in this short voyage; because Caesar made it his business to search out and provide for our entertainment, especially to please his dearly adored Imoinda, who was a sharer in all our adventures; we being resolved to make her chains as easy as we could, and to compliment the Prince in that manner that most obliged him.

As we were coming up again, we met with some Indians of strange aspects; that is, of a larger size, and other sort of features, than those of our country. Our Indian slaves, that rowed us, asked 'em some questions, but they could not understand us; but showed us a long cotton string, with several knots on it; and told us, they had been coming from the mountains so many moons as there were knots; they were habited in skins of a strange beast, and brought along with 'em bags of gold dust (which, as well as they could give us to understand, came streaming in little small channels down the high mountains, when the rains fell) and offered to be the convoy to anybody, or persons, that would go to the mountains. We carried these men up to Parham, where they were kept till the Lord-Governor came. And because all the country was mad to be going on this golden adventure, the Governor, by letters, commanded (for they sent some of the gold to him) that a guard should be set at the mouth of the River of Amazons (a river so called, almost as broad as the River of Thames), and prohibited all people from going up that river, it conducting to those mountains of gold. But we going off for England before the project was further prosecuted, and the Governor being drowned in a hurricane, either the design died, or the Dutch have the advantage of it. And 'tis to be bemoaned what his Majesty lost by losing that part of America.

Though this digression is a little from my story, however since it contains some proofs of the curiosity and daring of this great man, I was content to omit nothing of his character.

It was thus, for some time we diverted him; but now Imoinda began to

show she was with child, and did nothing but sigh and weep for the captivity of her lord, herself, and the infant yet unborn; and believed, if it were
so hard to gain the liberty of two, 'twould be more difficult to get that for
three. Her griefs were so many darts in the great heart of Caesar; and taking
his opportunity one Sunday, when all the whites were overtaken in drink,
as there were abundance of several trades, and slaves for four years, that
inhabited among the Negro houses; and Sunday was their day of debauch
(otherwise they were a sort of spies upon Caesar), he went pretending out
of goodness to 'em, to feast amongst 'em; and sent all his music, and
ordered a great treat for the whole gang, about three hundred Negroes;
and about a hundred and fifty were able to bear arms, such as they had,
which were sufficient to do execution with spirits accordingly. For the
English had none but rusty swords, that no strength could draw from a
scabbard; except the people of particular quality, who took care to oil 'em
and keep 'em in good order. The guns also, unless here and there one,
or those newly carried from England, would do no good or harm; for 'tis
the nature of that country to rust and eat up iron, or any metals, but gold
and silver. And they are very unexpert at the bow, which the Negroes and
the Indians are perfect masters of.

Caesar, having singled out these men from the women and children,
made a harangue to 'em, of the miseries, and ignominies of slavery; counting up all their toils and sufferings, under such loads, burdens, and
drudgeries, as were fitter for beasts than men; senseless brutes, than
human souls. He told 'em, it was not for days, months, or years, but for
eternity; there was no end to be of their misfortunes. They suffered not like
men who might find a glory and fortitude in oppression; but like dogs
that loved the whip and bell, and fawned the more they were beaten. That
they had lost the divine quality of men, and were become insensible asses,
fit only to bear; nay, worse: an ass, or dog, or horse having done his duty,
could lie down in retreat, and rise to work again, and while he did his duty,
endured no stripes; but men, villainous, senseless men, such as they, toiled
on all the tedious week till Black Friday; and then, whether they worked
or not, whether they were faulty or meriting, they promiscuously, the
innocent with the guilty, suffered the infamous whip, the sordid stripes,
from their fellow-slaves, till their blood trickled from all parts of their
body; blood, whose every drop ought to be revenged with a life of some
of those tyrants, that impose it. 'And why,' said he, 'my dear friends and
fellow-sufferers, should we be slaves to an unknown people? Have they
vanquished us nobly in fight? Have they won us in honourable battle?
And are we, by the chance of war, become their slaves? This would not
anger a noble heart, this would not animate a soldier's soul; no, but we are

bought and sold like apes, or monkeys, to be the sport of women, fools, and cowards; and the support of rogues and runagades, that have abandoned their own countries, for rapine, murders, thefts, and villainies. Do you not hear every day how they upbraid each other with infamy of life, below the wildest savages; and shall we render obedience to such a degenerate race, who have no one human virtue left, to distinguish 'em from the vilest creatures? Will you, I say, suffer the lash from such hands?' They all replied, with one accord, 'No, no, no; Caesar has spoke like a great captain; like a great king.'

After this he would have proceeded, but was interrupted by a tall Negro of some more quality than the rest, his name was Tuscan; who, bowing at the feet of Caesar, cried, 'My Lord, we have listened with joy and attention to what you have said; and, were we only men, would follow so great a leader through the world. But oh! consider we are husbands and parents too, and have things more dear to us than life; our wives and children unfit for travel, in these unpassable woods, mountains, and bogs; we have not only difficult lands to overcome, but rivers to wade, and monsters to encounter; ravenous beasts of prey.' – To this, Caesar replied that honour was the first principle in Nature, that was to be obeyed; but as no man would pretend to that, without all the acts of virtue, compassion, charity, love, justice, and reason; he found it not inconsistent with that, to take equal care of their wives and children as they would of themselves; and that he did not design, when he led them to freedom, and glorious liberty, that they should leave that better part of themselves to perish by the hand of the tyrant's whip. But if there were a woman among them so degenerate from love and virtue to choose slavery before the pursuit of her husband, and with the hazard of her life, to share with him in his fortunes, that such a one ought to be abandoned, and left as a prey to the common enemy.

To which they all agreed – and bowed. After this, he spoke of the impassable woods and rivers; and convinced 'em, the more danger, the more glory. He told them that he had heard of one Hannibal, a great captain, had cut his way through mountains of solid rocks; and should a few shrubs oppose them, which they could fire before 'em? No, 'twas a trifling excuse to men resolved to die, or overcome. As for bogs, they are with a little labour filled and hardened; and the rivers could be no obstacle, since they swam by nature, at least by custom, from their first hour of their birth. That when the children were weary they must carry them by turns, and the woods and their own industry would afford them food. To this they all assented with joy.

Tuscan then demanded what he would do? He said, they would travel towards the sea, plant a new colony, and defend it by their valour; and when they could find a ship, either driven by stress of weather, or guided by Providence that way, they would seize it, and make it a prize, till it had transported them to their own countries; at least they should be made free in his kingdom, and be esteemed as his fellow-sufferers, and men that had the courage and the bravery to attempt, at least, for liberty; and if they died in the attempt, it would be more brave, than to live in perpetual slavery.

They bowed and kissed his feet at this resolution, and with one accord vowed to follow him to death. And that night was appointed to begin their march; they made it known to their wives, and directed them to tie their hamaca about their shoulder, and under their arm like a scarf; and to lead their children that could go, and carry those that could not. The wives who pay an entire obedience to their husbands obeyed, and stayed for 'em, where they were appointed. The men stayed but to furnish themselves with what defensive arms they could get; and all met at the rendezvous, where Caesar made a new encouraging speech to 'em, and led 'em out.

But, as they could not march far that night, on Monday early, when the overseers went to call 'em all together, to go to work, they were extremely surprised, to find not one upon the place, but all fled with what baggage they had. You may imagine this news was not only suddenly spread all over the plantation, but soon reached the neighbouring ones; and we had by noon about six hundred men, they call the militia of the county, that came to assist us in the pursuit of the fugitives. But never did one see so comical an army march forth to war. The men, of any fashion, would not concern themselves, though it were almost the common cause; for such revoltings are very ill examples, and have very fatal consequences often-times in many colonies. But they had a respect for Caesar, and all hands were against the Parhamites (as they called those of Parham Plantation), because they did not, in the first place, love the Lord-Governor; and secondly, they would have it, that Caesar was ill used, and baffled with; and 'tis not impossible but some of the best in the country was of his council in this flight, and depriving us of all the slaves; so that they of the better sort would not meddle in the matter. The Deputy-Governor, of whom I have had no great occasion to speak, and who was the most fawning fair-tongued fellow in the world, and one that pretended the most friendship to Caesar, was now the only violent man against him; and though he had nothing, and so need fear nothing, yet talked and looked bigger than any man. He was a fellow, whose character is not fit to be mentioned with the worst of the slaves. This fellow would lead his army forth to meet Caesar, or rather to pursue him; most of their arms were of those sort of cruel whips they call 'Cat with Nine Tails'; some had rusty useless guns for show; others old basket-hilts, whose blades had never seen the light in this age; and others had long staffs, and clubs. Mr Trefry went along, rather to be a mediator than a conqueror, in such a battle; for he foresaw, and knew if by fighting they put the Negroes into despair, they were a sort of sullen fellows, that would drown, or kill themselves before they would yield; and he advised that fair means was best. But Byam was one that abounded his own wit, and would take his own measures.

It was not hard to find these fugitives; for as they fled they were forced to fire and cut the woods before 'em, so that night or day they pursued 'em by the light they made, and by the path they had cleared. But as soon as Caesar found he was pursued, he put himself in a posture of defence, placing all the women and children in the rear; and himself, with Tuscan by his side, or next to him, all promising to die or conquer. Encouraged thus, they never stood to parley, but fell on pell-mell upon the English, and killed some, and wounded a great many; they having recourse to their whips, as the best of their weapons. And as they observed no order, they perplexed the enemy so sorely, with lashing 'em in the eyes; and the women and children, seeing their husbands so treated, being of fearful cowardly dispositions, and hearing the English cry out, 'Yield, and live, yield and be pardoned!' they all run in amongst their husbands and fathers, and hung about 'em, crying out, 'Yield, yield; and leave Caesar to their revenge', that by degrees the slaves abandoned Caesar, and left him only Tuscan and his heroic Imoinda; who, grown big as she was, did nevertheless press near her lord, having a bow, and a quiver full of poisoned arrows, which she managed with such dexterity, that she wounded several, and shot the Governor into the shoulder; of which wound he had like to have died, but that an Indian woman, his mistress, sucked the wound, and cleansed it from the venom. But however, he stirred not from the place till he had parleyed with Caesar, who he found was resolved to die fighting, and would not be taken; no more would Tuscan, or Imoinda. But he, more thirsting after revenge of another sort, than that of depriving him of life, now made use of all his art of talking, and dissembling; and besought Caesar to yield himself upon terms, which he himself should propose, and should be sacredly assented to and kept by him. He told him, it was not that he any longer feared him, or could believe the force of two men, and a young heroine, could overcome all them, with all the slaves now on their side also; but it was the vast esteem he had for his person; the desire he had to serve so gallant a man, and to hinder himself from the reproach hereafter, of having been the occasion of the death of a prince, whose valour and magnanimity deserved the empire of the world. He protested to him, he looked upon this action, as gallant and brave; however tending to the prejudice of his lord and master, who would by it have lost so considerable a number of slaves; that this flight of his should be looked on as a heat of youth, and a rashness of a too forward courage, and an unconsidered impatience of liberty, and no more; and that he laboured in vain to accomplish that which they would effectually perform, as soon as any ship arrived that would touch on his coast. 'So that if you will be pleased,' continued he, 'to surrender yourself, all imaginable respect shall be paid you; and yourself, your wife, and child, if it be born, shall depart free out of our land.' But Caesar would hear of no composition; though Byam urged, if he pursued, and went on in his design, he would inevitably perish, either by great snakes, wild beasts, or hunger; and he ought to have regard to his wife, whose condition required ease, and not the fatigues of tedious travel, where she could not be secured from being devoured. But Caesar told him, there was no faith in the white men, or the gods they adored; who instructed 'em in principles so false, that honest men could not live amongst 'em; though no people professed so much, none performed so little; that he knew what he had to do when he dealt with men of honour; but with them a man ought to be eternally on his guard, and never to eat and drink with Christians without his weapon of defence in his hand; and, for his own security, never to credit one word they spoke. As for the rashness and inconsiderateness of his action he would confess the Governor is in the right; and that he was ashamed of what he had done, in endeavouring to make those free, who were by nature slaves, poor wretched rogues, fit to be used as Christian's tools; dogs, treacherous and cowardly, fit for such masters; and they wanted only but to be whipped into the knowledge of the Christian gods to be the vilest of all creeping things; to learn to worship such deities as had not power to make 'em just, brave, or honest. In fine, after a thousand things of this nature, not fit here to be recited, he told Byam, he had rather die than live upon the same earth with such dogs. But Trefry and Byam pleaded and protested together so much, that Trefry believing the Governor to mean what he said, and speaking very cordially himself, generously put himself into Caesar's hands, and took him aside, and persuaded him, even with tears, to live, by surrendering himself, and to name his conditions. Caesar was overcome by his wit and reasons, and in consideration of Imoinda, and demanding what he desired, and that it should be ratified by their hands in writing, because he had perceived that was the common way of contract between man and man, amongst the whites. All this was performed, and Tuscan's pardon was put in, and they surrendered to the Governor, who walked peaceably down into the plantation with 'em, after giving order to bury their dead. Caesar was very much toiled with the bustle of the day; for he had fought like a fury, and what mischief was done, he and Tuscan performed alone;

and gave their enemies a fatal proof that they durst do anything, and feared no mortal force.

But they were no sooner arrived at the place, where all the slaves receive their punishments of whipping, but they laid hands on Caesar and Tuscan, faint with heat and toil; and, surprising them, bound them to two several stakes, and whipped them in a most deplorable and inhuman manner, rending the very flesh from their bones; especially Caesar, who was not perceived to make any moan, or to alter his face, only to roll his eyes on the faithless Governor, and those he believed guilty, with fierceness and indignation; and, to complete his rage, he saw every one of those slaves, who, but a few days before, adored him as something more than mortal, now had a whip to give him some lashes, while he strove not to break his fetters; though, if he had, it were impossible. But he pronounced a woe and revenge from his eyes, that darted fire, that was at once both awful and terrible to behold.

When they thought they were sufficiently revenged on him, they untied him, almost fainting, with loss of blood, from a thousand wounds all over his body; from which they had rent his clothes, and led him bleeding and naked as he was; and loaded him all over with irons; and then rubbed his wounds, to complete their cruelty, with Indian pepper, which had like to have made him raving mad; and, in this condition, made him so fast to the ground that he could not stir, if his pains and wounds would have given him leave. They spared Imoinda, and did not let her see this barbarity committed towards her lord, but carried her down to Parham, and shut her up; which was not in kindness to her, but for fear she should die with the sight, or miscarry; and then they should lose a young slave, and perhaps the mother.

You must know, that when the news was brought on Monday morning, that Caesar had betaken himself to the woods, and carried with him all the Negroes, we were possessed with extreme fear, which no persuasions could dissipate, that he would secure himself till night; and then, that he would come down and cut all our throats. This apprehension made all the females of us fly down the river, to be secured; and while we were away, they acted this cruelty. For I suppose I had authority and interest enough there, had I suspected any such thing, to have prevented it; but we had not gone many leagues, but the news overtook us that Caesar was taken and whipped like a common slave. We met on the river with Colonel Martin, a man of great gallantry, wit, and goodness, and whom I have celebrated in a character of my new comedy, by his own name, in memory of so brave a man. He was wise and eloquent and, from the fineness of his parts, bore a great sway over the hearts of all the colony. He was a friend to Caesar, and resented this false dealing with him very much. We carried him back to Parham, thinking to have made an accommodation; when he came, the first news we heard was that the Governor was dead of a wound Imoinda had given him; but it was not so well. But it seems he would have the pleasure of beholding the revenge he took on Caesar; and before the cruel ceremony was finished, he dropped down; and then they perceived the wound he had on his shoulder was by a venomed arrow; which, as I said, his Indian mistress healed, by sucking the wound.

We were no sooner arrived, but we went up to the plantation to see Caesar whom we found in a very miserable and unexpressable condition; and I have a thousand times admired how he lived, in so much tormenting pain. We said all things to him, that trouble, pity, and good-nature could suggest; protesting our innocency of the fact, and our abhorrence of such cruelties. Making a thousand professions of services to him, and begging as many pardons for the offenders, till we said so much, that he believed we had no hand in his ill treatment; but told us, he could never pardon Byam; as for Trefry, he confessed he saw his grief and sorrow, for his suffering, which he could not hinder, but was like to have been beaten down by the very slaves, for speaking in his defence. But for Byam, who was their leader, their head – and should, by his justice, and honour, have been an example to 'em – for him, he wished to live, to take a dire revenge of him, and said, 'It had been well for him, if he had sacrificed me, instead of giving me the contemptible whip.' He refused to talk much, but begging us to give him our hands, he took 'em, and protested never to lift up his, to do us any harm. He had a great respect for Colonel Martin, and always took his counsel, like that of a parent, and assured him, he would obey him in anything, but his revenge on Byam. 'Therefore,' said he, 'for his own safety, let him speedily dispatch me; for if I could dispatch myself, I would not, till that justice were done to my injured person, and the contempt of a soldier. No, I would not kill myself, even after a whipping, but will be content to live with that infamy, and be pointed at by every grinning slave, till I have completed my revenge; and then you shall see that Oroonoko scorns to live with the indignity that was put on Caesar.' All we could do could get no more words from him; and we took care to have him put immediately into a healing bath, to rid him of his pepper; and ordered a chirurgeon to anoint him with healing balm, which he suffered, and in some time he began to be able to walk and eat; we failed not to visit him every day, and, to that end, had him brought to an apartment at Parham.

The Governor was no sooner recovered, and had heard of the menaces of Caesar, but he called his council; who (not to disgrace them, or burlesque the government there) consisted of such notorious villains as Newgate never transported; and, possibly originally were such, who understood neither the laws of God or man; and had no sort of principles to make 'em worthy the name of men. But at the very council-table, would contradict and fight with one another, and swear so bloodily that 'twas terrible to hear, and see 'em. (Some of 'em were afterwards hanged, when the Dutch took possession of the place, others sent off in chains). But calling these special rulers of the nation together, and requiring their counsel in this weighty affair, they all concluded, that (damn 'em) it might be their own cases; and that Caesar ought to be made an example to all the Negroes, to fright 'em from daring to threaten their betters, their lords and masters: and, at this rate, no man was safe from his own slaves; and concluded, *nemine contradicente*, that Caesar should be hanged.

Trefry then thought it time to use his authority, and told Byam his command did not extend to his lord's plantation; and that Parham was as much exempt from the law as Whitehall; and that they ought no more to touch the servants of the Lord — (who there represented the King's person) than they could those about the King himself; and that Parham was a sanctuary; and though his lord were absent in person, his power was still in being there; which he had entrusted with him, as far as the dominions of his particular plantations reached, and all that belonged to it; the rest of the country, as Byam was lieutenant to his lord, he might exercise his tyranny upon. Trefry had others as powerful, or more, that interested themselves in Caesar's life, and absolutely said he should be defended. So turning the Governor, and his wise council, out of doors (for they sat at Parham-House), they set a guard upon our lodging-place, and would admit none but those we called friends to us and Caesar.

The Governor having remained wounded at Parham, till his recovery was completed, Caesar did not know but he was still there; and indeed, for the most part, his time was spent there; for he was one that loved to live at other people's expense; and if he were a day absent, he was ten present there; and used to play, and walk, and hunt, and fish with Caesar. So that Caesar did not at all doubt, if he once recovered strength, but he should find an opportunity of being revenged on him. Though, after such a revenge, he could not hope to live; for if he escaped the fury of the English mobile, who perhaps would have been glad of the occasion to have killed him, he was resolved not to survive his whipping; yet he had some tender hours, a repenting softness, which he called his fits of coward, wherein he struggled with love for the victory of his heart, which took part with his charming Imoinda there; but, for the most part, his time was passed in melancholy thought, and black designs; he considered, if he should do this deed, and die, either in the attempt or after it, he left his lovely Imoinda a prey, or at best a slave, to the enraged multitude; his great heart could not endure that thought. 'Perhaps,' said he, 'she may be first ravished by every brute, exposed first to their nasty lusts, and then a shameful death.' No, he could not live a moment under that apprehension, too insupportable to be borne. These were his thoughts, and his silent arguments with his heart, as he told us afterwards; so that now resolving not only to kill Byam, but all those he thought had enraged him; pleasing his great heart with the fancied slaughter he should make over the whole face of the plantation. He first resolved on a deed, that (however horrid it at first appeared to us all) when we had heard his reasons, we thought it brave and just. Being able to walk, and, as he believed, fit for the execution of his great design, he begged Trefry to trust him into the air, believing a walk would do him good; which was granted him, and taking Imoinda with him, as he used to do in his more happy and calmer days, he led her up into a wood, where, after (with a thousand sighs, and long gazing silently on her face, while tears gushed, in spite of him, from his eyes) he told her his design first of killing her, and then his enemies, and next himself, and the impossibility of escaping, and therefore he told her the necessity of dying; he found the heroic wife faster pleading for death than he was to propose it, when she found his fixed resolution; and, on her knees, besought him, not to leave her a prey to his enemies. He (grieved to death), yet pleased at her noble resolution, took her up, and embracing of her with all the passion and languishment of a dying lover, drew his knife to kill this treasure of his soul, this pleasure of his eyes; while tears trickled down his cheeks, hers were smiling with joy she should die by so noble a hand, and be sent into her own country (for that's their notion of the next world) by him she so tenderly loved, and so truly adored in this: for wives have a respect for their husbands equal to what any other people pay a deity; and when a man finds any occasion to quit his wife, if he love her, she dies by his hand; if not, he sells her, or suffers some other to kill her. It being thus, you may believe the deed was soon resolved on; and 'tis not to be doubted, but the parting, the eternal leave-taking of two such lovers, so greatly born, so sensible, so beautiful, so young, and so fond, must be very moving, as the relation of it was to me afterwards.

All that love could say in such cases, being ended; and all the intermitting irresolutions being adjusted, the lovely, young, and adored victim lays herself down before the sacrificer; while he, with a hand resolved, and a heart breaking within, gave the fatal stroke; first, cutting her throat, and then severing her, yet smiling, face from that delicate body, pregnant as it was with fruits of tenderest love. As soon as he had done, he laid the body decently on leaves and flowers, of which he made a bed, and concealed it under the same cover-lid of Nature; only her face he left yet bare to look on. But when he found she was dead, and past all retrieve, never more to bless him with her eyes, and soft language; his grief swelled up to rage; he tore, he raved, he roared, like some monster of the wood, calling on the loved name of Imoinda; a thousand times he turned the fatal knife that did the deed, toward his own heart, with a resolution to go immediately after her; but dire revenge, which was now a thousand times more fierce in his soul than before, prevents him; and he would cry out, 'No; since I have sacrificed Imoinda to my revenge, shall I lose that glory which I have purchased so dear, as the price of the fairest, dearest, softest creature that ever Nature made? No, no!' Then, at her name, grief would get the ascendant of rage, and he would lie down by her side, and water her face with showers of tears, which never were wont to fall from those eyes. And however bent he was on his intended slaughter, he had not power to stir from the sight of this dear object, now more beloved, and more adored than ever.

He remained in this deploring condition for two days, and never rose from the ground where he had made her sad sacrifice; at last, rousing from her side, and accusing himself of living too long, now Imoinda was dead, and that the deaths of those barbarous enemies were deferred too long, he resolved now to finish the great work; but offering to rise, he found his strength so decayed, that he reeled to and fro, like boughs assailed by contrary winds; so that he was forced to lie down again, and try to summons all his courage to his aid; he found his brains turn round, and his eyes were dizzy; and objects appeared not the same to him they were wont to do; his breath was short; and all his limbs surprised with a faintness he had never felt before. He had not eat in two days, which was one occasion of his feebleness, but excess of grief was the greatest; yet still he hoped he should never recover vigour to act his design; and lay expecting it yet six days longer; still mourning over the dead idol of his heart, and striving every day to rise, but could not.

In all this time you may believe we were in no little affliction for Caesar, and his wife; some were of opinion he was escaped never to return; others thought some accident had happened to him. But however, we failed not to send out a hundred people several ways to search for him; a party of about forty went that way he took; among whom was Tuscan, who was perfectly reconciled to Byam. They had not gone very far into the wood, but they smelt an unusual smell, as of a dead body; for stinks must be very noisome that can be distinguished among such a quantity of natural sweets, as every inch of that land produces. So that they concluded they should find him dead, or somebody that was so; they passed on towards it, as loathsome as it was, and made such rustling among the leaves that lie thick on the ground, by continual falling, that Caesar heard he was approached; and though he had, during the space of these eight days, endeavoured to rise, but found he wanted strength, yet looking up, and seeing his pursuers, he rose, and reeled to a neighbouring tree, against which he fixed his back; and being within a dozen yards of those that advanced, and saw him; he called out to them, and bid them approach no nearer, if they would be safe. So that they stood still, and hardly believing their eyes, that would persuade them that it was Caesar that spoke to 'em, so much was he altered; they asked him what he had done with his wife, for they smelt a stink that almost struck them dead. He, pointing to the dead body, sighing, cried, 'Behold her there.' They put off the flowers that covered her with their sticks, and found she was killed, and cried out, 'O monster! that hast murdered thy wife.' Then asking him why he did so cruel a deed, he replied, he had no leisure to answer impertinent questions. 'You may go back,' continued he, 'and tell the faithless Governor, he may thank Fortune that I am breathing my last; and that my arm is too feeble to obey my heart, in what it had designed him.' But his tongue faltering, and trembling he could scarce end what he was saying. The English, taking advantage by his weakness, cried, 'Let us take him alive by all means.' He heard 'em; and, as if he had revived from a fainting, or a dream, he cried out, 'No, Gentlemen, you are deceived; you will find no more Caesars to be whipped; no more find a faith in me. Feeble as you think me, I have strength yet left to secure me from a second indignity.' They swore all anew, and he only shook his head, and beheld them with scorn; then they cried out, 'Who will venture on this single man? Will nobody?' They stood all silent while Caesar replied, 'Fatal will be the attempt to the first adventurer; let him assure himself', and, at that word, held up his knife in a menacing posture. 'Look ye, ye faithless crew,' said he, ''tis not life I seek, nor am I afraid of dying.'; and at that word, cut a piece of flesh from his own throat, and threw it at 'em, 'yet still I would live if I could, till I had perfected my revenge. But oh! it cannot be; I feel life gliding from my eyes and heart, and if I make not haste, I shall fall a victim to the shameful whip.' At that, he ripped up his own belly; and took his bowels and pulled 'em out, with what strength he could; while some, on their knees imploring, besought him to hold his hand. But when they saw him tottering, they cried out, 'Will none venture on him?' A bold English cried, 'Yes, if he were the Devil.' (taking courage when he saw him almost dead), and swearing a horrid oath for his farewell to the world, he rushed on Caesar, with his armed hand met him so fairly, as stuck him to the heart, and he fell dead at his feet. Tuscan, seeing that, cried out, 'I love thee, O Caesar! and therefore will not let thee die, if possible.' And, running to him, took him in his arms; but, at the same time, warding a blow that Caesar made at his bosom, he received it quite through his arm; and Caesar having not the strength to pluck the knife forth, though he attempted it, Tuscan neither pulled it out himself, nor suffered it to be pulled out; but came down with it sticking in his arm; and the reason he gave for it was because the air should not get into the wound. They put their hands across, and carried Caesar between six of 'em, fainted as he was; and though they thought dead, or just dying; and they brought him to Parham, and laid him on a couch, and had the chirurgeon immediately to him, who dressed his wounds, and sewed up his belly, and used means to bring him to life, which they effected. We ran all to see him; and, if before we thought him so beautiful a sight, he was now so altered, that his face was like a death's-head blacked over; nothing but teeth, and eye-holes. For some days we suffered nobody to speak to him, but caused cordials to be poured down his throat, which sustained his life; and in six or seven days he recovered his senses. For, you must know, that wounds are almost to a miracle cured in the Indies; unless wounds in the legs, which rarely ever cure.

When he was well enough to speak, we talked to him, and asked him some questions about his wife, and the reasons why he killed her; and he then told us what I have related of that resolution, and of his parting; and he besought us, we would let him die, and was extremely afflicted to think it was possible he might live: he assured us, if we did not dispatch him, he would prove very fatal to a great many. We said all we could to make him live, and gave him new assurances; but he begged we would not think so poorly of him, or of his love to Imoinda, to imagine we could flatter him to life again; but the chirurgeon assured him, he could not live, and therefore he need not fear. We were all (but Caesar) afflicted at this news, and the sight was ghastly; his discourse was sad; and the earthly smell about him was so strong, that I was persuaded to leave the place for some time (being myself but sickly, and very apt to fall into fits of dangerous illness upon any extraordinary melancholy). The servants, and Trefry, and the chirurgeons, promised all to take what possible care they could of the life of Caesar; and I, taking boat, went with other company to Colonel Martin's, about three days' journey down the river; but I was no sooner gone, but the Governor taking Trefry, about some pretended earnest business, a day's journey up the river, having communicated his design to one Banister, a wild Irishman, and one of the council, a fellow of absolute barbarity, and fit to execute any villainy, but was rich. He came up to Parham, and forcibly took Caesar, and had him carried to the same post where he was whipped, and causing him to be tied to it, and a great fire made before him, he told him, he should die like a dog, as he was. Caesar replied, this was the first piece of bravery that ever Banister did, and he never spoke sense till he pronounced that word; and, if he would keep it, he would declare, in the other world, that he was the only man, of all the whites, that ever he heard speak truth. And turning to the men that had bound him, he said, 'My friends, am I to die, or to be whipped?' And they cried, 'Whipped! no; you shall not escape so well.' And then he replied, smiling, 'A blessing on thee'; and assured them, they need not tie him, for he would stand fixed, like a rock; and endure death so as should encourage them to die. 'But if you whip me,' said he, 'be sure you tie me fast.'

He had learned to take tobacco; and when he was assured he should die, he desired they would give him a pipe in his mouth, ready lighted, which they did; and the executioner came, and first cut off his members, and threw them into the fire; after that, with an ill-favoured knife, they cut off his ears and his nose, and burned them; he still smoked on, as if nothing had touched him; then they hacked off one of his arms, and still he bore up, and held his pipe; but at the cutting off the other arm, his head sunk, and his pipe dropped; and he gave up the ghost, without a groan or a reproach. My mother and sister were by him all the while, but not suffered to save him; so rude and wild were the rabble, and so inhumane were the justices, who stood by to see the execution, who after paid dearly enough for their insolence. They cut Caesar in quarters, and sent them to several of the chief plantations. One quarter was sent to Colonel Martin, who refused it, and swore, he had rather see the quarters of Banister, and the Governor himself, than those of Caesar, on his plantations, and that he could govern his Negroes without terrifying and grieving them with frightful spectacles of a mangled king.

Thus died this great man, worthy of a better fate, and a more sublime wit than mine to write his praise: yet, I hope, the reputation of my pen is considerable enough to make his glorious name to survive to all the ages, with that of the brave, the beautiful, and the constant Imoinda.

21. Aphra Benn

The Widow Ranter, or, The History of Bacon in Virginia.
(published 1690)

Dramatis Personae

Indian King, called Cavarnio
Bacon, General of the English
Colonel Wellman, Deputy Governor
Colonel Downright, a loyal honest Councillor
Hazard, friend known to Friendly many years in England
Friendly, friend known to Hazard many years in England
Dareing, Lieutenant General to Bacon
Fearless, Lieutenant General to Bacon
Dullman, a Captain
Timerous, a Cornet, Justice of the Peace, and very great coward
Whimsey, a Justice of the Peace, and very great coward
Whiff, a Justice of the Peace, and very great coward
Boozer, a Justice of the Peace, and very great coward
Brag, a Captain
Grubb, one Complained on by Captain Whiff for calling his wife
    Whore. A petitioner against Brag
Parson Dunce, formerly a farrier fled from England, and Chaplain to the
    Governor
Clerk
Jack, a sea-boy
Seaman
Indian Queen, called Semernia, beloved by Bacon
Madam Surelove, beloved by Hazard
Mrs Chrisante, daughter to Col. Downright
Widow Ranter, in love with Dareing
Mrs Flirt
Mrs Whimsey
Mrs Whiff
Nell, maid in Mrs Flirt's house
Jenny, the Widow Ranter's maid
Anaria, Semernia's maid
Cavaro, Semernia's servant
Indians
Jeffery, a coachman

Soldiers
Attendants.

Scene: Virginia, in Bacon's Camp

———

I.i

A room with several tables
Enter Hazard in a travelling habit, and a sea-boy carrying
his portmanteau

Hazard What town's this, boy?
Boy Jamestown, master.
Hazard Take care my trunk be brought ashore tonight, and there's for your pains.
Boy God bless you, master.
Hazard What do you call this house?
Boy Mrs Flirt's, master, the best house for commendation in all Virginia.
Hazard That's well. Has she any handsome ladies, sirrah?
Boy Oh! She's woundily handsome herself, master, and the kindest gentlewoman – look here she comes master – God bless you. Mistress, I have brought you a young gentleman here.

Enter Mrs Flirt

Mrs Flirt That's well, honest Jack – sir, you are most heartily welcome.
Hazard Madam, your servant. [*Salutes her*]
Mrs Flirt Please you to walk into a chamber, sir?
Hazard By and by, madam, but I'll repose here a while for the coolness of the air.
Mrs Flirt This is a public room, sir, but 'tis at your service.
Hazard Madam, you oblige me.
Mrs Flirt A fine-spoken person – a gentleman I'll warrant him. Come, Jack, I'll give thee a cogue of brandy for old acquaintance. [*Exeunt Landlady and Boy*].

Hazard pulls out pen, ink and paper, and goes to write; enter Friendly

Friendly Here, Nell, a tankard of cool drink quickly.

Enter Nell

Nell You shall have it, sir. [*Exit, re-enter with a drink, re-exit*]
Friendly Hah! Who's that stranger? He seems to be a gentleman.

Hazard If I should give credit to mine eyes, that should be Friendly.

Friendly Sir, you seem a stranger, may I take the liberty to present my service to you?

Hazard If I am not mistaken, sir, you are the only man in the world whom I would soonest pledge. You'll credit me if three years absence has not made you forget Hazard.

Friendly Hazard, my friend! Come to my arms and heart.

Hazard This unexpected happiness o'erjoys me. Who could have imagined to have found thee in Virginia? I thought thou hadst been in Spain with thy brother.

Friendly I was so till ten months since, when my uncle, Colonel Friendly, dying here, left me a considerable plantation; and faith I find diversions not altogether to be despised. The God of Love reigns here, with as much power, as in courts or popular cities. But, prithee, what chance, (fortunate for me) drove thee to this part of the New World?

Hazard Why (faith) ill company, and that common vice of the town, gaming, soon run out my younger brother's fortune, for imagining like some of the luckier gamesters to improve my stock at the Groom-Porters, ventured on and lost all. My elder brother, an errant Jew, had neither friendship, nor honour enough to support me, but at last was mollified by persuasions and the hopes of being for ever rid of me, sent me hither with a small cargo to seek my fortune, –

Friendly And begin the world withal.

Hazard I thought this a better venture than to turn sharping bully, cully in prentices and country squires, with my pocket full of false dice, your high and low Flats and Bars, or turn broker to young heirs; take up goods, to pay ten-fold at the death of their fathers, and take fees on both sides; or set up all night at the Groom-Porters begging his Honour to go a guinea the better of the lay. No, Friendly, I had rather starve abroad then live pitied and despised at home.

Friendly Thou art in the right, and art come just in the nick of time to make thy fortune. Wilt thou follow my advice?

Hazard Thou art too honest to command anything, anything that I shall refuse.

Friendly You must know then, there is about a mile from Jamestown a young gentlewoman – no matter for her birth, her breeding's the best this world affords – she is married to one of the richest merchants here. He is old and sick, and now gone into England for the recovery of his health, where he'll e'en give up the ghost. He has writ her word he finds no amendment, and resolves to stay another year. The letter I accidentally took up and have about me; 'tis easily counterfeited and will be of great use to us.

Hazard Now do I fancy I conceive thee.

Friendly Well, hear me first. You shall get another letter writ like this character, which shall say you are his kinsman, that is come to traffic in this country, and 'tis his will you should be received into his house as such.

Hazard Well, and what will come of this?

Friendly Why, thou art young and handsome, she young and desiring; 'twere easy to make her love thee, and if the old gentleman chance to die, you guess the rest, you are no fool.

Hazard Aye, but if he should return –

Friendly If – why if she love you, that other will be but a slender bar to thy happiness. For if thou canst not marry her, thou mayst lie with her, (and Gad) a younger brother may pick out a pretty livelihood here that way, as well as in England. Or if this fail, there thou wilt find a perpetual visitor the Widow Ranter, a woman bought from the ship by old Colonel Ranter; she served him half a year, and then he married her, and dying in a year more, left her worth fifty thousand pounds sterling, besides plate and jewels. She's a great gallant, but assuming the humour of the country gentry, her extravagancy is very pleasant; she retains something of her primitive quality still, but is good natured and generous.

Hazard I like all this well.

Friendly But I have a further end in this matter. You must know there is in the same house a young heiress, one Colonel Downright's daughter, whom I love, I think not in vain. Her father indeed has an implacable hatred to me, for which reason I can but seldom visit her, and in this affair I have need of a friend in that house.

Hazard Me you're sure of.

Friendly And thus you'll have an opportunity to manage both our amours. Here you will find occasion to show your courage as well as express your love, for at this time the Indians, by our ill management of trade, whom we have armed against ourselves, very frequently make war upon us with our own weapons, though often coming by the worst are forced to make peace with us again, but so, as upon every turn they fall to massacring us wherever we lie exposed to them.

Hazard I heard the news of this in England, which hastens the new Governor's arrival here, who brings you fresh supplies.

Friendly Would he were landed. We hear he is a noble gentleman.

Hazard He has all the qualities of a gallant man, besides he is nobly born.

Friendly This country wants nothing but to be peopled with a well-born race to make it one of the best colonies in the world. But for want of a Governor we are ruled by a Council, some of which have been perhaps transported criminals, who having acquired great estates are now become Your Honour and Right Worshipful, and possess all places of authority.

There are amongst 'em some honest gentlemen who now begin to take upon 'em, and manage affairs as they ought to be.

Hazard Bacon, I think, was one of the Council.

Friendly Now you have named a man indeed above the common rank. By nature generous, brave, resolved, and daring, who, studying the lives of the Romans and great men, that have raised themselves to the most elevated fortunes, fancies it easy for ambitious men to aim at any pitch of glory. I've heard him often say, 'Why cannot I conquer the universe as well as Alexander? Or like another Romulus form a new Rome, and make myself adored?'

Hazard Why might he not? Great souls are born in common men, sometimes as well as princes.

Friendly This thirst of glory cherished by sullen melancholy, I believe was the first motive that made him in love with the young Indian Queen, fancying no hero ought to be without his princess, and this was the reason why he so earnestly pressed for a commission, to be made General against the Indians, which long was promised him. But they, fearing his ambition, still put him off, till the grievances grew so high, that the whole country flocked to him, and begged he would redress them. He took the opportunity, and led them forth to fight, and vanquishing, brought the enemy to fair terms, but now instead of receiving him as a conqueror, we treat him as a traitor.

Hazard Then it seems all the crime this brave fellow has committed, is serving his country without authority.

Friendly 'Tis so, and however I admire the man, I am resolved to be of the contrary party, that I may make an interest in our new Governor. Thus stands affairs, so that after you have seen Madam Surelove, I'll present you to the Council for a commission.

Hazard But my kinsman's character –

Friendly He was a Leicestershire younger brother, came over hither with a small fortune, which his industry has increased to a thousand pound a year, and he is now Colonel John Surelove, and one of the Council.

Hazard Enough.

Friendly About it then, Madam Flirt to direct you.

Hazard You are full of your Madams here.

Friendly Oh, 'tis the greatest affront imaginable, to call a woman Mistress, though but a retail brandymonger. – Adieu! – One thing more, tomorrow is our country-court, pray do not fail to be there, for the rarity of the entertainment. But I shall see you anon at Surelove's where I'll salute thee as my first meeting, and as an old acquaintance in England – here's company, farewell.

Exit

Enter Dullman, Timerous, and Boozer; Hazard sits at a table and writes.

Dullman Here, Nell! Well Lieutenant Boozer, what are you for?

Enter Nell

Boozer I am for cooling Nants, Major.

Dullman Here, Nell, a quart of Nants, and some pipes and smoke.

Timerous And do ye hear, Nell, bid your Mistress come in to joke a little with us, for, adzoors, I was damnable drunk last night, and am better at the petticoat than the bottle today.

Dullman Drunk last night, and sick today, how comes that about, Mr Justice? You use to bear your brandy well enough.

Timerous Aye your shire-brandy I'll grant you, but I was drunk at Colonel Downright's with your high burgundy claret.

Dullman A pox of that paulter liquor, your English French wine, I wonder how the gentlemen do to drink it.

Timerous Aye, so do I. 'Tis for want of a little Virginia breeding. How much more like a gentleman 'tis, to drink as we do, brave edifying punch and brandy, – but they say the young noblemen now and sparks in England begin to reform, and take it for their mornings draught, get drunk by noon, and despise the lousy juice of the grape.

Enter Mrs Flirt

Dullman Come, Landlady, come, you are so taken up with Parson Dunce, that your old friends can't drink a dram with you? What no smutty catch now, no gibe or joke to make the punch go down merrily, and advance trading? Nay, they say, Gad forgive ye, you never miss going to church when Mr Dunce preaches – but here's to you. [*drinks*]

Mrs Flirt Lords, your Honours are pleased to be merry – but my service to your Honour. [*drinks*]

Hazard Honours? Who the devil have we here? Some of the wise Council at least, I'd sooner took 'em for hoggerds. [*aside*]

Mrs Flirt Say what you please of the Doctor, but I'll swear he's a fine gentleman, he makes the prettiest sonnets, nay, and sings 'em himself to the rarest tunes.

Timerous Nay, the man will serve for both soul and body, for they say he was a farrier in England, but breaking turned Life-guard man, and his horse dying, he counterfeited a deputation from the Bishop, and came over here a substantial orthodox. But, come, where stands the cup? – Here, my service to you, Major.

Mrs Flirt Your Honours are pleased – but methinks Doctor Dunce is a very edifying person, and a gentleman, and I pretend to know a gentleman, – for I myself am a gentlewoman. My father was a Baronet, but undone in the late rebellion – and I am fain to keep an ordinary now, Heaven help me.

Timerous Good lack, why see how virtue may be belied – we heard your Father was a tailor, but trusting for old Oliver's funeral, broke, and so came hither to hide his head, – but my service to you. What, you are never the worse?

Mrs Flirt Your Honour knows this is a scandalous place, for they say your Honour was but a broken exciseman, who spent the King's money to buy your wife fine petticoats, and at last, not worth a groat, you came over a poor servant, though now a Justice of Peace, and of the Honourable Council.

Timerous Adzoors, if I knew who 'twas said so, I'd sue him for *Scandalum Magnatum*.

Dullman Hang 'em, scoundrels, hang 'em, they live upon scandal, and we are scandal-proof. They say, too, that I was a tinker and running the country, robbed a gentleman's house there, was put into Newgate, got a reprieve after condemnation, and was transported hither – and that you, Boozer, was a common pick-pocket, and being often flogged at the cart's-tail, afterwards turned evidence, and when the times grew honest was fain to fly.

Boozer Aye, aye, Major, if scandal would have broke our hearts, we had not arrived to the honour of being Privy-Councillors – but, come, Mrs Flirt, what never a song to entertain us?

Mrs Flirt Yes, and a singer too newly come ashore.

Timerous Adzoors, let's have it then

Enter Girl, who sings; they bear the bob.

Hazard Here, maid, a tankard of your drink.

Mrs Flirt Quickly, Nell, wait upon the gentleman.

Dullman Please you, sir, to taste of our liquor – my service to you. I see you are a stranger and alone, please you to come to our table?

Hazard rises and comes.

Mrs Flirt Come sir, pray sit down here, these are very Honourable persons I assure you. This is Major Dullman, Major of His Excellency's own regiment, when he arrives, this Mr Timerous, Justice a Peace in Quorum, this Captain Boozer, all of the Honourable Council.

Hazard With your leave, gentlemen. [*sits*]

Timerous My service to you, sir. [*drinks*] What have you brought over any cargo, sir, I'll be your customer.
Boozer Aye, and cheat him too, I'll warrant him. [*aside*]
Hazard I was not bred to merchandising, sir, nor do intend to follow the drudgery of trading.
Dullman Men of fortune seldom travel hither, sir, to see fashions.
Timerous Why, brother, it may be the gentleman has a mind to be a planter. Will you hire yourself to make a crop of tobacco this year?
Hazard I was not born to work, sir.
Timerous Not work, sir, Zoors your betters have worked, sir. I have worked myself, sir, both set and stripped tobacco, for all I am of the Honourable Council. Not work, quotha – I suppose, sir, you wear your fortune upon your back, sir?
Hazard Is it your custom here, sir, to affront strangers? I shall expect satisfaction. [*rises*]
Timerous Why does anybody here owe you anything?
Dullman No, unless he means to be paid for drinking with us – ha, ha, ha.
Hazard No, sir, I have money to pay for what I drink. Here's my club – my Guinea, [*flings down a Guinea*] I scorn to be obliged to such scoundrels.
Boozer Hum – call men of Honour scoundrels – [*rises in huff*]
Timerous Let him alone, let him alone, brother, how should he learn manners, he never was in Virginia before?
Dullman He's some Covent-Garden bully.
Timerous Or some broken citizen turned factor.
Hazard Sir, you lie, and you're a rascal. [*flings the brandy in's face*]
Timerous Adzoors, he has spilled all the brandy.

Timerous runs behind the door, Dullman and Boozer strike Hazard.

Hazard I understand no cudgel-play, but wear a sword to right myself. [*draws, they run off*]
Mrs Flirt Good heavens, what quarrelling in my house?
Hazard Do the persons of quality in this country treat strangers thus?
Mrs Flirt Alas, sir, 'tis a familiar way they have, sir.
Hazard I'm glad I know it, – pray, madam, can you inform one how I may be furnished with a horse and a guide to Madam Surelove's?
Mrs Flirt A most accomplished lady, and my very good friend, you shall be immediately.

Exeunt

I.ii

Enter Wellman, Downright, Dunce, Whimsey, Whiff, and others

Wellman Come, Mr Dunce, though you are no Councillor, yet your counsel may be good in time of necessity, as now.

Dunce If I may be worthy advice, I do not look upon our danger to be so great from the Indians, as from young Bacon, whom the people have nick-named Fright-all.

Whimsey Aye, aye, that same Bacon, I would he were well hanged. I am afraid that, under pretence of killing all the Indians, he means to murder us, lie with our wives, and hang up our little children, and make himself Lord and King

Whiff Brother Whimsey, not so hot. With leave of the Honourable board, my wife is of opinion that Bacon came seasonably to our aid, and what he has done was for our defence. The Indians came down upon us, and ravished us all, men, women, and children.

Wellman If these grievances were not redressed we had our reasons for it. It was not that we were insensible, Captain Whiff, of what we suffered from the insolence of the Indians. But all knew what we must expect from Bacon if that by lawful authority he had arrived to so great a command as General, nor would we be huffed out of our commissions.

Downright 'Tis most certain that Bacon did not demand a commission out of a design of serving us, but to satisfy his ambition and his love, it being no secret that he passionately admires the Indian Queen, and under the pretext of a war, intends to kill the King, her husband, establish himself in her heart, and on all occasions have himself a more formidable enemy, than the Indians are.

Whimsey Nay, nay, I ever foresaw he would prove a villain.

Whiff Nay, and he be thereabout, my Nancy shall have no more to do with him.

Wellman But, gentlemen, the people daily flock to him, so that his army is too considerable for us to oppose by anything but policy.

Downright We are sensible gentlemen that our fortunes, our honours, and our lives are at stake, and therefore you are called together to consult what's to be done in this grand affair, till our Governor and forces arrive from England. The truce he made with the Indians will be out tomorrow.

Whiff Aye, and then he intends to have another bout with the Indians. Let's have patience, I say till he has thrummed their jackets, and then to work with your politics as soon as you please.

Downright Colonel Wellman has answered that point good Captain

Whiff. 'Tis the event of this battle we ought to dread, and if won or lost will be equally fatal for us, either from the Indians or from Bacon.

Dunce With the permission of the Honourable board, I think I have hit upon an expedient that may prevent this battle. Your Honours shall write a letter to Bacon, where you shall acknowledge his services, invite him kindly home, and offer him a commission for General –

Whiff Just my Nancy's counsel – Doctor Dunce has spoken like a cherubin, he shall have my voice for General, what say you, brother Whimsey?

Whimsey I say, he is a noble fellow, and fit for a General.

Dunce But conceive me right, gentlemen, as soon as he shall have rendered himself, seize him and strike off his head at the fort.

Whiff Hum! his head – brother.

Whimsey Aye, aye, Doctor Dunce speaks like a cherubin.

Wellman Mr Dunce, your counsel, in extremity, I confess is not amiss, but I should be loth to deal dishonourably with any man.

Downright His crimes deserve death, his life is forfeited by law, but shall never be taken by my consent by treachery. If, by any stratagem, we could take him alive, and either send him for England to receive there his punishment, or keep him prisoner here till the Governor arrive, I should agree to't, but I question his coming in upon our invitation.

Dunce Leave that to me.

Whimsey Come, I'll warrant him, the rogue's as stout as Hector, he fears neither Heaven nor Hell.

Downright He's too brave and bold to refuse our summons, and I am for sending him for England and leaving him to the King's mercy.

Dunce In that you'll find more difficulty, sir, to take him off here will be more quick and sudden, for the people worship him.

Wellman I'll never yield to so ungenerous an expedient. The seizing him I am content, in the extremity wherein we are, to follow. What say you, Colonel Downright? Shall we send him a letter now while this two days, truce lasts, between him and the Indians?

Downright I approve it.

All And I, and I, and I.

Dunce If your Honours please to make me the messenger, I'll use some arguments of my own to prevail with him.

Wellman You say well, Mr Dunce, and we'll dispatch you presently.

Whiff Ah, Doctor, if you could but have persuaded Colonel Wellman and Colonel Downright to have hanged him – [*Exeunt Wellmam, Downright and all but Whimsey, Whiff and Dunce*]

Whimsey Why, brother Whiff, you were for making him a General but now.

Whiff The counsels of wise statesmen, brother Whimsey, must change as causes do, d'ye see?

Dunce Your Honours are in the right, and whatever those two leading Councillors say, they would be glad if Bacon were dispatched, but the punctillio of honour is such a thing.

Whimsey Honour, a pox on't, what is that honour that keeps such a bustle in the world, yet never did good as I heard of?

Dunce Why 'tis a foolish word only, taken up by great men, but rarely practised – but if you would be great men indeed –

Whiff If we would, Doctor, name, name the way.

Dunce Why, you command each of you a company. When Bacon comes from the camp, as I am sure he will (and full of this silly thing called honour will come unguarded too), lay some of your men in ambush along those ditches by the Savannah about a mile from the town, and as he comes by, seize him, and hang him upon the next tree.

Whiff Hum – hang him! a rare plot.

Whimsey Hang him – we'll do't, we'll do't sir, and I doubt not but to be made General for the action – I'll take it all upon myself. [*aside*]

Dunce If you resolve upon this, you must about it instantly. Thus I shall at once serve my country, and revenge myself on the rascal for affronting my dignity once at the Council-Table, by calling me farrier.

Exit

Whiff Do you know, brother, what we are to do?

Whimsey To do, yes, to hang a General, brother, that's all.

Whiff All, but is it lawful to hang any General?

Whimsey Lawful, yes, that 'tis lawful to hang any General that fights against law.

Whiff But in what he has done, he has served the King and our country, and preserved all our lives and fortunes.

Whimsey That's all one, brother. If there be but a quirk in the law offended in this case, though he fought like Alexander, and preserved the whole world from perdition, yet if he did it against law, 'tis lawful to hang him. Why what, brother, is it fit that every impudent fellow that pretends to a little honour, loyalty and courage, should serve his King and country against the law? No, no, brother, these things are not to be suffered in a Civil Government by law established, – wherefore let's about it –

Exeunt

I.iii

Surelove's house.
Enter Ranter and her coachman

Ranter Here, Jeffrey, ye drunken dog, set your coach and horses up, I'll not go till the cool of the evening, I love to ride in fresco.

Enter Boy

Coachman Yes after hard drinking [*aside*] it shall be done, madam.
Ranter How now, boy, is Madam Surelove at home?
Boy Yes, madam.
Ranter Go tell her I am here, sirrah.
Boy Who are you, pray, forsooth?
Ranter Why, you son of baboon, don't you know me?
Boy No, madam, I came over but in the last ship.
Ranter What from Newgate or Bridewell? From shoving the fumbler, sirrah, lifting or filing the cly?
Boy I don't understand this country-language, forsooth, yet.
Ranter You rogue, 'tis what we transport from England first – go ye dog, go tell your lady the Widow Ranter is come to dine with her – [*Exit Boy*] I hope I shall not find that rogue Dareing here, snivelling after Mrs Chrisante. If I do, by the Lord, I'll lay him thick, pox on him, why should I love the dog, unless it be a judgement upon me.

Enter Surelove and Chrisante

My dear, jewel how dost do? As for you, gentlewoman, you are my rival, and I am in rancour against you till you have renounced my Dareing.
Chrisante All the interest I have in him, madam, I resign to you.
Ranter Aye – but your house, lying so near the camp, gives me mortal fears – but prithee, how thrives thy amour with honest Friendly?
Chrisante As well as an amour can, that is absolutely forbid by a father on one side, and pursued by a good resolution on the other.
Ranter Hey Gad, I'll warrant for Friendly's resolution, what, though his fortune be not answerable to yours, we are bound to help one another – here boy – some pipes and a bowl of punch. You know my humour, madam, I must smoke and drink in a morning, or I am mawkish all day.
Surelove But will you drink punch in a morning?
Ranter Punch, 'tis my morning's draught, my table-drink, my treat, my regalio, my everything, ah, my dear Surelove, if thou wouldst but refresh

and cheer thy heart with punch in a morning, thou wouldst not look thus cloudy all the day.

Enter pipes and a great bowl; she falls to smoking.

Surelove I have reason, madam, to be melancholy, I have received a letter from my husband, who gives me an account that he is worse in England than when he was here, so that I fear I shall see him no more, the doctors can do no good on him.

Ranter A very good hearing. I wonder what the Devil thou hast done with him so long? An old fusty weather-beaten skeleton, as dried as stock-fish, and much of the hue. Come, come, here's to the next, may he be young, Heaven, I beseech thee. [*drinks*]

Surelove You have reason to praise an old man, who died and left you worth fifty thousand pound.

Ranter Aye, Gad – and what's better sweetheart, died in good time too, and left me young enough to spend this fifty thousand pound in better company – rest his soul for that too.

Chrisante I doubt 'twill be all laid out in Bacon's mad Lieutenant General Dareing.

Ranter Faith, I think I could lend it the rogue on good security.

Chrisante What's that, to be bound body for body?

Ranter Rather that he should love nobody's body besides my own, but my fortune is too good to trust the rogue, my money makes me an infidel.

Chrisante You think they all love you for that.

Ranter For that, aye, what else? If it were not for that, I might sit still and sigh, and cry out, a miracle! a miracle! at sight of a man within my doors.

Enter Maid

Maid Madam, here's a young gentleman without would speak with you.

Surelove With me, sure thou'rt mistaken, is it not Friendly?

Maid No madam 'tis a stranger.

Ranter 'Tis not Dareing, that rogue, is it?

Maid No, madam.

Ranter Is he handsome? Does he look like a gentleman?

Maid He's handsome and seems a gentleman.

Ranter Bring him in then, I hate a conversation without a fellow, – hah – a good handsome lad indeed.

Enter Hazard with a letter

Surelove With me, sir, would you speak?

Hazard If you are Madam Surelove.

Surelove So I am called.

Hazard Madam I am newly arrived from England, and from your husband my kinsman bring you this – [*gives a letter*]

Ranter Please you to sit, sir.

Hazard She's extremely handsome – [*aside, sits down*]

Ranter Come, sir, will you smoke a pipe?

Hazard I never do, madam –

Ranter Oh fie upon't, you must learn then, we all smoke here, 'tis a part of good breeding. Well, well, what cargo, what goods have ye? Any points, lace, rich stuffs, jewels? If you have I'll be your chafferer, I live hard by, any-body will direct you to the Widow Ranter's.

Hazard I have already heard of you, madam.

Ranter What, you are like all the young fellows, the first thing they do when they come to a strange place, is to enquire what fortunes there are.

Hazard Madam, I had no such ambition:

Ranter Gad, then you're a fool, sir, but come, my service to you. We rich widows are the best commodity this country affords, I'll tell you that.

Surelove [*this while she reads the letter*] Sir, my husband has recommend-ed you here in a most particular manner, by which I do not only find the esteem he has for you, but the desire he has of gaining you mine, which on a double score I render you, first for his sake, next for those merits that appear in yourself.

Hazard Madam, the endeavours of my life shall be to express my gratitude for this great bounty.

Enter Maid

Maid Madam, Mr Friendly's here.

Surelove Bring him in.

Hazard Friendly, – I had a dear friend of that name, who I hear is in these parts – pray Heaven it may be he.

Ranter How, now, Charles.

Enter Friendly

Friendly Madam, your servant – Hah! should not I know you for my dear friend Hazard? [*Embracing him*]

Hazard Or you're to blame, my Friendly.

Friendly Prithee, what calm brought thee ashore?

Hazard Fortune de la guerre, but, prithee, ask me no questions in so good company, where a minute lost from this conversation is a misfortune not to be retrieved.

Friendly Do'st like her, rogue? [*softly aside*]

Hazard Like her! Have I sight, or sense? Why, I adore her.

Friendly My Chrisante, I heard your father would not be here today, which made me snatch this opportunity of seeing you.

Ranter Come, come, a pox of this whining love, it spoils good company.

Friendly You know, my dear friend, these opportunities come but seldom, and therefore I must make use of 'em.

Ranter Come, come, I'll give you a better opportunity at my house tomorrow, we are to eat a buffalo there, and I'll secure the old gentleman from coming.

Friendly Then I shall see Chrisante once more before I go.

Chrisante Go – Heavens – whither my Friendly?

Friendly I have received a commission to go against the Indians, Bacon being sent for home.

Ranter But will he come when sent for?

Friendly If he refuse, we are to endeavour to force him.

Chrisante I do not think he will be forced, not even by Friendly.

Friendly And, faith, it goes against my conscience to lift my sword against him, for he is truly brave, and what he has done, a service to the country, had it but been by authority.

Chrisante What pity 'tis there should be such false maxims in the world, that noble actions how ever great, must be criminal for want of a law to authorise 'em.

Friendly Indeed 'tis pity that when laws are faulty they should not be mended or abolished.

Ranter Hark ye, Charles, by Heaven, if you kill my Dareing I'll pistol you.

Friendly No, widow, I'll spare him for your sake. [*They join with Surelove*]

Hazard Oh, she is all divine, and all the breath she utters serves but to blow my flame.

Enter Maid

Maid Madam, dinner's on the table.

Surelove Please you, sir, to walk in – come, Mr Friendly. [*she takes Hazard*]

Ranter Prithee, good wench, bring in the punch-bowl.

Exeunt

II.i

A pavilion.
Discovers the Indian King and Queen sitting in state,
with guards of Indians, men and women attending; to them Bacon
richly dressed, attended by Dareing, Fearless, and other officers;
he bows to the King and Queen, who rise to receive him.

King I am sorry, sir, we meet upon these terms, we who so often have embraced as friends.

Bacon How charming is the Queen? [*aside*] War, sir, is not my business, nor my pleasure. Nor was I bred in arms; my country's good has forced me to assume a soldier's life, and 'tis with much regret that I employ the first effects of it against my friends. Yet whilst I may – whilst this cessation lasts, I beg we may exchange those friendships, sir, we have so often paid in happier peace.

King For your part, sir, you've been so noble, that I repent the fatal difference that makes us meet in arms. Yet though I'm young, I'm sensible of injuries; and oft have heard my grandsire say that we were monarchs once of all this spacious world, till you, an unknown people landing here, distressed and ruined by destructive storms, abusing all our charitable hospitality, usurped our right and made your friends your slaves.

Bacon I will not justify the ingratitude of my forefathers, but finding here my inheritance, I am resolved still to maintain it so, and by my sword which first cut out my portion, defend each inch of land with my last drop of blood.

Queen Ev'n his threats have charms that please the heart. [*aside*]

King Come, sir, let this ungrateful theme alone, which is better disputed in the field.

Queen Is it impossible there might be wrought an understanding betwixt my lord and you? 'Twas to that end I first desired this truce, myself proposing to be mediator, to which my Lord Cavarnio shall agree, could you but condescend. I know you're noble and I have heard you say our tender sex could never plead in vain.

Bacon Alas! I dare not trust your pleading, madam. A few soft words from such a charming mouth would make me lay the conqueror at your feet as a sacrifice for all the ills he has done you.

Queen How strangely am I pleased to hear him talk. [*aside*]

King Semernia, see – the dancers do appear. Sir, will you take your seat? [*to Bacon*]

He leads the Queen to a seat, they sit and talk.

Bacon Curse on his sports that interrupted me, my very soul was hovering at my lip, ready to have discovered all its secrets. But oh! I dread to tell her of my pain, and when I would, an awful trembling seizes me, and she can only from my dying eyes, read all the sentiments of my captive heart. [*sits down, the rest wait*]

*Enter Indians that dance antics; after the dance the King seems
in discourse with Bacon, the Queen rises, and comes forth.*

Queen The more I gaze upon this English stranger, the more confusion struggles in my soul. Oft I have heard of love, and oft this gallant man (when peace had made him pay his idle visits) has told a thousand tales of dying maids. And ever when he spoke, my panting heart, with a prophetic fear in sigh replied, 'I shall fall such a victim to his eyes.'

Enter an Indian

Indian [*to the King*] Sir here's a messenger from the English Council desires admittance to the General.
Bacon [*to the King*] With your permission, sir, he may advance.

Re-enter Indian with Dunce

Dunce All health and happiness attend your honour. This from the Honourable Council. [*gives him a letter*]
King I'll leave you till you have dispatched the messenger, and then expect your presence in the Royal tent.   *Exeunt King, Queen, and Indians*
Bacon Lieutenant, read the letter. [*to Dareing*]
Dareing [*reads*] Sir, the necessity of what you have acted makes it pardonable, and we could wish we had done the country, and ourselves so much justice as to have given you that commission you desired. We now find it reasonable to raise more forces, to oppose these insolences, which possible yours may be too weak to accomplish, to which end the Council is ordered to meet this evening, and desiring you will come and take your place there, and be pleased to accept from us a commission to command in chief in this war. Therefore send those soldiers under your command to their respective houses, and haste, sir, to your affectionate friends –
Fearless Sir, I fear the hearts and pen did not agree when this was writ.
Dareing A plague upon their shallow politics! Do they think to play the old game twice with us?
Bacon Away, you wrong the Council, who of themselves are honourable

gentlemen, but the base coward fear of some of them puts the rest on tricks that suit not with their nature.

Dunce Sir, 'tis for noble ends you're sent for, and for your safety I'll engage my life.

Dareing By Heaven and so you shall – and pay it too with all the rest of your wise-headed Council.

Bacon Your zeal is too officious now. I see no treachery, and can fear no danger.

Dunce Treachery! Now Heavens forbid, are we not Christians, sir, all friends and countrymen? Believe me, sir, 'tis honour calls you to increase your fame, and he who would dissuade you is your enemy.

Dareing Go cant, sir, to the rabble – for us – we know you.

Bacon You wrong me when you but suspect for me, let him that acts dishonourably fear. My innocence, and my good sword's my guard.

Dareing If you resolve to go, we will attend you.

Bacon What, go like an invader? No Dareing, the invitation's friendly, and as a friend, attended only by my menial servants, I'll wait upon the Council, that they may see that, when I could command it, I came a humble suppliant for their favour. You may return, and tell 'em I'll attend.

Dunce I kiss your Honour's hands – [*goes out*]

Dareing 'Sdeath will you trust the faithless Council, sir, who have so long held you in hand with promises, that curse of statesmen, that unlucky vice that renders even nobility despised.

Bacon Perhaps the Council thought me too aspiring, and would not add wings to my ambitious flight.

Dareing A pox of their considering caps, and now they find that you can soar alone, they send for you to nip your spreading wings. Now, by my soul, you shall not go alone.

Bacon Forbear, lest I suspect you for a mutineer; I am resolved to go.

Fearless What, and send your army home? A pretty fetch.

Dareing By Heaven, we'll not disband – not till we see how fairly you are dealt with. If you have a commission to be General, here we are ready to receive new orders, if no – we'll ring 'em such a thundering peal shall beat the town about their treacherous ears.

Bacon I do command you not to stir a man, till you're informed how I am treated by 'em. – Leave me all – [*Exeunt officers*]

While Bacon reads the letter again, to him the Indian Queen, with women waiting.

Queen Now, while my Lord's asleep in his pavilion, I'll try my power with the General, for an accommodation of a peace. The very dreams of war fright my soft slumbers that used to be employed in kinder business.

Bacon Ha! – The Queen – What happiness is this presents itself which all my industry could never gain?

Queen Sir – [*approaching him*]

Bacon Pressed with the great extremes of joy and fear I trembling stand, unable to approach her.

Queen I hope you will not think it fear in me, though tim'rous as a dove, by nature framed, nor that my Lord, whose youth's unskilled in war, can either doubt his courage, or his forces, that makes me seek a reconciliation on any honourable terms of peace.

Bacon Ah, madam! If you knew how absolutely you command my fate, I fear but little honour would be left me, since whatsoe'er you ask me I should grant.

Queen Indeed I would not ask your honour, sir, that renders you too brave in my esteem. Nor can I think that you would part with that – no, not to save your life.

Bacon I would do more to serve your least commands than part with trivial life.

Queen Bless me! Sir, how came I by such a power?

Bacon The gods and nature gave it you in your creation, formed with all the charms that ever graced your sex.

Queen Is't possible? Am I so beautiful?

Bacon As Heaven, or angels there.

Queen Supposing this, how can my beauty make you so obliging?

Bacon Beauty has still a power over great souls, and from the moment I beheld your eyes, my stubborn heart melted to compliance, and from a nature rough and turbulent, grew soft and gentle as the God of Love.

Queen The God of Love! What is the God of Love?

Bacon 'Tis a resistless fire, that's kindled thus – [*takes her by the hand and gazes on her*] at every gaze we take from fine eyes, from such bashful looks, and such soft touches – it makes us sigh – and pant as I do now, and stops the breath whene'er we speak of pain.

Queen Alas, for me if this should be love! [*aside*]

Bacon It makes us tremble, when we touch the fair one, and all the blood runs shiv'ring through the veins. The heart's surrounded with a feeble languishment, the eyes are dying, and the cheeks are pale. The tongue is falt'ring, and the body fainting.

Queen Then I'm undone, and all I feel is love. [*aside*] If love be catching, sir, by looks and touches, let us at distance parley. Or rather let me fly, for within view is too near – [*aside*]

Bacon Ah! she retires – displeased, I fear, with my presumptuous love. Oh pardon, fairest creature. [*kneels*]

Queen I'll talk no more. Our words exchange our souls, and every look fades all my blooming honour, like sunbeams, on unguarded roses. Take all our kingdoms – make our people slaves, and let me fall beneath your conquering sword. But never let me hear you talk again or gaze upon your eyes – [*goes out*]

Bacon She loves! By Heaven, she loves! And has not art enough to hide her flame, though she have cruel honour to suppress it. However I'll pursue her to the banquet.

Exit

— ——

II.ii

The Widow Ranter's hall.
Enter Surelove, fanned by two Negroes, followed by Hazard

Surelove This Madam Ranter is so prodigious a treater – oh! I hate a room that smells of a great dinner, and what's worse a dessert of punch and tobacco. What, are you taking leave so soon, cousin?

Hazard Yes, madam, but 'tis not fit I should let you know with what regret I go – but business will be obeyed.

Surelove Some letters to dispatch to English ladies you have left behind – come cousin, confess.

Hazard I own I much admire the English beauties, but never yet have put their fetters on –

Surelove Never in love – oh then you have pleasure to come.

Hazard Rather a pain when there's no hope attends it.

Surelove Oh such diseases quickly cure themselves.

Hazard I do not wish to find it so; for even in pain I find a pleasure too.

Surelove You are infected then, and came abroad for cure.

Hazard Rather to receive my wounds, madam.

Surelove Already, sir? Whoe'er she be, she made good haste to conquer, we have few here boast that dexterity.

Hazard What think you of Chrisante, madam?

Surelove I must confess, your love and your despair are there placed right, of which I am not fond of being made a confidante, [*coldly*] since I'm assured she can love none but Friendly.

Hazard Let her love on, as long as life shall last, let Friendly take her, and the universe, so I had my next wish, – [*sighs*] madam, it is yourself that I adore, – I should not be so vain to tell you this, but that I know you've found the secret out already from my sighs.

Surelove Forbear, sir, and know me for your kinsman's wife, and no more.

Hazard Be scornful as you please, rail at my passion, and refuse to hear it; yet I'll love on, and hope, in spite of you, my flame shall be so constant and submissive, it shall compel your heart to some return.

Surelove You're very confident of your power I perceive, but if you chance to find yourself mistaken, say your opinion and your affectation were mis-applied, and not that I was cruel –

Exit

Hazard Whate'er denials dwell upon your tongue, your eyes assure me that your heart is tender. [*goes out*]

Enter the bagpiper, playing before a great bowl of punch, carried between two Negroes, a highlander dancing after it, the Widow Ranter led by Timerous, Chrisante by Dullman, Mrs Flirt and Friendly all dancing after it; they place it on the table.

Dullman This is like the noble widow all over, i'faith.

Timerous Aye, aye, the widow's health in a full ladle, Major, [*drinks*] – but a pox on't what made that young fellow here, that affronted us yesterday, Major? [*while they drink about*]

Dullman Some damned sharper that would lay his knife aboard your Widow Cornet.

Timerous Zoors, if I thought so, I'd arrest him for 'salt and battery, lay him in prison for a swingeing fine and take no bail.

Dullman Nay, had it not been before my Mrs here, Mrs Chrisante, I had swinged him for his yesterday's affront, – ah, my sweet Mrs Chrisante – if you did but know what a power you have over me –

Chrisante Oh you're a great courtier, Major.

Dullman Would I were anything for your sake, madam.

Ranter Thou art anything, but what thou shouldst be. Prithee, Major, leave off being an old buffoon, that is a lover turned to ridicule by age, consider thyself a mere rolling tun of Nants, – a walking chimney, ever smoking with nasty mundungus, – and then thou hast a countenance like an old worm-eaten cheese.

Dullman Well Widow, you will joke, ha, ha, ha –

Timerous Gadzoors, she's pure company, ha, ha –

Dullman No matter for my countenance – Colonel Downright likes my estate and is resolved to have it a match.

Friendly Dear Widow, take off your damned Major, for if he speak another

word to Chrisante, I shall be put past all my patience, and fall foul upon
him.

Ranter 'Slife, not for the world – Major I bar love-making within my territories, 'tis inconsistent with the punch-bowl. If you'll drink, do, if not be
gone.

Timerous Nay, Gadzooks, if you enter me at the punch-bowl, you enter
me in politics – well 'tis the best drink in Christendom for a Statesman.
[*they drink about, the bagpipe playing*]

Ranter Come, now you shall see what my highland valet can do –

A Scots dance

Dullman So – I see let the world go which way it will, Widow, you are
resolved for mirth, – but come – to the conversation of the times.

Ranter The times, why, what a Devil ails the times, I see nothing in the
times but a company of coxcombs that fear without a cause.

Timerous But if these fears were laid and Bacon were hanged, I look upon
Virginia to be the happiest part of the world, Gadzoors, – why there's
England – 'tis nothing to't – I was in England about six years ago, and was
showed the Court of Aldermen, some were nodding, some saying nothing,
and others very little to purpose, but how could it be otherwise, for they
had neither bowl of punch, bottles of wine or tobacco before 'em to put life
and soul into 'em as we have here. Then for the young gentlemen – their
farthest travels is to France or Italy, they never come hither.

Dullman The more's the pity by my troth. [*drinks*]

Timerous Where they learn to swear Mor-blew, Mor-Dee:

Friendly And tell you how much bigger the Louvre is then Whitehall; buy
a suit à-la-mode, get a swinging cap of some French Marquis, spend all
their money and return just as they went.

Dullman For the old fellows, their business is usury, extortion, and undermining young heirs.

Timerous Then for young merchants, their exchange is the tavern, their
warehouse the playhouse, and their bills of exchange billet-douxs, where
to sup with their wenches at the other end of the town. Now judge you
what a condition poor England is in, for my part I look upon't as a lost
nation, Gadzoors.

Dullman I have considered it, and have found a way to save all yet.

Timerous As how, I pray?

Dullman As thus, we have men here of great experience and ability – now
I would have as many sent into England as would supply all places, and
offices, both civil and military, d'ye see, their young gentry should all travel

hither for breeding, and to learn the mysteries of State.

Friendly As for the old covetous fellows, I would have the tradesmen get in their debts, break and turn troupers.

Timerous And they'd be soon weary of extortion, Gadzoors.

Dullman Then for the young merchants, there should be a law made, none should go beyond Ludgate.

Friendly You have found out the only way to preserve that great kingdom. [*drinking all this while, sometimes*]

Timerous Well, Gadzoors, 'tis a fine thing to be a good Statesman

Friendly Aye Cornet, which you had never been had you stayed in old England.

Dullman Why, sir, we were somebody in England.

Friendly So I heard, Major.

Dullman You heard, sir? What have you heard? He's a kidnapper that says he heard anything of me – and so my service to you – I'll sue you sir for spoiling my marriage here, by your scandals with Mrs Chrisante, but that shan't do sir. I'll marry her for all that, and he's a rascal that denies it.

Friendly S'death, you lie, sir – I do.

Timerous Gadzoors, sir, lie to a Privy Councillor, a Major of horse, brother, this is an affront to our dignities, draw and I'll side with you. [*they both draw on Friendly, the ladies run off*]

Friendly If I disdain to draw, 'tis not that I fear your base and cowardly force, but for the respect I bear you as Magistrates, and so I leave you –

Timerous An arrant coward, Gadzoors. [*goes out*]

Dullman A mere poltroon, and I scorn to drink in's company.

Exeunt, putting up their swords

II.iii

A savannah, or large heath.
Enter Whimsey, Whiff, and Boozer, with some soldiers, armed

Whimsey Stand – stand – and hear the word of command – do ye see yon copse, and that ditch that runs along Major Dullman's plantation?

Boozer We do.

Whimsey Place your men there, and lie flat on your bellies, and when Bacon comes (if alone) seize him, d'y' see?

Whiff Observe the command now, (if alone) for we are not for blood-shed.

Boozer I'll warrant you for our parts. [*Exeunt all but Whimsey and Whiff*]

Whimsey Now we have ambushed our men, let's light our pipes and sit down and take an encouraging dram of the bottle. [*pulls out a bottle of brandy out of his pocket – they sit*]

Whiff Thou art a knave and hast emptied half the bottle in thy leathern pockets, but, come, here's young Fright-all's health.

Whimsey What, wilt drink a man's health thou'rt going to hang?

Whiff 'Tis all one for that, we'll drink his health first, and hang him afterwards, and thou shalt pledge me d'ye see, and though 'twere under the gallows.

Whimsey Thou'rt a traitor for saying so, and I defy thee.

Whiff Nay, since we are come out like loving brothers to hang the General, let's not fall out among ourselves, and so here's to you [*drinks*] though I have no great maw to this business.

Whimsey Prithee, brother Whiff, do not be so villainous a coward, for I hate a coward.

Whiff Nay, 'tis not that – but my wife, my Nancy dreamt tonight she saw me hanged.

Whimsey 'Twas a cowardly dream, think no more on't, but as dreams are expounded by contraries, thou shalt hang the General.

Whiff Aye – but he was my friend, and I owe him at this time a hundred pounds of tobacco.

Whimsey Nay, then I'm sure thou'dst hang him if he were thy brother.

Whiff But hark – I think I hear the neighing of horses. Where shall we hide ourselves, for if we stay here, we shall be mauled damnably? [*Exeunt both behind a bush, peeping*]

Enter Bacon, Fearless and three or four footmen

Bacon Let the groom lead the horses o'er the savannah. We'll walk it on foot, 'tis not a quarter of a mile to the town and here the air is cool.

Fearless The breezes about this time of the day begin to take wing and fan refreshment to the trees and flowers.

Bacon And at these hours how fragrant are the groves.

Fearless The country's well, were but the people so.

Bacon But, come, let's on – [*they pass to the entrance*]

Whimsey There, boys – [*the soldiers come forth and fall on Bacon*]

Bacon Hah! Ambush –

Draws; Fearless and footmen draw; the soldiers, after a while fighting, take Bacon and Fearless, they having laid three or four dead

Whiff So, so, he's taken now we may venture out.

Whimsey But are you sure he's taken?

Whiff Sure can't you believe your eyes? Come forth, I hate a coward. Oh, sir, have we caught your mightiness?

Bacon Are you the authors of this valiant act? None but such villainous cowards dar'st have attempted it.

Whimsey Stop his railing tongue.

Whiff No, no, let him rail, let him rail now his hands are tied, ha, ha. Why, good General Fright-all, was nobody able, d'ye think, to tame the roaring lion?

Bacon You'll be hanged for this!

Whimsey Come, come, away with him to the next tree.

Bacon What mean you, villains?

Whiff Only to hang your Honour a little, that's all. We'll teach you sir, to serve your country against law.

As they go off, enter Dareing with soldiers

Dareing Hah – my General betrayed – this I suspected.

His men come in, they fall on, release Bacon and Fearless and his man, who get swords. Whimsey's party put Whimsey and Whiff before 'em, striking 'em as they endeavour to run on this side or that, and forcing 'em to bear up, they are taken after some fighting.

Fearless Did not the General tell you rogues, you'd be all hanged?

Whiff Oh Nancy, Nancy, how prophetic are thy dreams?

Bacon Come, let's on –

Dareing 'Sdeath, what mean you, sir?

Bacon As I designed – to present myself to the Council.

Dareing By Heavens, we'll follow then to save you from their treachery. 'Twas this that has befallen you that I feared, which made me at a distance follow you.

Bacon Follow me still, but still at such a distance as your aids may be assisting on all occasion. Fearless, go back and bring your regiment down, and, Dareing, let your Sergeant with his party guard these villains to the Council. [*Exeunt Bacon Dareing and Fearless*]

Whiff A pox on your Worship's plot.

Whimsey A pox on your forwardness to come out of the hedge.

Exeunt officers with Whimsey and Whiff

II.iv

The Council-Table
Enter Colonel Wellman, Colonel Downright, Dullman, Timerous,
and about seven or eight more; seat themselves

Wellman You heard Mr Dunce's opinion gentlemen, concerning Bacon's coming upon our invitation. He believes he will come, but I rather think, though he be himself undaunted, yet the persuasions of his two Lieutenant-Generals, Dareing and Fearless, may prevent him. Colonel, have you ordered our men to be in arms?

Enter a soldier

Downright I have, and they'll attend further order on the savannah.
Soldier May it please your Honours, Bacon is on his way, he comes unattended by any but his footmen and Colonel Fearless.
Downright Who is this fellow?
Wellman A spy I sent to watch Bacon's motions.
Soldier But there is a company of soldiers in ambush on this side of the savannah to seize him as he passes by.
Wellman That's by no order of the Council.
All No, no, no order.
Wellman Nay, 'twere a good design if true.
Timerous Gadzoors, would I had thought on't for my troop.
Downright I am for no unfair dealing in any extremity.

Enter a messenger in haste [with Brag]

Messenger An't please, your Honours, the saddest news – an ambush being laid for Bacon, they rushed out upon him, on the savannah, and after some fighting took him and Fearless.
Timerous Is this your sad news – 'zoors, would I had had a hand in't.
Brag When on a sudden, Dareing and his party fell in upon us, turned the tide – killed our men and took Captain Whimsey and Captain Whiff pris'ners, the rest run away, but Bacon fought like a fury.
Timerous A bloody fellow.
Downright Whimsey and Whiff? They deserve death for acting without order.
Timerous I'm of the Colonel's opinion, they deserve to hang for't.
Dullman Why brother, I thought you had wished the plot had been yours but now?

Timerous Aye, but the case is altered since that, good brother.

Wellman Now he's exasperated past all hopes of a reconciliation.

Dullman You must make use of the statesman's refuge, wise dissimulation.

Brag For all this, sir, he will not believe but that you mean honourably, and no persuasions could hinder him from coming, so he has dismissed all his soldiers, and is ent'ring the town on foot.

Wellman What pity 'tis a brave man should be guilty of an ill action.

Brag But the noise of his danger has so won the hearts of the mobile, that they increase his train as he goes and follow him in the town like a victor. [*Exit*]

Wellman Go wait his coming – he grows too popular, and must be humbled.

Timerous I was ever of your mind Colonel.

Wellman Aye right or wrong – but what's your counsel now?

Timerous E'en as it used to be, I leave it to wiser heads.

Enter Brag

Brag Bacon, sir, is ent'ring.

Timerous Gadzoors, would I were safe in bed.

Dullman Colonel, keep in your heat and treat calmly with him.

Wellman I rather wish you would all follow me. I'd meet him at the head of all his noisy rabble, and seize him from the rout.

Downright What men of authority dispute with rake-hells? 'Tis below us, sir.

Timerous To stake our lives and fortunes against their nothing.

Enter Bacon, after him the rabble with staves and clubs
bringing in Whimsey and Whiff, bound

Wellman What means this insolence? What, Mr Bacon do you come in arms?

Bacon I'd need, sir, come in arms, when men that should be honourable can have so poor designs to take my life.

Wellman Thrust out his following rabble.

First Rabble We'll not stir till we have the General safe back again.

Bacon Let not your loves be too officious – but retire –

First Rabble At your command, we vanish – [*The rabble retire*]

Bacon I hope you'll pardon me, if in my own defence I seized on these two murderers.

Downright You did well, sir, 'twas by no order they acted. Stand forth and hear your sentence – in time of war we need no formal trials to hang knaves that act without order.

Whiff Oh mercy, mercy, Colonel – 'twas Parson Dunce's plot.

Downright Issue out a warrant to seize Dunce immediately. You shall be carried to the fort to pray

Whimsey Oh, good your Honour, I never prayed in all my life,

Downright From thence drawn upon a sledge to the place of execution, where you shall hang till you are dead – and then be cut down and –

Whimsey Oh hold – hold – we shall never be able to endure half this.[*kneeling*]

Wellman I think th'offence needs not so great punishment, their crime, sir, is but equal to your own, acting wthout commission.

Bacon 'Tis very well explained sir, – had I been murdered by commission, then the deed had been approved, and now, perhaps, I am beholding to the rabble for my life.

Wellman A fine pretence to hide a popular fault, but for this once we pardon them and you.

Bacon Pardon, for what? By Heaven, I scorn your pardon. I've not offended honour nor religion.

Wellman You have offended both in taking arms.

Bacon Should I stand by and see my country ruined, my King dishonoured, and his subjects murdered, hear the sad cries of widows and of orphans? You heard it loud, but gave no pitying care to't, and till the war and massacre was brought to my own door, my flocks and herds surprised, I bore it all with patience. Is it unlawful to defend myself against a thief that breaks into my doors?

Wellman And call you this defending of yourself?

Bacon I call it doing of myself that right, which upon just demand the Council did refuse me. If my ambition, as you're pleased to call it, made me demand too much, I left myself to you.

Wellman Perhaps we thought it did.

Bacon Sir you affront my birth. I am a gentleman, and yet my thoughts were humble – I would have fought under the meanest of your parasites –

Timerous There's a bob for us brother. [*to Dullman*]

Bacon But still you put me off with promises – and when compelled to stir in my defence, I called none to my aid, and those that came, 'twas their own wrongs that urged 'em.

Downright 'Tis feared sir, under this pretence you aim at government.

Bacon I scorn to answer to so base an accusation. The height of my ambition is to be an honest subject.

Wellman An honest rebel, sir –

Bacon You know you wrong me, and 'tis basely urged – but this is trifling – here are my commissions.

Throws down papers. Downright reads.

Downright To be General of the forces against the Indians, and blank commissions for his friends.

Wellman Tear them in pieces – are we to be imposed upon? Do ye come in hostile manner to compel us?

Downright Be not too rough, sir, let us argue with him.

Wellman I am resolved I will not.

Timerous Then we are all dead men, Gadzoors! He will not give us time to say our prayers.

Wellman We every day expect fresh force from England, till then, we of ourselves shall be sufficient to make defence, against a sturdy traitor.

Bacon Traitor, 'sdeath traitor – I defy ye, but that my honour's yet above my anger; I'd make you answer me that 'traitor' dearly. [*Rises*]

Wellman Hah – am I threatened? Guards, secure the rebel. [*Guards seize him*]

Bacon Is this your honourable invitation? Go – triumph in your short lived victory, the next turn shall be mine.

Exeunt guards with Bacon

A noise of fighting; enter Bacon; Wellman's guards beat back by the rabble, Bacon snatches a sword from one, and keeps back the rabble, Timerous gets under the table.

Downright What means this insolence!

Rabble We'll have our General, and knock that fellow's brains out, and hang up Colonel Wellman.

All Aye, aye, hang up Wellman. [*The rabble seize Wellman, and Dullman, and the rest*]

Dullman Hold, hold gentleman, I was always for the General.

Rabble Let's barbecue this fat rogue.

Bacon Begone, and know your distance to the Council. [*The rabble let 'em go*]

Wellman I'd rather perish by the meanest hand, than owe my safety poorly thus to Bacon. [*In rage*]

Bacon If you persist still in that mind I'll leave you, and conquering, make you happy 'gainst your will. *Exeunt Bacon and rabble, hollowing* 'à Bacon, à Bacon'.

Wellman Oh villainous cowards, who will trust his honour with sycophants so base? Let us to arms – by Heaven I will not give my body rest, till I've chastised the boldness of this rebel. [*Exeunt Wellman, Downright and the rest, all but Dullman, Timerous peeps from under the table*]

Timerous What is the roistering Hector gone, brother?

Dullman Aye, aye, and the Devil go with him. [*Looking sadly, Timerous comes out*]

Timerous Was there ever such a bull of Bashan? Why, what if he should come down upon us and kill us all for traitors?

Dullman I rather think the Council will hang us all for cowards – ah – oh – a drum – a drum – oh [*He goes out*]

Timerous This is the misery of being great, we're sacrificed to every turn of stage.

─────

III.i

The Country Court, a great table, with papers, a clerk writing
Enter a great many people of all sorts, then Friendly,
after him Dullman

Friendly How now, Major? What, they say Bacon scared you all out of the Council yesterday. What say the people?

Dullman Say? They curse us all, and drink young Fright-all's health, and swear they'll fight through fire and brimstone for him.

Friendly And tomorrow will hallow him to the gallows, if it were his chance to come there.

Dullman 'Tis very likely. Why, I am forced to be guarded to the Court now, the rabble swore they would de Wit me, but I shall hamper some of 'em. Would the Governor were here to bear the brunt on't, for they call us the evil Councillors. [*Enter Hazard, goes to Friendly*] Here's the young rogue that drew upon us too, we have rods in piss for him, i'faith.

Enter Timerous with bailiffs, whispers to Dullman,
after which to the bailiffs.

Timerous Gadzoors, that's he, do your office.

Bailiffs We arrest you, sir, in the King's name, at the suit of the Honourable Justice Timerous.

Hazard Justice Timerous, who the Devil's he?

Timerous I am the man sir, d'ye see, for want of a better; you shall repent, Gadzoors, your putting of tricks upon persons of my rank and quality.

[*After he has spoke he runs back as afraid of him*]

Hazard Your rank and quality!

Timerous Aye, sir, my rank and quality. First I am one of the Honourable Council, next a Justice of Peace in Quorum, Cornet of a troop of horse d'ye see, and Church-warden.

Friendly From whence proceeds this Mr Justice? You said nothing of this at Madam Ranter's yesterday; you saw him there, then you were good friends?

Timerous Aye, however I have carried my body swimmingly before my mistress, d'ye see, I had rancour in my heart, Gadzoors.

Friendly Why, this gentleman's a stranger, and but lately come ashore.

Hazard At my first landing I was in company with this fellow and two or three of his cruel brethren, where I was affronted by them, some words passed and I drew –

Timerous Aye, aye, sir, you shall pay for't, – why – what sir, cannot a civil magistrate affront a man, but he must be drawn upon presently?

Friendly Well, sir, the gentleman shall answer your suit, and I hope you'll take my bail for him.

Timerous 'Tis enough – I know you to be a civil person.

Timerous and Dullman take their places, on a long bench placed behind the table; to them Whimsey and Whiff; they seat themselves; then Boozer and two or three more, who seat themselves; then enter two bearing a bowl of punch, and a great ladle or two in it; the rest of the stage being filled with people

Whiff Brothers, it has been often moved at the bench, that a new punch bowl should be provided, and one of a larger circumference, when the bench sits late about weighty affairs, oftentimes the bowl is emptied before we end.

Whimsey A good motion; clerk set it down.

Clerk Mr Justice Boozer, the Council has ordered you a writ of ease, and dismiss Your Worship from the bench.

Boozer Me from the bench, for what?

Whimsey The complaint is, brother Boozer, for drinking too much punch in the time of hearing trials.

Whiff And that you can neither write nor read, nor say the Lord's Prayer.

Timerous That your warrants are like a brewer's tally: a notch on a stick, if a special warrant, then a couple. Gadzoors, when His Excellency comes he will have no such Justices.

Boozer Why, brother, though I can't read myself, I have had Dalton's *Country-Justice* read over to me two or three times, and understand the

law. This is your malice, brother Whiff, because my wife does not come to
your warehouse to buy her commodities, – but no matter, to show I have
no malice in my heart, I drink your health – I care not this, I can turn
lawyer and plead at the board. [*Drinks, all pledge him and hum.*]

Dullman Mr Clerk, come, to the trials on the docket. [*Clerk reads*]

Clerk The first is between his Worship Justice Whiff and one Grubb.

Dullman Aye, that Grubb's a common disturber, brother, your cause is a
good cause if well managed, here's to't. [*Drinks*]

Whiff I thank you, brother Dullman, – read my petition. [*Drinks*]

Clerk The petition of Captain Thomas Whiff showeth, whereas Gilbert
Grubb calls his Worship's wife Ann Grabb 'whore', and said he would
prove it. Your petitioner desires the Worshipful bench to take it into consideration, and your petitioner shall pray, etc. Here's two witnesses have
made *affidavit vive voce*, an't like Your Worships.

Dullman Call Grubb.

Clerk Gilbert Grubb, come into the Court.

Grubb Here.

Whimsey Well, what can you say for yourself, Mr Grubb.

Grubb Why an't like Your Worship, my wife invited some neighbours'
wives to drink a cagg of cider, now Your Worship's wife, Madam Whiff,
being there fuddled, would have thrust me out of doors, and bid me go
to my old whore, Madam Whimsey, meaning Your Worship's wife. [*To
Whimsey*]

Whimsey Hah! My wife called whore! She's a jade and I'll arrest her husband here - in an action of debts.

Timerous Gadzoors, she's no better than she should be, I'll warrant her.

Whiff Look ye, brother Whimsey, be patient, you know the humour of my
Nancy when she's drunk, but when she's sober, she's a civil person, and
shall ask your pardon.

Whimsey Let this be done and I am satisfied. And so here's to you.
[*drinks*]

Dullman Go on to the trial.

Grubb I being very angry said, indeed, I would prove her a greater whore
than Madam Whimsey.

Clerk An't like, Your Worships, he confesses the words in open court.

Grubb Why, an't like, Your Worships, she has had two bastards. I'll prove
it.

Whiff Sirrah, sirrah, that was when she was a maid, not since I married her
my marrying her made her honest.

Dullman Let there be an order of court to sue him, for *Scandalum
Magnatum*.

Timerous Mr Clerk, let my cause come next.

Clerk The defendant's ready, sir. [*Hazard comes to the board*]

Timerous Brothers of the bench take notice, that this Hector here coming into Mrs Flirt's ordinary where I was, with my brother Dullman and Lieutenant Boozer. We gave him good counsel to fall to work, now my gentleman here was affronted at this, forsooth, and makes no more to do but calls us scoundrels, and drew his sword on us, and had not I defended myself by running away, he had murdered me, and assassinated my two brothers.

Whiff What witness have you, brother?

Timerous Here's Mrs Flirt and her maid Nell, – besides we may be witness for one another I hope; our words may take.

Clerk Mrs Flirt and Nell are sworn. [*They stand forth*]

Whimsey By the oaths that you have taken, speak nothing but the truth.

Mrs Flirt An't please, Your Worships, Your Honours came to my house, where you found this young gentleman, and Your Honours invited him to drink with Your Honours. Whereafter some opprobrious words given him, Justice Dullman and Justice Boozer struck him over the head; and after that, indeed, the gentleman drew.

Timerous Mark that, brother, he drew.

Hazard If I did, it was *se defendendo*.

Timerous Do you hear that, brothers? He did in defiance.

Hazard Sir, you ought not to sit Judge and accuser too.

Whiff The gentleman's i'th' right, brother, you cannot do it according to law.

Timerous Gadzoors, what new tricks, new quirks?

Hazard Gentlemen, take notice, he swears in court.

Timerous Gadzoors, what's that to you, sir.

Hazard This is the second time of his swearing.

Whimsey What, do you think we are deaf sir? Come, come, proceed.

Timerous I desire he may be bound to his good behaviour, fined and deliver up his sword, what say you, brother? [*Jogs Dullman who nods*]

Whimsey He's asleep, drink to him and waken him. You have have missed the cause by sleeping, brother. [*Drinks*]

Dullman Justice may nod, but never sleeps, brother – you were at – deliver his sword – a good motion, let it be done. [*Drinks*]

Hazard No, gentlemen, I wear a sword to right myself.

Timerous That's fine i'faith, Gadzoors, I have worn a sword this dozen year and never could right myself.

Whiff Aye, 'twould be a fine world if men should wear swords to right themselves, he that's bound to the peace shall wear no sword.

Whimsey I say he that's bound to the peace ought to wear no peruke, they may change 'em for black or white, and then who can know them.

Hazard I hope, gentlemen, I may be allowed to speak for myself.

Whiff Aye, what can you say for yourself, did you not draw your sword, sirrah?

Hazard I did.

Timerous 'Tis sufficient he confesses the fact, and we'll hear no more.

Hazard You will not hear the provocation given.

Dullman 'Tis enough, sir, you drew –

Whimsey Aye, aye, 'tis enough he drew – let him be fined.

Friendly The gentleman should be heard, he's a kinsman, too, to Colonel John Surelove.

Timerous Hum – Colonel Surelove's kinsman.

Whiff Is he so, nay, then all the reason in the world he should be heard, brothers.

Whimsey Come, come Cornet, you shall be friends with the gentleman. This was some drunken bout I'll warrant you.

Timerous Ha, ha, ha – so it was, Gadzoors.

Whiff Come drink to the gentleman, and put it up.

Timerous Sir, my service to you, I am heartily sorry for what's passed, but it was in my drink. [*Drinks*]

Whimsey You hear his acknowledgements, sir, and when he is sober he never quarrels. Come sir sit down, my service to you.

Hazard I beg your excuse, gentlemen – I have earnest business.

Dullman Let us adjourn the court, and prepare to meet the regiments on the savannah.

All go but Friendly and Hazard.

Hazard Is this the best court of judicature your country affords?

Friendly To give it its due, it is not. But how does thy amour thrive?

Hazard As well as I can wish, in so short a time.

Friendly I see she regards thee with kind eyes, sighs and blushes.

Hazard Yes, and tells me I am so like a brother she had – to excuse her kind concern – then blush so prettily, that, Gad, I could not forbear making a discovery of my heart.

Friendly Have a care of that, come upon her by slow degrees, for I know she's virtuous. But come let's to the savannah, where I'll present you to the two Colonels, Wellman and Downright, the men that manage all till the arrival of the Governor.

III.iii

The savannah or heath
Enter Wellman, Downright, Boozer, and officers

Wellman Have you dispatched the scouts to watch the motions of the enemies? I know that Bacon's violent and haughty, and will resent our vain attempts upon him; therefore we must be speedy in prevention.
Downright What forces have you raised since our last order?
Boozer Here's a list of 'em, they came but slowly in, till we promised every one a bottle of brandy.

Enter officer and Dunce

Officer We have brought Mr Dunce here, as Your Honour commanded us. After strict search we found him this morning in bed with Madam Mrs Flirt.
Downright No matter, he'll exclaim no less against the vices of the flesh, the next Sunday.
Dunce I hope, sir, you will not credit the malice of my enemies.
Wellman No more, you are free, and what you counselled about the ambush was both prudent and seasonable, and perhaps I now wish it had taken effect.

Enter Friendly and Hazard

Friendly I have brought an English gentleman to kiss your hands, sir, and offer you his service, he is young and brave, and kinsman to Colonel Surelove.
Wellman Sir, you are welcome, and to let you see you are so, we will give you your kinsman's command, Captain of a troop of horse-guards, and which I am sure will be continued to you when the Governor arrives.
Hazard I shall endeavour to deserve the honour, sir.

Enter Dullman, Timerous, Whimsey and Whiff, all in buff,
scarf and feather

Downright So gentlemen, I see you're in a readiness.
Timerous Readiness! What means he, I hope we are not to be drawn out to go against the enemy, Major?
Dullman If we are, they shall look a new Major for me.
Wellman We were debating, gentlemen, what course were best to pursue against this powerful rebel.

Friendly Why, sir, we have forces enough, let's charge him instantly, delays are dangerous.

Timerous Why, what a damned fiery fellow's this?

Downright But if we drive him to extremities, we fear his siding with the Indians.

Dullman Colonel Downright has hit it; why should we endanger our men against a desperate termagant? If he love wounds and scars so well, let him exercise on our enemies – but if he will needs fall upon us, 'tis then time for us enough to venture our lives and fortunes.

Timerous How, we go to Bacon, under favour I think 'tis his duty to come to us, an you go to that, Gadzoors.

Friendly If he do, 'twill cost you dear, I doubt, Cornet. I find by our list, sir, we are four thousand men.

Timerous Gadzoors, not enough for a breakfast for that insatiate Bacon, and his two Lieutenant Generals, Fearless and Dareing. [*Whiff sits on the ground with a bottle of brandy*]

Whimsey A morsel, a morsel.

Wellman I am for an attack, what say you, gentlemen, to an attack? – What, silent all? – What say you, Major?

Dullman I say, sir, I hope my courage was never in dispute. But, sir, I am going to marry Colonel Downright's daughter here – and should I be slain in this battle 'twould break her heart; – besides, sir, I should lose her fortune. [*Speaks big*]

Wellman I'm sure here's a Captain will never flinch. [*To Whimsey*]

Whimsey Who I, an't like Your Honour?

Wellman Aye, you.

Whimsey Who I? ha, ha, ha! Why did Your Honour think that I would fight?

Wellman Fight, yes? Why else do you take commissions?

Whimsey Commissions! O Lord, O Lord, take commissions to fight! ha ha ha; that's a jest, if all that take commissions should fight –

Wellman Why do you bear arms then?

Whimsey Why, for the pay, to be called Captain, noble Captain, to show, to cock and look big and bluff as I do; to be bowed to thus as we pass, to domineer, and beat our soldiers. 'Fight', quotha, ha ha ha.

Friendly But what makes you look so simply, Cornet?

Timerous Why, a thing that I have quite forgot, all my accounts for England are to be made up, and I'm undone if they be neglected – else I would not flinch for the stoutest he that wears a sword – [*Looks big*]

Downright What say you, Captain Whiff? [*Whiff almost drunk*]

Whiff I am trying, Colonel, what mettle I'm made on. I think I am valiant,

I suppose I have courage, but I confess 'tis a little of the d--- breed, but a little inspiration from the bottle, and the leave of my Nancy, may do wonders.

Enter Seaman in haste

Seaman An't please, Your Honours, Fright-all's officers have seized all the ships in the river, and rid now round the shore, and had by this time secured the sandy beach, and landed men to fire the town, but that they are high in drink aboard the ship called *The Good Subject*. The Master of her sent me to let Your Honours know, that a few men sent to his assistance will surprize them, and retake the ships.

Wellman Now, gentlemen, here's a brave occasion for emulation – why writ not the Master?

Dullman Aye, had he writ, I had soon been amongst them, i'faith; but this is some plot to betray us.

Seaman Keep me here, and kill me if it be not true.

Downright He says well – there's a brigantine and a shallop ready, I'll embark immediately.

Friendly No, sir, your presence is here more necessary, let me have the honour of this expedition.

Hazard I'll go your volunteer, Charles.

Wellman Who else offers to go?

Whimsey A mere trick to kidnap us, by Bacon. If the Captain had writ –

Timerous Aye, aye, if he had writ –

Wellman I see you're all base cowards, and here cashier ye from all commands and offices.

Whimsey Look ye, Colonel, you may do what you please, but you lose one of the best dressed officers in your whole camp, sir –

Timerous And in me, such a head piece.

Whiff I'll say nothing, but let the State want me.

Dullman For my part I am weary of weighty affairs. [*In this while Wellman, Downright, Friendly and Hazard talk*]

Wellman Command what men you please, but expedition makes you half a conqueror. [*Exeunt Friendly and Hazard*]

Enter another Seaman with a letter, gives it to Downright, he and Wellman read it

Downright Look ye now, gentlemen, the Master has writ.

Dullman Has he – he might have writ sooner, while I was in command, – if he had –

Whimsey Aye, Major – if he had – but let them miss us –

Wellman Colonel, haste with your men and reinforce the beach, while I follow with the horse, – Mr Dunce, pray let that proclamation be read concerning Bacon, to the soldiers.

Dunce It shall be done, sir. [*Exit Downright and Wellman*]

The scene opens and discovers a body of soldiers.

Dunce Gentlemen, how simply you look now.

Timerous Why, Mr Parson, I have a scruple of conscience upon me, I am considering whether it be lawful to kill, tho' it be in war; I have a great aversion to't, and hope it proceeds from religion.

Whiff I remember the fit took you just so, when the Dutch besieged us, for you could not then be persuaded to strike a stroke.

Timerous Aye, that was because they were Protestants as we are, but, Gadzoors, had they been Dutch Papists, I had mauled them, but conscience –

Whimsey I have been a Justice of Peace this six years and never had a conscience in my life.

Timerous Nor I neither, but in this damned thing of fighting.

Dunce Gentlemen, I am commanded to read the declaration of the Honourable Council to you. [*To the soldiers*]

All Hum hum hum –

Boozer Silence – silence –

Dunce reads.

Dunce By an order of Council dated May the 10th 1670: To all gentlemen soldiers, merchants, planters, and whom else it may concern. Whereas Bacon, contrary to law and equity, has, to satisfy his own ambition, taken up arms, with a pretence to fight the Indians, but indeed to molest and enslave the whole colony, and to take away their liberties and properties; this is to declare, that whoever shall bring this traitor dead or alive to the Council shall have three hundred pounds reward. And so God save the King.

All A Council, Council! Hah – [*Hollow*]

Enter a Soldier hastily

Soldier Stand to your arms, gentlemen, stand to your arms, Bacon is marching this way.

Dunce Hah – what numbers has he?

Soldier About a hundred horse, in his march he has surprized Colonel Downright, and taken him prisoner.

All Let's fall on Bacon – let's fall on Bacon, hay – [*Hollow*]

Boozer We'll hear him speak first – and see what he can say for himself.

All Aye, aye, we'll hear Bacon speak – [*Dunce pleads with them*]

Timerous Well, Major, I have found a stratagem shall make us four the greatest men in the colony. We'll surrender ourselves to Bacon, and say we disbanded on purpose.

Dullman Good –

Whiff Why, I had no other design in the world in refusing to fight.

Whimsey Nor I, d'ye think I would have excused it with the fear of disordering my cravat string else?

Dunce Why, gentlemen, he designs to fire Jamestown, murder you all, and then lie with your wives, and will you slip this opportunity of seizing him?

Boozer He's a termagant rogue, neighbours – we'll hang the dog.

All Aye, aye, hang Bacon, hang Bacon.

Enter Bacon, and Fearless, some soldiers leading in. Downright bound; Bacon stands and stares a while on the regiments, who are silent all

Bacon Well, gentlemen – in order to your fine declaration, you see I come to render myself –

Dunce How came he to know of our declaration?

Whimsey Rogues, rogues among ourselves – that inform.

Bacon What are ye silent all, – not a man lift his hand in obedience to the Council to murder this traitor, that has exposed his life so often for you? Hah, what not for three hundred pound, – you see I've left my troops behind, and come all wearied with the toils of war, worn out by summer's heats and winter's colds, marched tedious days and nights through bogs and fens as dangerous as your clamours, and as faithless, – what though 'twas to preserve you all in safety, no matter, you should obey the grateful Council, and kill this honest man that has defended you?

All Hum, hum hum.

Whiff The General speaks like a gorgon.

Timerous Like a cherubin, man.

Bacon All silent yet – where's that mighty courage that cried so loud but now 'A Council à Council'? Where is your resolution, cannot three hundred pound excite your valour, to seize that traitor Bacon who has bled for you? –

All A Bacon, à Bacon, à Bacon – [*Hollow*]

Downright Oh, villanous cowards – oh the faithless multitude!

Bacon What say you, Parson – you have a forward zeal?

Dunce I wish my coat, sir, did not hinder me, from acting as becomes my zeal and duty.

Whimsey A plaguy rugid dog – that Parson –

Bacon Fearless, seize me that canting knave from out the herd, and next those honourable officers. [*Points to Dullman, Whimsey, Whiff and Timerous; Fearless seizes them, and gives them to the soldiers, and takes the proclamation from Dunce and shows Bacon, they read it*]

Dullman Seize us, sir, you shall not need, we laid down our commissions on purpose to come over to Your Honour.

Whiff We ever loved and honoured Your Honour.

Timerous So entirely, sir – that I wish I were safe in Jamestown for your sake, and Your Honour were hanged. [*Aside*]

Bacon This fine piece is of your penning, Parson – though it be countenanced by the Council's names – Oh ingratitude – burn – burn the treacherous town – fire it immediately.

Whimsey We'll obey you, sir –

Whiff Aye, aye, we'll make a bonfire on't, and drink Your Honour's health round about it. [*They offer to go*]

Bacon Yet hold, my revenge shall be more merciful. I ordered that all the women of rank shall be seized and brought to my camp. I'll make their husbands pay their ransoms dearly; they'd rather have their hearts bleed than their purses.

Fearless Dear General, let me have the seizing of Colonel Downright's daughter; I would fain be plundering for a trifle called a maiden-head.

Bacon On pain of death, treat them with all respect; assure them of the safety of their honour. Now, all that will follow me shall find a welcome, and those that will not may depart in peace.

All Hay, à General, à General, à General. [*Some soldiers go off, some go to the side of Bacon*]

Enter Dareing and soldiers with Chrisante, Surelove, Mrs Whimsey, and Mrs Whiff, and several other women

Bacon Successful Dareing, welcome; what prizes have ye?

Dareing The fairest in the world, sir, I'm not for common plunder.

Downright Hah, my daughter and my kinswoman!

Bacon 'Tis not with women, sir, nor honest men like you that I intend to combat; not their own parents shall not be more indulgent, nor better safeguard to their honours, sir. But 'tis to save the expense of blood, I seize on their most valued prizes

Downright But, sir, I know your wild Lieutenant-General has long loved my Chrisante, and perhaps, will take this time to force her to consent.

Dareing I own I have a passion for Chrisante, yet by my General's life – or her fair self – what now I act is on the score of war, I scorn to force the maid I do adore.

Bacon Believe me, ladies, you shall have honourable treatment here.

Chrisante We do not doubt it, sir, either from you or Dareing. If he love me – that will secure my honour, or if he do not, he's too brave to injure me.

Dareing I thank you for your just opinion of me, madam.

Chrisante But, sir, 'tis for my father I must plead. To see his reverend hands in servile chains – and then perhaps, if stubborn to your will, his head must fall a victim to your anger.

Downright No, my good pious girl, I cannot fear ignoble usage from the General – and if thy beauty can preserve thy fame, I shall not mourn in my captivity.

Bacon I'll ne'er deceive your kind opinion of me – ladies I hope you're all of that opinion too.

Surelove If seizing us, sir, can advance your honour, or be of any use considerable to you, I shall be proud of such a slavery.

Mrs Whimsey I hope, sir, we shan't be ravished in your camp.

Dareing Fie, Mrs Whimsey, do soldiers use to ravish?

Mrs Whiff Ravish – marry I fear 'em not, I'd have 'em know I scorn to be ravished by any man!

Fearless Aye o' my conscience, Mrs Whiff, you are too good natured.

Dareing Madam, I hope you'll give me leave to name love to you, and try by all submissive ways to win your heart?

Chrisante Do your worst, sir, I give you leave, if you assail me only with your tongue.

Dareing That's generous and brave, and I'll requite it.

Enter Soldier in haste

Soldier The truce being ended, sir, the Indians grow so insolent as to attack us even in our camp, and have killed several of our men.

Bacon 'Tis time to check their boldness. Dareing, haste, draw up our men in order, to give 'em battle, I rather had expected their submission. The country now may see what they're to fear, since we that are in arms are not secure. [*Exeunt, leading the ladies*]

IV.i

*A temple, with an Indian god placed upon it, priests and
priestesses attending.*
*Enter Indian King on one side attended by Indian men, the Queen
enters on the other side with women, all bow to the idol, and divide
on each side of the stage, then, the music playing louder, the priest and
priestesses dance about the idol, with ridiculous postures and crying
(as for incantations) thrice repeated:*

> Agah Yerkin,
> Agah Boah,
> Sulen Tawarapah,
> Sulen Tawarapah.

*After this soft music plays again, then they sing something fine,
after which the priests lead the King to the altar, and the priestessess,
the Queen. They take off little crowns from their heads, and offer
them at the altar*

King Invoke the god, of our Quiocto to declare, what the event shall be of
this our last war against the English General.

*Soft music ceases; the music changes to confused tunes, to which the
priest and priestess dance antickly singing between; the same
incantation as before, and then dance again, and so invoke again
alternately; which dance ended a voice behind the altar cries,
while soft music plays:*

> The English General shall be,
> A captive to his enemy;
> And you from all your toils be freed,
> When by your hand the foe shall bleed:
> And ere the sun's swift course be run,
> This mighty conquest shall be won.

King I thank the gods for taking care of us. Prepare new sacrifice against
the evening, when I return a conqueror, I will myself perform the office of
a priest.
Queen Oh, sir, I fear you'll fall a victim first.
King What means Semernia, why are thy looks so pale?
Queen Alas, the oracles have double meanings, their sense is doubtful,
and their words enigmas. I fear, sir, I could make a truer interpretation –

King How, Semernia! By all thy love, I charge thee as you respect my life, to let me know your thoughts.

Queen Last night I dreamed a lion, fell with hunger, spite of your guards slew you, and bore you hence.

King This is thy sex's fear, and no interpretation of the oracle.

Queen I could convince you farther.

King Hast thou a secret thou canst keep from me, thy soul a thought that I must be stranger to? This is not like the justice of Semernia. Come unriddle me the oracle.

Queen The English General shall be a captive to his enemy. He is so, sir, already to my beauty, he says he languishes for love of me.

King Hah – the General my rival – but go on –

Queen And you from all your war be freed. Oh, let me not explain that fatal line, for fear it mean, you shall be freed by death.

King What, when by my hand the foe shall bleed? – away – it cannot be –

Queen No doubt my Lord, you'll bravely sell your life, and deal some wounds where you'll receive so many.

King 'Tis love, Semernia, makes thee dream, while waking I'll trust the gods, and am resolved for battle.

Enter an Indian

Indian Haste, haste, great sir, to arms. Bacon with all his forces is prepared, and both the armies ready to engage.

King Haste to my General bid him charge 'em instantly. I'll bring up the supplies of stout Teroomians, those so well skilled in the envenomed arrow. [*Exit Indian*] – Semernia – words but poorly do express the griefs of parting lovers – 'tis with dying eyes, and a heart trembling – thus – [*Puts her hand on his heart*] They take a heavy leave, – one parting kiss, and one love pressing sigh, and then farewell - but not a long farewell; I shall return victorious to thy arms, – commend me to the Gods and still remember me. [*Exit*]

Queen Alas! What pity 'tis I saw the General, before my fate had given me to the King – but now – like those that change their gods, my faithless mind 'twixt two opinions wavers. While to the gods my monarch I commend, my wand'ring thoughts in pity of the General makes that zeal cold, declined – ineffectual. If for the General I implore the deieties, methinks my prayers should not ascend the skies since honour tells me 'tis an impious zeal.

Which way soever my devotions move,
I am too wretched to be heard above.   [*Goes in, all exeunt*]

IV.ii

Shows a field of tents, seen at some distance through the trees of a
wood, drums, trumpets and the noise of battle with hollowing.
The Indians are seen with battleaxes to retreat, fighting, from the
English and all go off, when they re-enter immediately beating back the
English, the Indian King at the head of his men, with bows and arrows,
Dareing being at the head of the English.
They fight off; the noise continues less loud as more at distance.
Enter Bacon with his sword drawn, meets Fearless with his sword drawn.

Fearless Haste, haste, sir, to the entrance of the wood. Dareing's engaged past hope of a retreat, vent'ring too far, pursuing of the foe; the King in ambush with his poisoned archers, fell on and now we're dangerously distressed.
Bacon Dareing is brave, but he's, withal, too rash, come on and follow me to his assistance – [*They go out*]

A hollowing within, the fight renews. Enter the Indians beaten back
by Bacon, Dareing and Fearless; they fight off. The noise of fighting
continues a while, this still behind the wood
Enter Indians flying over the stage, pursued by the King

King Turn, turn ye fugitive slaves, and face the enemy. Oh, villains, cowards, deaf to all command by Heaven. I had my rival my in view and aimed at nothing but my conquering him. Now like a coward I must fly with cowards, or like a desperate madman fall, thus singly midst the numbers.
[*Follows the Indians*]

Enter Bacon enraged, with his sword drawn, Fearless, and
Dareing following him

Bacon Where is the King? Oh, ye perfidious slaves, how have you hid from my just revenge? Search all the brakes, the furzes and the trees, and let him not escape on pain of death.
Dareing We cannot do wonders, sir.
Bacon But you can run away –
Dareing Yes, when we see occasion – yet – should any but my General tell me so – by Heaven, he should find I were no starter.
Bacon Forgive me, I'm mad – the King's escaped, hid like a trembling slave in some close ditch, where he will sooner starve than fight it out.

Re-enter Indians running over the stage, pursued by the King
who shoots them as they fly, some few follow him

King All's lost – the day is lost – and I'm betrayed – Oh, slaves, that even wounds can't animate. [*In rage*]
Bacon The King!
King The General here, by all the powers betrayed by my own men.
Bacon Abandoned as thou art I scorn to take thee basely. You shall have soldier's chance, sir, for your life, since chance so luckily has brought us hither. Without more aids we will dispute the day: this spot of earth bears both our armies' fates. I'll give you back the victory I have won, and thus begin anew, on equal terms.
King That's nobly said – the powers have heard my wish! You, sir, first taught me how to use a sword, which heretofore has served me with success, but now – 'tis for Semernia that it draws, a prize more valued than my Kingdom, sir –
Bacon Hah, Semernia!
King Your blushes do betray your passion for her.
Dareing 'Sdeath, have we fought for this, to expose the victor to the conquered foe?
Fearless What fight a single man – our prize already?
King Not so, young man, while I command a dart.
Bacon Fight him, by Heaven, no reason shall dissuade me, and he that interrupts me is a coward, whatever be my fate, I do command ye to let the King pass freely to his tents.
Dareing The Devil's in the General.
Fearless 'Sdeath, his romantic humour will undo us.

They fight and pause

King You fight as if you meant to outdo me this way, as you have done in generosity.
Bacon You're not behind hand with me, sir, in courtesy. Come, here's to set us even –

Fight again

King You bleed apace.
Bacon You've only breached a vein, and given me new health and vigour by it.

They fight again, wounds on both sides, the King staggers,

Bacon takes him in his arms, the King drops his sword

Bacon How do you, sir?
King Like one – that's hovering between Heaven and Earth, I'm – mounting – somewhere – upwards – but giddy with my flight, – I know not where.
Bacon Command my surgeons, – instantly – make haste. Honour returns and love all bleeding's fled. *Exit Fearless*
King Oh, Semernia, how much more truth had thy divinity than the predictions of the flattering oracles. Commend me to her – I know you'll – visit – your fair captive sir, and tell her – oh – but death prevents the rest. [*Dies*]

Enter Fearless

Bacon He's gone – and now like Cæsar I could weep over the hero I myself destroyed.
Fearless I'm glad for your repose I see him there – 'twas a mad hot brained youth and so he died.
Bacon Come bear him on your shoulders to my tent, from whence with all the solemn state we can, we will convey him to his own pavilion.

Enter a Soldier

Soldier Some of our troops, pursuing of the enemy even to their temples, which they made their sanctuary, finding the Queen at her devotion there with all her Indian ladies, I'd much ado to stop their violent rage from setting fire to the holy pile.
Bacon Hang 'em immediately that durst attempt it, while I myself will fly to rescue her.
Goes out, they bear off the King's body. Exeunt all

Enter Whimsey pulling in Whiff, with a halter about his neck

Whimsey Nay, I'm resolved to keep thee here till his Honour the General comes, – what to call him traitor, and run away after he had so generously given us our freedom, and listed us cadees for the next command that fell in his army – I'm resolved to hang thee –
Whiff Wilt thou betray and peach thy friend? Thy friend that kept thee company all the while thou wert a prisoner – drinking at my own charge –
Whimsey No matter for that, I scorn ingratitude and therefore will hang thee – but as for thy drinking with me – I scorn to be behind hand with

thee in civility and therefore here's to thee. [*Takes a bottle of brandy out of his pocket, drinks*]

Whiff I can't drink.

Whimsey A certain sign thou won't be hanged.

Whiff You used to be à my side when a Justice, let the cause be how it would. [*Weeps.*]

Whimsey Aye – when I was a Justice I never minded honesty, but now I'll be true to my General, and hang thee to be a great man.

Whiff If I might but have a fair trial for my life –

Whimsey A fair trial – come, I'll be thy Judge – and if thou can'st clear thyself by law I'll acquit thee, sirrah. Sirrah, what can'st thou say for thyself for calling his Honour rebel? [*Sits on a drum head.*]

Whiff 'Twas when I was drunk, an't like Your Honour.

Whimsey That's no plea, for if you kill a man when you are sober you must be hanged when you are drunk, hast thou any thing else to say for thyself, why sentence may not pass upon thee?

Whiff I desire the benefit of the clergy.

Whimsey The clergy, I never knew anybody that ever did benefit by 'em, why thou canst not read a word.

Whiff Transportation then –

Whimsey It shall be to England then – but hold – who's this?

Dullman creeping from a bush

Dullman So, the danger's over, I may venture out, – pox on't I would not be in this fear again, to be Lord –

Enter Timerous with battleaxe, bow and arrows, and feathers on his head

Dullman Chief Justice of our court. Why, how now, Cornet – what in dreadful equipage? Your battleaxe bloody, with bow and arrows?

Timerous I'm in the posture of the times, Major – I could not be idle where so much action was. I'm going to present myself to the General with these trophies of my victory here –

Dullman Victory – what victory? Did not I see thee, creeping out of yonder bush – where thou wert hid all the fight – stumble on a dead Indian, and take away his arms?

Timerous Why, didst thou see me?

Dullman See thee, aye – and what a fright thou wert in, till thou wert sure he was dead.

Timerous Well, well, that's all one – Gadzoors, if every man, that pass for valiant in a battle, were to give an account how he gained his reputation, the world would be but thinly stocked with heroes. I'll say he was a great war Captain, and that I killed him hand to hand, and who can disprove me?

Dullman Disprove thee – why that pale face of thine, that has so much of the coward in't.

Timerous 'Shaw, that's with loss of blood – Hah, I am overheard, I doubt – who's yonder – [*Sees Whimsey and Whiff*] how, brother Whiff, in a hempen cravat-string?

Whimsey He called the General traitor and was running away, and I'm resolved to peach.

Dullman Hum – and one witness will stand good in law, in case of treason –

Timerous Gadzoors, in case of treason he'll be hanged if it be proved against him, were there ne'er a witness at all, but he must tried by a Council of War, man – come, come let's disarm him – [*They take away his arms, and pull a bottle of brandy out of his pocket*]

Whiff What, I hope you will not take away my brandy, gentlemen, my last comfort.

Timerous Gadzoors, it's come in good time – we'll drink it off. Here, Major – [*Drinks, Whiff takes him aside*]

Whiff Hark ye, Cornet – you are my good friend, get this matter made up before it come to the General.

Timerous But this is treason, neighbour.

Whiff If I hang – I'll declare upon the ladder, how you killed your war captain.

Timerous Come, brother Whimsey – we have been all friends and loving magistrates together, let's drink about, and think no more of this business.

Dullman Aye, aye, if every sober man in the nation should be called to account of the treason he speaks in's drink, the lord have mercy upon us all – put it up – and let us, like loving brothers, take an honest resolution to run away together; for this same Fright-all minds nothing but fighting.

Whimsey I'm content, provided we go all to the Council and tell them (to make our peace) we went in obedience to the proclamation to kill Bacon, but the traitor was so strongly guarded we could not effect it, but mum – who's here –

To them, enter Ranter and Jenny, as man and footman

Ranter Hah, our four Reverend Justices – I hope the blockheads will not know me – gentlemen, can you direct me to Lieutenant General Dareing's tents?

Whiff Hum, who the devil's this? That's he that you see coming this way. 'Sdeath, yonder's Dareing – Let's slip away before he advances. [*Exeunt all but Ranter and Jenny*]

Jenny I am scared with those dead bodies we have passed over. For God's sake, madam, let me know your design in coming.

Ranter Why, now I'll tell thee. My damned mad fellow, Dareing – who has my heart and soul – loves Chrisante, has stolen her, and carried her away to his tents. She hates him, while I am dying for him.

Jenny Dying, madam! I never saw you melancholy.

Ranter Pox on't, no. Why should I sigh and whine, and make myself an ass, and him conceited? No, instead of snivelling I'm resolved –

Jenny What madam?

Ranter Gad, to beat the rascal, and bring off Chrisante.

Jenny Beat him madam? What a woman beat a Lieutenant General?

Ranter Hang 'em, they get a name in war from command, not courage. How know I but I may fight? Gad, I have known a fellow kicked from one end of the town to t'other, believing himself a coward, at last forced to fight, found he could, got a reputation and bullied all he met with, and got a name, and a great commission.

Jenny But if he should kill you, madam?

Ranter I'll take care to make it as comical a duel as the best of 'em; as much in love as I am, I do not intend to die its martyr.

Enter Dareing and Fearless

Fearless Have you seen Chrisante since the fight?

Dareing Yes, but she is still the same, as nice and coy as fortune, when she's courted by the wretched, yet she denies me, so obligingly she keeps my love still in its humble calm.

Ranter Can you direct me, sir, to one Dareing's tent? [*Sullenly*]

Dareing One Dareing? He has another epithet to his name.

Ranter What's that, rascal, or coward?

Dareing Hah, which of thy stars, young man, has sent thee hither, to find that certain fate they have decreed?

Ranter I know not what my stars have decreed, but I shall be glad if they have ordained me to fight with Dareing – by thy concern thou shouldst be he?

Dareing I am. Prithee, who art thou?

Ranter Thy rival, though newly arrived from England, and came to marry fair Chrisante, whom thou hast ravished, for whom I hear another lady dies.

Dareing Dies for me?

Ranter Therefore resign her fairly – or fight me fairly –

Dareing Come on, sir – but hold – before I kill thee, prithee, inform me who this dying lady is?

Ranter Sir, I owe ye no courtesy, and therefore will do you none by telling you – come, sir, for Chrisante – draw. [*They offer to fight; Fearless steps in*]

Fearless Hold – what mad frolick's this? – sir, you fight for one you never saw [*to Ranter*] and you for one that loves you not. [*to Dareing*]

Dareing Perhaps she'll love him as little.

Ranter Gad, put it to the trial, if you dare – if thou be'st generous, bring me to her, and whom she does neglect shall give the other place.

Dareing That's fair. Put up thy sword – I'll bring thee to her instantly. [*Exeunt*]

———

IV.iii

A tent
Enter Chrisante and Surelove

Chrisante I'm not so much afflicted for my confinement, as I am that I cannot hear of Friendly.

Surelove Art not persecuted with Dareing?

Chrisante Not at all, though he tells me daily of his passion, I rally him, and give him neither hope nor despair – he's here.

Enter Dareing, Fearless, Ranter and Jenny

Dareing Madam, the complaisance I show, in bringing you my rival, will let you see how glad I am to oblige you every way.

Ranter I hope the danger I have exposed myself to for the honour of kissing your hand, madam, will render me something acceptable – here are my credentials – [*Gives her a letter*]

Chrisante [*reads*] Dear creature, I have taken this habit to free you from an impertinent lover, and to secure the damned rogue Dareing to myself. Receive me as sent by Colonel Surelove from England to marry you – favour me – no more – your Ranter – Hah, Ranter? [*aside*]. Sir you have too good a character, from my cousin Colonel Surelove, not to receive my welcome. [*Gives Surelove the letter*]

Ranter Stand by, General – [*Pushes away Dareing and looks big and takes Chrisante by the hand and kisses it*]

Dareing 'Sdeath, sir, there's room enough – at first sight so kind? Oh, youth – youth and impudence, what temptations are you – to villanous woman?

Chrisante I confess, sir, we women do not love these rough fighting fellows, they're always scaring us with one broil or other.

Dareing Much good may do you with your tame coxcomb.

Ranter Well, sir, then you yield the prize?

Dareing Aye, Gad, were she an angel, that can prefer such a callow fop as thou before a man – take her and domineer. [*They all laugh*] – 'Sdeath, am I grown ridiculous?

Fearless Why hast thou not found the jest? By Heaven, 'tis Ranter, 'tis she that loves you. Carry on the humour. [*aside*] Faith, sir, if I were you, I would devote myself to Madam Ranter.

Chrisante Aye, she's the fittest wife for you, she'll fit your humour.

Dareing Ranter – Gad, I'd sooner marry a she bear, unless for a penance for some horrid sin, we should be eternally challenging one another to the field, and ten to one she beats me there; or if I should escape there, she would kill me with drinking.

Ranter Here's a rogue – does your country abound with such ladies?

Dareing The Lord forbid, half a dozen would ruin the land, debauch all the men, and scandalize all the women.

Fearless No matter, she's rich.

Dareing Aye, that will make her insolent.

Fearless Nay, she's generous too.

Dareing Yes, when she's drunk, and then she'll lavish all.

Ranter A pox on him – how he vexes me.

Dareing Then such a tongue – she'll rail and smoke till she choke again, then six gallons of punch hardly recovers her, and never but then is she good natured.

Ranter I must lay him on –

Dareing There's not a blockhead in the country that has not –

Ranter – What? –

Dareing – been drunk with her.

Ranter I thought you had meant something else sir. [*In huff*]

Dareing Nay – as for that – I suppose there's no great difficulty.

Ranter 'Sdeath, sir, you lie – and you're a son of a whore. [*Draws and fences with him, and he runs back round the stage*]

Dareing Hold – hold virago – dear Widow, hold, and give me thy hand.

Ranter Widow!

Dareing 'Sdeath, I knew thee by instinct, Widow though I seemed not to do so, in revenge for the trick you put on me in telling me a lady died for me.

Ranter Why, such an one there is, perhaps she may dwindle forty or fifty years – or so – but will never be her own woman again that's certain.

Surelove This we are all ready to testify, we know her.

Chrisante Upon my life, 'tis true.

Dareing Widow I have a shrewd suspicion, that you yourself may be this dying lady.

Ranter Why so, coxcomb?

Dareing Because you took such pains to put yourself into my hands.

Ranter Gad, if your heart were but half so true as your guess, we should conclude a peace before Bacon and the Council will – besides this thing whines for Friendly and there's no hopes. [*To Chrisante*]

Dareing Give me thy hand, Widow, I am thine – and so entirely, I will never – be drunk out of thy company – Dunce is in my tent – prithee, let's in and bind the bargain.

Ranter Nay, faith, let's see the wars at an end first.

Dareing Nay, prithee, take me in the humour, while thy breeches are on – for I never liked thee half so well in petticoats.

Ranter Lead on General, you give me good encouragement to wear them. [*Exeunt*]

V.i

The savannah in sight of the camp; the moon rises
Enter Friendly, Hazard and Boozer, and a party of men

Friendly We are now in the sight of the tents.

Boozer Is not this a rash attempt, gentlemen, with so small force to set upon Bacon's whole army?

Hazard Oh, they are drunk with victory and wine; there will be naught but revelling tonight.

Friendly Would we could learn in what quarter the ladies are lodged, for we have no other business but to release them – but hark – who comes here?

Boozer Some scouts, I fear, from the enemy.

Enter Dullman, Timerous, Whimsey and Whiff, creeping as in the dark

Friendly Let's shelter ourselves behind yonder trees – lest we be surprised.

Timerous Would I were well at home – Gadzoors – if e'er you catch me a-cadeeing again, I'll be content to be set in the forefront of the battle for hawk's meat.

Whimsey Thou'rt afraid of every bush.

Timerous Aye, and good reason too: Gadzoors, there may be rogues hid – prithee, Major, do thou advance.

Dullman No, no, go on – no matter of ceremony in these cases of running away. [*They advance*]

Friendly They approach directly to us, we cannot escape them – their numbers are not great – let us advance. [*They come up to them*]

Timerous Oh, I am anihilated.

Whiff Some of Fright-all's scouts; we are lost men. [*They push each other foremost*]

Friendly Who goes there?

Whimsey Oh, they'll give us no quarter; 'twas long of you, Cornet, that we ran away from our colours.

Timerous Me – 'twas the Major's ambition here – to make himself a great man with the Council again.

Dullman Pox o' this ambition, it has been the ruin of many a gallant fellow.

Whiff If I get home again, the height of mine shall be to top tobacco; would I'd some brandy.

Timerous Gadzoors, would we had, 'tis the best armour against fear – hum – I hear nobody now – prithee, advance a little.

Whimsey What, before a horse officer?

Friendly Stand on your lives –

Timerous Oh, 'tis impossible – I am dead already.

Friendly What are ye? Speak – or I'll shoot.

Whimsey Friends to thee – who the devil are we friends to?

Timerous E'en who you please, Gadzoors.

Friendly Hah – Gadzoors – who's there? Timerous?

Timerous Hum – I know no such scoundrel – [*Gets behind*]

Dullman Hah – that's Friendly's voice.

Friendly Right – thine's that of Dullman – who's with you?

Dullman Only Timerous, Whimsey and Whiff, all valiantly running away from the arch rebel that took us prisoners.

Hazard Can you inform us where the ladies are lodged?

Dullman In the hither quarter in Dareing's tents; you'll know them by lanthorns on every corner – there was never better time to surprize them – for this day Dareing's married, and there's nothing but dancing and drinking.

Hazard Married! To whom?

Dullman That I ne'er inquired.

Friendly 'Tis to Chrisante, friend – and the reward of my attempt is lost.

Oh, I am mad, I'll fight away my life, and my despair shall yet do greater wonders, than even my love could animate me too. Let's part our men, and beset his tents on both sides. [*Friendly goes out with a party*]

Hazard Come, gentlemen, let's on –

Whiff On sir – we on sir? –

Hazard Aye, you on, sir – to redeem the ladies.

Whiff Oh, sir, I am going home for money to redeem my Nancy.

Whimsey So am I, sir.

Timerous I thank my stars I am a bachelor. Why, what a plague is a wife?

Hazard Will you march forward?

Dullman We have achieved honour enough already, in having made our campaign here – [*Looking big*]

Hazard 'Sdeath, but you shall go – put them in the front, and prick them on – if they offer to turn back run them through.

Timerous Oh, horrid – [*The soldiers prick them on with their swords*]

Whiff Oh, Nancy, thy dream will yet come to pass.

Hazard Will you advance, sir? [*Pricks Whiff*]

Whiff Why, so we do, sir; the devil's in these fighting fellows. [*Exeunt*]

An alarm at a distance. Within: To arms, to arms, the enemy's upon us!
A noise of fighting, after which enters Friendly with his party,
retreating and fighting, from Dareing and some soldiers, Ranter fighting
like a fury by his side, he putting her back in vain; they fight out
Re-enter Dareing with Friendly all bloody; several soldiers
enter with flambeaux

Dareing Now, sir – what injury have I ever done you, that you should use this treachery against me?

Friendly To take advantage, any way, in war was never counted treachery – and had I murdered thee, I had not paid thee half the debt I owe thee.

Dareing You bleed too much to hold too long a parley – come to my tent, I'll take a charitable care of thee.

Friendly I scorn thy courtesy, who against all the laws of honour and of justice, hast ravished innocent ladies.

Dareing Sir, your upbraiding of my honour shall never make me forfeit it, or esteem you less. Is there a lady here you have a passion for?

Friendly Yes, on a nobler score than thou darest own.

Dareing To let you see how you're mistaken, sir, who e'er that lady be whom you affect, I will resign, and give you both your freedoms.

Friendly Why, for this courtesy, which shows thee brave, in the next fight I'll save thy life, to quit the obligation.

Dareing I thank you, sir – come to my tent – and when we've dressed your wounds, and yielded up the ladies, I'll give you my passport for your safe conduct back, and tell your friends i'th' town we'll visit them i'th' morning.
Friendly They'll meet you on your way, sir –
Dareing Come, my young soldier, now thou'st won my soul.

An alarm beats
Enter at another passage Boozer with all the ladies; they pass over the
stage, while Hazard, Downright, beating back a party of soldiers;
Dullman, Timerous, Whimsey, and Whiff, pricked on by their party
to fight, so that they lay about them like madmen
Bacon, Fearless and Dareing come in, rescue their men, and fight
out the other party, some falling dead
Bacon, Fearless and Dareing return tired, with their swords drawn
Enter soldier running

Soldier Return, sir, where your sword will be more useful – a party of Indians, taking advantage of the night, have set fire on your tents, and born away the Queen.
Bacon Hah, the Queen! By Heaven, this victory shall cost them dear; come, let us fly to rescue her. [*Goes out*]

Scene changes to Wellman's tent
Enter Wellman, Brag, Grub and Officers

Wellman I cannot sleep my impatience is so great, to engage this haughty enemy, before they have reposed their weary limbs. Is not yon ruddy light the morning's dawn?
Brag 'Tis, and please Your Honour.
Wellman Is there no news of Friendly yet, and Hazard?
Brag Not yet – 'tis thought they left the camp tonight, with some design against the enemy.
Wellman What men have they?
Brag Only Boozer's party, sir.
Wellman I know they are brave, and mean to surprise me with some handsome action.

Enter Friendly

Friendly I ask a thousand pardons, sir, for quitting the camp without your leave.

Wellman Your conduct and your courage cannot err; I see thou'st been in action by thy blood.

Friendly Sir I'm ashamed to own these slender wounds, since without more my luck was to be taken, while Hazard did alone effect the business; the rescuing of the ladies.

Wellman How got ye liberty?

Friendly By Dareing's generosity, who sends you word he'll visit you this morning.

Wellman We are prepared to meet him.

Enter Downright, Hazard, ladies, Whimsey, Whiff, Dullman,
Timerous looking big; Wellman embraces Downright

Wellman My worthy friend, how am I joyed to see you!

Downright We owe our liberties to these brave youths, who can do wonders when they fight for ladies.

Timerous With our assistance, ladies.

Whimsey For my part I'll not take it as I have done. Gad, I find when I am damnable angry I can beat both friend and foe.

Whiff When I fight for my Nancy here – adsfish I'm a dragon.

Mrs Whiff Lord you need not have been so hasty.

Friendly Do not upbraid me with your eyes Chrisante, but let these wounds assure you I endeavoured to serve you, though Hazard had the honour on't.

Wellman But ladies we'll not expose you in the camp, – a party of our men shall see you safely conducted to Madam Surelove's; 'tis but a little mile from our camp.

Friendly Let me have that honour, sir.

Chrisante No, I conjure you, let your wounds be dressed. Obey me if you love me, and Hazard shall conduct us home.

Wellman He had the toil, 'tis fit he have the recompense.

Whiff He the toil, sir. What did we stand for – cyphers?

Whimsey The very appearance I made in the front of the battle awed the enemy.

Timerous Aye, aye, let the enemy say how I mauled 'em – but, Gadzoors, I scorn to brag.

Wellman Since you've regained your honour so gloriously – I restore you to your commands, you lost by your seeming cowardice.

Dullman Valour is not always in humour, sir.

Wellman Come, gentlemen, since they're resolved to engage us, let's set our men in order to receive 'em. [*Exeunt all but the four Justices*]

Timerous Our commissions again – you must be bragging, and see what comes on't; I was modest ye see and said nothing of my prowess.

Whiff What a devil, does the Colonel think we are made of iron, continually to be beat on the anvil?

Whimsey Look, gentlemen, here's two evils – if we go we are dead men, if we stay we are hanged – and that will disorder my cravat-string – therefore the least evil is to go – and set a good face on the matter as I do – [*Goes out singing*]

V.ii

A thick wood
Enter Queen dressed like an Indian man, with a bow in her
hand and quiver at her back, Anaria her confidante disguised so too,
and about a dozen Indians led by Cavaro

Queen I tremble yet. Dost think we're safe Cavaro?

Cavaro Madam, these woods are intricate and vast, and 'twill be difficult to find us out – or, if they do, this habit will secure you from the fear of being taken.

Queen Dost think if Bacon find us he will not know me? Alas my fears and blushes will betray me.

Anaria 'Tis certain, madam, if we stay we perish; for all the wood's surrounded by the conqueror.

Queen Alas 'tis better we should perish here, than stay to expect the violence of his passion, to which my heart's too sensibly inclined.

Anaria Why do you not obey its dictates then? Why do you fly the conqueror?

Queen Not fly – not fly the murderer of my Lord?

Anaria What world, what resolution can preserve you, and what he cannot gain by soft submission, force will at last o'ercome.

Queen I wish there were in nature one excuse either by force or reason to compel me: – For, oh, Anaria – I adore this General – take from my soul a truth – till now concealed – at twelve years old – at the Pauwmungian court I saw this conqueror. I saw him young and gay as newborn spring, glorious and charming as the midday's sun. I watched his looks, and list'ned when he spoke, and thought him more than mortal.

Anaria He has a graceful form.

Queen At last a fatal match concluded was, between my lord and me. I gave my hand, but oh how far my heart was from consenting, the angry gods are witness.

Anaria 'Twas pity.

Queen Twelve tedious moons I passed in silent languishment; honour endeavouring to destroy my love, but all in vain, for still my pain returned whenever I beheld my conqueror, but now when I consider him as murderer of my Lord -[*fiercely*] I sigh and wish – some other fatal hand had given him his death – but now there's a necessity I must be brave and overcome my heart: What if I do? Ah, whither shall I fly? I have no Amazonian fire about me, all my artillery is sighs and tears, the earth my bed, and Heaven my canopy. [*Weeps; after a noise of fighting*] Hah, we are surprised. Oh, whither shall I fly? And yet methinks a certain trembling joy, 'spite of my soul, 'spite of my boasted honour, runs shivering round my heart.

Enter an Indian

Indian Madam, your out-guards are surprised by Bacon, who hews down all before him, and demands the Queen with such a voice and eyes so fierce and angry, he kills us with his looks.

Cavaro Draw up your poisoned arrows to the head, and aim them at his heart, sure some will hit.

Queen Cruel Cavaro, – would 'twere fit for me to contradict thy justice. [*Aside*]

Bacon [*within*] The Queen, ye slaves, give me the Queen and live!

He enters furiously beating back some Indians, Cavaro's party going to shoot, the Queen runs in

Queen Hold, hold, I do command ye.

Bacon flies on 'em as they shoot and miss him, and fights like a fury, and wounds the Queen in the disorder; beats them all out

Queen Hold thy commanding hand, and do not kill me, who would not hurt thee to regain my Kingdom – [*He snatches her in his arms; she reels*]

Bacon Hah – a woman's voice – what art thou? Oh, my fears!

Queen Thy hand has been too cruel to a heart – whose crime was only tender thoughts for thee.

Bacon The Queen! What is't my sacreligious hand has done?

Queen The noblest office of a gallant friend, thou'st saved my honour and hast given me death.

Bacon Is't possible! Ye unregarding gods, is't possible?

Queen Now I may love you without infamy, and please my dying heart by gazing on you.

Bacon Oh I am soft – for ever lost – I find my brain turn with the wild confusion.

Queen I faint – oh lay me gently on the earth. [*Lays her down*]

Bacon Who waits – [*Turns in rage to his men*] make of the trophies of the war a pile, and set it all on fire, that I may leap into consuming flames – while all my tents are burning round about me. [*Wildly*] Oh, thou dear prize, for which alone I toiled. [*Weeps and lies down by her*]

Enter Fearless with his sword drawn

Fearless Hah, on the earth – how do you sir?

Bacon What wouldst thou?

Fearless Wellman, with all the forces he can gather, attacks us even in our very camp. Assist us, sir, or all is lost.

Bacon Why, prithee, let him make the world his prize, I have no business with the trifle now; it now contains nothing that's worth my care, since my fair Queen – is dead, – and by my hand.

Queen So charming and obliging is thy moan, that I could wish for life to recompense it; but oh, death falls – all cold – upon my heart like mildews on the blossoms.

Fearless By Heaven, sir, this love will ruin all – rise, rise and save us yet.

Bacon Leave me, what e'er becomes of me – lose not thy share of glory – prithee, leave me.

Queen Alas, I fear, thy fate is drawing on, and I shall shortly meet thee in the clouds; till then – farewell – even death is pleasing to me, while thus – I find it in thy arms – [*Dies*]

Bacon There ends my race of glory and of life. [*An alarm at distance – continues a while*] Hah – Why should I idly whine away my life, since there are nobler ways to meet with death? – Up, up, and face him then – hark – here's the soldiers knell – and all the joys of life – with thee I bid farewell – [*Goes out.*]

The Indians bear off the body of the Queen; the alarm continues
Enter Downright, Wellman, and others swords drawn

Wellman They fight like men possessed – I did not think to have found them so prepared.

Downright They've good intelligence – but where's the rebel?

Wellman Sure he's not in the fight? Oh that it were my happy chance to meet him, that while our men look on, we might dispatch the business of the war. Come, let's fall in again now we have taken breath. [*They go out*]

Enter Dareing and Fearless hastily, with their swords drawn, meet Whimsey, Whiff, with their swords drawn, running away

Dareing How now, whither away? [*In anger*]
Whimsey Hah, Dareing here – we are pursuing of the enemy, sir, stop us not in the pursuit of glory. [*Offer to go*]
Dareing Stay – I have not seen you in my ranks today.
Whiff Lord, does your Honour take us for starters?
Fearless Yes, sirrah, and believe you are now rubbing off – confess, or I'll run you through.
Whiff Oh mercy, sir, mercy, we'll confess.
Whimsey What will you confess? – we were only going behind yon hedge to untruss a point; that's all.
Whiff Aye, your Honours will smell out the truth if you keep us here long.
Dareing Here, carry the prisoners to my tent. [*Exeunt soldiers with Whimsey & Whiff*]

Enter Ranter without a hat, and sword drawn; Dareing angrily goes the other way

Ranter A pox of all ill luck, how came I to lose Dareing in the fight? Ha – who's here? – Dullman and Timerous dead – the rogues are counterfeits – I'll see what moveables they have about them, all's lawful prize in war. [*Takes their money, watches and rings; goes out*]
Timerous What, rob the dead? – Why, what will this villanous world come to?

Clashing of swords just as they were going to rise; enter Hazard bringing in Ranter

Hazard Thou couldst expect no other fate young man, thy hands are yet too tender for a sword.
Ranter Thou look'st like a good natured fellow – use me civilly, and Dareing shall ransom me.
Hazard Doubt not a generous treatment. [*Goes out*]
Dullman So, the coast is clear, I desire to remove my quarters to some place of more safety – [*They rise and go off*]

Enter Wellman and soldiers hastily

Wellman 'Twas this way Bacon fled. Five hundred pound for him who finds the rebel. [*Go out*]

Scene changes to a wood
Enter Bacon and Fearless, with their swords drawn, all bloody

Bacon 'Tis just, ye gods! That when you took the prize for which I fought, fortune and you should all abandon me.
Fearless Oh fly, sir, to some place of safe retreat, for there's no mercy to be hoped if taken. What will you do? I know we are pursued. By Heaven, I will not die a shameful death.
Bacon Oh they'll have pity on thy youth and bravery, but I'm above their pardon.

A noise is heard within: This way – this way – hay – hollow.

Fearless Alas, sir, we're undone – I'll see which way they they take. [*Exit*]
Bacon So near! Nay then to my last shift. [*Undoes the pommel of his sword.*] Come, my good poison, like that of Hannibal, long I have borne a noble remedy for all the ills of life. [*Takes poison*] I have too long survived my Queen and glory, those two bright stars that influenced my life are set to all eternity. [*Lies down*]

Enter Fearless, runs to Bacon and looks on his sword

Fearless – Hah – what have ye done?
Bacon Secured myself from being a public spectacle upon the common theatre of death.

Enter Dareing and soldiers

Dareing Victory, victory, they fly, they fly, where's the victorious General?
Fearless Here – taking his last adieu.
Dareing Dying? Then wither all the laurels on my brows, for I shall never triumph more in war, where is the wounds?
Fearless From his own hand by what he carried here, believing we had lost the victory.
Bacon And is the enemy put to flight my hero? [*Grasps his neck*]
Dareing All routed horse and foot. I placed an ambush, and while they were pursuing you, my men fell on behind and won the day.
Bacon Thou almost makes me wish to live again, if I could live now fair

Semernia's dead – but oh – the baneful drug is just and kind and hastens
me away – now while you are victors make a peace – with the English
Council – and never let ambition – love – or interest make you forget as I
have done – your duty – and allegiance – farewell – a long farewell –
[*Dies embracing their necks*]
Dareing So fell the Roman Cassius – by mistake –

Enter soldiers with Dunce, Timerous and Dullman

Soldier An't please, Your Honour, we took these men running away.
Dareing Let 'em loose – the wars are at an end, see where the General
lies – that great souled man, no private body e'er contained a nobler, and
he that could have conquered all America, finds only here his scanty length
of earth – go bear the body to his own pavilion. [*Soldiers go out with the
body*] Though we are conquerers we submit to treat, and yield upon conditions. You, Mr Dunce, shall bear our articles to the Council –
Dunce With joy I will obey you.
Timerous Good General, let us be put in the agreement.
Dareing You shall be obliged – [*Exeunt Dareing, Dunce, Dullman and
Timerous; as Fearless goes out, a soldier meets him*]
Soldier What does your Honour intend to do with Whimsey and Whiff,
who are condemned by a Council of War?

Enter Dareing, Dullman, Timerous, Fearless and officers

Dareing You come too late, gentlemen, to be put into the articles, nor am
I satisfied you're worthy of it.
Dullman Why did not you, sir, see us lie dead in the field?
Dareing Yes, but I see no wound about you.
Timerous We were stunned with being knocked down. Gadzoors, a man
may be killed with the butt end of a musket, as soon as with the point of a
sword. [*Enter Dunce*]
Dunce The Council, sir, wishes you health and happiness, and sends you
these signed by their hands – [*Gives papers; Dareing reads*] that you shall
have a general pardon for yourself and friends; that you shall have all new
Commissions, and Dareing to command as General; that you shall have
free leave to inter your dead General, in Jamestown, and to ratify this – we
will meet you at Madam Surelove's house which stands between the armies,
attended only by our officers. The Council's noble and I'll wait upon
them. *Exit Dunce*

V.iii

A grove near Madam Surelove's
Enter Surelove weeping, Wellman, Chrisante, Mrs Flirt, Ranter
as before, Downright, Hazard, Friendly, Boozer, Bragg

Wellman How long, madam, have you heard the news of Colonel Surelove's death?
Surelove By a vessel last night arrived.
Wellman You should not grieve when men so old pay their debt to nature. You are too fair not to have been reserved for some young love's arms.
Hazard I dare not speak – but give me leave to hope.
Surelove The way to oblige me to't, is never more to speak to me of love till I shall think it fit –
[*Wellman speaks to Downright*]
Wellman Come, you shan't grant it – 'tis a hopeful youth.
Downright You are too much my friend to be denied – Chrisante, do you love Friendly? Nay, do not blush – till you have done a fault, your loving him is none – Here take her, young man, and with her all my fortune – when I am dead, sirrah – not a groat before – unless to buy ye baby clouts.
Friendly He merits not this treasure, sir, can wish for more.

Enter Dareing, Fearless, Dunce and officers; they meet Wellman and
Downright who embrace 'em; Dullman and Timerous stand

Dareing Can you forgive us, sir, our disobedience?
Wellman Your offering peace, while yet you might command it, has made such kind impressions on us, that now you may command your propositions; your pardons are all sealed and new commissions.
Dareing I'm not ambitious of that honour, sir, but in obedience will accept your goodness, but, sir, I hear I have a young friend taken prisoner by Captain Hazard whom I entreat you'll render me,
Hazard Sir – here I resign him to you. [*Gives him Ranter*]
Ranter Faith, General, you left me but scurvily in battle.
Dareing That was to see how well you could shift for yourself; now I find you can bear the brunt of a campaign you are a fit wife for a soldier.
All A woman – Ranter!
Hazard Faith, madam, I should have given you kinder quarter if I had known my happiness.
Mrs Flirt I have a humble petition to you, sir.
Surelove In which we all join.

Mrs Flirt An't please you, sir, Mr Dunce has long made love to me and on promise of marriage has [*Simpers*]
Downright What has he, Mrs Flirt?
Mrs Flirt Only been a little familiar with my person, sir –
Wellman Do you hear Parson – you must marry Mrs Flirt.
Dunce How, sir, a man of my coat, sir, marry a brandymonger?
Wellman Of your calling, you mean, a farrier and no parson – [*Aside to him*] she'll leave her trade – and spark it above all the ladies at church. No more – take her and make her honest.

Enter Whimsey and Whiff stripped; cries

Wellman Bless me, what have we here?
Whimsey Why, an't like, Your Honours, we were taken by the enemy – hah Dareing here and Fearless?
Fearless How now – gentlemen were not you two condemned to be shot for running from your colours?
Downright From your colours.
Fearless Yes, sir, they were both listed in my regiment.
Downright Then we must hang them for deserting us.
Whimsey So out of the frying pan – you know where, brother –
Whiff Aye – he that's born to be hanged – you know the rest, a pox of these proverbs.
Wellman I know ye well – you're all rank cowards, but once more we forgive ye, your places in the Council shall be supplied by these gentlemen of sense and honour. The Governor when he comes shall find the country in better hands than he expects to find it.
Whimsey A very fair discharge.
Whiff I'm glad 'tis no worse, I'll home to my Nancy.
Dullman Have we exposed our lives and fortunes for this?
Timerous Gadzoors, I never thrived since I was a statesman, left planting, and fell to promising and lying, I'll to my old trade again, bask under the shade of my own tobacco, and drink my punch in peace.
Wellman Come, my brave youths, let all our forces meet,
To make this country happy, rich, and great;
Let scanted Europe see that we enjoy
Safer repose, and larger worlds than they.

NOTES

1. Text: *Cabala, Mysteries of State in Letters of the Great Ministers of K. James and K. Charles. Wherein much of the public manage of affairs is related*, 1654, 4o.
Wing C183, UMI microfilm reel 57.
Copy-text: British Library Thomason Tracts E.221 (3), p. 260.
Tilbury] Town on the north bank of the River Thames, where the English army amassed to defend the country against the threatened invasion by the Spanish Armada.
published 1654] Although this speech was delivered by Elizabeth I in 1588, the text itself is recorded by a third party and not published until sixty-six years later. It is related in a letter from Dr Leonel Sharp to the Duke of Buckingham (257–62). The manuscript version is reproduced in Marcus, Mueller and Rose (2000, 325–6), and significant variants have been noted below.
we] It is customary for English monarchs to refer to themselves in the plural, comprising their personal self and their political self. The manuscript version employs first person singular here.
And therefore . . . amongst you all] MS version reads 'Wherefore I am come among you at this time but for my recreation and pleasure, being resolved, in the midst and heat of the battle to live and die amongst you all' (Marcus, Mueller and Rose 2000, 326).
Parma] Alessandro Farnese, Duke of Parma, leader of the Spanish campaign on the European mainland.
Spain] King Philip II of Spain.
Lieutenant General] Robert Dudley, Earl of Leicester, Elizabeth I's favourite.
Not doubting . . . of my people] MS version reads 'Not doubting but by your concord in the camp and valour in the field and your obedience to myself and my general, we shall shortly have a famous victory over these enemies of my God and of my kingdom' (Marcus, Mueller and Rose 2000, 326).

2. Text: *Her Protection for Women*, 1589, 4o.
STC 644, UMI microfilm reel 165.
Copy-text: UMI microfilm of sole extant copy at Henry E. Huntington Library, sigs. A4r to Bv; B3r to B3v; Cr to C2r; C4v to Dr.
late surfeiting lover] Anger is writing in response to a misogynistic publication entitled *Boke his Surfeit in Love* (now lost).
Venerians] Lechers
choleric] Angry.

Ne] Nor.

a-railing] Attacking verbally.

Paul's steeple and Charing Cross] Ecclesiastical landmarks in London

Aetna] Volcano dominating town of Catania in Sicily.

Boreas] Classical god of the North Wind.

lists] Limits.

last] Shoemaker's implement for stretching leather.

silly] In this period it means innocent and simple, rather than frivolous and stupid.

Apollo] Classical god of the sun, music, poetry and medicine; often figured as the ideal of masculine beauty.

cravened] Bereft of courage, as in a fighting cock no longer able to face his opponent.

jades] Worn out and, therefore, ill-tempered horses; also used in this period as an insulting term for women.

Venus] Classical goddess of love, mother of Cupid and renowned for her great beauty.

Hesiodus] Hesiod, Greek poet of the 8th century BC, author of the two earliest Classical accounts of the creation, *Theogony* and *Works and Days*, in which he claims that women were sent by the gods as a punishment to man.

noddies] Foolish individuals.

Clytemnestra] Wife of Agamemnon, leader of the Greek troops in the Trojan War. She and her lover Aegisthus murdered Agamemnon on his return from the war.

Ariadne] Princess of Crete who helped the Athenian, Theseus, against the interest of her father, King Minos. Theseus had come to face the double danger of the fierce half-human, half bull Minotaur, who lived in a complex labyrinth out of which no human being could escape. Ariadne gave Theseus a ball of string, which he unravelled on his journey through the labyrinth, whilst she kept hold of the other end. Thus, having defeated the Minotaur, Theseus found his way out easily and took the waiting Ariadne away with him.

Delilah] Woman who discovered and the secret that Samson's strength lay in his hair (Judges 16:4–30).

Jezebel] Pagan wife of King Ahab who was torn to pieces by dogs because she refused to change her religion (1 Kings 22).

Nero] Claudius Tiberius Nero, 1st century Roman Emperor famous for his appetites and excesses.

In principio] At first.

huswifery] The art of good housekeeping.

Malum malo additum efficit malum peius] 'Evil added to evil makes a greater evil'.

Magnificat] Hymn sung by the Virgin Mary after the Annunciation (Luke 1:46–55). Implicitly, this hymn is without fault, and to seek to correct it is an act of great arrogance.

sithence] Since.

ex confessio] 'By their own confession.'

Contra principium non est disputandum] 'There is no argument against principle'.

Primum est optimum] 'First is best'.

Non plus] A state of confusion.

lawns] Fine linen or cotton fabrics.

drawn-works] Pieces of cloth decorated by drawing out threads to make a pattern.

periwigs] Fashionable headdress of false hair.

galled . . . winch] Proverbial. A 'gall' was a sore caused by chafing, and 'winch' means to kick out.

peradventure] Perhaps.

3. Text: *A Discourse of Life and Death. Written in French by Ph. Mornay . . . done in English by the Countess of Pembroke*, 1592, 4o.
STC 18138, UMI microfilm reel 440.
Copy-text: British Library C.57.d.16, sigs. A2r–A3r; Cr–C2r; C2v–C3v; D2r–D3v; Ev–E3r.

Ph. Mornay] Philippe Mornay, Seigneur du Plessis-Marly, friend of Sir Philip Sidney, and author of the original text in 1576.

published 1592] A note at the end of the text says 'The 13th of May 1590 at Wilton'.

descried] Perceived from a distance.

Penelope's web] Wife of Odysseus, one of Greek heroes in the Trojan War, Penelope remained faithful to her husband during his twenty-year absence from their home in Ithaca. She was plagued by suitors who encroached ruinously upon her hospitality. To stave off their attentions, she promised to answer them once she had finished weaving a funeral shroud for her father-in-law, Laertes. Each night she unpicked the work that she had done during the day.

fain] Rather.

travails] Labours.

impostume] Abscess.

jostling] 1592: iustling

hap] Luck (good or bad).

vizard] Mask

Hecate] Goddess of magic and spells, she is said to preside over crossroads, an ideal location for sorcery.

ere] Before.

retrait] Military signal for retiring.

4. Text: Speech at the Dissolving of Parliament, printed in John Stow, *The Annals of England*, London, 1615.
STC 23338, UMI microfilm reel 1434.
Copy-text: British Library shelfmark L.7.g.11, p. 765.

Lords . . . House] The two Houses of Parliament. At this time the Lords comprised senior members of the aristocracy and clergy, whereas the Commons were elected by a small elite of wealthy landowners.

commonweal] Common good.

travail] Work, effort; 1615: travell.

but one only excepted] that is, King Henry VIII.

doubt] Suspicion.

that King] Philip II of Spain

so mighty a Protector] that is, God.

returning into the country] The return of MPs to their constituencies.

maritane shire] Maritime county, that is, one which borders the sea.

bands] Troops of armed men.

want . . . rooms] that is, deficiency of numbers is to be made up by recruiting new soldiers to replace those no longer present.

5. Text: *Her majesty's most princely answer delivered by herself at the court at Whitehall, on the last day of November 1601, when the speaker of the Lower House of Parliament, assisted with the greatest part of the knights and burgesses, had presented their humble thanks for her free and gracious favour in preventing and reforming of sundry grievances by abuse of many grants commonly called monopolies. The same being taken verbatim in writing by A. B., as near as he could possibly set it down.* London, 1601.
STC7578, UMI microfilm reel 783.
Copy-text: Emmanuel College, Cambridge, shelfmark 330.4.36

Mr Speaker] The presiding officer of the House of Commons.

ere] Before.

conceits] Notions, ideas, thoughts.

aught] 1601: ought.

thrallers] Enslavers.

glozing] Deceptively flattering.

pass] Care.

we think . . . we list] that is, whatever we choose to do is lawful.

vaunting] Boastful.

6. Text: 'A Dialogue between two shepherds, Thenot and Piers, in Praise of Astrea', in Francis Davison (ed.), *A Poetical Rapsody containing diverse sonnets, odes, elegies, madrigals, and other poesies, both in rhyme and measured verse*, 1602.
STC 6373, UMI microfilm 643.
Copy-text: Bodleian Library Mal. 384, sigs. B5r to B6r.

Title] According to the original, this dialogue was 'made by the excellent Lady, the Lady Mary Countess of Pembroke, at the Queen's Majesty's being at her house at Anno 15 . . .' (B5r).

Astrea] A complimentary epithet for Queen Elizabeth I, Astrea was the personification of Justice in Classical mythology. She operated on earth during the Golden Age (see note to Text 8, p. 441) engendering justice and virtue amongst mankind. When wickedness entered the world, she was transformed into the constellation Virgo.

Momus] Classical personification of sarcasm and censure.

there] First edition has 'three'; I have retained the emendation of the 1611 edition.

manly palm . . . maiden bay] Palm and bay were emblems of victory and poetic excellence. Hannay, Kinnamon and Brennan (1998, 320) note that these two metaphors praise the Queen's two bodies, as monarch and virgin.

7. Text: *Salve Deus Rex Judaeorum. Containing, 1 The Passion of Christ. 2 Eve's Apology in defence of Women. 3 The Tears of the Daughters of Jerusalem. 4. The Salutation and Sorrow of the Virgin Mary. With diverse other things not unfit to be read.* 1611, 4o.

STC 15227, UMI microfilm reel 1929.

'To the Virtuous Reader' copy-text: Bodleian Library shelfmark Vet. A2 f99, sig. f3

Sisera] 1611: Cesarus.

Esther] 1611: Hester.

Salve Deus Rex Judaeorum copy-text: British Library shelfmark C.71.h.15, sigs Ar to Hv.

sith] Since.

Cynthia] Complimentary reference to Queen Elizabeth I, calling her by one of the names of the chaste goddess of the moon.

great Countess] Margaret Clifford, Countess of Cumberland and chief dedicatee of Lanyer's volume.

pardon, madam] Reference to a supposed commission to write 'To Cookeham'.

Phoebe] Personification of the moon.

Ne] Nor.

Bridegroom] Reference to Christ as husband of the Church. Woods (1993, 54) identifies the source of this as Christ's parable of the bridegroom (Matt. 25:1–13) and the Song of Solomon.

Froward] Perverse, ill-tempered.

tabernacle] Temple.

turtle-dove] Symbol of never-failing love.

that Queen's for whom proud Troy was sold] Helen of Troy (see note to Text 2)

Lucrece . . . Tarquin] A chaste roman matron raped by the King's son. Lucrece reported the rape to her husband and then committed suicide. This led to an insurrection by Junius Brutus and the subsequent expulsion of Tarquin's family Rome.

Antonius . . . Cleopatra . . . Octavia] Mark Antony, one of the triumvirate of Rome (with Octavius and Lepidus) c. 42 BC, spurned his wife Octavia, sister of Octavius, in favour of the Egyptian Queen Cleopatra. This led to war with Octavius and, ultimately, Antony's suicide after his defeat at the Battle of Actium, c. 31 BC. Antony lost at Actium as a result of pursuing Cleopatra's ship, which fled from the site of the battle.

Rosamund] Mistress of the 12th century King Henry II, supposedly poisoned by Queen Eleanor of Aquitaine.

Matilda] Virtuous woman pursued by King John in the 13th century.

Icarus] Son of the artist and early engineer Daedalus. They escaped from incarceration by using sets of wings designed by Daedalus and made from wax and feathers. Against his father's advice, Icarus flew too close to the sun, the wax melted, the wings fell apart and Icarus plunged to his death.

silly] See note to Text 2, p. 434.

mewed up] Confined.

Phaeton] Semi-divine offspring of the Sun, he asked to drive his father's chariot across the Heavens. The task was too difficult for him and he was struck down by a thunderbolt when his incompetence threatened the Earth and the Heavens.

widow's mite] Proverbial symbol of great personal generosity (Mark 12:41–4; Luke 21:1–4).

Gethsemane] Garden where Jesus spent his last night and where he was betrayed by Judas Iscariot.

sons of Zedebus] James and John.

glass] Hour-glass, a metaphor for a person's life-span.

David . . . Solomon . . . his wilful son] David, his son Solomon and grandson Rehoboam turned from God during their reigns (1 Chron. and 2 Chron.).

Thy betrayer] Judas Iscariot.

trothless] Lacking integrity.

bills] Long staff with a hook-shaped blade.

ruth] Pity.

Egypt's King] God sent down successive plagues on Egypt, the last and worst being the death of the firstborn, until the King agreed to let the Jewish slaves leave the country under the leadership of Moses (Exodus 8–13).

owly] Short-sighted.

wicked caitiff] Judas Iscariot; caitiff means wretch or coward.

imbrue] Stain.

witness thy wife] See Matt. 27:19.

Saul] Saul, King of Israel, planned to murder David, whom God had chosen as his successor (1 Sam. 18).

robes of honour] Scarlet robes, a symbol of royalty, mockingly placed on Jesus by Herod's soldiers.

Jesse flower] A 'Jesse Tree' representing the geanealogy of Christ as descended from the root of Jesse was a popular church ornament at this time (1 Sam. 16; Isa. 10:1).

Gabriel] Archangel who delivered the Annunciation (Luke 1:26–30).

house of Jacob] Jacob, also called Israel, was the father of the Jewish race (Gen. 25–6).

Simon of Cyrene] See Matt. 27:3.

Golgotha] Literally, the place of skulls (Matt. 27:33).

Joseph] Joseph of Arimathea (Mark 15:43).

Marys] Mary Magdalene and Mary the mother of James (Mark 16:1–4).

keys] Saint Peter is traditionally the gatekeeper of Heaven.

spouse of Christ] Margaret, Countess of Cumberland. See above note

Scythian women] Woods notes (1993, 114) that Lanyer credits the women with the victory gained by Alexander the Great over King Darius of Persia in 331 BC.

laurel] Symbol of poetic excellence and of victory.

Deborah . . . Joachim's wife] See Biblical references in 'To the Virtuous Reader'.

Ethiopian Queen . . . Queen of Sheba] See 1 Kings 10:1–13.

niceness] Fastidiousness.

Jasper] Bright jewel featured in Revelations 4:3.

winged beasts so full of eyes] Seraphim described in Revelations 4:8.

Phoenix] Brilliantly coloured bird, connected with sun-worship in Ancient Egypt and a symbol of resurrection and rebirth. Only one Phoenix existed at a time and so the bird was the source of its own birth and death. The old Phoenix gathered together spices and aromatic plants to make itself a funeral pyre, which was set alight when the sun paused at the sumptuous vision of the doomed bird. The new Phoenix was born out of the cooling ashes.

fishermen] The disciples Peter, James and John.

manna] Food which miraculously appeared to sustain the Israelites in the desert after they had escaped enslavement in Egypt.

Stephen] First Christian martyr, stoned to death (Acts 7:55–60).

Laurence] Christian martyr burned to death.

Andrew] Martyred by crucifixion.

by the sword . . . his head] John the Baptist, beheaded at the behest of Herod's step-daughter and her mother.

Arctic Star] North Star or Pole Star, the key astronomical guide for sailors.

'To Cookeham' copy-text: British Library shelfmark C.71.h.15, sigs. H2r to Ir.

Cookeham] 'Crown manor leased to the Countess of Cumberland's brother, William Russell of Thornhaugh, where the Countess resided periodically until 1605 or shortly after' (Woods 1993, 130).

the Muses] Nine female figures in Classical mythology, who presided over the creative arts. Their names and responsibilities were: Melpomene (tragedy); Thalia (comedy); Clio (history); Erato (poetry accompanied by the flute); Terpsichore (dance); Urania (astronomy); Polyhymnia (hymns and sacred verse); Euterpe (poetry accompanied by the lyre); Calliope (epic poetry). However, the term 'muse' could also refer to an individual poet's particular source of inspiration, be it imaginary or an actual person.

Pallas] 1613: palace.

Pallas] Pallas Athena, Ancient Greek goddess of wisdom, the arts and war.

Philomela] Name for the nightingale, from the name of the Princess raped by her brother-in-law Tereus. He cut out her tongue to prevent her telling his wife Procne but Philomela figured her misfortunes in a piece of needlework. She and her sister Procne gained revenge on Tereus by serving him the body of his son at dinner. When he pursued the women, the gods turned them into birds. Procne became a swallow and Philomela a nightingale. Sometimes spelt without the terminal 'a'.

descry] Perceive from a distance.

Phoebus] Personification of the sun.

mount his holy hill] Reference to Moses receiving the ten commandments (Exodus 24:13–18 and 25:32–3).

often sing] Reference to David's authorship of the Psalms.

Joseph . . . pinèd brethren] Joseph, second youngest son of Jacob, was sold into slavery in Egypt. He rose to power, which enabled him to provide his family with grain during seven year famine (Gen. 45).

that sweet lady] 'Anne, Countess of Dorset, the Countess of Cumberland's daughter. She was the product of two great families, the Cliffords, earls of Cumberland (on her father's side) and the Russells, earls of Bedford (on her mother's side); she married into a third, the Sackvilles, earls of Dorset' (Woods 1993, 134).

Fortune] Personification of the concept, partly drawn from Classical mythology, is often figured as a blind and, hence, inconstant woman. The vagaries of Fortune are also expressed as a constantly turning wheel.

swarthy, rivelled ryne] Dark, roughly textured bark.

Echo] In Classical mythology, a nymph deprived of the power of speech by Juno, except for the ability to repeat the last words spoken to her.

8. Text: *The Tragedy of Mariam, the Fair Queen of Jewry*, 1613, 4o.
   STC 4613, UMI microfilm reel 830.
   Copy-text: Henry E. Huntington Library, shelfmark 80841.

his son by Doris] 1613: his sonne by Salome.

Idumean] Native of Idumea and a descendant of Esau, or Edom. As the Idumeans, or Edomites, were not descended from Jacob they were not considered true Jews and so the term is employed pejoratively by Mariam and Alexandra to refer to Herod and his family.

Hircanus] John Hircanus, last of the Hasmonean dynasty.

Antony] Mark Antony. See note to Text 7, p. 437.

Caesar] Octavius, later Augustus, Caesar. See note to Text 7, p. 437.

Rome's last hero . . . Pompey's life was gone] Weller and Ferguson (1994, 153) suggest that this refers to Julius Caesar's reaction to the dead Pompey's severed head, detailed in Plutarch's *Lives*.

loveliest] 1613: lowlyest.

ruth] Pity.

mine] 1613: maide.

vaunt-courier] A messenger sent to prepare the way or announce the arrival of another.

Edomite . . . Judah's race] Alexander details Mariam's descent from Jacob and David to confirm her position in the royal dynasty of Judea as one of birthright rather than marriage.

famed] 1613: fain'd.

ere] Before.

caitiff] Wretch.

blood is red] Edom means 'red stuff'. Esau earned the name when he sold his birthright to his brother Jacob for a red venison stew (Gen. 25:29–34). Herod, like his ancestor, craves red stuff but this is blood rather than stew.

ephod] Jewish priestly garment.

Alexander] The references to 'Alexander' are confusing. Both Mariam's son and father were called Alexander and so the Alexander of whom Mariam speaks is her son, whereas Alexandra is speaking of her husband, Mariam's father.

Felicity] The personification of good fortune.

Table] A board on which portraits of Mariam and Aristobolus were painted.

she that fled] See note to Text 7, p. 437.

seek] 1613: leeke.

choler] Anger.

fumish] Irascible.

twit] Taunt.

no boot] No use.

miss her merit] Get her just deserts.

lets] Hindrances.

Moses' laws] Divorce was a male privilege under Mosaic law (Deut. 24:1–4).

O more] 1613: a more.

proper] Own.

Obodas] Slothful king of Arabia.

gratitude] Favour, grace. This meaning is chiefly Scottish and now obsolete.

wisest Prince . . . her husband's head] Solomon, in Proverbs 12:4.

Joshua . . . Gibonites] See Joshua 9:23.

swim] 1613: swine.

the holy Ark] The Ark of the Covenant, which held the two tablets of stone bearing the Ten Commandments.

land of Ham] Egypt. The Egyptians were descended from Noah's second son, Ham.

Except] Unless.

fond] Foolish.

fain] Rather.

If] 1613: 0f.

for expectation of variety] Because she did not expect to be.

Golden Age] Classical equivalent of the Christian pre-lapsarian world, described by Hesiod; also used figurately for any idealised bygone era.

Jesse's son and valiant Jonathan] David and Jonathan, whose friendship was opposed by King Saul, Jonathan's father (1 Sam. 19:1–10).

quick buried] Buried alive.

overpassed] 1613: operpast.

fear] 1613: leare.

falchion] A broad sword.

Octavius] Octavius Caesar, later the Emperor Augustus Caesar.

phys'nomy] Physiognomy, that is, the face viewed as an index to the mind or character.

dastard] An ignoble coward.

stoop] 1613: scope.

trumpet's . . . ground] Annual Jewish festivals, such as the Passover and the offering of the first fruits.

trophy] A structure erected on a battlefield and hung with riches or spoils.

whilom] Previous.

it skills not how] It does not matter how.

exception] 1613: expectation.

list] Wish.

list] Listen.

too fast] 1613: so fast.

bate] Lessen.

blast] Something transient.

sped] Served by.

attend] Expect.

tuition] Protection, care.

Ophir] Legendary place in Arabia, where fine gold, perfume and precious stones were to be found (1 Kings 9:28 and 10:11).

Tyrus] A city famous for its silk, glass and purple dye industry. In 63 BC, Tyre came under the rule of Mark Antony, who demanded the return of Jewish property taken by the Tyrians and forbade any damage to be done to the city.

I] 1613: he.

our] 1613: his.

detect] Expose to scandal.

stickler] Mediator.

peculiar] Particular to one person only.

Joshua-like the season stays] See Joshua 10:12–14.

Ediles] Two subordinate officials of the plebs, who superintended the common temple (aedes) and the cult of the plebs, that of Ceres. They also took responsibility for urban adminstration and the public games.

Livia] Livia Drusilla, wife of Octavius Caesar.

Phasaelus] Herod's brother, who killed himself when taken as a prisoner of war

froward] Peevish, perverse of humour.

rate] Scold.

poison] 1613: passion.

Hyssop] A plant used in Jewish purification rites.

plain] Honest.

wheel of Fortune] See note to Text 7, p. 440.

cozen] Trick, dupe.

heav'nly] 1613: heavy.

sot] Fool.

Achitophel] Achitophel joined forces with Absalom against his father, David. When Achitophel's counsels were rejected by Absalom, he hanged himself (2 Sam. 17:23).

base mechanic traffic] The lowest form of commercial transaction.

our] 1613: your.

Cham's servile curse] This appears to be a conflation of more than one biblical curse, that of Eve for her transgression in Eden (Gen. 4:16) and that of Ham, or Cham, cursed to servitude after bringing his brothers to observe their father Noah drunk and naked (Gen. 9:21–5).

endued] Invested.

Die quoth you] 1613: words attributed to Herod.

refell] Repel.

rebate] Blunt.

quondam] Previously.

limes] A reference to catching with birdlime. This sticky substance was put on trees and bushes to catch birds.

sable] Heraldic term for black.

prate] Chatter.

The holy David . . . a queen] See 2 Sam. 11.

the wisest man of men] Solomon, who had a prodigious harem (1 Kings 11:3).

Asuerus . . . the Persian throne] See Esther 2.

Ate] Goddess of evil.

As] 1613: At.

prove] Try.

Paphos' queen] Venus, goddess of love, who was born out of the sea foam, off the island of Paphos.

drawn] In the first instance, 'taken away', in the second, 'manipulated'.

hap] Luck (good or bad).

Sara's lap] Sara was the wife of Abraham; her lap is perhaps the equivalent of Abraham's bosom, denoting Heaven.

cup of wrath] See Jeremiah 25:9–38.

Gerarim] Cerasano and Wynne-Davies (1996, 194) gloss this as Mount Gerazim, the mountain upon which Abraham was instructed to sacrifice Isaac (Gen. 21–22).

Phoenix] See note to Text 7, p. 439.

pick-thank] One who curries favour.

Go on] 1613: words attributed to Nuntio.

host] Army.

Armenian guide] Perhaps referering to the duplicity of Armenia Minor at the time of the play's events.

moi'ty] Contraction of moiety, a part.

grandam] Female ancestor.

Abel] Son of Adam and Eve, slain by his brother Cain (Gen. 3:2–25).

grandam Sara . . . beldame age] See Gen. 20:1–7.

Saturn] Father of Jupiter, associated with wisdom and melancholy.

Jove] Classical King of the gods, alternatively known as Jupiter.

Leda] Woman seduced by Jove in the shape of a swan.

Mars] Classical god of war.

Venus] See note to Text 2, p. 434.

Sol] The sun.

physic's god] Apollo. See note to Text 2, p. 434.

empiric] An untrained practitioner or quack.

queen of love] Venus; see note to Text 2, p. 434.

Hermes] In Classical mythology, messenger of the gods, famed for his wit.

Paphian goddess] Venus. See note above.

Mercurius] Hermes. See note above.

Cynthia] Goddess of the moon.

stained the virgin earth] Cain. See note above.

9. Text: *A Muzzle for Melastomus, the cynical baiter of, and foul mouthed barker against, Evah's Sex* 1617, 4o.
   STC 23058, UMI microfilm reel 939
   Copy-text: Bodleian Library shelfmark 40 L 69 (4) Art., pp. 3 to 13
   Melastomus] Slanderer, literally 'Black-mouth'.
   Ironica] Lewalski (1996, 14) identifies this as figure of speech termed the 'dry mock' by George Puttenham in *The Art of English Poesy*, 1598.
   Saint Augustine] Christian writer in the 4th and early 5th centuries and Bishop of Hippo in Roman Africa, he is seen as one of the 'fathers' of the Early Church.
   Hevah] Eve.

Eusebius] Greek Christian writer in the 3rd and 4th centuries, his *Ecclesiastical History* is credited as first history of the Early Church.

Cephas] Alternative name for the Apostle Peter.

Ecclesiastes] 21st book of the Old Testament.

First, the efficient cause . . .] Lewalski (1996, 17) identified the causes as those laid down in Aristotle's *Physics* 2.3. The efficient cause is the agent; the material cause is the matter; the formal cause is the pattern; and the final cause is the end or aim.

10. Text: *Pamphilia to Amphilanthus*, in *The Countess of Montgomery's Urania*, 1621, folio.
STC 26051, UMI microfilm reel 980.
Copy-text: Bodleian Library shelfmark M 5.6 (2) Art., sigs. Aaaar to Ffff4v.

Venus] See note to Text 2, p. 434.

hie] Hasten.

willow] Symbol of the unrequited lover.

Sir God, your boyship] Disdainful mode of address to Cupid.

contraries] Properties of hot, cold, wet and dry; in combination these made up the four humours, which were thought to govern the human condition. See note to Text 19, p. 453.

worth] Pritchard (1996, 36) suggests a pun on 'Wroth' here and elsewhere in the poems.

list] Wishes.

lightsome] Radiant.

vade] Fade.

Phoebus] Personification of the sun.

Mars] See note to Text 8, p. 443; also the name of the red planet.

Fortune] See note to Text 7, p. 440.

for] 1621: forth. MS emendation in Wroth's own copy, taken from facsimile reprint (Roberts 1996).

ere] Before.

descried] Perceived from a distance.

a biding crave] Ask for leave to stay.

gloze] Flattery.

room] Place.

Argus] Mythological figure with a multitude of eyes, some of which stayed open even when he slept. He was employed by Hera to keep watch over Io, one of Zeus's lovers, but Hermes used his magic to lull Argus into shutting all of his eyes. Io escaped and Hera, in her anger, turned Argus into a peacock, hence the 'eyes' in a peacock's tail.

Goodwins] Sand banks off the east coast of Kent.

Diana] Classical goddess of the moon, famed for her chastity and, therefore, a natural opposite to Venus.

springing] 1621: Spring. MS emendation in Wroth's own copy, taken from facsimile reprint (Roberts 1996).

cozen] Trick, dupe.

travail] Labour.

thread of love] Reference to Ariadne's method of helping Theseus. See note to Text 2, p. 434.

impostures] Deceptions.

Silvia] Generic name for a wood nymph.

myrtle] Evergreen shrub sacred to Venus and, hence, an emblem of love.

Philomel] Nightingale. See note to Text 7, p. 439.

Popish law] Catholic doctrine.

Juno] In Classical mythology, the Queen of the gods, who also presided over women in childbirth. She was the wife of Jupiter and known for her envy of Jupiter's many lovers.

Jove . . .Jupiter] See note to Text 8, p. 443.

Genius] In Classical mythology, the presiding spirit connected with a place or institution.

11. Text: *A Chain of Pearl, or A Memorial of the Peerless Graces, and Heroic Virtues of Queen Elizabeth, of Glorious Memory*, 1630, 4o.
STC 20388, UMI microfilm reel 971.
Copy-text: Microfilm of Henry E. Huntington Library copy, pp. 1 to 3; 6 to 7; 9 to 10.

Mary] Elizabeth's half-sister and predecessor, Mary I.

maugre] Despite.

Romist] Roman Catholic.

Bull] Edict issued in February 1570 by Pope Pius V, excommunicating Elizabeth.

Felton] John Felton posted a copy of the Bull on the Bishop of London's gate.

Northumberland] Thomas Percy, 7th Earl of Northumberland.

Westmoreland] Charles Neville, 6th Earl of Westmoreland.

moe] More.

In open field] Reference to the rebellion of the Northern Earls in 1569.

recusants] Those, especially Roman Catholics, who refuse to attend Church of England services.

banged] Greer et al. (1988, 86) gloss this as Elizabeth's Act of 1571 which made the giving of absolution by Catholic priests punishable by death.

Bull was baited] Pun on the popular contemporary sport of bull-baiting, where a tethered bull was attacked by dogs.

golden bridle of Bellerophon] A hero in Classical mythology, Bellerophon was given this magical bridle, which tamed the winged horse Pegasus; here a symbol of self-restraint.

Siren] Female monster in Classical mythology, whose enchanting voice lured sailors and their ships off course to their destruction.

the King her brother] Edward VI.

momentany] Transitory.

Golden Age] See note to Text 8, p. 441.

Parry] Thomas Parry, Elizabeth's servant during the reign of Edward VI, who implicated her in plots to depose the King.

great Henry] Henry VIII.

Virginia] American colony named in honour of Elizabeth, originally founded in 1585.

Spain's King] Philip II.

distaff] Cleft stick used for spinning thread; symbolic of domestic (and, hence, traditionally feminine) work. The female dynastic line is referred to as the 'distaff' side.

12. Text: *A True Copy of the Petition of the Gentlewomen, and Tradesmen's wives, in and about the City of London. Delivered, to the Honourable, the Knights, Citizens and Burgesses, of the House of Commons in Parliament, the 4th of February, 1641. Together with their several reasons why their sex ought thus to petition, as well as the men; and the manner how both their petition and reasons was delivered. Likewise the answer which the Honourable Assembly sent to them by Mr. Pym, as they stood at the House door.* 4o.
Wing T2656, UMI microfilm reel 24.
Copy-text: British Library Thomason Tracts E.134[17]

House of Peers] House of Lords. See note to Text 4, p. 435.

arch-enemy] William Laud, Archbishop of Canterbury, imprisoned in 1641 but not executed until 1645.

as they have done in Ireland] The Catholic rebellion in Ireland, October 1641.

bloody wars in Germany] The Thirty Years' War, 1618–48, most of which was fought on German soil.

His Majesty's late Northern Army] The Second Bishop's War in Scotland, 1640.

Episcopal persecutions] Laud's campaign to root out Puritanism and impose Arminianism, a version of Protestantism barely removed from Catholicism.

the Queen's court] Charles I's Queen, Henrietta Maria, kept a separate court in which she and many of her ladies openly maintained their Catholic faith.

thorow] Through.

Mr Pym] John Pym, MP, a long-standing opponent of Arminianism.

13. Text: *A Vision, wherein is manifested the cure of the Kingdom*, 1648, 4o.
Wing P2810, UMI microfilm reel 83.
Copy-text: British Library Thomason Tracts E.537 (24), sigs A2r to A4v.

Remonstrance] *The Remonstrance and Resolution of the Right Honourable and Truly Valiant, Lieutenant-General Cromwell*, September 1648.

travailing woman] A woman in labour.

potsherd] Broken piece of earthenware.

giving it up to the people] Trill, Chedgzoy and Osborne (1997, 166) identify this as a reference to *An Argument of the Free People of England*, by John Lilburne, leader of the Leveller movement during the Civil War.

Charles your Lord] King Charles I.

14. Text: *Strange and Wonderful News from Whitehall*, 1654, 4o.
Wing T2034 UMI microfilm reel 39.
Copy-text: British Library Thomason Tracts E.224 (3).

Mr Powel] Vavasour Powell, Puritan preacher sympathetic to the Fifth Monarchist movement.

ordinary] Inn serving simple fare at a fixed price.

little toast in small beers] Morsel of bread, browned at the fire and served in a cup of weak beer.

Four horns] 1654: fair horns.

Lord Protector] Oliver Cromwell.

—s] Presumably 'Oliver's'.

the relator] The person who has transcribed Anna's prophecies.

orison] Prayer.

Gideon] Gideon was appointed by God to deliver the Israelites from servitude to the Midianites and the worship of the pagan god Baal (Judges 6–8).

you seem to do] 1654: you seem to do.

15. Text: *The Case of Madam Mary Carleton, lately styled 'The German Princess', truly stated: with an historical relation of her birth, education, and fortunes; in an appeal to His Illustrious Highness Prince Rupert.* 1663, 12o.
Wing C586A, UMI microfilm reel 2037.
Copy-text British Library shelfmark 1606/1589, sigs. Br to B11v; C8r to C9v; D2r to D4v; D8r to D11r

Prince Rupert] Cousin of Charles I (his parents were Elisabeth, Charles's sister, and Frederick, Elector Palatine) and a Royalist general the English Civil War, he became part of the English court on the Restoration of Charles II.

femes covert] Literally 'hidden' or 'covered' woman, this term denotes the practice in English law whereby a married woman's legal identity was subsumed into that of her husband.

submiss] Submissive.

superstructure] That is, that which was built upon these foundations.

mechanic and base] See note to Text 8, p. 442.

fiddler ... *Whore of Canterbury*] This pamphlet, published before the trial, ultimately proved more accurate that Mary Carleton's account of her origins.

Newgate] Prison in London.

my governess] Previously Carleton has described how she was taken under the wing of a Mrs Margaret Hammond, whom she met whilst visiting the exiled Charles II's court.

Elysium] Paradise, ideal world.

heroines] 1663: Heroinas.

princess ... loss of the design] Todd and Spearing (1996, 151) note that the first is Queen Christina of Sweden (1626–89) who abdicated in 1654 to travel through Europe in male attire; they do not gloss the second.

travail] Labour.

appurtenant] Accessory.

catch-dolt] Confidence trickster.

bewrayed] Exposed, betrayed.

irrefragable] Incontrovertible.

Dutch] Deutsch (that is, German).

tide-boat] That is, one that travelled up the Thames with the tide.

the Exchange . . . Cornhill] Area of London devoted to trade, especially luxury goods, coffee houses and taverns.

telling of brass farthings] Counting out coins of small denomination.

80000li. per annum] £80,000 a year.

the Fates] In classical mythology, three women who determined human lives; usually depicted as drawing, spinning and cutting a thread which represented the life-span.

Durham Yard] Fashionable residential area of London.

Hyde Park] Highly fashionable place to visit and be seen.

the right hand] The position of honour.

divertissement] Entertainment.

liber intentare **. . . in her own name**] Free to use the law to gain redress for a grievance.

heaven for women] Todd and Spearing (1996, 154) note that this is a popular concept, originating from Fynes Moryson's *Itinerary* (1617), that 'England is in generall said to be the hell of Horses, the Purgatory of Servants and the Paradice of Women'.

dowers] Married woman's property. A woman brought a sum of money and/or property (a dowry) to her marriage in return for the means to live for the rest of her life (jointure). In England everything owned by a woman on the day of her marriage and any she inherited subsequently became the property of her husband.

cum fueris Romae, Romano vivite more] That is, 'when in Rome, do as the Romans do'.

bruited] Rumoured, put about.

Fanchurch Street] Wide street in London now called Fenchurch Street.

prentices] Specifically an apprentice; used to imply youthful curiosity and lack of discretion.

May-game] Trivial diversion.

pasquils] Public lampoons.

A Westminster-wedding] A ballad printed in 1663, supposedly by John Carleton

chimeras] Fantastical creatures or, proverbially, impossible goals.

sword and feather] Distinguishing features of Cavalier garb, a large feather being worn in a broad-brimmed hat.

coffee-house] Not simply a place of refreshment; the coffee-house of the late 17th and 18th centuries was a key location for literary and political conversation, and the dissemination of news and opinion.

slams] Insults, possibly deriving from an obsolete word for refuse. It is a derivation of the German 'schlamm' meaning mud; interestingly the immediate context draws particular attention to this derivation.

maugre] despite

16. Text: *Poems* by Katherine Philips, 1667, folio.
    Wing P2033, UMI microfilm 748.
    Copy-text: Newberry Library shelfmark Case Y.185.P.513, pp. 1-2; 11-13; 18-19; 21-6; 32-3; 36-9; 58-9; 70-1; 74-7; 82-5; 88-91; 106; 111-13; 128-30; 134; 136-7; 139-41; 148-9; 153-4.

double murther] Of the King's personal and political bodies.

Vavasor Powell] See note to Text 14, p. 447.

But I . . . sceptres fly] In agreement with Thomas (1990, 70), I have retained these two lines from the 1664 edition.

Duchess of York] Anne Hyde, daughter of the Earl of Clarendon and wife of Charles II's brother James, later King James II.

Queen of Bohemia] Elisabeth, eldest sister of Charles I, who died in England in 1662. She had married Frederick Elector Palatine in 1613. He accepted the crown of Bohemia, against the wishes of the Hapsburgs, the European imperial dynasty, thereby precipitating the Thirty Years War.

losing one] Frederick and Elisabeth went into exile in Holland after Frederick's army was defeated by Imperial forces at the battle of the White Mountain in 1620.

Fortune] See note to Text 7, p. 440.

Henry Lawes] Leading English composer who set several of Philips's poems to music.

lyre] Ancient Greek harp.

laurel] See note to Text 7, p. 438.

Lucasia] Literary sobriquet for Mrs Anne Owen.

election] Reference to the Calvinist doctrine of election in which God chooses those who will receive spiritual and temporal benefits, regardless of their desert.

fairy Red-cross Knight] Hero of the first book of Edmund Spenser's *The Faerie Queene* (1590).

cypress] Tree symbolising mourning.

Orinda] Literary sobriquet for Katherine Philips.

practick] Practical.

burning-glass] A lens which intensifies the sun's rays in order to burn the object on which they are focused.

Wiston Vault] Thomas (1990, 343) identifies this as belonging to the Wogans of Pembrokeshire, the family of Katherine Philips's mother-in-law, Anne.

the Seal] The poem describes a badge which Thomas (1990, 343) suggests is the symbol of their 'society'.

Moses' bush] See Exodus 3:2–4.

Mr Cartwright] William Cartwright, Cavalier poet and playwright who died in 1643.

descry] Perceive at a distance.

Mrs M. A.] Mary Aubrey.

Lieger] Permanent resident.

Antenor] Literary sobriquet for Colonel James Philips, Katherine's husband.

glass] Mirror.

turtles] Turtle-doves. See note to Text 7, p. 437.

reflux] Flowing back.

viol] Early string instrument played with a bow.

pelf] Trumpery or trash.

Golden Age] See note to Text 8, p. 441.

Hyde Park] See note to Text 15, p. 445.

Rosania] Literary sobriquet for Mary Aubrey.

transmigrations] The journey of a soul, on the death of one body, into another.

a period of] An end to.

squibs] Small fireworks, usually arranged on ropes or lines.

Mrs Philips] Anne Wogan, wife of Hector Philips and mother of Colonel James Philips.

fifteen pledges] Fifteen children.

her son H. P.] Hector Philips, born and died in 1655.

Hermes' seal] An airtight seal, believed to have been invented by the legendary alchemist Hermes Trismegistus.

17. Text: *The Convent of Pleasure* in Margaret Cavendish, *Plays, Never Before Printed* 1668, folio.
    Wing N867, UMI microfilm 674
    Copy-text: Trinity College, Cambrige, shelfmark H.18.41 (plays individually paginated).

brouilleries] Hubbub.

vot'ress] Woman devoted to a religious life.

deboist] Debauched.

silk-damask] Rich fabric woven with elaborate designs.

plate] Utensils for table and domestic use, originally of silver or gold.

taffety] A variant of taffeta, in this period meaning a glossy, lustrous cloth, usually silk.

reaves] Strips of split wood.

franchipane] Frangipane, perfume made from red jasmine.

Turkey carpets] Richly coloured deep pile carpets, cut to resemble velvet, imported from Turkey.

fine holland] High quality linen fabric.

diaper] Simply patterned linen fabric.

shifts] Underskirts.

devotes] Nuns; here, the inmates of the convent.

Jupiter] See note to Text 10, p. 445.

mopes] Foolish expressions.

make legs] Bow.

gorgets] Pieces of clothing for the neck and breast.

a pretty shift] A good attempt , with a pun on 'shift' (see note above).

mistress . . . servant] As Bowerbank and Mendelson note (2000, 111), 'mistress' and 'servant' were, according to seventeenth-century courtship conventions, technical terms for a male suitor and the female object of his love. Cavendish eschews the obvious opportunity for comic irony by leaving the audience no wiser than Lady Happy as to the Prince's true identity at this point.

masque] Elaborate dramatic entertainment, reserved for royalty and high nobility.

mean] Poor.

botcher] Cobbler or tailor who does repairs.

bush] Sign of the vintner.

jointure] See note to Text 15, p. 448.

prentices] See note to Text 15, p. 448.

journeyman] Skilled tradesman working under a master craftsman.

choleric] Hot-tempered.

vapours] Depression of spirits.

spleen] Abdominal organ regarded as the seat of melancholy.

Juno] See note to Text 10, p. 445.

butler . . . taps] The butler was in charge of the wine and beer in the household; here, this butler is considered worth less than the drips from the casks under his charge.

sola] Alone.

pastoral] Literary or dramatic form which portrays its characters as shepherds leading an idealised country life.

planets seven] Shaver (1999, 235) identifies these as the moon, Mercury, Venus, the sun, Mars, Jupiter and Saturn.

transmigrate] See note to Text 16, p. 450.

cerusse] Paint or cosmetic with a white lead base.

hatchments] Panel bearing a coat of arms.

Written by my Lord Duke] MS addition in copy-text.

scrips of corduant] Leather purses.

oaten pipe] Traditional musical instrument of the shepherd.

Holmby] Shaver (1999, 238) identifies this as the family estate of sir Christopher Hatton, favourite of Queen Elizabeth, and the place where Charles I was imprisoned by Parliament.

wassail] Spiced ale or wine served in a large bowl.

by my Lord Duke] MS addition in copy-text.

Hymen] Classical god of marriage.

Mars] See note to Text 8, p. 443.

Neptune] Classical god of the sea.

Fates] See note to Text.

May-dew] Bowerbank and Mendelson (2000, 125) gloss this as 'dew gathered at dawn on May-day, thought to have cosmetic properties'.

Beshrew me] Exclamation.

coz'ning] Tricking.

orient pearls] Pearls of great lustre.

Apollo] See note to Text 2, p. 434.

ambergris] Waxy substance used as a fixative in perfumery.

you will quit me] You will excuse me.

V.ii] Bowerbank and Mendelson's copy-text has 'Written by my Lord Duke' (2000, 129) although this is not present in the copy-text used here.

fidle fadle] Expression of contempt.

The Practice of Piety] Shaver (1999, 245) identifies this as a popular instructive tract by Sir Lewis Bailey, which ran to many editions throughout the 17th century.

Gazette] News-sheet, often viewed as an unreliable source of gossip.

Ods body] Oath meaning 'God's body'.

ballets] Ballads.

There's much . . . cup and the lip] Proverbial. The more familiar version is 'There's many a slip 'twixt cup and lip'.

hautboys] Oboe players and/or their instruments. From the French, 'hautbois', literally 'high wood'.

bed-rid] Bedridden.

solus] Alone.

marry] Oath, contraction of 'by the Virgin Mary'.

through] 1621: your. MS emendation in copy-text.

18. Text: *An Essay to Revive the Ancient Education of Gentlewomen*, 1673, 4o.
Wing M309, UMI microfilm 697
Copy-text: British Library 1031.g.19, pp. 3–4; 8–9; 21–3; 41–3.
The Lady Mary . . . Duke of York] See note to Text 16, p. 449.
sots] Fools.
endued] Invested.
I am a man] Makin assumes a masculine narrative voice.
Minerva] Roman name for Pallas Athena. See note to Text 7, p. 439.
quibble and droll] Make fun.
Nine Muses] See note to Text 7, p. 439.
parts of the world] All taken from Classical mythology, except America, which, although feminine in form, is in fact named after the male explorer Amerigo Vespucci.
Ex quovis liguo non fit Minerva] Teague (1998, 164) translates this as 'Minerva does not make branches in every place', that is, everyone does not have the same intellectual capacity.
whisk] Neckerchief.
Circe's cup] In Classical mythology, an island sorceress who, by means of a magic potion, turned her male visitors into beasts befitting their characters.
drils] Mandrils.
cark] Toil.
Princess Elisabeth] Daughter of Henrietta Maria and Charles I, named after her aunt, Elisabeth of Bohemia. See note to Text 16, p. 449.
Accompts] Accounts.
Visibles] Displays.
Limning] Painting or sketching.
20 l. per annum] £20 a year.
Mr Mason's coffee-house . . . Fleet Street] Hostelries in commercial areas of London. See also note to Text 15, p. 448.

19. Text: Anne Bradstreet, *Several Poems*, 1678, 8o.
Wing B4166, UMI microfilm reel 759.
Copy-text British Library shelfmark C.39.b.48(1), pp. 43–68; 192–202; 236.
du Bartas] Guillaume du Bartas, 16th century French poet.
sweet-tongued Greek / Who lisped at first] Demosthenes (384–322 BC); as a child he spoke with a stammer, but grew up to be the greatest of all Athenian orators.
Calliope] See note to Text 7, p. 439.
bays] See note to Text 6, p. 436.
other] This is part of a series of poems which begins with dialogues by the four elements (fire, water, air and earth) and the four humours (blood, choler, phlegm and melancholer) and ends with the four seasons (spring, summer, autumn and winter).

Phlegm] Humour causing sluggishness.

Blood] Humour causing optimism.

Choler] Humour causing anger; also known as yellow bile.

Melancholer] Humour causing depression; also known as black bile.

Aurora] Goddess of the dawn.

betime] Early.

throughly] Thoroughly.

Gillyflowers] Clove-scented pinks.

silliness] Innocence.

cark] Toil.

Statist] Statesman.

fifth commandment] 'Honour thy father and thy mother' (Exodus 21:12).

crudities] Imperfectly digested food.

flux] The effects of dysentery.

glass] See note to Text 7, p. 438.

pike] Weapon consisting of a long pole with a sharp blade at the end, used in the forefront of the troops in pitched battle.

corslet] Body armour.

glozing] Flattering.

ruffins] Fiends.

roarers] Bullies.

pounce] Powder.

Adonis] Youth of legendary beauty.

Sardanapalus] Descendant of Ninus, the mythical founder of the ancient city of Nineveh (c. 2182 BC), he was the last and worst of a long line of slothful, debauched and ineffective rulers.

masques] See note to Text 17, p. 450.

Cavalier] Supporter of the Royalist cause.

ague] Fever.

quinsy] Form of tonsilitis.

two-fold pox] Syphilis, which attacks the skin and the nervous system.

Bedlam] St Mary of Bethlehem Hospital in London, a notorious lunatic asylum in this period.

staved] Beaten.

reines] Kidneys.

strangury] Painful urinary disease.

quarton ague] Fever which attacks every fourth day.

megrim] Variant of migraine.

bis pueri senes] 'Old men are children again'.

celestial she] Queen Elizabeth I.

France and Holland . . . Philip and Albertus] Reference to late 16th century hostilities between England and Spain, involving King Philip II of Spain and Albert, Archduke of Austria.

a prince . . . heaven's angry hand] Death of Prince Henry, Prince of Wales, 1612.

a plot to blow up nobles] The gunpowder plot, 1605.

Rhe . . . Palatinate for ever lost] Protestant losses in the Thirty Years War (1618–48).

a Prince to live . . . strangers' hands] Charles II in exile.

one stabbed] George Villiers, Duke of Buckingham, assassinated in 1628.

some . . . heads] Thomas Wentworth, Earl of Strafford and William Laud, Archbishop of Canterbury, executed in 1641 and 1645 repectively.

Popish hellish miscreants] The Irish Rebellion of 1641.

King] Charles I.

usurper] Oliver Cromwell.

almond-tree] Metaphor for grey hairs.

golden bowl and silver cord] See Eccles. 12:6.

Hengist] 5th century leader of the Jutes who treacherously turned against his ally Vortigern, King of Celts, to take Kent from him and establish a new dynasty there.

Canutus] King Canute, or Cnut, 11th century King of England, reputed to have demonstrated the limit of his powers by ordering the tide to turn.

Norman] Specifically, William the Conqueror who successfully invaded England in 1066.

Maud and Stephen] Rivals for the English crown in the 12th century. Maud claimed superior right as daughter of Henry I, whereas Stephen, the incumbent King, was his nephew. Their dispute led to civil war in England.

Barons rise] Reference to King John and Magna Carta 1215.

Edward] Edward II, 14th century English King deposed (and subsequently murdered) in favour of his young son, who became Edward III.

Richard] Richard II, 15th century English King deposed (and subsequently murdered) in favour of Henry Bolingbroke, Duke of Lancaster, who became Henry IV.

Richmond] Henry Tudor, Earl of Richmond who defeated Richard III at the Battle of Bosworth field in 1485, to become Henry VII.

the Boar] Richard, Duke of Gloucester who reigned as Richard III in the mid 15th century. As Shakespeare's play *Richard III* (1597) demonstrates, he was generally thought to have murdered his way to the throne, including his nephews, sons of Edward IV.

Armado] The Spanish Armada, defeated by the English fleet in 1588.

Nor is it . . . prevent it speedily] Old England repeats the list of historical incidents detailed above, only to show that her current trouble is considerably worse.

Alcie's son] Stephen. See note above.

nephews slew] See note above.

Edward third . . . Henry fifth] English Kings who led victorious forces against the French at the battles of Crècy (1346) and Agincourt (1415), respectively.

Beelzebub] Chief devil, often depicted as Lucifer's deputy.

Clarence' hapless son] Edward Earl of Warwick, executed in 1499 for supporting a plot to depose Henry VII.

Jane] Lady Jane Dudley (neè Grey) the Protestant 'nine days queen', deposed in 1554 by the Catholic Mary I and later executed.

paralize] Embellish.

Hydras] In Classical mythology, the Hydra was a nine-headed serpent.

after-clap] Subsequent shock.

Germany . . . Ireland . . . Rochelle] Sites of doctrinally-motivated warfare in the 17th century. See notes on p. 454.

calcined] Reduced to a powder.

Strafford] See note on p. 454.

Laud] See note on p. 454.

Metropolitan] Ruled by the Church.

Gideon] See Judges 7: 18, 20.

Mero's curse] See Judges 5: 23.

Baal] Pagan god of the Old Testament.

Rochets] Ecclesiastical vestment.

Essex] Robert Devereux, 3rd Earl of Essex, Parliamentary leader between 1642 and 1645.

pursevants] State messenger with the power to execute royal warrants.

catchpoles] Petty office of the law.

polled] Plundered.

Gog] Proverbially heathen prince defeated by the Israelites (Ezek. 38–39); here a reference to the Islamic Turkish Empire.

Abraham's seed] Christendom.

Canaanite] Pagan people from whom the Israelites took the Promised Land.

even feet] Pun on the physical and metrical meanings.

20. Text: *Oroonoko, or The Royal Slave*, 1688, 8o.
Wing B1766a UMI microfilm 121
Copy-text: Bodleian Library shelfmark Vet. A3f. 726(1).

Surinam] On the northern coast of South America, this colony was founded in 1651 by Lord Willoughby, the absent 'English Governor' to whom Behn subsequently refers.

marmosets . . . cousheries] Both of these natives of tropical America are usually referred to as 'marmosets'. However, it is likely that the first are, strictly speaking, tamarins and the second *Hapalidae* or true marmosets, which are distinctive for their ear tufts and mane (hence 'the form and fashion of a lion').

his Majesty's Antiquary's] Gallagher (2000, 38) suggests that this refers to the museum of the Royal Society, founded by Charles II for the promotion of scientific inquiry.

Indian Queen] Eponymous character of the play by John Dryden and Sir Robert Howard, premiered in 1664 and revived in 1668.

ell] Now obsolete unit of measurement equalling 45 inches.

nice] Fastidious.

savannahs] An open plain scattered with drought-resistant trees.

Coramantien] Nation on the Gold Coast of Africa.

field of Mars] Battlefield; see note to Text 8, p. 443.

Moor] Generic term for black Africans.

deplorable . . . monarch] Reference to the execution of Charles I.

statuary] Sculptor.

bating] Except.

politic maxims] Wise sayings.

Venus] See note to Text 2, p. 434.

chagrin] 1688: Shagrien.

grave relations] Elders.

parley] Conversation or discourse, usually with military overtones suggesting a discussion of terms with the enemy.

pass regardless by, and were paid] 1688: pass, were regardless by, and paid.

antic] Fantastic or bizzare.

ere] Before.

citrons] Fruit related to the lemon, but larger and less acid.

complaisance] Politeness, deference or obligation.

maugre] Despite.

effects] 1688: efforts.

this person] That is, the ship's captain.

asseveration] Solemn or emphatic assertion.

parole] Word of honour, especially that of a prisoner of war that he will not take action against his captives in order to secure his freedom.

pickaninnies] Small children of Black African origin; term now considered offensive.

vest] In this context a robe or gown.

Backearay] White person. Gallagher (2000, 68) sugests this could derive from the Ibo 'backra', meaning master.

brown holland] Plain linen fabric.

Caesar] Oroonoko is named after Julius Caesar (100–44 BC), Roman general, statesman and dictator. He was stabbed to death by a group of senators, led by Cassius and Brutus (see note to Text 21, p. 460), concerned by his increasing personal popularity and power.

japanned] Varnished or lacquered.

Picts] Ancient tribe of Northern Britain.

Lives of the Romans] Historical work by Plutarch (c. 46–120 AD), popular in the 17th century.

pitching the bar] Competition to throw a heavy bar the furthest.

Alexander] Alexander the Great (356–323 BC), leader of the Scythian Empire.

late Majesty, of sacred memory] Charles II.

purlings] Action and/or sound made by running water.

ravishing] 1688: raving.

Mall here] 1688: Marl, hear. Gallagher (2000, 77) suggests this is the tree-lined Mall in St James's Park, London.

fruit-bearing] 1688: fruity-bear.

Sometimes we would go surprising] In this paragraph, 1688 variously uses male and female pronouns to refer to the tigress; these have been standardised.

outvie] Outdo, surpass.

dams] Mothers, specifically in relation to animals.

chus'd] chose.

Harry Martin, the great Oliverian] Supporter of Oliver Cromwell and a signatory to the warrant for the execution of Charles I.

numb eel] Electric eel.

polled] Possibly took a show of hands.

taffety] See note to Text 17, p. 450.

stuff-suit] Suit made of woollen fabric.

burning glass] concave lens or mirror for concentrating the sun's rays upon an object to achieve combustion.

runagades] Obsolete form of 'renegades'.

Hannibal] Carthaginian general who cut his way through the Alps in 218 BC during his campaign to invade Italy; he committed suicide in 183 BC after his army was defeated by the Romans.

hamaca] Obsolete form of 'hammock'.

basket-hilts] Swords with wickerwork protection for the hand.

pell-mell] In disorder or confusion.

Colonel Martin . . . new comedy] George Marteen, hero of Behn's *The Younger Brother, or, The Amorous Jilt*, which premiered posthumously in 1696.

chirurgeon] Early form of surgeon.

nemine contradicente] Unanimously.

mobile] Common people, rabble, populace.

gushed] 1688: gust.

ghastly] 1688: gashly.

noisome] Ill-smelling and noxious.

death's head] Figure or representation of a skull as an emblem of mortality.

21. Text: *The Widow Ranter*, or, *The History of Bacon in Virginia*, 1690, 4o. Wing B1774, UMI Microfilm 1056.
Copy-text National Library of Scotland, shelfmark Bute.38.

Justice a Peace in Quorum] Full title of a JP.

sirrah] Term of address to men or boys, implying authority in the speaker.

woundily] Extremely.

cogue] Small wooden cup.

Groom-porters] Officer of the English Royal Household, in charge of gaming within the court.

sharping bully] Aggressive swindler.

cully in] Dupe.

prentices] See note to Text 15, p. 448.

high and low Flats and Bars] False dice.

pay ten-fold at the death of their fathers] Swindle heirs out of their inheritance.

go a guinea at the better of the lay] Place a bet.

Gad] Oath. The play contains a number of such corruptions of blasphemous oaths.

plate] See note to Text 17, p. 450.

Alexander] See note to Text 20, p. 456.

Romulus] Legendary founder of Rome, he was suckled in infancy by a she-wolf, together with his twin brother, Remus.

retail brandymonger] Seller of brandy to the public.

Nants] Brandy, from Nantes in France.

adzoors] Oath.

shire-brandy] Inferior form produced in England.

paulter] Indifferent.

sparks] Young men of fashion.

catch] Song.

hoggerds] Swine-keepers, hence low-class persons.

Life-guard man] Soldier in the Life-Guards.

fain to] Obliged to.

ordinary] See note to Text 14, p. 447.

trusting for old Oliver's funeral] Hoping to make a profit from the trade associated with such a state occasion.

groat] Coin of minimal value.

Scandalam Magnatum] Malicious utterance or publication against a person of dignity.

bear the bob] Sing the chorus.

'zoors] Oath.

quotha] Says he.

factor] Retailer, middle-man.

huffed] Bullied.

thrummed] Torn or cut.

Hector] Leader of the Trojan forces during the Trojan war, he was eventually slain by the divinely protected Achilles; proverbially an aggressive person.

punctillio] Minute point of detail.

a pox on't] Curse, wishing venereal disease upon the recipient.

in fresco] Outdoors, in the fresh air.

shoving . . . the cly] Pickpocketing; stealing; secreting stolen goods.

mawkish] Nauseous.

regalio] Variant of regalo, choice food or drink.

stock-fish] Cured and dried fish.

points] Cords used to hold up breeches.

chafferer] Dealer.

Fortune de la Guerre] Fortune of war.

anticks] Grotesque dances.

salt and battery] Assault and battery.

tun] Large cask or barrel.

mundungus] Foul smelling tobacco.

'slife] Oath.

Gadzooks] Oath.

coxcombs] Vain and foolish men.

by my troth] By my honour.

Mor-Blew, Mor-Dee] Timerous's attempts to pronounce French oaths.

bills of exchange] Means of raising money or credit; an early form of cheque.

Gadzoors] Oath.

troupers] Staunch supporters.

poltroon] Coward.

maw] Stomach.

rail] Attack verbally.

mobile] See note to Text 20, p. 457.

rake-hells] Dissolute individuals.

sedge] Coarse grass.

a bob] Rebuke or insult.

bull of Bashan] See Psalm 22:12–15.

de Wit] Todd (1996, 455) identifies him as Johan de Wit, a 17th-century Dutch statesman who was torn apart by an unruly mob.

rods in piss] Birch rods were kept in urine to harden them.

Dalton's Country-Justice] Todd (1996, 456) identifies this as Michael Dalton's *The Country Justice*, first published in 1618 and republished in updated edition throughout the 17th century.

affidavits viva voce] Contradiction in terms; an affidavit is a sworn written statement and viva voce means by word of mouth.

cagg] Small cask.

jade] See note to Text 2, p. 434.

se defendo] In self-defence.

peruke] Long curly wig.

buff, scarf and feather] Military uniform.

Termagant] In medieval times, an imaginary Islamic deity; here an aggressive person.

d—] Damned.

brigantine] Small swift sailing vessel.

shallop] Large heavy boat sometimes charged with guns.

Dutch Papists] The Netherlands were staunchly Protestant at this period. Timerous's boast is, therefore, empty.

A Council, a Council] Signifies the mob's support for the Council.

gorgon] Fearsome mythological female monsters, with snakes for hair.

rugid] Shabby.

would fain be] Would rather be.

Quiocto] Todd (1996, 457) suggests this is a variant of Quioco, a second-tier deity in the Indian hierarchy.

ere] Before.

fell] Deadly.

Teroomians] Walden (1993, 85) suggests a corruption of 'Siouxians', the Sioux having a reputation as fierce warriors.

brakes] Clumps of bracken.

furzes] Gorse bushes.

starter] Coward.

Caesar] Julius Caesar. See note to Text 20, p. 456.

cadees] Early form of cadet or caddie, a junior officer.

peach] Impeach.

benefit of the clergy] The advantage of belonging to a profession which was exempted from the jurisdiction of ordinary courts of law.

'shaw] Exclamation.

hempen cravat-string] Hanging-rope.

mum] Hush.

'sdeath] Oath.

hawk's meat] Soldiers first in line of fire, whose corpses would be food for birds of prey.

long of you] Due to you.

lanthorns] Lanterns.

flambeaux] Torches.

parley] Formal debate in the context of armed hostilities.

adsfish] Oath.

conjure] Beseech.

cyphers] Nonentities.

Pauwmungian] Walden (1993, 111) suggests a reference to the Pamunkey Tribe who inhabited the banks of the Pamunkey river.

Amazonian] In Classical mythology, the Amazons were a race of warrior women.

untruss a point] Undo his trousers (to relieve himself).

moveables] Personal property.

pommel] Round knob at the hilt of a sword.

Hannibal] See note to Text 20, p. 457.

Cassius] Roman general, an ally of Brutus, who committed suicide in 42 BC, thinking their forces had been defeated by those of Octavius and Mark Antony.

baby clouts] Baby clothes.

BIOGRAPHICAL NOTES

Elizabeth I (1533–1603)
Daughter of King Henry VIII and his second wife, Anne Boleyn, she inherited the crown in 1558, after the death of her half-sister, Mary, daughter of King Henry VIII and his first wife, Catherine of Aragon. Originally declared a bastard by her father after the execution of her mother for adultery, Elizabeth became the longest-serving and, arguably, the most successful English monarch in the Early Modern period. She was educated by the humanist Roger Ascham, under whose tutelage she learned Latin and Greek. She also knew French, Italian, Spanish, German, Flemish and Welsh. Perhaps inevitably, her great learning and personal creativity expressed itself in her political duties, which is one of the reasons why three of her speeches are included here. However, some of her literary works and translations do survive, including a Chorus from Seneca's *Hercules Oetaeus*. Her talent for creating a carefully staged political persona, and perhaps particularly her commitment to her role as a virgin queen, 'married' to her country, which allowed her to toy with, yet finally reject, all her suitors, meant that she inevitably became the object of other writers' pens. After her death she served as an appropriate inspiration for talented women of the period; more than one of the writers included in this anthology draws upon the myth of the Virgin Queen.
   See: Hackett (1995); Levin (1998); Teague (1987, 1992)

Jane Anger (fl. 1588)
Little is known of Jane Anger beyond this one publication. The fortuitous correspondence between the author's name and the subject matter of the pamphlet, to which the pamphlet itself draws attention (see p. 2) has led some scholars (see, for example, Purkiss 1992) to conclude that it is indeed a pseudonym. However, Simon Shepherd has shown that the name was borne by a number of Englishwomen at the time of the pamphlet's publication, although none of these can be positively identified as the author (Shepherd 1984, p. 30).
   See: Shepherd (ed.) (1984); Henderson and McManus (eds) (1987)

Mary Sidney Herbert, Countess of Pembroke (1561–1621)
Mary Sidney Herbert was the third daughter of Sir Henry Sidney and Mary Dudley, eldest daughter of the Duke of Northumberland. In 1577 she married Henry Herbert, 2nd Earl of Pembroke, and went to live at his house at Wilton, where she established a library. She had three children, William, Philip and Anne. However, her closest relationship was with her brother, Sir Philip Sidney, and during the 1580s they began

work on a metrical translation of the Psalms of David. He did not live to see them completed as he died unexpectedly from a wound sustained whilst fighting the Spanish in the Netherlands in 1586. Mary finished the work, although she did not have it published, and she also produced three more translations: Francis Petrarch's *Triumph of Death*, Philippe Mornay's *Discourse of Life and Death*, and Robert Garnier's *The Tragedy of Antonie*. The last two were published in a single volume in 1592. Four original poems survive, two in manuscript and two printed, one of which is included in this anthology. After her brother's death, she gave patronage a number of the leading poets of the day, including Samuel Daniel and Michael Drayton. The death of Mary's husband in 1601 meant that much of her time was then taken up administering the estates which he had left to her. In the last years of her life, she commissioned the building of Houghton House in Bedfordshire, where she died in 1621.

See: Hannay (1990); Hannay, Kinnamon and Brennan (eds) (1998); Lamb (1990)

Aemilia Lanyer (1569–1645)

Daughter of Giovanni Baptista Bassano, a court musician, and Margaret Johnson, Aemilia was born into a family of Venetian Jewish émigrés. She was brought up in the household of Susan, Countess of Kent, where she received a higher standard of education than was usual for a woman of her status. She spent some time at court, becoming the mistress of Henry Carey, 1st Baron Hunsdon, until she fell pregnant in 1592 and was married off to Alphonso Lanyer, who was a member of another family of court musicians. The child, a son, was born in 1593 and named Henry. Her second child, Odillya, was born in 1598, although she died less than a year later. The Lanyers were not particularly wealthy and the publication of *Salve Deus Rex Judaeorum*, with its numerous dedications, may have been an attempt to gain patronage. As Woods notes, however, there is no evidence that the attempt was successful (1993, p. xxvii). Alphonso died in 1613 and Aemilia was thrown into dispute with his family over his estate. In 1617 she set up a school in St Giles-in-the-Field, which lasted until 1619 and put her in constant conflict with her landlord over rent and repairs. She seems to have spent some of the ensuing time with her son and his family, until he predeceased her in 1633; she died twelve years later.

See: Woods (ed.) (1993); Purkiss (ed.) (1994)

Elizabeth Cary, 1st Viscountess Falkland (1585–1639)

Daughter of the lawyer Laurence Tanfield and Elizabeth Symondes, Elizabeth was an only child with an appetite for learning, especially foreign languages. She attracted the praise of the poets Michael Drayton and John Davies, both of whom may have tutored her. In 1602 she was married to Sir Henry Cary, later 1st Viscount Falkland, and bore him eleven children, including the poet and Royalist hero Lucius Cary, 2nd Viscount Falkland. Her husband was a staunch Protestant and, when she converted publicly to Catholicism in 1626, he disowned her. She lived in relative poverty for the rest of her life, despite securing the support of some of the most influential women at court, including Queen Henrietta Maria. The Falklands appear to have been reconciled just before Henry's death in 1633, although Elizabeth then went on to incur the wrath of Church and State, as she successfully sent four of her daughters and two of her sons to the Continent to be received into the Catholic faith. Elizabeth's periods of literary activity occurred outwith the years she was nursing her children. Before her marriage she translated Abraham Ortelius's *The Mirror of the World*, which survives in manuscript. In the early years of her marriage she wrote two plays, although only the published version of the second, *The Tragedy of Mariam*, is extant. A lengthy history of Edward II, written in 1626, survives in manuscript, and this is the likely source of two printed versions published in 1680, for a long time erroneously attributed to her husband. Her translation of the pro-Catholic *The Reply of the Most Illustrious Cardinal of Perron*, dedicated to Queen Henrietta Maria, was published in 1630. When Elizabeth Cary died in 1639, the Queen allowed her body to be buried in her private chapel.

See: Hodgson-Wright (ed.) (2000); Weller and Ferguson (eds) (1994)

Rachel Speght (c. 1597->1630)

Born circa 1597, daughter of the Calvinist Minister James Speght, Rachel married William Procter late in 1621. She bore two children, Rachel in 1627 and William in 1630. Her marriage appears to mark the end of her publishing career, which began in 1617, with *A Muzzle for Melastomus*, and ended in 1621, with *Mortality's Memorandum*, the latter being prompted by the death of her mother. The most recent scholarship has not found any record of her death or burial.

See: Lewalski (ed.) (1996)

Lady Mary Wroth (c. 1586–c. 1651)

Daughter of Robert Sidney and Barbara Gamage, she was born into a notable literary dynasty, having Mary Sidney Herbert, Countess of Pembroke (q.v.) and Sir Philip Sidney as her aunt and uncle. She spent much of her childhood at her aunt's home, although she also regularly visited her father in the Netherlands, where he was Governor of Flushing. In 1604 she became part of Queen Anna's court circle and a regular performer in court masques. She married Sir Robert Wroth in the same year and, although the marriage does not seem to have been happy, it was relatively short; he died in 1614, leaving her with a young son, James (who died in 1616), and massive debts. She entered into (or possibly resumed) an affair with her cousin, William Herbert, by whom she had two natural children, William and Catherine. Mary was dismissed from court and it seems that she never regained a place there. She died circa 1651, having constantly struggled with the debt left to her by her husband. Some time between 1618 and 1620, she began her literary career in earnest, although her first and only publication was to cause further scandal. *The Countess of Montgomery's Urania*, a prose romance, was published together with *Pamphilia to Amphilanthus* in 1621. It was withdrawn from sale because its readership soon began to recognise figures and recent events from the Jacobean court. Lord Denny, in particular, objected to the portrayal of himself and his family and wrote a scathing poem attacking Wroth, to which she replied in kind. The rest of Wroth's oeuvre, part two of the *Urania* and a pastoral play, *Love's Victory*, was not published in her lifetime, although the latter is available in two modern editions: Brennan (ed) (1988) and Cerasano and Wynne-Davies (eds) (1996).

See: Lamb (1990); Miller (1996); Roberts (1983)

Diana Primrose (fl. 1630)

Little is known of Diana Primrose beyond this one publication. In the nineteenth century, John Gough Nichols took the name to be a pseudonym for Anne Clifford, Countess of Dorset and Pembroke, and this has recently been considered again as a serious proposition (McBride 1999, n.p.). Conversely, Greer et al point out that the name Primrose belonged to a family of considerable note in the early seventeenth century, although they cannot place a family member called Diana (Greer et al. 1988, p. 83).

See: Greer, Medoff, Sansone and Hastings (eds) (1988); McBride (1999)

Anne Stagg (fl. 1641)

Biographical details of this woman, beyond those given by the pamphlet to which her name is appended, are as yet unknown.

See: Orchard (1999)

Elizabeth Poole (fl. 1648-9)

Possibly a seamstress from Abington, in 1645 she joined the Particular Baptists, a sect, with their roots in Calvinism, who threatened the structure of society by advocating adult baptism and encouraging parents to renounce their rights to impose baptism upon their infant children. She was the author of two pamphlets dealing with the issue of the trial and execution of Charles I, the first being included in this collection. The second, *An Alarum of War* (1649), was published after his execution. It warned of the dire consequences that would befall those who had failed to heed her first prophecy.

See: Gillespie (1999b)

Anna Trapnel (fl. 1642-58)

She was born in Stepney, the daughter of a shipwright, William Trapnel. In January 1642 she experienced a revelation at the Baptist church of John Simpson, in Aldgate, London, and by 1652 had become a supporter of the Fifth Monarchist movement. Two years later, she accompanied the preacher, Vavasor Powell, when he was summoned to Whitehall to face questions about his preaching activities. She fell into a twelve-day trance, which is chronicled in *Strange and Wonderful News from Whitehall* (1654) and *The Cry of a Stone* (1654). Large crowds gathered to hear her prophesy and, under the protection of being God's instrument, she was able to express criticism of Oliver Cromwell's government. She then went to preach in Cornwall, where she was arrested and imprisoned, eventually ending up in Bridewell gaol in London. Whilst in prison, *A Legacy for Saints* (1654) was published and details of her experiences in Cornwall appeared in *Anna Trapnel's Report and Plea* (1654). Later that year, she was released and recommenced prophesying, revisiting Cornwall in 1656 and then falling into another trance the following year, details of which appeared in *A Voice for the King of Saints* (1658) and a large untitled folio volume in the Bodleian Library, Oxford.

See: Drake (1995); Graham, Hinds, Hobby and Wilcox (eds) (1989); Trill (1999)

Mary Carleton (1639/42–73)

Despite her eloquently argued protestations, Mary Carleton was indeed English and of considerably humbler extraction than she claimed. She was born Mary Moders, in Canterbury, the daughter of a chorister, and had received an education beyond her class by ingratiating herself with children from better quality families. She married Thomas Stedman, a shoemaker, and then a Dover surgeon named Thomas Day. She was tried for bigamy but was excused as she had believed her first husband to be dead. In 1663, decking herself out as the 'German Princess', she married John Carleton, who was himself posing as the son of an earl. Almost immediately, the Carleton family discovered the cheat and brought her to trial for bigamy. However, they failed to produce adequate witnesses, most crucially Thomas Stedman himself, and Mary was acquitted. The trial produced a flurry of pamphlets, including two that have been attributed to Mary herself – *An Historical Narrative of the German Princess* and *The Case of Madam Mary Carleton*. Apparently, the trial did not persuade her away from her career of deception, fraud and theft. In 1673 she was tried and executed, prompting another flurry of pamphlets, all claiming to expose the truth of her identity.

See: Todd and Spearing (eds) (1994); Kietzman (1999)

Katherine Philips (1631–64)

She was born in London, the daughter of John Fowler and Katherine Oxenbridge, and, at the age of eight, was sent to the fashionable boarding school run by Mrs Salmon in Hackney, where she probably became acquainted with the works of the Cavalier playwright, William Cartwright. When her father died, her mother married Hector Philips of Porth Eynon in Wales. In 1647 Katherine married Colonel James Philips, Hector's eldest son by a previous marriage and forty years her senior. Katherine and James had two children, Hector, born in 1647, who lived only a few weeks, and Katherine, born in 1656. After her marriage, Katherine divided her time between her husband's house at Cardigan and London. She also established a society of friendship – a literary coterie that precipitated many of her most passionate poems. The survival rate of her poetry is impressive; numerous manuscripts in her and others' handwriting exist, and the published collection of her poems ran to five editions. Her earliest publications were prefaces to collections of works by Henry Vaughan and William Cartwright in 1651. Her next foray into the public eye came in 1663 when, having accompanied her husband to Dublin, the Earl of Orrery persuaded her to allow her translation of Pierre Corneille's *Pompey* to be staged. It was a great success and the text was published immediately in London and Dublin. A pirated edition of her poems was published in 1664, and she hurried to London to oversee publication of an authorised edition. It was here that she caught smallpox and died, leaving the last act of her translation of Corneille's *Horace* unfinished. Her poems and plays were published together for the first time in 1667.

See: Thomas (1990)

Margaret Cavendish, Duchess of Newcastle (1623–73)

She was born Margaret Lucas, youngest child of Thomas Lucas of Colchester and Elizabeth Leighton. Whilst in her teens, she became a Maid of Honour to Queen

Henrietta Maria and, at twenty, she followed the Queen into exile during the English Civil Wars. During her sojourn on the Continent, she met her future husband, William Cavendish. Margaret's marriage brought cultural as well as socio-economic advantages, for Cavendish was not only a writer himself, but also encouraged and collaborated with his wife. Her output was both varied and prolific. She wrote in all the major genres, plus biography, autobiography and epistolary works, and produced fourteen separate titles in twenty years, beginning with a volume of poetry in 1653. She was also something of an eccentric in behaviour and dress, which attracted rather uncharitable attention from her contemporaries, including Samuel Pepys and Dorothy Osborne. Nevertheless, she has the distinction of being the first woman to visit the Royal Society and is one of the few women writers of this period to oversee fully the publication of her work.

See: Jones (1988); Battigelli (1998); Bowerbank and Mendelson (eds) (1999)

Bathsua Makin (1600–<75)

She was the daughter of Henry Reginald, headmaster of a school at St Mary Axe in London, where Bathsua received a good education along with the boy pupils. She was married in 1622 and had three children, born between 1623 and 1629. In 1637 her father died and left her his books. Makin was able to put her education to good use. She was awarded a lifetime pension of £40 per year by Charles I for tutoring his daughter, the Princess Elizabeth, between 1639 and 1644. Five years later, she had gained the patronage of Lucy, Countess of Huntingdon, and also, possibly, taught her. Makin's letters and elegies, pertaining to her relationship with the Countess, survive in manuscript in the Huntington Library, California. Two further examples of Makin's linguistic dexterity were published, the first being *Musa Virginea Graeco-Latino-Gallica* in 1616, and, 57 years later, *The Essay to Revive the Ancient Education of Gentlewomen*. The latter represented another attempt to provide an education for others and an income for herself. The level of her hands-on involvement in the school she advertises in *The Essay* is difficult to determine, given that she would have been seventy-three at the time. As yet, no record of her death has been found.

See: Brink (1991); Teague (1998)

Anne Bradstreet (1612–72)

Born in Northamptonshire to Thomas Dudley and Dorothy York, Anne spent much of her early life in noble households, where her father, and then her husband, held posts, including, in 1619, that of the 4th Earl of Lincoln, the son of Elizabeth Clinton. In 1621, Simon Bradstreet joined the household and, in 1628, after Anne survived an attack of smallpox, they were married. For a short time, they lived in the household of the Dowager Countess of Warwick. However, increasing disillusionment, amongst the nonconformist gentry and nobility, with the policies of Charles I, led to a large-scale emigration to New England and, in 1630, a group of ships left Southampton, bound for Massachusetts, with the Dudleys and the Bradstreets on board. Reaching dry land did not mark the end of Anne's travels, however. For several years, she moved further and further inland, following her husband's and father's ambitions to increase their property and political power within the colony. (Both Thomas Dudley and Simon Bradstreet became Governors of Massachusetts.) From their arrival at the unpromising Salem, a town riddled with death and disease, the Bradstreets moved to Charlestown, then Newton (Cambridge), Ipswich and, finally, Andover, where Anne bore eight children and spent the rest of her days. Her earliest poetry dates from her sojourn in Newton, although most of the poems included in the pirated *Tenth Muse* (1650) were written in Ipswich. The revisions and additions which appeared in the posthumous *Several Poems* (1678) were composed in Andover, as was her substantial corpus of mainly devotional manuscript writing, which was not published in her lifetime.

See: Caldwell (1999); Martin (1984); Stanford (1974)

Aphra Behn (1640–89)

Many of the details of Aphra Behn's life, beyond her literary career, are sketchy and speculative. Current scholarship concludes that she was the daughter of John and Amy Johnson, and probably travelled to Surinam in 1663 with her family. Aphra stayed only two months in the colony, as her father had died on the voyage out and the family continued to Surinam simply to wait for a ship to take them back to England. By 1666, she had married a Mr Behn and it is likely that she was widowed soon after her marriage, as, in that year, she travelled to Flanders, employed as an agent of the Crown in Flanders. When she returned to England in 1667, she began frequenting the London theatrical and literary scene. By 1668, she had met John Dryden and in 1670 she had successfully offered a play, *The Forced Marriage*, for production. This was fortuitous for she was in debt and still unpaid for her work in Flanders. She then began to carve out a name for herself as an influential professional writer in the literary milieu of post-Restoration London, publishing novels, poetry and plays. Indeed, she was one of the most prolific playwrights of her age, second only to John Dryden. However, her money problems stayed with her, and by the mid 1680s she also had to deal with the expense attendant upon poor health. She died in 1689 and was buried in 'Poet's Corner' at Westminster Abbey.

See: Duffy (1977); Goreau (1980); Mendelson (1987)

BIBLIOGRAPHY

References

Anderson, Misty G. (1999), 'Tactile Places: Materialising Desire in Margaret Cavendish and Jane Barker', *Textual Practice* 13 (2): 329–52.

Andreadis, Harriette (1989), 'The Sapphic-Platonics of Katherine Philips', *Signs* 15 (1): 34–60.

Andreadis, Harriette (1999), 'The Erotics of Female Friendship in Early Modern England' in Susan Frye and Karen Robertson (eds), *Maids, Mistresses, Cousins and Queens: Women's Alliances in Early Modern England*, New York and Oxford: Oxford University Press, pp. 241–58.

Barthes, Roland (1977), 'From Work to Text' in *Image, Music, Text*, selected and trans. Stephen Heath, London: Fontana.

Battigelli, Anna (1998), *Margaret Cavendish and the Exiles of the Mind*, Lexington: University Press of Kentucky.

Benson, Pamela Joseph (1992), *The Invention of the Renaissance Woman: The Challenge of Female Independence in the Literature and Thought of Italy and England*, Pennsylvania: Pennsylvania State University Press.

Bowerbank, Sylvia and Sara Mendelson (eds) (1999), *Paper Bodies: a Margaret Cavendish Reader*, Peterborough, ON and London: Broadview Press.

Brennan, Michael G. (ed.) (1988), *Lady Mary Wroth's Love's Victorie: The Penshurst Manuscript*, London: Roxburghe Club.

Brink, Jean R. (1991), 'Bathsua Reginald Makin; "Most Learned Matron"', *Huntington Library Quarterly* 54: 313–26.

Caldwell, Patricia (1999), 'Contextual Material on *The Tenth Muse*', *Renaissance Women On Line*, http://www.wwp.brown.edu/sitemap.html.

Callaghan, Dympna (1994), 'Re-Reading Elizabeth Cary's *The Tragedie of Mariam, the Faire Queene of Jewry*' in Margo Hendricks and Patricia Parker (eds), *Women, 'Race', and Writing in the Early Modern Period*, London: Routledge, pp. 163–77.

Cerasano, S. P. and Marion Wynne-Davies (eds) (1996), *Renaissance Drama by Women: Texts and Documents*, London and New York: Routledge.

Davies, John (1612), *The Muses Sacrifice*, London.

Drake, Valerie (1995), 'Trapnel, Anne, fl. 1642', in *The Dictionary of National Biography on CD-ROM*, Oxford: Oxford University Press, n.p.

Duffy, Maureen (1977), *The Passionate Shepherdess: Aphra Behn 1640–1689*, London: Cape.

Easton, Celia (1990) 'Excusing the Breach of Nature's Laws: the Discourse of Denial and Disguise in Katherine Philips' Friendship Poetry', *Restoration: Studies in English Literary Culture 1660–1700* 14(1): 1–14.

Ellis, John H. (ed.) (1962), *The Works of Anne Bradstreet in Prose and Verse*, Gloucester, MA: Peter Smith.

Ezell, Margaret J. M. (1987), *The Patriarch's Wife: literary evidence and the history of the family*, Chapel Hill and London: University of North Carolina Press.

Findlay, Alison, Stephanie Hodgson-Wright and Gweno Williams (1999a), '"The Play is ready to be Acted": women and dramatic production, 1570–1670', *Women's Writing* 6(1): 129–48.

Findlay, Alison, Stephanie Hodgson-Wright and Gweno Williams (1999b), *Women Dramatists 1550–1670: Plays in Performance*, Lancaster: Lancaster University Television.

Findlay, Alison, Stephanie Hodgson-Wright and Gweno Williams (2000), '(En) Gendering Performance: Staging Plays by Early Modern Women' in Jane Donawerth and Adele Seeff (eds), *Crossing Boundaries: Attending to Early Modern Women*, London: Associated University Presses and Newark: University of Delaware Press, pp. 289–308.

Frohock, Richard (1996), 'Violence and Awe: the foundations of Government in Aphra Behn's New World Settings', *Eighteenth-Century Fiction* 8 (4): 437–52.

Gallagher, Catherine (ed.) (2000), *Oroonooko*, Bedford Cultural Editions, London: Macmillan Press.

Gillespie, Katharine (1997), 'Anna Trapnel's Window on the Word: The Domestic Sphere of Public Dissent in Seventeenth-Century Nonconformity', *Bunyan Studies* 7: 49–72.

Gillespie, Katharine (1999a), '"This briny ocean will o'erflow your shore": Anne Bradstreet's 'Second World' Atlanticism and national narratives of literary history', *Symbiosis* 3 (2): 99–118.

Gillespie, Katharine (1999b), 'Contextual Materials on *A Vision: Wherein is Manifested the Disease and Cure of the Kingdom*', *Renaissance Women On Line*, http://www.wwp.brown.edu/sitemap.html.

Gim, Lisa (1999) '"Faire Eliza's Chaine": Two Female Writers' Literary Links to Queen Elizabeth I' in Susan Frye and Karen Robertson (eds), *Maids and Mistresses, Cousins and Queens: Women's Alliances in Early Modern England*, New York and Oxford: Oxford University Press.

Graham, Elspeth, Hilary Hinds, Elaine Hobby and Helen Wilcox (eds) (1989), *Her Own Life: Autobiographical Writings by Seventeenth-Century Englishwomen*, London: Routledge.

Greer, Germaine, Jeslyn Medoff, Melinda Sansone and Susan Hastings (eds) (1988), *Kissing the Rod: An Anthology of Seventeenth-Century Women's Verse*, London: Virago.

Goreau, Angeline (1980), *Reconstructing Aphra*, New York: Dial.

Guibbory, Achsah (1996), 'The Gospel according to Aemilia: Women and the sacred in Aemilia Lanyer's *Salve Deus Rex Judaeorum*' in Helen Wilcox, Richard Todd and Alasdair Macdonald (eds), *Sacred and Profane: Secular and Devotional Interplay in Early Modern British Literature*, Amsterdam: VU University Press, pp. 105–126.

Habermas, Jurgen (1962, trans. 1989), *The Structural Transformation of the Public Sphere*, trans. Thomas Burger, Cambridge: Polity Press.

Hackett, Helen (1995) *Virgin Mother, Maiden Queen*, Basingstoke: Macmillan.

Hannay, Margaret P. (1990), *Philip's Phoenix: Mary Sidney, Countess of Pembroke*, Oxford and New York: Oxford University Press.

Hannay, Margaret P., Noel J. Kinnamon, and Michael G. Brennan (eds) (1998), *The Collected Works of Mary Sidney Herbert, Countess of Pembroke 1561–1621*, vol. 1, Oxford: Clarendon Press.

Henderson, Katherine Usher and Barbara F. McManus (eds) (1985), *Half Humankind: Contexts and Texts of the Controversy about Women in England, 1540–1640*, Urbana and Chicago: University of Illinois Press.

Hobby, Elaine (1988), *Virtue of Necessity: English Women's Writing 1649–88*, London: Virago.

Hobby, Elaine (1991), 'Katherine Philips: Seventeenth-Century Lesbian Poet' in Elaine Hobby and Chris White (eds), *What Lesbians Do in Books*, London: The Women's Press, pp. 183–204.

Hodgson-Wright, Stephanie (ed.) (2000), *Elizabeth Cary: The Tragedy of Mariam*, Peterborough, ON and London: Broadview Press.

Ingram, Randall (2000), 'First Words and Second Thoughts: Margaret Cavendish, Humphrey Moseley, and "the Book"', *Journal of Medieval and Early Modern Studies* 30(1): 101–124.

Jones, J. R. (1980), from *Britain and Europe in the Seventeenth Century* rpt. in W. R. Owens (ed.), *Seventeenth-Century England: A Changing Culture*, London: Open University Press, pp. 45–60.

Jones, Kathleen (1988), *A Glorious Fame: The Life of Margaret Cavendish, Duchess of Newcastle 1623–1673*, London: Bloomsbury.

Kietzman, Mary Jo (1999), 'Defoe Masters the Serial Subject', *English Literary History* 66 (3): 677–705.

Lamb, Mary Ellen (1986), 'The Countess of Pembroke and the Art of Dying' in Mary Beth Rose (ed.), *Women in the Middle Ages and the Renaissance: Literary and Historical Perspectives*, New York: Syracuse University Press, pp. 207–26.

Lamb, Mary Ellen (1990), *Gender and Authorship in the Sidney Circle*, Madison, WI: University of Wisconsin Press.

Lewalski, Barbara K. (1991), 'Re-Writing Patriarchy and Patronage: Margaret Clifford, Anne Clifford, and Aemilia Lanyer', *The Yearbook of English Studies*, 21: 87–106.

Lewalski, Barbara K. (ed.) (1996), *The Polemics and Poems of Rachel Speght*, Oxford: Oxford University Press.

Lewalski, Barbara K. (1997), 'Female Text, Male Reader Response: Contemporary Marginalia in Rachel Speght's *A Mouzell for Melastomus*', in Claude J. Summers and Ted-Larry Pebworth (eds), *Representing Women in Renaissance England*, Columbia, MO: University of Missouri Press, pp. 136–62

Levin, Carole (1998) '"We Princes, I tell you, are set on stages": Elizabeth I and dramatic self-representation', in S. P. Cerasano and Marion Wynne-Davies (eds), *Readings in Renaissance Women's Drama: Criticism, History, and Performance 1594–1998*, London and New York: Routledge, pp. 113–124.

Limbert, Claudia A. (1991), 'Katherine Philips: Controlling a Life and Reputation', *South Atlantic Review* 56: 27–42.

McBride, Kari Boyd (1999), 'Contextual Material on *A Chain of Pearl*', *Renaissance Women On Line*, http://www.wwp.brown.edu/sitemap.html.

McDowell, Paula (1998), *The Women of Grub Street: Press, Politics and Gender in the London Literary Marketplace 1678–1730*, Oxford: Clarendon Press.

Magnusson, A. Lynne (1991), '"His Pen With My Hand": Jane Anger's Revisionary Rhetoric', *English Studies in Canada*, 17 (3): 269–81.

Marcus, Leah, Janel Mueller and Mary Beth Rose (eds) (2000), *Elizabeth I: Collected Works*, Chicago and London: University of Chicago Press.

Martin, Wendy (1984), An American Triptych: *Anne Bradstreet, Emily Dickinson, and Adrienne Rich*, Chapel Hill: University of North Carolina Press.

Meehan, Johanna (ed.) (1995), *Feminists Read Habermas: Gendering the Subject of Discourse*, London and New York: Routledge.

Mendelson, Sara Heller (1987), *The Mental World of Stuart Women: Three Studies*, Brighton: Harvester.

Miller, Naomi J. (1990), 'Rewriting Lyric Fictions: The Role of the Lady in Lady Mary Wroth's *Pamphilia to Amphilanthus*' in Anne M. Haselkorn and Betty S. Travitsky (eds), *The Renaissance Englishwoman in Print: Counterbalancing the Canon*, Amherst: University of Massachusetts Press, pp. 295–310.

Miller, Naomi J. (1996), *Changing the Subject: Mary Wroth and Figurations of Gender in Early Modern England*, Lexington: University of Kentucky Press.

Mintz, Susannah B. (1998), 'Katherine Philips and the Space of Friendship', *Restoration: Studies in English Literary Culture 1660–1700* 22 (2): 62–78.

Orchard, Chris (1999), 'Contextual Materials on *A True Copy of The Petition of Gentlewomen*', *Renaissance Women On Line*, http://www.wwp.brown.edu/sitemap.html.

Pritchard, R. (ed.) (1996), *Lady Mary Wroth: Poems*, Keele: Keele University Press.

Purkiss, Diane (ed.) (1994), *Salve Deus Rex Judaeorum* in *The Plays of Elizabeth Cary and the Poems of Aemilia Lanyer*, London: Pickering and Chatto.

Purkiss, Diane (ed.) (1998), *Three Tragedies by Renaissance Women*, London: Penguin.

Raber, Karen (1995), 'Gender and the Political Subject in *The Tragedy of Mariam*', *Studies in English Literature 1500–1900* 35 (2): 321–41.

Revard, Stella P. (1997), 'Katherine Philips, Aphra Behn and the Female Pindaric', in Claude J. Summers and Ted-Larry Pebworth (eds), *Representing Women in Renaissance England*, Columbia, MO: University of Missouri Press, pp. 227–41.

Roberts, Josephine (ed.) (1983), *The Poems of Lady Mary Wroth*, London: Louisiana State University Press.

Shannon, Laurie J. (1994), '*The Tragedie of Mariam*: Cary's Critique of the Terms of Founding Social Discourses', *English Literary Renaissance* 24: 135–53.

Shaver, Anne (ed.) (1999), *The Convent of Pleasure and Other Plays*, Baltimore, MD: Johns Hopkins University Press.

Shepherd, Simon (ed.) (1984), *The Women's Sharp Revenge: Five Women's Pamphlets from the Renaissance*, London: Fourth Estate.

Spender, Dale (1986), *Mothers of the Novel: 100 Good Writers before Jane Austen*, London: Pandora.

Stanford, Ann (1974), *Ann Bradstreet: The Worldly Puritan*, New York: Burt Franklin and Co.

Teague, Frances (1987), 'Elizabeth I' in Katherina M. Wilson (ed.), *Women Writers of the Renaissance and Reformation*, London: University of Georgia Press, pp. 522–47.

Teague, Frances (1992), 'Queen Elizabeth in her Speeches' in S. P. Cerasano and Marion Wynne-Davies (eds), *Gloriana's Face: Women, Public and Private in the English Renaissance*, London: Harvester Wheatsheaf, pp. 63–78.

Teague, Frances (1998), *Bathsua Makin: Woman of Learning*, London: Associated University Presses.

Thomas, Patrick (ed.) (1990), *The Collected Works of Katherine Philips, The Matchless Orinda*, vol. 1 *The Poems*, Stump Cross: Stump Cross Books.

Todd, Janet and Elizabeth Spearing (eds) (1994), *Counterfeit Ladies: The Life and Death of Mal Cutpurse; The Case of Madam Mary Carleton*, London: William Pickering.

Todd, Janet (ed.) (1995), *The Works of Aphra Behn*, vol. 3 *The Fair Jilt and Other Short Stories*, London: Pickering & Chatto; Columbus: Ohio State University Press.

Todd, Janet (ed.) (1996a), *The Works of Aphra Behn*, vol. 7 *The Plays 1682–96*, London: Pickering & Chatto; Columbus: Ohio State University Press.

Todd, Janet (1999), 'A Spectacular Death: History and Story in *The Widow Ranter*' in Janet Todd (ed.), *Aphra Behn*, London: Macmillan, pp. 73–84.

Trill, Suzanne, Kate Chedgzoy and Melanie Osborne (eds) (1997), *Lay by Your Needles Ladies, Take the Pen: Writing Women in England 1500–1700*, London: Arnold.

Trill, Suzanne (1999), 'Contextual Material on *Strange and Wonderful News from White-hall*', *Renaissance Women On Line*, http://www.wwp.brown.edu/sitemap.html.

Walden, Aaron R. (ed.) (1993), *The Widow Ranter: or, The History of Bacon in Virginia. A Tragi-Comedy by Aphra Behn*, London: Garland Publishing.

Weller, Barry and Margaret W. Ferguson (eds) (1994), *The Tragedy of Mariam with The Lady Falkland: Her Life*, London: University of California Press.

Widdowson, Peter (1999), *Literature*, London: Routledge.

Woods, Susanne (ed.) (1993), *The Poems of Aemilia Lanyer: Salve Deus Rex Judaeorum*, Oxford: Oxford University Press.

Wroth, Lady Mary (1997), *The Countess of Montgomery's Urania*, in The Early Modern Englishwoman: A Facsimile Library of Essential Works, Part 1, vol. 10, selected and introduced by Josephine Roberts, Aldershot: Scolar Press; Brookfield, VT: Ashgate Publishing.

Zook, Melinda (1999), 'Contextualizing Aphra Behn: plays, politics and party, 1679–1689' in Hilda L. Smith (ed.), *Women Writers and the Early Modern British Political Tradition*, Cambridge: Cambridge University Press, pp. 75–93.

Further Reading

Monographs

Barash, Carol (1996), *English Women's Poetry, 1646–1714: Politics, Community, and Linguistic Authority*, Oxford: Clarendon Press.

Beilin, Elaine V. (1987), *Redeeming Eve: Women Writers of the English Renaissance*, Princeton, NJ: Princeton University Press.

Berry, Philippa (1989), *Of Chastity and Power: Elizabethan Literature and the Un-married Queen*, London: Routledge.

Cotton, Nancy (1980), *Women Playwrights in England 1363–1750*, Lewisburg: Bucknell University Press.

Crawford, Patricia (1993), *Women and Religion in England 1500–1720*, London: Routledge.

Diamond, Elin (1997), *Unmaking Mimesis: Essays on feminism and theater*, London: Routledge.

Eales, Jacqueline (1998), *Women in early modern England, 1500–1700*, London: UCL Press.

Ezell, Margaret J. M. (1993), *Writing Women's Literary History*, London: Johns Hopkins University Press.

Findlay, Alison and Stephanie Hodgson-Wright, with Gweno Williams (2000), *Women and Dramatic Production 1550–1700*, London and New York: Longman.

Greer, Germaine (1995), *Slip-shod Sybils: Recognition, Rejection and the Woman Poet*, London: Viking.

Gutierrez, Nancy (1991), 'Valuing *Mariam*: Genre Study and Feminist Analysis', *Tulsa Studies in Women's Literature* 10 (2): 233–51.

Hinds, Hilary (1996), *God's Englishwomen: Seventeenth-century radical sectarian writing and feminist criticism*, Manchester and New York: Manchester University Press.

Krontiris, Tina (1992), *Oppositional Voices: Women as Writers and Translators of Literature in the English Renaissance*, London: Routledge.

Lewalski, Barbara K. (1993), *Writing Women in Jacobean England*, London: Harvard University Press.

Mack, Phyllis (1992), *Visionary Women: Ecstatic Prophecy in Seventeenth-Century England*, Berkeley: University of California Press.

Mendelson, Sara and Patricia Crawford (1997), *Women in Early Modern England*, Oxford: Oxford University Press.

Pearson, Jacqueline (1988), *The Prostituted Muse: Images of Women & Women Dramatists 1642–1737*, New York: Harvester Wheatsheaf.

Smith, Hilda L. (1982), *Reason's Disciples: Seventeenth-Century English Feminists*, Urbana, Chicago and London: University of Illinois Press.

Ulrich, Laurel Thatcher (1991), *Good Wives: Image and Reality in the Lives of Women in Northern New England 1650–1750*, New York: Random House.

Waller, Gary (1993), *The Sidney Family Romance: Mary Wroth, William Herbert and the Early Modern Construction of Gender*, Detroit: Wayne State University Press.

Warnicke, Retha (1983), *Women of the English Renaissance and Reformation*, Westport, CT: Greenwood Press.

Woodbridge, Linda (1984), *Women and the English Renaissance*, Chicago: University of Illinois Press.

Collections of Essays

Brant, Clare and Diane Purkiss (eds) (1992), *Women, Texts and Histories 1575–1760*, London: Routledge.

Cerasano, S. P. and Marion Wynne-Davies (eds) (1992), *Gloriana's Face: Women, Public and Private in the English Renaissance*, London: Harvester Wheatsheaf.

— (eds) (1998), *Readings in Renaissance Women's Drama: Criticism, History, and Performance 1594–1998*, London: Routledge.

Chedgzoy, Kate, Melanie Hansen and Suzanne Trill (eds) (1998), *Voicing Women: Gender and Sexuality in Early Modern Women's Writing*, 2nd edition, Edinburgh: Edinburgh University Press.

Grossman, Marshall (ed.) (1998), *Aemilia Lanyer: Gender, Genre, and the Canon*, Lexington, KY: University Press of Kentucky.

Grundy, Isobel and Susan Wiseman (eds) (1992), *Women, Writing, History 1640–1740*, London: B. T. Batsford.

Hageman, Elizabeth H. and Sarah Jayne Steen (guest eds) (1996), *Shakespeare Quarterly* 47 (4), special issue on 'Teaching Judith Shakespeare'.

Hannay, Margaret Patterson (1985) (ed.), *Silent but for the Word: Tudor Women as Patrons, Translators and Writers of Religious Works*, Kent, OH: Kent State University Press.

Hutner, Heidi (ed.) (1993), *Rereading Aphra Behn: History, Theory and Criticism*, Charlottesville and London: University Press of Virginia.

Kelly, Joan (1984), *Women, History, Theory: the Essays of Joan Kelly*, Urbana: University of Chicago Press.

Levin, Carole and Patricia A. Sullivan (eds) (1995), *Political Rhetoric, Power, and Renaissance Women*, Albany, NY: State University of New York Press.

Miller, Naomi and Gary Waller (eds) (1991), *Reading Mary Wroth: Representing Alternatives in Early Modern England*, Knoxville: University of Tennessee Press.

Pacheco, Anita (ed.) (1998), *Early Women Writers: 1660–1720*, London and New York: Longman.

Rose, Mary Beth (ed.) (1986), *Women in the Middle Ages and the Renaissance: Literary and Historical Perspectives*, London: Syracuse University Press.

Todd, Janet (ed.) (1996b), *Aphra Behn Studies*, Cambridge: Cambridge University Press.

Todd, Janet (ed.) (1999), *Aphra Behn*, London: Macmillan.

Wilcox, Helen (ed.) (1996), *Women and Literature in Britain 1500–1700*, Cambridge: Cambridge University Press.

Wynne-Davies, Marion (guest ed.) (1999), *Women's Writing* 6 (1), special issue on Renaissance drama by women.

Individual Essays and Articles

Athley, Stephanie and Daniel Cooper Alarcón (1995), '*Oroonoko's* Gendered Economies of Honor/Horror: Reframing Colonial Discourse Studies in the Americas' in Michael Moon and Cathy Davidson (eds), *Subjects and Citizens: Nation, Race and Gender from Oroonoko to Anita Hill*, Durham, NC: Duke University Press, pp. 27–55.

Ballaster, Ros (1992), 'New Hystericism: Aphra Behn's *Oroonoko*: The Body, the Text and the Feminist Critic', in Isobel Armstrong (ed.), *New Feminist Discourses: Critical Essays on Theories and Texts*, London: Routledge, pp. 283–95.

Blackstock, Carrie Galloway (1997), 'Ann Bradstreet and Performativity: Self-Cultivation, Self-Deployment', *Early American Literature* 32 (3): 222–48.

Bonin, Erin Lang (2000), 'Margaret Cavendish's Dramatic Utopias and the Politics of

Gender', *Studies in English Literature 1500–1900* 40 (2): 339–54.

Cowell, Pattie (1994), 'Early New England Women Poets: Writing as Vocation', *Early American Literature* 19: 103–21.

Ferguson, Margaret (1992), 'The Spectre of Resistance' in David Scott Kastan and Peter Stallybrass (eds), *Staging the Renaissance: Reinterpretations of Elizabethan and Jacobean Drama*, pp. 233–50.

Ferguson, Margaret (1994), 'News from the New World: Miscegenous Romance in Aphra Behn's *Oroonoko* and *The Widow Ranter*' in David Lee Miller, Sharon O'Dair, and Harold Weber (eds), *The Production of English Renaissance Culture*, Ithaca: Cornell University Press, pp. 151–89.

Green, Janet M. (1997), '"I My Self": Queen Elizabeth's Oration at Tilbury Camp', *Sixteenth-Century Journal*, 28 (2): 421–45.

Helm, J. L. (1993), 'Bathsua Makin's *An Essay to Revive the Antient Education of Gentlewomen* in the Canon of Seventeenth-Century Educational Reform Tracts', *Cahiers Elisabethains* 44: 45–51.

Hodgson-Wright, Stephanie (1999), 'Early Feminism' in Sarah Gamble (ed.), *The Icon Critical Dictionary of Feminism and Post-Feminism*, London: Icon Press, pp. 3–15.

Iwanisziw, Susan B. (1998), 'Behn's Novel Investment in *Oroonoko*: Kingship, Slavery and Tobacco in English Colonialism', *South Atlantic Review* 63 (2): 75–98.

Jankowski, Theodora A. (1998), 'Pure Resistance: Queer(y)ing Virginity in William Shakespeare's *Measure for Measure* and Margaret Cavendish's *The Convent of Pleasure*', *Shakespeare Studies* 26: 218–55.

Kietzman, Mary Jo (1999), 'Defoe Masters the Serial Subject', *English Literary History* 66 (3): 677–705.

Martin, Wendy (1979), 'Anne Bradstreet's Poetry: A Study of Subversive Piety', in Sandra Gilbert and Susan Gubar (eds), *Shakespeare's Sisters: Feminist Essays on Women Poets*, London: Indiana University Press, pp. 20–31.

Mihoko, Suzuki (1993), 'The Case of Mary Carleton: Representing the Female Subject', *Tulsa Studies in Women's Literature* 12(1): 61–83.

Miller, Naomi J. (1997), 'Domestic Politics in Elizabeth Cary's *The Tragedy of Mariam*', *Studies in English Literature 1500–1900* 37 (2): 353–69.

Payne, Linda R. (1991), 'Dramatic Dreamscape: Women's Dreams and Utopian Vision in the Works of Margaret Cavendish, Duchess of Newcastle' in Mary Anne Schofield and Cecilia Macheski (eds), *Curtain Calls: British and American Woman and the Theater 1660–1820*, Athens: Ohio University Press, pp. 18–33.

Pearson, Jacqueline (1985), '"Women may discourse . . . as well as men": Speaking and silent women in the plays of Margaret Cavendish, Duchess of Newcastle', *Tulsa Studies in Women's Literature* 4: 33–45.

Rivero, Albert J. (1999), 'Aphra Behn's *Oroonoko* and the 'Blank Spaces' of Colonial Fictions', *Studies in English Literature 1500–1900* 39 (3): 443–64.

Roberts, Jeanne (1997), 'Convents, Conventions and Contraventions: *Loves Labor's Lost* and *The Convent of Pleasure*', in M. J. Collins (ed.), *Shakespeare's Sweet Thunder: Essays on the Early Comedies*, Newark: University of Delaware Press, pp. 140–64.

Steibel, Arlene (1992), 'Not since Sappho: The Erotic in Poems of Katherine Philips and Aphra Behn' in Claude J. Summers (ed.), *Homosexuality in Renaissance and Enlightenment England*, pp. 153–71.

Waller, Gary (1991), 'Mother/Son, Father/Daughter, Brother/Sister, Cousins: The Sidney Family Romance', *Modern Philology* 88 (4): 401–14.

Anthologies of Primary Texts
Aughterson, Kate (ed.) (1995), *Renaissance Woman: A Sourcebook*, London and New York: Routledge.
Fitzmaurice, James, Josephine A. Roberts, Carole L. Barash, Eugene R. Cunnar and Nancy A. Gutierrez (eds) (1997), *Major Women Writers of the Seventeenth Century*, Ann Arbor: University of Michigan Press.
Keeble, N. H. (ed.) (1994), *The Cultural Identity of Seventeenth-Century Woman: A Reader*, London and New York: Routledge.
Mahl, Mary R. and Helene Koon (eds) (1977), *The Female Spectator: English Women Writers Before 1800*, London: Indiana University Press.
Martin, Randall (ed.) (1997), *Women Writers in Renaissance England*, London and New York: Longman.
Salzman, Paul (ed.) (2000), *Early Modern Women's Writing: An Anthology 1560–1700*, Oxford: Oxford University Press.

INDEX OF THEMES

Numbers indicate texts, not pages